Parades and the
Politics of the Street

EARLY AMERICAN STUDIES

Richard S. Dunn, Director, Philadelphia Center for
Early American Studies, Series Editor

A complete list of books in the series is available
from the publisher

Parades and the Politics of the Street

Festive Culture in the Early American Republic

Simon P. Newman

PENN

University of Pennsylvania Press

Philadelphia

10 9 8 7 6 5 4 3 2 1

Published by
University of Pennsylvania Press
Philadelphia, Pennsylvania 19104-6097

Library of Congress Cataloging-in-Publication Data

Newman, Simon Peter.
    Parades and the politics of the street : festive culture in the
early American republic / Simon P. Newman.
        p.   cm.—(Early American studies)
    Includes bibliographical references and index.
    ISBN 0-8122-3399-9 (alk. paper)
    1. United States—Politics and government—1783–1809.   2. United
States—Politics and government—1775–1783.   3. Festivals—Political
aspects—United States—History—18th century.   4. Political
culture—United States—History—18th century.   5. Festivals—
Political aspects—United States—History—19th century.
6. Political culture—United States—History—19th century.
I. Title. II. Series.
E310.N49   1997
973.4—dc21   97-5392
                                                                  CIP

For P. and M.

with love and thanks for all of the penny-a-churching,
along the byways and back roads of Suffolk,
where it all began

Contents

Illustrations

Preface

HISTORIANS HAVE WRITTEN A GREAT DEAL about the political history of the revolutionary and early national periods of United States history. For two centuries the political beliefs and partisan conflicts of Americans in the late eighteenth century have fascinated us, and scholars have explored this field in far greater depth, perhaps, than have those working in any other era in the political history of the United States.

Yet something is missing from this voluminous literature. Armed with an apparent assumption that government and politics were an elite affair, many of these historians have devoted themselves to the philosophies and policies of George Washington, Thomas Jefferson, John Adams, James Madison, Alexander Hamilton and other early national leaders. In the process, however, they have all but ignored those who were ruled, apparently regarding these Americans as essentially powerless spectators who were outside of and thus in some sense apart from the political process. As a result these political histories are dominated by the words and actions of the ruling elite, the great owners of land, material goods, and enslaved people.[1]

A few historians, including Alfred Young, Jesse Lemisch, Gary Nash, Rhys Isaac, and Linda Kerber, have sought to broaden this narrow conception of political history by exploring the political lives of ordinary Americans.[2] Yet in their published work and in their classrooms many historians persist in privileging the words and actions of the ruling elite, and writing as if poor, lower, and even middling sort Americans had no political existence or none worthy of mention.[3] Moreover, the myriad accounts of popular political belief and practice that filled early national newspapers have been all but ignored by most of those who study the political history of the early republic.[4]

The work of a generation of English historians underscores the folly of such an omission.[5] E. P. Thompson is of seminal importance here, with his extraordinary sensitivity to the agency of common English folk within their political world.[6] Arguing that they would take to the streets in defense of traditional rights and customs, Thompson argued that one can trace in their rites, symbols, and language the formation of a homogeneous working class and working-class consciousness. John Brewer has explored the involvement of these ordinary folk in eighteenth-century partisan politics.[7] George Rudé has written extensively on popular movements and crowd actions in the eighteenth and early nineteenth centuries, exploring their utility as a tool of disaffected members of the lower social orders. Focusing almost exclusively on such phenomena as strikes, riots, and rebellions, Rudé paid scant attention to the numerous less violent forms of crowd activity, however political and partisan they may have been.[8] Tim Harris, in contrast, included some of these more peaceable demonstrations and audiences, and has established how commonplace were the diverse and often highly politicized crowd activities of late seventeenth-century England.[9] Mark Harrison has done much the same for the late eighteenth and early nineteenth centuries.[10]

Perhaps the most comprehensive treatment of the evolution of popular political ritual per se has come from Nicholas Rogers. The heavily ritualized festive calendar of late seventeenth-century England was intended, he has argued, "to legitimize the political order, [and] to imbue it with drama and dignity." But the decades around the turn of eighteenth century "saw a significant broadening of the boundaries of the political nation," and the emergence of "a dynamic and contentious political culture, centered around royal and national anniversaries, in which the populace itself was a vigorous participant." During these years early modern provincialism and a large measure of elite control faded away, and a significant rise in partisan strife encouraged the lower orders to take a greater role in politics in the public sphere.[11]

By the late eighteenth century the early modern festive calendar had been transformed by crowds who worked within the parameters of traditional rites and celebrations in order to make known their own opinions, beliefs, and demands; these crowds created and populated new, highly politicized festivals commemorating such events as the defeat of the Excise Bill and Admiral Edward Vernon's birthday. Often these new partisan celebrations proved more popular than royal anniversaries. Thompson and Brewer focused their attention on the oppositional politics of the lower orders, while Harris and Harrison encouraged us to consider the celebrations and ceremonies in support of the ruling elite. Rogers has combined these approaches by showing that festive culture was the site of battle between different partisan groups and their supporters in England, including Whigs who celebrated the anniversaries of the discovery of the Gunpowder

Plot and William's landing in 1688, and Tories who commemorated the anniversary of the martyrdom of Charles I and celebrated the anniversary of the Restoration.[12]

In this book I have attempted to build upon the work and methods of these historians in order to move our discussion of early national politics beyond Congress and the studies of elite leaders like Washington and Jefferson, and into the streets and public places of the new republic. It was, I shall argue, in their rich array of parades, festivals, civic feasts, badges, and songs that most Americans experienced national politics. I contend that ordinary men and women were active participants in their political world, and that a national popular political culture and political parties were created, at least in part, by ordinary Americans participating in celebrations of George Washington's birthday, Independence Day, and the French Revolution. This book will explore the political world of ordinary men and women during the epochal decade between the ratification of the Federal Constitution and the inauguration of Thomas Jefferson.

* * *

This book began at Princeton University, and I am grateful for the help of many friends and teachers who helped me during the early stages, especially David Bell, Jane Dailey, Marcus Daniel, David Nirenberg, Jean-Yves Le Saux, the late Gene Sheridan, Chris Stansell, Lawrence Stone, Susan Whyman and Sean Wilentz. It has been John Murrin, with his great sense of humor and his infectious enthusiasm for early American history, who has taught me the most, and I am fortunate to call him both teacher and friend.

As it has for many early Americanists, the Philadelphia Center for Early American Studies has become my academic home-away-from-home. During my first residence at the Center in 1989–91 my colleagues Aaron Fogleman, Rosalind Remer, Peter Thompson, and especially Susan Branson and Alison Games gave freely of their expertise and friendship. I returned to the Center in 1994–95 and completed this book as a University of Pennsylvania Mellon Fellow. For all their help during this second sojourn I thank Rosanne Adderly, John Bezís Selfa, George Boudreau, Jacob Cogan, Kon Dierks, Richard Dunn, Ruth Herndon, Dan Kilbride, Susan Klepp, Gabrielle Lanier, Leslie Patrick and Igor, Liam Riordan, Billy Smith, Susan Stabile, Cami Townsend, Susan Thibedeau, and Cynthia Van Zandt. Thanks also to Roger Abrahams, Carroll Smith-Rosenberg, and especially my coffee companion Sally Gordon, each of whom made this year at Penn both enjoyable and productive.

Other friends and colleagues who have helped me develop this book include Kathy Brown, Joe Henry, Reg Horsman, Tom Humphrey, Allan Kulikoff, Ted Pearson, Jim Tagg, David Waldstreicher, and especially Alfred Young. I shall always be grateful to my friend Caroline Goddard, who endured interminable discussions of late eighteenth-century American political culture and introduced me to all kinds of new approaches and theory. Rick Beeman and Paul Gilje furnished me with valuable readings of my manuscript; Gerry Krieg created the maps; and Jerry Singerman and Alison Anderson at the University of Pennsylvania Press have helped me through the process of publication with patience and much good humor.

For all the assistance they gave me while I was researching this book, I would like to thank the folks at Princeton's Firestone Library, the University of Pennsylvania's Van Pelt Library, Founder's Memorial Library at Northern Illinois University, the Newberry Library, the Massachusetts Historical Society, the Historical Society of Pennsylvania, the American Antiquarian Society, the South Carolina Historical Society, the Vermont Historical Society, the American Philosophical Society, and the Library Company of Philadelphia.

I have presented portions of what follows at annual meetings of the American Historical Association, the Institute of Early American History and Culture, and the Organization of American Historians, and at the Social History Workshop of the University of Chicago, the Philadelphia Center for Early American Studies Seminar, the Newberry Library Early American History Seminar, and the History Seminar at Syracuse University. An earlier version of Chapter Three appeared as "'*Principles* or *Men?*' George Washington and the Political Culture of National Leadership, 1776–1801," in the *Journal of the Early Republic* 12 (1992): 477–507, reprinted by permission.

This book is dedicated to my parents. Together with my sister Clare, my brothers Giles, Jeremy, and Tim, and my nephew Christopher, they have given me the love and support that has made the book possible.

Introduction:
The Significance of Popular
Political Culture

AT DAWN ON THE COLD AND WINTRY MORNING of Thursday, the twenty-fourth of January, 1793, the people of Boston were awakened by the thunderous roar of an artillery salute fired by a local militia company to signal the beginning of a day of public festivity and rejoicing. On this joyful day there were no classes for the city's school children, and under the direction of their teachers they assembled in their hundreds and paraded through the streets, after which they were rewarded with cakes on which were impressed the words "Liberty" and "Equality." [1]

Later that morning a much larger group of adults formed their own procession behind decorated carriages bearing eight hundred loaves of bread, two hogsheads of punch, and an enormous roasted ox decorated with red, white, and blue ribbons and a gilded sign that read "PEACE OFFERING TO LIBERTY AND EQUALITY." Behind these carriages marched two men holding aloft the French and American flags, the members of the committee elected by townspeople to organize the day's festivities, craftsmen and artisans bearing the flags and colors of their trades, a musical band, a dozen white-robed butchers, and several hundred men in well ordered ranks.

As the procession wound through the streets of Boston, many residents stood and watched it pass and then took up the rear. They halted three times, to salute with three cheers the home of the French Consul, to pay homage to the stump of the liberty tree, and to conduct a brief ceremony renaming Oliver's Dock as Liberty Square. The procession ended in the open area around the State House, where the butchers set about carving up the ox, and participants and spectators joined in a great public feast. While they enjoyed this repast the townspeople were entertained by the band that had provided music for the procession: the musicians had taken up position in the balcony of the State House, and they now regaled their audience with various tunes, the most popular of which was the French Revolutionary anthem, the "Ça Ira." At the same time two large balloons were raised from Market Square, one trailing the American flag, the other the motto "Liberty and Equality."

While this popular feast was taking place yet another procession began, starting out from the State House and ending at Faneuil Hall. Led by Lieutenant Governor Adams and French Consul Letombe, this was a gathering of the city's mercantile and professional elite. When they arrived at Faneuil Hall these men found several allegorical statues of Liberty, Fame, Justice, and Peace, an emblem of the Rights of Man, and a banner proclaiming "LIBERTY & EQUALITY." Meanwhile, in taverns and halls around the city, militia companies and gatherings of artisans and mechanics held their own celebratory feasts, lauding the day with enthusiastic toasts.

The final procession of the day was a rather more spontaneous affair. Following the great civic feast a group of seafarers took possession of the horns of the roasted ox and marched with them to the liberty pole that stood in the newly named Liberty Square. Once there these impoverished men announced their intention of paying to have the horns gilded and mounted atop the liberty pole, in honor of the Boston celebration and the event it commemorated. As darkness fell, hundreds of lamps and candles illuminated both the State House and the home of the French Consul, and on Copps Hill fireworks and a large bonfire lit up the evening sky.

*   *   *

What did this great civic festival mean to the Bostonians who staged it and to their fellow townspeople who either took part in the processions and feasts or watched them? Nominally the celebration honored the French army's defeat of Prussian invaders at the Battle of Valmy, a victory that had secured the immediate future of the fragile republican revolution in France. But why did some Bostonians choose to commemorate this event in such a fashion, and what can we learn from their celebration? For during the years between the ratification of the Federal Constitution and the inauguration of Thomas Jefferson, the streets and public places of the American republic were filled with an extraordinarily diverse array of such feasts, festivals, and parades.[2] While some—like Boston's Valmy festival—celebrated the French Revolution, others commemorated the anniversary of American independence; many honored George Washington, while some paid tribute to John Adams, Thomas Jefferson, and other public figures; still more voiced popular support of or opposition to the policies and principles of the political parties that took shape during this volatile decade.

The richest source of data for the parades, festivals, and public celebrations of this era is the extraordinarily rich accounts that filled the columns of the early national newspapers. Newspapers constituted the principal source of news and information for many American citizens and were vital to these festive occasions, for while many Americans were taking part in or watching these events, even more were reading about them in local or more distant newspapers.[3] There had been a veritable explosion in the number of newspapers printed and available in late eighteenth-century America, from the forty odd that had served some three million colonists on the eve of the revolution to well over one hundred by the early 1790s and more than two hundred by the turn of the century, and most of their editors printed myriad reports of parades, feasts, and festivals from both far and near.[4]

The rites[5] and festivals of the new republic and the expansion of popular print culture thus went hand-in-hand. Festive culture required both participants and an audience, and by printing and reprinting accounts of July Fourth celebrations and the like newspapers contributed to a greatly enlarged sense of audience: by the end of the 1790s those who participated in these events knew that their actions were quite likely going to be read about and interpreted by citizens far beyond the confines of their own community.[6] This sharing of information made possible the emergence of a common national language of ritual activity. This symbiotic relationship between the early national press and an emerging national festive culture furnished the people who mounted, participated in, and watched these rites and festivals with an awareness that they were acting on both a local and a national stage.[7]

The sheer number of parades, feasts, and festivals that took place in the last decade of the eighteenth century, the ubiquity of the cockades, flags, liberty caps, and liberty trees that added texture to such events, and the press coverage devoted to all the rites and symbols of festive culture all bear witness to the tremendous vitality and enormous significance of this aspect of life in the early republic. Yet we know little about the place, role, and meaning of these rites and festivals in the lives of late eighteenth-century Americans. What was this festive culture all about? Who mounted, participated in, and watched these parades and festivals, and who wore the badges, flew the flags, and sang the songs of this vibrant popular culture? Why were they reported on such a large scale and with such enthusiasm in the early national press? What was the significance of these activities, and what did they mean to those who participated in them? What sorts of contests were fought over and within these rites and festivals, what was their connection to the frenzied politics of the 1790s, and did they contribute to the drawing of partisan lines and the creation of the republic's first political parties?

This book represents my attempt to address these questions, by means of a description of the full range of public ritual and festive culture in the years between 1789 and 1801, and an interpretation of the nature and the significance of these activities. I have read complete runs of over fifty late eighteenth-century newspapers, and have sampled incomplete runs of a further twenty-five. Contemporary magazines, manuscript correspondence, journals, and diaries have furnished me with additional information, as have the printed journals, correspondence, and diaries of such diverse characters as the Maine midwife Martha Ballard and the Virginia planter and president Thomas Jefferson. My research has uncovered thousands of descriptions, references to, and impressions of July Fourth festivities, celebrations of the birthday of George Washington, French Revolutionary festivals, and other similar events; many thousands of the toasts drunk by those who attended them; and innumerable references to the songs, badges, flags, and so forth that were such important components of early national popular culture.

Working through this rich body of data it became clear to me that these rites and symbols constituted a vital part of the political lives of ordinary Americans in the era of the first political party system. The term "ordinary" is somewhat problematic, given its implication that all those who did not participate in politics by means of parades and festivals were in some sense "extraordinary." Here and throughout this work the term "ordinary" conveys a sense of the commonplaceness of the political activities that I am describing. When Americans participated in a July Fourth celebration as enthusiastic spectators, or took part in a public meeting disavowing the Jay Treaty, or sang the "Marseillaise" in a theater, they were not behaving in an abnormal or even an unusual fashion. This was the regular and routine stuff of popular politics, and it is in this sense that these activities and those who participated in them were commonplace and essentially ordinary.[8]

Yet for all that these badges, songs, parades, and festivals were a routine part of early national political life, they have been ignored in favor of the words, writings, and actions of elite political leaders in the large majority of the political histories of the early national United States. Elite is perhaps as problematic a term as ordinary, even when employed to describe those at the summit of the hierarchical and deferential society of late eighteenth-century America.[9] Yet the word has utility as a descriptive label for those white men who believed that their birth, education, financial independence, and professional experience all qualified them as "natural" rulers, eminently well suited to hold positions of power and authority in the society and government of the early republic. This was a large and flexible category that might include Southern planters, successful port city merchants, lawyers, businessmen, and large-scale landholders.

These members of the elite were not, however, the only people to practice politics in the early republic. Public ritual and festive culture were vital elements of political life, and if we are to understand American politics in the age of the first political party system, we need to learn more about these aspects of the political lives of ordinary Americans. For rulers and ruled alike in late eighteenth-century America, parades, feasts, and festivals were essential components of early national popular political culture. "Popular," "political," and "culture" are each sufficiently amorphous to make clarification of this compound term a necessary yet highly problematic endeavor, and it is extremely difficult to do more than provide a rough working definition, which nonetheless may aid readers in their attempt to understand the nature and significance of early national political ritual. The most important component of the triad is the word "culture," the base term that is qualified by "popular" and "political." In his volume of definitions, Raymond Williams refused to define the word "culture," observing that "it is the range and overlap of meanings that is significant."[10] With this in mind I have worked within the parameters set by those historians and anthropologists who see culture in terms of signifying and symbolic systems, and thus not as "some static artifact, but rather a continuous process of sense-making."[11] Crudely put, culture is the web of meanings spun in and around the rites and symbols that are the subject of this book.

"Popular" is a term with many meanings, and it is often used by historians and anthropologists to refer "to the beliefs and customs of groups socially defined as 'the people,'" or to "a literary or visual style considered 'low,' or comic or 'naive.'" Following Natalie Zemon Davis I have employed a related yet rather more general definition; I use "popular" to refer to "beliefs . . . practices and festivities widely dispersed in a given society." [12] Politics may be defined in a similarly broad fashion, including "any action, formal or informal, taken to affect the course or behavior of government or the community," and consequently the range of activities that might be described as political is extraordinarily broad. Individuals and groups may join together to take political action in any number of ways and in just as many locations, for political behavior is neither rooted in any one location nor exclusive to any particular social group.[13]

When these terms are combined as "popular political culture," the essential meaning becomes rather more focused while yet retaining much of the breadth and range of my unwieldy explanations of its constituent parts. As both a conceptual category and a set of actual events, popular political culture allows us to see and make some sense of the ways in which politics extended far beyond the ruling elite, for in their parades, festivals, civic feasts, songs, crowd actions, and badges many ordinary Americans ventured into an arena in which "politics assumed both shape and significance." [14] Public ritual and festive culture was one of many such spheres or arenas of interaction accessible to white women, some African American men and women, and both urban and rural poor white men. Different Americans enjoyed very different levels of participation in popular politics, yet it was in this unequal and contested arena that early national popular political culture coalesced.

The creation of a national popular political culture in the 1790s was made possible by the social and political upheavals that had accompanied the preceding quarter century of resistance, revolution, and nation-building, all of which had complicated the relationship between rulers and ruled in colonial America. The American War for Independence had occasioned an extraordinary crisis of elite power and authority: Loyalist gentry fled; ideologies of radical republicanism erupted among white working men; slaves threw down their tools and ran; bloody civil war tore large parts of the country apart; civilian and military leaders pleaded for ordinary men and women to fight for or support rival armies; and opposing groups campaigned for the support of the populace in their struggles to gain control of the new nation's government.

The riots and rebellions that had shaken America during the 1770s and 1780s had made Carl Becker's question of who should rule at home seem very real in the minds of those elite Americans who struggled to prevent their slaves from running away to the British, or fired on angry crowds from Fort Wilson in Philadelphia, or paid to quell Shay's Rebellion in Massachusetts.[15] As the new system of republican government took shape in the 1790s, the insurgencies and popular disorders of the preceding quarter century were fresh in the minds of members of the ruling elite, some of whom were not slow to follow Washington in associating rebellion with a surfeit of popular political activity.[16]

Once opened, however, Pandora's box could never again be closed: resistance and revolution had moved the locus of politics further out into the public sphere, thereby forever changing the political significance of the people out-of-doors. During the 1790s the rites and festivals that comprised the out-of-doors political activity of ordinary Americans became an essential part of the political process, and this regularization of popular politics is at the heart of this book.[17]

The detailed descriptions of parades, festivals, civic feasts, and other rites that filled contemporary newspapers yield a wealth of information about the political world of ordinary Americans as it was played out in this vital public arena. Popular political culture furnished many different Americans with the means to exercise some measure of political power— calling their leaders to account, demanding action, pressuring for change, championing ideals and sacred values, and preventing the enactment of certain policies. Thus these common folk affirmed that they were far more than simple subjects of power; in these rites and festivals they continually demonstrated that power was not inherent in a single individual or a small group, but was instead exercised in the negotiations between rulers and ruled that took place in public places and print as much as in congressional and state assembly chambers.[18]

This is not to say that rural farm folk, craftsmen and artisans, middling sorts, impoverished white men, white women of different classes, and free or enslaved black Americans enjoyed the same kind or the same amount of political power as each other or as powerful elite leaders, but neither does it mean that all these folk were completely powerless. Politics was comprised of a chorus of many different voices, some loud and some soft, sometimes in harmony yet often in discord. These voices featured both arguments within the ranks of the ruling elite and highly ritualized public expressions of popular opinion about the government and its policies. The former included the pamphlet wars, partisan newspaper editorials, and congressional wranglings that have filled so many of the political histories of this era. The latter included such things as celebrations of the French Revolution that were so enthusiastic as to make condemnation by the government and its supporters all but impossible, and popular demands that elected leaders conform to republican—rather than aristocratic or even monarchical—standards of behavior. In this concordance of many different voices we can learn much about the politics of the American population as a whole.[19]

The loudest voices of all belonged to white men, and throughout the new nation white males regularly mounted public displays, parades, civic feasts, and the like.[20] However, the success of these rites and festivities was contingent on the stability of certain keywords, concepts, and symbols that allowed those present to perceive and interpret the event. These interpretations could vary. When the white men of a militia company paraded behind a liberty cap on the Fourth of July, the success of their parade and the political message it expressed was measured in part by the enthusiasm of their audience. That audience, both on the day and later when reading about it in newspapers, might include white men of the lower sort, white women of different classes, and perhaps even black Americans, all of whom were familiar with both the rite and the symbol, who could interact in certain limited ways with the men who marched, and who could interpret what they saw or read about on their own terms.

A process of negotiation is revealed in the scores of newspaper accounts of the rites and symbols of popular political culture: negotiation between political rulers and the ordinary folk on the streets, and between those who mounted and participated in festive and ritual culture and those who gave it life and vibrancy as they watched, cheered, and read about the events. It was in this public sphere that many ordinary Americans took part in popular political culture, and it was there that they experienced, participated in, and to a certain extent created their government and its policies. This popular political culture was, then, a shared political language, and it is this shared way of practicing politics that is the subject of this book.

It is important to remember, however, that for late eighteenth-century Americans the burning of John Jay in effigy, or participating in an open-air civic feast in honor of a French military victory, or breaking windows on July Fourth were no more political than participants wanted them to be, and one must be wary of describing as political those Americans who may have primarily been interested in the festive aspects of public occasions and holidays. Anybody who has joined any kind of political march, protest, or crowd action can attest to the fact that participants in these events may range in sentiment from deep commitment to almost total apathy. Nonetheless, it is all but impossible for these people, whatever their original motives for taking part, to avoid making public political statements by and through their participation: both their presence and their participation involve some degree of politicization and an expression of political identity and power in a public setting. One might have taken part in an avowedly Democratic Republican July Fourth celebration in rural New Jersey in the late 1790s with the intention of enjoying a holiday and eating and drinking to excess. However, the symbols and the rhetoric of the celebration would have been avowedly partisan, and both fellow participants and those who read about the event in their newspapers would have regarded it as a partisan event. Given that, it is difficult to accept that many people failed to realize or ignored the political character of their actions.

The badges and songs and the parades and festivals that comprised popular political culture furnished Americans with regular opportunities to participate in and read about political life. It was by means of these rites and symbols that many assumed their political and partisan identities: the young apprentice Benjamin Tappan was typical in the way he "had taken his stand" in "politics" not by joining a political party or by voting, but rather by participating in a large French Revolutionary civic feast in 1794.[21] As described in newspapers and other sources, a great many of the civic festivals of the 1790s were explicitly political events, in which participants and observers articulated a variety of opinions about the policies, the personnel, and even the system of their government. The political parties of the early national polity were in part created in these public settings, the product of negotiation between interests, classes, and to a lesser degree races and sexes that took place in the contested terrain of the public sphere.[22]

*   *   *

The turbulent years between 1788 and 1801 were of tremendous significance in American political history. It was during this decade that the first truly national popular political culture began to develop and a national political party system began to take shape. In the festivals, rites, and symbols of popular politics, ordinary Americans played a vital role in these processes, helping to form local and national political parties, and helping create a new way of doing politics. The politics of ordinary Americans became a regularized part of the political process, and what follows is an exploration of both the nature and the significance of this development.

This book begins with a chapter that traces the English and American Revolutionary contexts for the development of a national popular political culture. The second, third, and fourth chapters comprise a detailed investigation of popular politics in the 1790s: chapter two deals with the ways early national Americans celebrated their first three presidents; chapter three explores the popular politics of Independence Day; and chapter four chronicles American celebrations of the French Revolution. The fifth chapter details some of the other ways in which badges, songs and symbols functioned in the day-to-day political life of the new republic, and the conclusion elaborates on the meaning of these data and the significance of this study.

I

Resistance, Revolution, and Nationhood:

The Origins of a National Popular Political Culture

PEOPLE FROM THREE CONTINENTS CREATED the new societies of mainland British North America, bringing a wide array of beliefs and traditions to the communities that spanned out from Chesapeake Bay, the Delaware and Hudson River Valleys, and the rugged coastlines of New England. Yet while ethnic and racial diversity were defining characteristics of this world, in vital ways it was the cultural heritage of the English that dominated in British North America. It was English culture that played the principal role in the formation of an American popular political culture.[1]

This is not to say that the political culture of England remained of abiding interest to those who inhabited the New World. Once in America settlers were confronted by the sweltering heat of the Carolinas, the heavily wooded and dangerous backcountry, and the cold and harsh terrain of New England. The Old World seemed far away, and many colonists had neither the time nor the means to maintain an active interest in English politics and political culture. Descriptions of English celebrations of the monarch's birthday or the birth of a new member of the royal family, accounts of London's Whig celebrations during November, depictions of the Liberty Cap and similar popular radical symbols, and references to a variety of English and Scottish crowd actions all appeared in colonial newspapers, but on such an infrequent basis that it is clear that the festive rites mounted in England were no longer a part of everyday life in the colonies.[2]

While the colonists may have displayed little interest in the political world of parades, feasts, and crowd actions of a distant land, their lives remained informed by an English political cultural heritage that they transformed to suit local needs. In the process these colonists developed new,

local political cultures, informed by English traditions yet very much a
part of local identity in the New World. Perhaps because of the significant
differences among New England, the Middle Atlantic region, the Chesapeake Bay colonies, the deep South, and the backcountry, and because of
the lack of regular communication between these disparate regions, by the
middle of the eighteenth century a variety of different political cultures had
emerged in the mainland colonies, although all had some common elements of English festive culture.

During the French and Indian War there appeared the first signs of a
unification of these divergent regional political cultures as different colonists participated in strikingly similar rites of celebration and commemoration. The ensuing two decades of political crisis escalated this process:
the experiences of the resistance movement, the politicization of ordinary
folk, and the bringing into the polity—albeit to a limited degree—of white
women and black Americans combined to create a unified discourse of political activity. Drawing on English and regional American traditions of
crowd actions and festive and commemorative rites, all manner of Americans from Maine to Georgia participated in the politics of resistance, rebellion, and then nation-building. In fact success in the struggle to create
an independent nation was in part contingent on the creation of a unified
popular political culture that allowed Americans to act in concert. A brief
resurgence of provincialism in the aftermath of success in the war for independence temporarily weakened the move toward a national discourse
of popular politics and political activity, but the chaos of the 1780s and the
centralizing impulses that culminated in the Federal Constitution revitalized the move toward a national popular political culture.

*   *   *

Allegiance to the Crown united all the settlers in colonial British
North America (in theory if not in fact), and there were celebrations of the
birthdays of the monarch and of leading members of the royal family in all
the colonies. These events were, however, neither as widespread nor as enthusiastic as those mounted in Britain, and there appears to have been little
in the way of widespread commemoration beyond the coastal towns and
cities. Moreover, since these festivals were not conducted in the partisan
context of Hanoverian politics, they were quite unlike the highly politicized British celebrations which provided political parties with opportunities to rally popular support. Colonial celebrations generally were

organized by and for members of the local ruling elite, who drew some portion of their power and success from the monarch they celebrated. As such they may well have played a role in the process of Anglicization, wherein members of the colonial elite sought to enhance their power and privilege by recreating English rites and institutions.[3]

In New England the anti-monarchical heritage of the Puritans, together with their disdain for ostentatious public display, meant that large-scale celebrations of royal events were far less common than they were farther south. A small civic feast and toasts in celebration of Queen Anne's birthday, staged by a group of Bostonians and several English soldiers, prompted Samuel Sewall and his fellow justice Edward Bromfield to threaten to raise the militia in order to quell such "disorder."[4] Among people who had harbored regicides and despised royal interference in local affairs, such lack of sympathy for royalist festivities was hardly surprising. Thus celebrations of royal birthdays and the anniversaries of coronations often consisted of little more than cannon salutes fired by visiting ships of the Royal Navy, toasts by local and imperial officials, and the illumination of major public buildings.[5]

Royal festivals were more common in the middle Atlantic region, but they had little of the partisan character and public holiday atmosphere of English celebrations. By the mid-eighteenth century small but standardized celebrations had emerged in both New York City and Philadelphia. In New York City the day was generally observed "with the usual Demonstrations of Loyalty and Joy."[6] Colonial officials and "most of the principal Gentlemen and Inhabitants of this City" convened and drank loyal healths, while the ships in the harbor flew their colors and soldiers in the fort fired cannon salutes.[7] The governor of Pennsylvania orchestrated the celebrations in Philadelphia, hosting "a great entertainment" at which local worthies drank loyal toasts, and "a grand Ball" for the "Ladies" and "Gentlemen" of the elite.[8] In the background, English soldiers and later local militia men fired cannon, and ships in the Delaware raised their colors.[9]

In the Southern colonies, where the planter elite consciously emulated the lifestyles of the British gentry and aristocracy, royal celebrations played a much larger role in the festive calendar. The birthdays of the Queen or the Prince of Wales were deemed worthy of celebration in Annapolis, Williamsburg, and Charleston, where they inspired elite balls, feasts, and toasts accompanied by gunfire salutes, bonfires, and the illumination of windows.[10] In Charleston the birthday of the monarch was celebrated in similar style but on a grander scale than in Philadelphia, with a very large feast provided by the governor, loyal toasts, and a general illumination of the town.[11] By the mid-eighteenth century a militia review had been added, complete with military exercises, small arms and cannon fire, feasting and toasting by the men of the militia, and a separate ball "for the Ladies."[12]

The celebrations in the Virginia capital of Williamsburg were of a kind with those in Charleston, but given the size of the community they were on a decidedly smaller scale. Ships on the James River displayed their colors, the militia fired salutes, the governor hosted a ball, and "most of the Gentlemens and Other Houses of Note" were illuminated.[13] In Annapolis the king's birthday was celebrated in similar fashion, "with Firing of Guns" and "a Public Ball."[14] Throughout the colonies, elite balls and celebrations tended to dominate celebrations that were most common in the urban centers or the capitals of overwhelmingly rural colonies: there is little evidence to suggest that the birthday of the monarch was a large-scale popular holiday, as it was for the people of England.

In addition to celebrating the monarch's birthday, the residents of the colonies built on such English precedents as royal entries and the Lord Mayor of London's parade in order to fashion festive rites suited to local situations. When a new governor or a senior imperial official arrived from London, for example, he was formally welcomed by members of the colonial elite. When Sir Danvers Osborne arrived in New York City he was received by the Mayor, members of the Council, "and the greatest part of the gentlemen and Merchants of this City," while the entry of Sir William Pepperrell into Boston was marked by cannon salutes, a militia parade, and the flying of colors by the ships in the harbor.[15]

In Williamsburg the rites honoring a new governor changed little over the first three-quarters of the eighteenth century: the roar of cannon announced the arrival of the ship carrying the new governor, and when he disembarked he was met by the members of the council, the speaker, "and many other Gentlemen of distinction" who had gathered to welcome him into Williamsburg. After his commission was read and he had taken "the usual oaths," the governor and council feasted at a local tavern, and in the evening the town was illuminated.[16] Although relations between colonists and governors were often soured by internal political infighting and friction between London and the colonies, these kinds of celebratory rites remained an important part of local political life until the eve of independence. Celebration of the office of governor served local as well as imperial purposes, allowing the socio-economic elite to celebrate and uphold a well-ordered and peaceful government, as the local population watched the parade, cheered the new governor, and enjoyed the illuminated windows.

A series of long and bloody imperial wars, culminating in the French and Indian War, served to broaden popular participation in the increasingly unified rites of festive culture. On the one hand members of the colonial elite seized on celebrations to orchestrate popular support for the empire and its needs, while on the other ordinary folk commemorated losses and celebrated defeats with patriotic ardor. As a result, as the French and Indian War proceeded celebrations of British victories and festivities in honor of the sovereign grew decidedly larger in scale and occurred in many more locations than had been true in preceding years. A typical example occurred in Charleston in 1740, when the proclamation of a declaration of war against Spain prompted a parade including British soldiers, a host of local officials and judges, naval captains, heralds who read aloud the declaration, a small band, the lieutenant governor, local militia men, and whatever "Private Gentlemen" chose to join in. After the militia had fired their small arms and cannon in celebration, the elite retired for a feast hosted by the lieutenant governor, well satisfied that the colony was united for war.[17]

The early years of the French and Indian War brought major defeats for the colonies and Britain, together with a series of devastating attacks by the French and their Indian allies, and throughout British North America the colonists responded with the familiar rite of public fast days. In Virginia, for example, Lieutenant Governor Robert Dinwiddie set aside September 24, 1755 "for the solemn and public humiliation of ourselves before Almighty GOD . . . and more particularly for the Preservation of us from the Hands of our Enemies."[18] But it was in New England that these kinds of fast days had always played a particularly important role. In the absence of traditional Anglican festivals and saints' days, fast and feast days had long been central to the festive calendar, giving New Englanders the opportunity to gather and celebrate or commiserate over events of great significance to the community.[19]

When early defeats turned into sensational victories there were "extraordinary [celebrations] throughout *North-America*."[20] Given the immediacy of the French and the Spanish threat to the colonists, and the fact that a great many colonists were participating in the fight against these enemies, it is hardly surprising that British victories in the western hemisphere occasioned the greatest celebrations. The capture of Quebec, for example, was celebrated by the residents of Annapolis with cannon salutes at dawn, a militia parade in the early afternoon followed by another discharge of muskets and cannon, the illumination of the city in the evening, and a ball given by the governor for the local planter and merchant elite.[21] In New London, Connecticut the news of the surrender of Montreal was met by church bells and cannon fire, a general illumination of the town, loyal toasts, "and other demonstrations of joy."[22]

The death of George II during the waning years of this successful war prompted colonial commemoration of his passing and celebration of the accession of George III on a much larger than usual scale. With the colonial war-time economy booming, and an end to the French and Indian peril in sight, the rulers and many of the ruled seemed happy to proudly celebrate their membership in the powerful and successful British empire. The rites in Philadelphia marking the accession of the new monarch were typical. The "Gentlemen in public office, and other principal inhabitants" formed a procession and walked with the governor and clergy to the Court House, where they were received by British soldiers in formation. These groups, together with "a vast concourse of people," then heard the proclamation of George III's accession, which was greeted "by the Acclamations of all present," small arms fire from the soldiers, cannon fire from the fort, and the ringing of church bells. The governor, military officers, local government officials, merchants, "and other Gentlemen of the City" then repaired to several taverns for celebratory feasts and toasts.[23]

Many of the celebrations of royal events and anniversaries, British victories and the rites honoring British officials took place in the coastal towns and cities of the American colonies, urban areas that were in relatively close contact with Britain and with English political culture. As a result only a minority of colonists witnessed these events, for the large majority of the population were dispersed throughout the villages and farms of the northern colonies, the large and small plantations of the South, and the more isolated regions of the backcountry. Once outside of the seaboard towns and cities the rhythms and patterns of festive culture varied widely, although generally these rites were still informed by English precedents.

The militia played an important, albeit varied role in colonial political culture. With the French, Spanish, and Native American residents posing a real and often formidable threat to the safety of British colonists, adult white men in town and countryside alike gathered together on a regular basis in order to arm and train themselves for battle. But militia men were capable of transcending their defensive role. On occasion, when colonists who lived far from the loci of colonial political power in coastal towns and cities believed that their best interests were being threatened, well armed local men did not hesitate to take the law into their own hands, as Bacon's Rebellion in Virginia, the Regulators in the Carolinas, and Pennsylvania's Paxton Boys so vividly demonstrated.[24] (See Figure 1.)

More often than not, however, militia musters provided a tangible display of the commitment of ordinary white men to social stability and the preservation of law and order. For many rural colonists, the days on which the militia mustered provided one of the relatively infrequent occasions on which their community gathered together. While white men paraded, practiced shooting, and went through various military maneuvers, white women and occasionally African Americans gathered to watch. For all their political significance these were often highly social affairs: many militia men who joined professional British soldiers in action against Native Americans and their French allies had attended musters where militia men were so drunk that they could hardly keep hold of their muskets.

The mustering of the militia assumed an entirely different significance in the southern colonies, where the white population were just as concerned with the enforced subservience of a large enslaved population as they were with war against foreign enemies. Yet this did not prevent participants and observers from drawing on the traditions of English fairs and carnivals, turning southern militia musters into highly festive social occasions. As Rhys Issac has demonstrated, horse races and court day meetings were the occasions on which a widely scattered population drew together, and were central to southern festive culture.[25] In 1711 William Byrd went with his family "to the general muster of this county," prepared to watch competitions for running, cudgels, and wrestling, and to enjoy large quantities of food and drink.[26] A quarter century later residents of Hanover County, Virginia assembled to enjoy horse racing, country fiddlers, "Football-play," jumping, and wrestling, while every October a fair with a horse race and ball took place just outside Annapolis.[27]

For the relatively few white Southerners who lived close to a church and clergyman, church day provided both a venue and an occasion for the people of the community to gather together. More often, however, communal assembly was "intermittent rather than continuous" for the people of the colonial South, although on these rare occasions "the quest was above all for unanimity."[28] The planter elite presided over these affairs, graciously acknowledging deferential yeoman, while both groups expected the enthusiastic support of white female observers and demanded the obedience of enslaved black spectators. This reciprocal relationship between

Figure 1. The Paxton Expedition. Henry Dawkins, 1764. The Library Company of Philadelphia. This representation of Philadelphians preparing to repel the Paxton Boys' march in 1763 show something of the chaos and diversity of urban public displays, with men and women of different classes milling around and giving support as eager spectators.

planters and yeomen was also played out in elections in the southern colonies, where the ruling planter elite "treated" the deferential voters of their areas, thereby recognizing the role and power of the yeomanry in the process of government.[29]

In New England, however, the absence of this kind of alliance between yeoman and gentry made for a quite different political culture, and usually elections were far more staid affairs with little in the way of campaigning and often with quite low voter turnout.[30] The situation was somewhat different in the coastal towns of New England and the Middle Atlantic, where economic hardship and rising social tensions inflamed political passions as the eighteenth century wore on, as evidenced by the introduction of caucuses to draw up slates of candidates, political advertising, and the expansion of a political press.[31]

The festive culture of the political community in British North America was thus dominated by the white men who fired cannons on the king's birthday and drank to his health in local taverns, who went through maneuvers with the local militia, who attended elections as voters or observers, who participated in celebrations of imperial victories and who fêted high-ranking British officials. The level of their participation in all this culture was, however, dependent on both class and location: an indentured servant was no more likely to feast with the gentry who were welcoming a new governor than a yeoman farmer in the interior was to take part in the urban festivities in honor of the birthday of the monarch.

Neither white women nor men and women of color played a direct role in this festive culture, but they played an important role in the proceedings as spectators. White women of high and low rank attended militia musters, watched parades in honor of a great victory, and drank the king's health in lowly dram shops or at a governor's ball, and their presence sanctioned and enhanced these events. Public rites required large and enthusiastic audiences to bear witness to community solidarity in support of the male militia, the election of civil officers, or perhaps the celebration of the nation's monarch and British military prowess: although this did not translate into real and effective female power and agency, white women nonetheless played a role in the ritual world of popular politics.

Many African Americans lived on plantations and could not hope to attend the communal meetings of white society in the colonial South, although both free and enslaved blacks in the North were able to witness and occasionally participate in the festivals and celebrations mounted in or near their communities. On southern plantations slaves began the process of molding their own distinctive culture, while some black residents of the urban north created their own alternatives to a festive culture that often less than welcomed their participation. In New England, perhaps beginning in the early eighteenth century, free and enslaved black residents of Salem, Boston, Narragansett, and other towns began holding annual elections of "governors" or "kings," events that quickly turned into a festival with games, dances, and feasting.[32] In Albany and New York City black residents drew on African traditions of dancing, drumming, first harvest celebrations, and coming of age ceremonies for young adults in their transformation of Dutch celebrations of Pentecost: these Pinkster festivals usually lasted for several days and drew attendance from as far as forty miles away.[33]

The white residents of these northern towns, including the owners of those enslaved blacks who participated in King's or Pinkster's Day, appear to have condoned them as local variants of the traditional European festivals of inversion, when for a brief period those on the bottom of society appropriated power and rank to themselves. In fact slaveholders often made substantial contributions to these events, perhaps reasoning that a year of peaceful subservience was worth the expense of a short period of riotous excess.[34]

Revelry and symbolic upturning of the world were not, however, restricted to the black residents of northern towns. The celebration of the English Whig festival of November 5, the anniversary of the successful discovery of Guy Fawkes's plot to destroy James I and his Protestant Parliament, evolved into a day of carnivalesque celebration among the impoverished white residents of several northern towns, especially Boston. In England the day had been an integral part of the festive calendar since the mid-1620s, when large bonfires and the burning in effigy of the Pope and the devil by common folk had shown the depth of popular resentment against Charles I's Catholic Queen Henrietta Maria.[35] After the restoration of Charles II, many English men and women had deliberately mounted larger and more extensive celebrations of Gunpowder Treason Day than of the anniversary of the monarch's restoration: in England November 5 was a holiday that belonged to the people, in which they could articulate this clear warning to the restored Stuart monarch.[36]

There was, then, a longstanding English tradition of investing this traditionally anti-Catholic festival with contemporary political and religious significance, and by the late seventeenth century the Whigs had appropriated Gunpowder Treason Day and were employing it as an occasion for the celebration and affirmation of partisan ideologies and allegiances. This kind of politicization would resurface in New England during the mid-1760s, again in protest against the royal government in London. But colonial celebrations of Guy Fawkes Day, soon renamed Pope's Day, usually took place in a rather different context. In New York City the earliest records of observance of the day describe restrained commemoration by members of the elite, with members of the Council, Assembly, and Corporation and "the principal Gentlemen and Merchants" waiting on the Lieutenant Governor, drinking a series of Royal Healths, and then retiring through an illuminated city.[37] But within a few years it was more common for "a large Body of the Mobility" to assemble and parade through the town with effigies of the Devil, the Pope, and the Pretender, all of which they then burned on a large bonfire.[38]

It was in Boston, however, that the fifth of November was truly appropriated and reshaped by poor and working people. Populated by sailors, shipwrights, slaves, cordwainers, chairmakers, sailmakers, and shipjoiners, Pope's Day was a surprisingly carnivalesque event for Puritan New England, despite an ardently religious tone that contrasted starkly with the partisan political celebrations of Guy Fawkes Day in contemporary England.[39] The festivities centered around the activities of crowds of impoverished men from Boston's North and South Ends, who made effigies of the Pope, the Devil, and the Pretender, which they then paraded in rival processions attended by boys dressed as the "Devil's imps." "Voluntary" contributions were garnered from city residents to improve the platforms and effigies of the two groups, who then massed for what often degenerated into a pitched brawl. In 1752, for example, a mariner named John Crabb died at the hands of Abraham, a slave, and Thomas Chubb, another seafarer.[40] The victors from either North or South End seized the effigies of their vanquished opponents, took them back to their home ground, and then burned them alongside their own.[41]

The Boston elite appear to have been willing to tolerate this annual festival of inversion as a safety valve that allowed the lower orders to let off steam, and because the hated objects of their annual rampaging were Catholic and foreign. In New York City during the French and Indian War, Pope's Day revelers changed the course of their parade in order to exact tribute from a captured French general, a rite that can have done little to offend the city's Protestant elite.[42]

But by their very nature festivals of inversion empowered those who usually had little power, and there was always the possibility that crowds of black and white laborers, seafarers, and mechanics could transform the ideological thrust of Pope's Day. As imperial authorities began instituting policies unpopular with many colonists in the wake of the French and Indian War, Bostonians politicized their Pope's Day crowd actions and created a pattern of popular political activity that spread throughout the thirteen colonies. The process began during the Stamp Act crisis, when Boston's Patriot elite attempted to harness large-scale popular enthusiasm for and participation in the annual festival and deploy it against an unpopular British policy. From that point forward, as Patriot leaders confronted both the Loyalist elite and the mighty British empire itself, they constantly sought to strengthen their position by demonstrating that the majority of colonists supported them. From Boston to Charleston, Patriot leaders sought out the active support of lower and middling Americans, both male and female and on occasion black as well as white, in a popular political culture of parades, festivals, and crowd actions. This was as hazardous an undertaking as rebellion itself. For not only did it show unempowered Americans that the colonial elite were bitterly divided, but it also affirmed that they—slaves, women, laborers, sailors, mechanics, and small farmers —had political voices and political power.

This process began in Boston in 1765. Residents were experiencing a major depression in the wake of the French and Indian War, and it was not hard for the merchants and master craftsmen of the Loyal Nine (soon to become the Sons of Liberty) to convince Ebenezer McIntosh and other mechanics and artisans that the Stamp Act impinged on their liberty.[43] McIntosh was the leader of the South End Pope's Day crowd, and the support of McIntosh, other popular leaders, and the crowd of which he was a part was vital to the success of the protest movement: large-scale crowd actions, with women and children applauding them, demonstrated that the community had united in protest against British policies. During 1765 Bostonians participated in a series of well-organized crowd actions designed to prevent the act from going into effect by forcing the intended stamp distributor, a local merchant named Andrew Oliver, to resign his commission, and by destroying the stamped paper itself. To that end a crowd from Boston's South End attacked Oliver's home on August 14, 1765. This was as much crowd action as the Loyal Nine wanted, but the members of the crowd had their own agenda. They later regrouped and were then joined by their traditional adversaries from the North End, and together they razed Oliver's new office building to the ground.[44]

The Loyal Nine had sought no more than a show of force by a united community under their leadership, and they were quite content to have secured Oliver's resignation. But the underemployed and hungry people of Boston associated the Stamp Act with the accumulation of wealth by Lieutenant Governor Thomas Hutchinson, and his gross insensitivity toward Boston's long-suffering lower orders. Experienced in years of Pope's Day celebrations, the North and South Enders reassembled some days later and attacked Hutchinson's house.[45]

These lawless attacks on property horrified Patriot leaders who sought a change in British policy rather than in the social order, and they scrambled to regain control of the protest movement. By and large they were successful, and in November 1765 they were able to orchestrate a peaceful celebration of Pope's Day itself; the crowds of the South and North Ends added effigies of "stamp men" to their usual motley crew, met peacefully at King Street, and then marched to each other's home ground. But given that the mocking processions and pageantry of inversion that characterized the Pope's Day celebrations of ordinary Bostonians had provided the basis for popular protests against the Stamp Act, it was ultimately impossible for Patriot leaders to completely control subsequent protests or ignore the interests of the mariners, the laborers, the mechanics, and these men's families, whose support was so very essential. However loudly Samuel Adams might call for "NO MOBS," the people had a role in protest and they could not be ignored.[46]

Many of Boston's most important protests against British policy took place out of doors, in open public spaces. One of the most important of these venues, both for the display of symbols and as a meeting place, was beneath the branches of what soon became known as the liberty tree. In August 1765 effigies of stamp collectors and British ministers were hung from the branches of this large old elm tree, which stood at the intersection of Essex and Orange Streets in the heart of the South End, and when the hated stamps arrived in Boston the unfortunate Andrew Oliver was required to publicly resign his commission as collector of the stamp tax *under* the liberty tree. Oliver had previously offered to appease the angry Boston crowd by resigning in the courthouse, but this venue reeked too much of British authority, and McIntosh escorted the reluctant Oliver to the Liberty Tree.[47] When news of the fall of George Grenville's government reached Boston in September 1765, celebrations began at the liberty tree, on which a copper plate was fastened which memorialized the elm as "the Tree of Liberty."[48]

*　*　*

Just as Boston's Stamp Act protests drew on the customary inversion of Pope's Day celebrations, the liberty tree, under whose branches these protests were often enacted, drew on the ancient folk traditions of the may pole and its own rites of social inversion.[49] Under the branches of the liberty tree the normal order of things could be overturned, and it thus provided the perfect venue for theatrical attacks on British authority. Liberty trees and branchless liberty poles spread rapidly throughout mainland North America, and for the rest of the century they functioned as new venues for popular political culture, and as new bases of political power.

The liberty tree also served as an alternative to the gallows or "hanging tree." Standing on the Neck, no more than half a mile down Orange Street from the site of the liberty tree, Boston's gallows served as a very real symbol of the power of the state to punish those who broke the law. The liberty tree, however, represented the power of the people over those who transgressed the social and political codes of the governed. On both August 14 and November 1, 1765, Bostonians hung effigies of British ministers and stamp distributors, and a placard attached to the effigy of Andrew Oliver announced "It's a glorious sight to see a Stamp-man hanging on a tree." The liberty tree was the hanging tree of the people: if the state hung its enemies on the gallows, the people hung their opponents (in effigy) on the liberty tree, and, as the unfortunate Andrew Oliver discovered, they exacted vengeance below its branches.[50]

Boston's resistance movement was dependent on the participation of black and white seamen, laborers, mechanics, and women. While Patriot leaders sought to control the crowd and its theater of protest, their success remained contingent on the willing participation of large numbers of ordinary men and women. With an adult male population of about 3,000 in the 1760s, Boston's Patriot leaders occasionally found themselves confronting as many as 5,000 in meetings of "the whole Body of the People."[51] By themselves Boston's Patriot leaders were impotent against Britain, and it was angry biracial crowds of poor artisans, journeymen, apprentices, seamen, local farmers, and occasionally women who nullified the Stamp Act in 1765 and the Tea Act in 1773, drove the British army out in 1770, and began the war in 1775.[52]

The rites of resistance of the people of Boston quickly spread through the thirteen colonies.[53] Angry crowds assembled in protest against the Stamp Act, usually with effigies of stamp distributors and often around liberty trees and poles, in towns as far apart as Annapolis, New London, Newport, Philadelphia, New Brunswick, Charleston, New York City, and Portsmouth. Boston's political culture of resistance informed protest throughout the thirteen colonies, thereby laying one foundation of a new, American popular political culture in the coastal towns and cities of mainland British North America. Sitting at home or in a tavern or coffee house, a colonist could read about the similarity of rites of protest from far and near: all the Stamp Act protests listed above, for example, were reported in great detail in Charleston newspapers.[54]

The adoption of a liberty pole in New York City and the significance of this symbol to the local population provide another example of the development of American popular political culture. Liberty poles were even closer to may poles than liberty trees, for unlike a tree they could be erected by the community at a time and place of their choosing, allowing the crowd to publicly create a universal symbol of their dedication to the ideals and policies represented by liberty trees and poles. In the port cities of late eighteenth-century America, many liberty poles were fashioned from old ship masts, thus allowing the proletarian culture of seafarers to inform the rites of protest.

Between June 1766 and February 1770, five liberty poles were erected in New York City, beginning with the transmutation of a flag pole erected to honor the monarch and signify royal power in the province. The first liberty pole was dedicated by the Sons of Liberty as part of their celebrations of the repeal of the Stamp Act. A large public banquet was held on the commons, under the newly erected pole, in a festival echoed throughout the colonies. Four more liberty poles were erected at the same location, because Tory opponents and British soldiers—recognizing the symbolic significance of the liberty poles to the Patriot cause—regularly cut them down.[55] Although Tory judges sitting at Schenectady were unable to declare that the erection of a liberty pole in that town constituted a riot or a breach of the peace, others took the law into their own hands, destroying liberty trees and poles that they regarded as the focal points of popular sedition and treason.[56] In New York City, however, the Patriot population—from wealthy merchants to black seafarers—promptly replaced them.

Throughout the years of resistance, liberty poles and trees furnished Patriots of all classes with one of their most important meeting points. In Charleston, for example, in October 1768 a group of mechanics consecrated a large oak tree as their liberty tree and proceeded to toast the ninety-two members of the Massachusetts Assembly who had stood firm against the Townshend Act.[57] They met there with "other Inhabitants of Charles-Town" some eight months later to discuss and adopt a non-importation agreement, and then again shortly thereafter to discuss actions against those who refused to participate in the embargo.[58] A year later, more general meetings under this liberty tree discussed circular letters from other colonies about the Townshend duty on tea, the need to continue non-importation, and how to respond to the effective end of non-importation in the northern colonies.[59] In the spring of 1774 the tea crisis prompted "as great and respectable a Body of the Inhabitants" of Charleston to meet at their liberty tree "as have yet appeared upon any public occasion."[60] (See Figure 2.)

As resistance edged toward rebellion, white American men of different classes united in a variety of crowd actions, parades, feasts, songs, and toasts under liberty trees and poles, wherein they organized their opposition to new British policies and celebrated their defeat. These rites of resistance drew on a variety of ritual traditions: thus the residents of Norfolk, New York, Annapolis, Philadelphia, Charleston, Newbern, and Boston all used the familiar celebratory rites of firing cannon and muskets, displaying ships' colors, ringing church bells, parades, feasts, toasts, and illuminations in celebration of the repeal of the Stamp Act.[61]

The colonists drew on various local and Anglo-American traditions in their commemoration of Patriot victories and defeats. The fall of Grenville's ministry, for example, was celebrated in Philadelphia as a public holiday: church bells were rung throughout the city, happy crowds indulged "in congratulations on a revolution," and bonfires illuminated the evening skies.[62] Almost a decade later, on the day the Boston Port Act went into effect, the people of Philadelphia used familiar public rites to "express their sympathy and show their concern for their suffering brethren in the common cause of liberty."[63] Most shops and businesses were closed, church bells were muffled and rang solemn and mournful peals, ships in the harbor flew their flags at half mast, and people crowded into churches to in-

Figure 2. Raising the liberty pole. Engraving by John C. McRae based on an original work by F. A. Chapman, 1876. The Library Company of Philadelphia. Here the popular destruction of the symbols of royal rule are in the background, while in the foreground a multiracial crowd of men erect a liberty pole at the beginning of the war for independence. In the confusion, Tories look askance, young men enlist in the Continental army, and men, women, and children participate in one of the most important popular political rites of the late eighteenth century.

voke God's help.[64] These kinds of activities, drawing on familiar patterns of celebration and commemoration, were widely reported in newspapers throughout the colonies, and the circulation of this evolving discourse of political activity widened as Americans read about a unified resistance movement and discussed it in New England town meetings, outside Virginia court houses, and inside Philadelphia taverns.

In addition to newspapers, a variety of extra-legal organizations helped circulate information about popular political activity in the years after 1765. The Sons of Liberty, committees of correspondence, groups that enforced the embargo against trade with Britain, and new committees within the militia came into existence throughout the colonies, and they were in frequent communication with one another in order to coordinate the work of resistance. These organizations and the political power that they exercised were dependent on laborers, cordwainers, tailors, and carpenters, who joined with members of the elite in meetings of the radical and powerful committees formed by the Philadelphia militia during the 1770s.[65] The rites of resistance would have failed without this kind of interclass unity, which gave new political significance to familiar rites and new political power to those who participated in them.

In the town meetings of New England and in similar gatherings of the citizenry throughout the colonies, Patriot leaders read aloud communiqués received from similar organizations that detailed resistance activity, and then those present elected committees to draft responses. In addition, newspapers filled their pages with accounts of the crowd actions, meetings, feasts, toasts, resolutions, non-importation agreements, and sponsorship of domestic manufacturing undertaken by these Patriot organizations. The significance of these committees and newspapers in the communication of radical ideology has long been acknowledged, but their role in the transmission of the rites and symbols of popular political culture has been overlooked.[66]

There were a wide variety of ways in which Americans were able to participate in the political culture of resistance. Much of the resistance against Britain took the form of popular refusal to import, buy, or consume British goods, a form of economic pressure that was doomed to failure without the participation of all the colonies and most of their residents. These boycotts usually began when merchants and members of the Patriot elite met on public ground (often under liberty trees) to sign non-importation agreements, after which men and women of mixed social ranks combined to search out those who continued to import, buy, or use proscribed goods. This was a quite remarkable process of inter-class cooperation, uniting groups of laborers, craftsmen, merchants, and the elite in public action. The Sons of Liberty could not hope to enforce resistance on an unwilling populace: thus, when a Richmond merchant announced early in 1766 that he intended to abide by the Stamp Act and use stamped paper, the local Sons of Liberty were dependent on the active support of over four hundred white men of all ranks from the surrounding area for the success of their attempt to end this "matchless Impudence."[67]

White women, too, played a vital role in the politics of resistance. As members of the community who often had responsibility for the buying and selling of goods, women were deeply involved in the political culture of the 1760s and 1770s, and throughout the colonies they gathered to support the boycotts. The imperial crisis politicized women's position in the public sphere and enhanced their role in the popular politics of resistance and rebellion. In the fall of 1774, for example, Clementina Rind approvingly printed in the *Virginia Gazette* a plea by "A PLANTER'S WIFE" in South Carolina to "MY SISTERS AND COUNTRYWOMEN." Urging these women to forgo buying or using tea, the Planter's Wife asserted that women "cannot be tame spectators."[68] The women of Charleston heeded the call, subscribing to an agreement renouncing the use of tea in which they acknowledged their own role in securing "the Liberty of our Posterity."[69] Similarly, "upwards of 300 mistresses of Families" in Boston signed a petition pledging themselves to do without tea.[70] These women were actively involved in popular politics, and throughout the colonies many women took active stands in support of the Patriot cause. On occasion they published their agreements as examples for other women, and they engaged in crowd actions against recalcitrant merchants and shopkeepers.[71]

*   *   *

Civic feasts and toasts were an extremely important component of the newly emergent popular political culture throughout the angry American colonies, for they allowed those present to articulate their commitment, first to the Patriot cause and later to political causes and parties in the new republic. When Patriots sang their songs in private parlors and drank their toasts in dining rooms and taverns, they extended the realm of politics far outside colonial assemblies and governors' mansions, thereby aiding in the creation of a more truly popular political culture. In the years before in-

dependence, for example, men gathered in the great plantation houses of
Virginia could be found "toasting the Sons of America" and "singing 'Liberty Songs' as they call'd them."[72] Farther north, John Adams was only
one of many to sit in taverns and public houses and raise his glass to such
republican "sentiments" as the one offered by Robert Treat Paine on a
September evening in 1774: "May the collision of British Flint and American Steel produce that Spark of Liberty which shall illumine the latest posterity."[73] When George Washington was appointed by the Continental
Congress to command the new nation's army, leading members of the
Continental Congress and residents of Philadelphia could think of no
more appropriate rite than a feast at a Philadelphia tavern, where toasts to
the patriot cause were offered by all present.[74]

Relatively few of the toasts of the colonial era traveled farther than the
rooms in which they were offered. During the revolutionary and early national years however, newspapers played a vital role in broadcasting many
thousands of the toasts drunk at civic feasts and celebrations, thereby establishing them as a vital part of eighteenth-century political discourse.
These "sentiments" were of considerable significance not only to those
who drank them but also to others who then read them: one contemporary
observed that these toasts "may justly be denominated the criterions of
sentiment and truth," while another acknowledged that toasts were "in-
dicative of the public sentiment."[75]

A whole set of conventions surrounded the drinking of toasts in late
eighteenth-century America, investing them with extraordinary political
significance. Slates of toasts were often drunk at the conclusion of a civic
feast or sometimes after such ritual activity as the erection of a liberty pole.
Usually, but not always, it was an exclusively male group who raised their
glasses, and they drank toasts that had been thought out and written down
well in advance to ensure uniformity in sentiment. The minutes of the
Tammany Society's "Committee of Amusement," for example, reveal how
committee members created and transcribed the toasts for their annual
celebration of the anniversary of the evacuation of New York City by the
British well in advance of their civic feast.[76] Given the tradition that a person who disagreed with the sentiment could and should refuse to raise a
glass to a toast, it was extremely important that toasts be acceptable to all
present. One American newspaper reported with horror an occasion in
England when a "citizen rose and objected" that he could not in good
conscience join the company in drinking a toast honoring the resolutions
of a local corresponding society.[77]

What appeared as rites of sociability gave an impression of communal unity in support of often explicitly political causes, and a public display of disunity was to be avoided at all costs. "I was at my wits end to evade drinking" toasts at a New York city feast, claimed Alexander Anderson in the spring of 1795. The young man did not like alcohol, but he knew that to refuse to drink toasts with the rest of the company would give great offense, so he "threw the greatest part of the wine over my shoulder or under the table, and by that means contriv'd to drink but a small quantity."[78]

Given the fact that late eighteenth-century Americans were disinclined to raise their glasses to sentiments with which they did not agree, we can find in their toasts evidence about their beliefs, values, and objectives, whether they were elite merchants in New York City or yeoman militia on the Virginia frontier. Some toasts were blandly patriotic, as when Georgia's Chatham County militia celebrated Independence Day in 1785 by raising their glasses to "The United States of America," "The Governor and State of Georgia," and "The virtuous Militia of Georgia."[79] But on other occasions toasts went a good deal farther: they were actually used as evidence in London's treason trials of 1794, an example of the significance given by contemporaries to the words one uttered or agreed with when one was drinking.[80]

All classes of white men were able to take part in toasting rites, affirming their unity behind the Patriot cause, but it was generally non-elite Americans—white and black, male and female—who actually took to the streets in order to take direct action against British policy, thereby moving the diverse crowd actions of colonial America into a highly politicized national context. From the crowd of five hundred "Sailors, Boys and Negroes"[81] in Newport, Rhode Island who burned a small naval boat, to the crowd in Wilmington, Delaware who hung on the gallows a roasted ox presented to them by their pro-Stamp Act governor,[82] crowds throughout the colonies continually proved that without their active support resistance against Britain was futile.

This meant that people who were unused to enjoying a direct role in politics could now, whether by direct action and participation, spectatorship, or even calculated inaction, assume a political role. In Wilmington even "the very Negroes disdained to taste the Bait of Slavery which was laid for their Masters" by refusing to eat any of the tainted ox. It seems unlikely that any slave, however hungry he or she was, would have dared defy a white master or mistress by taking the meat, but the fact remains that this commentator was including slaves in this paean to the unity of the entire political community.[83]

Direct popular action climaxed in violent clashes between crowds of colonists and British soldiers, as in the Boston Massacre and the epochal clashes at Lexington and on the road to Boston. Others colonists gathered to commemorate crowd activities and those crowd members and bystanders who were killed by the British and their supporters: at least 2,000 Bostonians attended the funeral of Christopher Seider, killed by the Loyalist Ebenezer Richardson in February of 1770, and two months later some 10,000 of the city's residents walked six abreast in the funeral procession for the victims of the Massacre.[84]

This was a remarkably permeable political culture, one that was accessible to many different Americans. White women—especially those of the middling and upper classes—were deeply involved, as illustrated by the Williamsburg women who were wearing "homespun gowns,"[85] the northern women who manufactured cloth in their homes,[86] and the "female soldiers" of Connecticut who were prepared to tar and feather their opponents.[87] Newspapers often conjoined male and female political activity, as in one article that described Boston's female Association "against the use of East India Tea" and in the same breath announced that Massachusetts could raise 80,000 troops: clearly women's actions were an integral part of the popular political culture of resistance.[88] Without the support of others, the handful of elite and middling white men who comprised the Patriot leadership could achieve little, forcing them to acknowledge "the political principles" of American women.[89]

Black Americans built on long traditions of resistance as they participated in the theater of revolution in all their diversity, from Crispus Attucks and other free and enslaved residents of northern towns who participated in crowd actions, to the slaves on southern plantations who leaped into the political arena by fleeing from bondage after Governor Dunmore issued his revolutionary proclamation promising freedom to slaves who joined the British armies. During the colonial era black Americans had been excluded from most of the rites and celebrations of public ritual and festive culture or relegated to the less powerful and active roles of spectators. However, the revolutionary struggle allowed black Americans to employ their own political culture of resistance and celebration within the larger context of an evolving American political culture. Some sense of the full range of revolutionary possibilities comes across in the words of one black man who refused to move from the sidewalk next to Christ Church in Philadelphia to allow a white woman to pass, responding to her reprimand with the threat that she should wait and see what would happen when "Lord Dunmore and his black regiment come."[90] This politicization of African American men was gendered in a variety of different ways: this one white woman appears more as a victim than as a politically empowered agent in this encounter: moreover, for black women throughout British America empowerment and meaningful participation in the new American popular political culture was decidedly problematic.[91]

The success of Patriot resistance and eventually of rebellion itself was contingent on the active support and participation of people from all sections of the community, and in running away from plantations many black men and women were able to seize freedom and undermine the Patriot cause. On the other hand, throughout the 1760s and 1770s many colonial men and women of different races and social ranks affirmed their identification with the Patriot cause in the public rites of a nascent national popular political culture: attending a liberty tree meeting, hunting out those who broke the boycotts, drinking toasts, and singing songs of resistance.

*   *   *

With the coming of independence and the accompanying dislocation and hardship of seven years of full scale war, many of these rites of resistance appeared to lose relevance. But during the war years the trend toward a national discourse of political activity continued, as Americans throughout the nation gathered to celebrate the same events in often strikingly similar fashion. Once the war ended there was a hiatus of sorts: with a weak central government a national political culture appeared to have little relevance, and regional patterns began to reemerge. With the advent of the new federal union, however, a national political culture quickly flourished, building on the precedents of the years of resistance and revolution.

The declaration of American independence thus marked both an ending and a beginning, a point that was not lost on the many Americans who applauded the birth of the new republic with a mixture of old and new rites, customary and yet revolutionary. While some Americans first learned of the Declaration by reading it in a broadside or newspaper, many more heard it read aloud in town and country alike. In Boston the public reading of the Declaration from the balcony of the State House was "received with great joy" by "a great concourse of people," who then poured through the streets and tore down every picture or representation of "the king's arms, and every sign with any resemblance of it, pestle and mortar and crown, heart and crown, &c." that they could find, and then ceremoniously burned them all in King Street.[92] Much the same happened in Philadelphia, where the royal coat of arms that had graced the bench in the court room at the State House was torn down, dragged through the streets, and then burned, and in New York City, where an equestrian statue of George III was "laid prostrate in the dirt."[93] (See Figure 3.)

It was the anniversary of the Declaration of Independence that prompted many of the most extensive celebrations of the war-time years. John Adams recognized as much when he wrote to his wife Abigail that the second of July "will be celebrated, by succeeding generations, as the great anniversary Festival."[94] While Adams had the day wrong, he gauged the tenor of festive culture with great accuracy. Philadelphia, the erstwhile capital of the new nation, was host to some of the more extensive Independence Day celebrations. On the first anniversary Congress adjourned for the celebrations, which were announced by joyful peals of church bells. The merchant ships anchored on the Delaware mounted a colorful display of flags, while several warships fired thirteen-gun salutes in honor of the thirteen American states. When members of Congress and the state government, continental soldiers, and local militia units adjourned to taverns for civic feasts, artillery companies fired salutes to the toasts they offered. Cavalry, infantry, and artillery units paraded through the city, and in the evening thousands of candles illuminated the windows of city residents, while bonfires blazed and fireworks soared in the distance.[95] Few residents can have missed the irony of appropriating the rites employed a few years earlier in celebration of the monarch's birthday in this commemoration of the anniversary of the creation of a republic.

Celebrations of July Fourth continued in Philadelphia in the years that followed, although the hardships of the war and the confederation era often curtailed extensive celebratory rites. A shortage of candles, for example, occasionally prevented the illumination of windows, and in 1778 the Continental Congress advertised that it did "not expect . . . [that the inhabitants of Philadelphia] will illuminate their houses."[96] Throughout the nation members of the Patriot elite followed the example of Philadelphia and orchestrated their own Independence Day festivities, recognizing that these rites of celebration provided a valuable opportunity to draw attention to the Patriot cause and the need for national unity. These celebrations looked much the same in large towns and rural communities alike. In Albany, for example, the ninth anniversary of Independence was celebrated

Figure 3. Pulling down the statue of George III by the Sons of Freedom. Engraving by John C. McRae based on an original work by Johannes A. Oertel, 1876. The Library Company of Philadelphia. This engraving recaptures the power of the urban rites associated with resistance and revolution. While well-dressed Tories watch the proceedings with horror, a diverse crowd of New Yorkers destroy their town's most visible symbol of royal power. Almost two decades later, supporters of the French Revolution planted a liberty tree in the vacant space.

"with the usual demonstrations of joy." Townspeople watched a procession by the mayor, corporation, and "many respectable citizens" to Fort Orange, where local militia units fired a thirteen gun salute. In the evening the Corporation feasted at the City Tavern and drank "many patriotic toasts."[97] Sometimes it was the local militia who marched, but otherwise the rites were much the same in Hartford, Boston, Wilmington, Charleston, Elizabethtown, Newport, and even the frontier community of Lexington, Kentucky.[98]

But the elite could not hope to control all aspects of these early Independence Day festivities, for ordinary Americans were now used to a voice in the proceedings. The second anniversary of independence found crowds of ordinary Philadelphians out in the streets, celebrating the recent departure of the British army. While members of Congress staged their usual civic feasts, "a crowd of the vulgar" people of the city formed their own carnivalesque procession, featuring a prostitute whom they dressed in all the finery displayed in the Quaker city by the wives and mistresses of British officers during the preceding months. She wore "the Monstrous head dress of the Tory Ladies," and "occasioned much mirth," as these poorer men and women maligned elite women who had accompanied the British troops or betrayed the Patriot cause and enjoyed the good life in a city where many did not have enough to eat.[99] The fact that the target of popular abuse and the embodiment of both the enemy and the idea of betrayal were feminine suggests some measure of misogyny within this rite; nonetheless, this living female effigy earned the contempt of the crowd by virtue of her political affiliations, providing further evidence of the ways resistance and revolution had enlarged the political sphere and made political activity accessible to a wide range of women and men.

Crowds of ordinary Philadelphians were not slow to punish those who refused to celebrate July Fourth in an appropriate manner. When dusk fell they roamed the streets and broke the unilluminated windows of wealthier residents, who were presumed to have Tory sympathies. Many of these windows belonged to unfortunate Quakers, who were not always successful in keeping themselves above the fray. But Quaker merchants, in particular, appeared to the crowd to be living well while betraying the Patriot cause, and for this they paid dearly. In 1777, for example, the crowds broke "a great number"[100] of windows, with the Quakers Thomas and Sarah Fisher losing fifteen, Nicholas and Sarah Waln fourteen, and George Logan over fifty.[101] Throughout the nation poorer Americans without the means to participate in more elaborate celebrations commemorated the

Fourth in taverns or perhaps by breaking unilluminated windows. Especially among American sailors imprisoned in Britain and soldiers serving in the Continental Army, Independence Day was the year's most important festival.[102]

If Americans had thus created a day on which they could gather to affirm their allegiance to the new republic, they had also adopted a national hero, and whenever they gathered to feast and drink they raised their glasses to salute George Washington. The American Revolution created any number of credible heroes, but it was Washington who held the limelight. For while Paine, Jefferson, and the angry crowds who tore down Hanoverian crests and symbols had destroyed the images of royalty, popular faith in leaders who embodied popular values did not die so fast. Thus the rites that had been used to honor the Hanoverian monarchs were rehabilitated both for commemoration of the Fourth of July and in order to pay tribute to America's new "patriot king."

The transition began quickly, and as early as 1779 American Patriots in York, Pennsylvania were singing "GOD SAVE GREAT WASHINGTON! GOD DAMN THE KING," to the tune of "God Save the King."[103] Both during and after the Revolution, Washington received a hero's welcome wherever he went, from a militia parade and feast in Annapolis in 1781, to a procession in Boston that drew 24,000 spectators in 1788, to his triumphant entry into Philadelphia at the conclusion of the war in 1783.[104] On the latter occasion senior military officers and several militia corps met the general, and cannon and church bells welcomed the conquering chief into the national capital.[105]

On occasion, in direct emulation of the rites honoring British monarchs, some Americans celebrated Washington's birthday. In Williamsburg, for examples, two celebratory feasts were held at the Raleigh Tavern in 1779,[106] while in Richmond the day was celebrated in 1784 "with the usual demonstrations of joy."[107] All over the country at all manner of feasts and festivals, Americans drank to the health of "The Illustrious GEORGE WASHINGTON."[108] But most of the celebrations of Washington's birthday were in his native Virginia: little was made of the day elsewhere in the country, and the townspeople of Newport were unusual in doing so much as commemorating the day with the firing of a Federal salute of thirteen cannon.[109]

Yet for all their relatively small size and infrequency, celebrations of the anniversary of independence and of America's first citizen continued the process of uniting Americans in the creation of a national festive cul-

ture. Once the revolutionary war ended, however, these Americans were
no longer bound together by the threat of a large foreign army, dependence on a weak central government, or even the revolutionary committees of correspondence and patriot organizations that had held together
the resistance movement. Under these circumstances, the development of
a national political culture faltered, and local patterns of festive culture
enjoyed a limited resurgence. The locus of political power was with the
individual states rather than the weak central government of the Confederation, and it was in the state houses that politics was played out during
much of the 1780s. Political culture, in short, followed power in reverting
from national to local patterns, and many Americans celebrated their newly
acquired independence and the formation of their proud new republic in
local celebrations of essentially local events.

In Bennington, Vermont, for example, one of the largest political festivals of the 1780s was staged in commemoration of the anniversary of General John Stark's victory over a contingent of Hessians from General John
Burgoyne's army, a victory near Bennington that had culminated with the
surrender of an entire British army. The residents of the town assembled
at the court house, and a salute of eight cannons marked the formation of
a procession of local militia companies, government officials, and school
boys. Two orations rounded off the proceedings, which clearly had an
added significance for those local residents who had participated in, witnessed or perhaps nursed the wounded of this battle. But while the victory
at Bennington may have brought "great Glory" to Stark and his men in
1777, a decade later it had become just one of many battles fought in a long
and bloody war, and as such the festivities at Bennington were distinctly
local in character, and the anniversary was not commemorated elsewhere.[110]

Bostonians regularly celebrated the anniversary of several "local" military engagements, including the battle of Bunker Hill and the capture of
General John Burgoyne's army. The former was usually remembered with
formal rites appropriate for such a costly battle. Militia units from several
local towns assembled and paraded in Boston, and then heard "a pertinent
and judicious oration." After an artillery company had fired a salute, the
militia companies dispersed to inns and taverns throughout the city, where
they feasted and commemorated the bloody battle in their toasts.[111] Similar
rites marked the anniversary of the capture of Burgoyne's army, although
on these occasions the militia units often "performed a number of ma-
noeuvres and firings," commemorating the capture of a mighty British
army with a display of martial ability.[112]

Celebrations of the anniversary of the Franco-American victory at Yorktown were quite common in the southern states, but by far the most elaborate and extensive celebrations of local victories or revolutionary achievements took place in New York City.[113] Each November twenty-fifth city residents commemorated the anniversary of the departure of the British army in 1783. During the following decade, Evacuation Day was by far the most important date in the festive calendar of New York City, and increasingly small-scale celebrations continued well into the nineteenth century. Newspaper reports of the festivities rapidly acquired a formulaic tone, reporting "the usual demonstrations of joy"[114] on "the auspicious day."[115] The rites were familiar: bells pealed and cannons fired throughout the day, and ships on the Hudson and East Rivers displayed their colors. It was a holiday for all citizens, many of whom assembled in the morning to watch the militia parade through the city's major streets. Members of the Tammany Society, the First Flank Company of the 3rd Regiment, Captain Montagnie's infantry company, the New York Rangers, and the officers of assorted militia companies were only a few of the groups who would gather at taverns later in the day, to feast and toast "in convivial harmony."[116]

Thus in the years following the American victory at Yorktown popular political festivals and celebrations appeared to revert to essentially local patterns. It was not until the end of the 1780s that the ratification of the Federal Constitution reinvigorated national popular political culture. In the decade following ratification, the local celebrations and festivals of the Confederation era faded into relative insignificance, while a national political culture developed in more and larger celebrations of July Fourth and George Washington's birthday, festivals commemorating the achievements of the new French republic, and a revitalized politics of the streets. This development was hardly accidental. When the new Federal Constitution went into effect a great deal of political power shifted from the peripheries to the center, and for the first time since Yorktown many Americans began to take note of their national government, a government that now enjoyed the power to make a difference in their lives. Newspapers reported congressional speeches, presidential messages, and the reports of cabinet members, and national politics captured the limelight.[117]

Moreover, the powers inherent in this new national government were securely lodged in the hands of the "natural" elite, who would spend the coming years struggling among themselves over which of them should rule and what kind of nation they should preside over. But building on the precedents of their participation in resistance and revolution, ordinary

Americans continued to use the rites and symbols of America's emerging national political culture to make their own voices heard, and to contest the hegemony of the wealthy white men who ruled over them.

The shift from the localized political culture of the Confederation period to the contested centralized national political culture of the Federal era was perhaps best symbolized by the processions staged throughout America to celebrate the ratification of the Constitution. For these were festivals to celebrate a national political event, and they dwarfed the local celebrations of the recent past. They took place throughout the country, in perhaps the biggest display of national unity through festive culture since the Stamp Act crisis.

The largest and most widely reported celebration took place in Philadelphia, a "Grand Federal Procession" that was staged on July Fourth 1788. The procession was a magnificent spectacle, and Francis Hopkinson's detailed description filled a small pamphlet. The dawning of the auspicious day was saluted by the bells of Christ Church and a cannonade from a ship in the harbor. Ten fully decorated vessels spanned the harbor throughout the day, honoring the ten states that had ratified the Constitution. Those who were to march in the procession began assembling at eight o'clock in the morning, and the procession set off one and one-half hours later. Nine men "furnished with speaking trumpets" superintended the event, organizing the militia companies, tradesmen and craftsmen, government officials, clergymen, musical bands, students, lawyers, and all the various groups who comprised the eighty-eight parts of the parade. Charles Biddle recalled that he had never before seen "so much satisfaction expressed on every countenance as there was on this day," and it seemed clear that the people of Philadelphia had given a resounding vote of public approval to the new Federal Constitution.[118] (See Figure 4.)

But these processions were typical of the public events which were to comprise the popular political culture of the coming decade, in that they were accessible to a wide variety of citizens, who used their participation for their own political purposes. The Philadelphia procession exemplifies this, for although it appeared to function as a well-organized rite expressing popular support for and confidence in the new system of national government, many of the ordinary people who took part in the procession used their participation to voice their own partisan opinions. While several senior Pennsylvania judges carried a framed copy of the new constitution "in a lofty ornamented car, in the form of a large eagle," the lowly bricklayers who marched far behind them proudly carried a

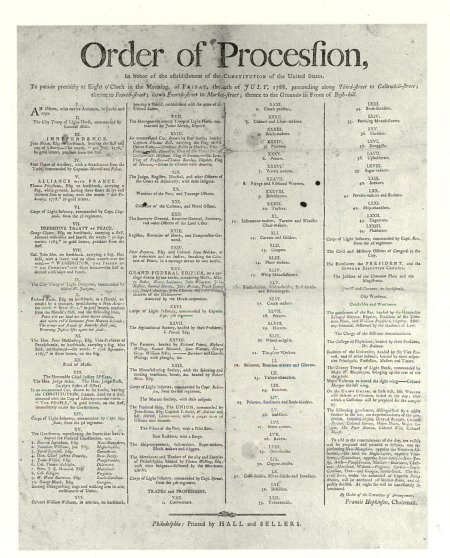

Figure 4. Order of Procession, in honor of the establishment of the Constitution of the United States. Hall and Sellers, Philadelphia, 1788. Library of the American Philosophical Society. Philadelphia's Grand Federal Procession was the most elaborate procession in honor of the ratification of the Federal Constitution, and one of the largest parades of the late eighteenth century. Almost all adult white male residents participated or were represented, and thousands of other Philadelphians endorsed the parade as spectators.

banner proclaiming "Both buildings and rulers are the work of our hands."
Even farther behind, the humble Biscuit Bakers' banner asked "May the
Federal Government revive our trade," and the flag of the Goldsmiths, Silversmiths, and Jewelers announced that "The purity, brightness, and so-
lidity of this metal is emblematical of that liberty which we expect from the
new Constitution." [119]

While many artisans, militia men, craftsmen, students, and other citizens were ready and willing to celebrate the ratification of the constitution,
their support of the new system of government was clearly conditional,
and they spelled out some of these conditions on the banners they carried.
Elsewhere citizens who were even more dubious about the new system
of government went much farther with their opposition. In Carlisle, supporters of the new constitution agreed to parade in honor of ratification
and threatened to break the unilluminated windows of Anti-Federalists,
prompting their opponents to gather to prevent the procession. A violent encounter led to the rout of the Federalists, and the Anti-Federalist
crowd—"a mob" [120] to their enemies, "the People" [121] to their friends—
spiked the Federalists' cannon, formally burned a copy of the Federal Constitution, and then paraded and burned in effigy the leading Federalists
Thomas McKean and James Wilson. [122]

Celebrations of ratification took place all over the country, from Baltimore to Boston, from Edenton in North Carolina to New Brunswick in
New Jersey, and from Chelsea in Connecticut to Charleston. [123] Although
few if any were as violent as that of Carlisle, most appear to have shared
some of the sense of contestation conveyed by the banners carried in Philadelphia's Federal Procession. These political contests within celebrations
of a unified polity set the stage for the epochal 1790s, a decade during
which an ever more national popular political culture of festivals, processions, civic feasts, and other rites filled America's streets and public places,
providing venues for partisan conflict and popular participation in the construction of national political parties.

It was during the 1790s, in villages and towns across the nation, that a
national popular political culture finally emerged. It was founded on British and colonial precedents, and had been fashioned by Patriots whose protests and celebrations had assumed a similar form throughout the thirteen
colonies. Their need for public displays of communal unity had required
the Patriot elite to encourage many different Americans to take part in parades, crowd actions, and all manner of festivals, so when a powerful new
national government was inaugurated in 1789 there already existed a tradi-

tion of popular involvement in the affairs of government. It is only by exploring the political badges, songs and toasts, the partisan parades, feasts, and crowd actions that we can begin to see what politics was all about for ordinary Americans. Only then can we begin to see how these Americans pulled politics out of the corridors of power and onto the streets of the new republic.

2

The Partisan Politics
of Popular Leadership

GEORGE WASHINGTON WAS OF PARAMOUNT importance in the political culture of late eighteenth-century America. His enormous popularity meant that the Virginia planter enjoyed considerable political power, that he occupied a central position in early national political rites and symbols, and that he had a profound impact on popular perceptions of the ways in which partisan leaders should conduct themselves in and out of office.[1] The development of Washington as a symbolic figure led to heated political debate over leadership within the early republic and partisan contests over the treatment and celebration of both the man and the symbol.

On the one hand, some Americans revered Washington as Cincinnatus reborn, an able yet retiring servant of the people whose very presence brought strength to the national government and safeguarded liberty and republicanism. On the other hand, many Americans recalled the antimonarchical, egalitarian republican rhetoric of the mid-1770s and were troubled by the dazzling aura that surrounded Washington. When James Wilson had spoken up in the Constitutional Convention to propose "that the Executive consist of a single person," his words had occasioned a "considerable pause" and Benjamin Franklin's somber warning "that it was a point of great importance."[2] To those present in the Pennsylvania State House, Washington was the obvious choice for president under the new system, and the power that would accrue to an office held by a man of such staggering popularity was a sobering thought. The Founders were familiar with the discourse of republicanism and its assumption of the inevitable degeneration of virtuous republican leadership, as had happened in Rome, the Italian city states, and most recently Great Britain itself.

The power of the new president, in the context of the ways in which he acted as head of state and the symbolic role he played in the emerging festive culture of the new republic, was thus integral to the discourse of early national partisan politics. In their participation in or critiques of the development of a partisan cult of Washington, and in their reactions to the ways in which Washington and then Adams and Jefferson conducted themselves and were received by others, ordinary Americans were able to take part in the construction of this political culture of national leadership: this was one more avenue into the public political sphere traveled by many ordinary Americans. Celebration of Washington—both as a real leader and as a symbolic figure—was at the heart of Federalist political culture. In contrast, the Democratic Republicans took issue with both the symbols and the rites surrounding it, and after contesting celebration of Washington they turned elsewhere to create an alternative festive culture.

The contest over partisan leadership was waged on several different levels. To begin with, elite leaders of the nascent Federalist and Democratic Republican parties argued over the most appropriate ways for their president to act and be treated, thus creating another contested arena in their struggle for control of the polity. With their conservative faith in social hierarchy, leaders and supporters of the Federalist party consciously melded the traditions and trappings of colonial celebrations of the monarch into a political culture around Washington, hoping to create a secular cult of Washington with rites and symbols that would strengthen their party and its plans for the new nation. Partisan opposition to this cult developed quickly, and a very real struggle developed among white men of all ranks for control over the content and meaning of celebrations staged in honor of Washington.

Through their participation in the struggle over the political culture of popular leadership, many ordinary Americans deepened their involvement in partisan politics in the public sphere. But ordinary Americans who involved themselves in celebrations of the anniversary of Washington's birthday, Adams's national leadership during the Quasi-War against France in 1797–1800, or Jefferson's inauguration were neither restrained nor defined by the politicking of partisan rulers, and their actions often represented far more than mere expressions of support for developing political parties and their leaders. While these aspects of popular political culture furnished Americans with opportunities to cheer publicly for a partisan leader, they simultaneously placed the policies and actions of political leaders in the public eye and revealed the dependence of these leaders on widespread and large-scale expressions of popular support. As a result, ordinary Americans gained some degree of power over the partisan politicking of their rulers, and the nature and style of political party leadership by Washington, Adams, and Jefferson was in part constructed by the ordinary folk of the new republic.

*   *   *

For generations before the outbreak of the American war for independence, the elite inhabitants of the port towns and cities of British America had staged and participated in ritual celebration of Queen Anne and the three Hanoverian kings. These events were far less common in the more rural areas inhabited by the large majority of the colonial population, and throughout British America royal birthday celebrations were smaller in scale and far less frequent than in Great Britain. This is not to say, however, that the festive rites used to honor monarchs were unknown to British North Americans: some may have remembered or heard tell of celebrations of the monarch's birthday in Great Britain, others born and raised in the colonies might have read in the newspapers of contemporary English celebrations, and a few may have witnessed or read about the festivals held in New York City, Philadelphia, or Charleston.

This collective memory may have gone beyond a shared consciousness of the appropriate ways to ritually honor the monarch, and encompassed a sense of the powers of ordinary folks within these events. For, just as emigrants to the American colonies brought with them their heritage of May poles and the Fifth of November, so too they may have remembered how the common folk in Britain had made partisan use of celebrations of their rulers, as when the parishioners of eighteen London churches had revived their celebrations of Queen Elizabeth's birthday as a deliberate affront against the unpopular Queen Henrietta Maria.[3]

The point here is that the explosion of celebrations of George Washington's birthday all over America in the 1790s, celebrations that bore a remarkable resemblance to royal birthday celebrations and allowed for a significant degree of popular voice and agency, attests to the strength of folk memory. At first it appeared that such memories would fade after Paine and Jefferson signed the death warrant for monarchical rule in the thirteen colonies, and when urban crowds executed George III in effigy, tearing down statues, tavern signs, and anything that symbolized royal power and rule. The Continental Congress assumed the powers and responsibilities of the monarch, and congressional leaders reconstructed the rites and symbols of traditional celebrations of royal birthdays in the newly created annual commemoration of the anniversary of independence. However, the celebration of an individual ruler did not die quickly, and in the ritual world of festive culture it was George Washington who "filled the king-shaped vacuum that followed the overthrow of George III."[4]

From the small and relatively private celebrations of his birthday in Virginia to the larger parades and festivals staged in his honor in the decade after Yorktown, Washington found himself the object of considerable popular celebration. But it was with his triumphant journey from Mount Vernon to his inauguration in New York City that these disconnected celebrations began the process of coalescence into a national political culture with Washington at its center, a political culture *of* Washington. The residents of many towns and villages between Mount Vernon and New York City welcomed the president-elect with parades and civic feasts, in a pattern of ritual behavior strikingly similar to the royal progresses of English monarchs to their coronations.[5]

Washington's most memorable reception was in New Jersey, where the women of Trenton erected a triumphal arch over a bridge leading into the city: eighteen feet high, fifteen feet wide, and ten feet long, the laurel-covered arch was an imposing edifice softened by the numerous flowers entwined in the laurel and evergreen branches. As Washington approached he saw a decorated sign hanging from the top of the arch memorializing the date of his famed victory over the Hessian occupants of the town during the Revolutionary War. Another sign spanned the entire top of the arch, proclaiming in large golden letters that "THE DEFENDER OF THE MOTHERS WILL ALSO PROTECT THEIR DAUGHTERS." After passing under the arch Washington came to the women who had constructed it, with their daughters standing before them. All were dressed in white, and while the mothers sang a welcoming ode the daughters scattered flowers across Washington's path. It was an extraordinary reception, and with characteristic élan Washington "made them a low bow [and] say'd the Ladies had done him a very great honour."[6] (See Figure 5.)

It was far more common for Washington to be greeted by men, who would "meet their beloved general with peals of thunder, and honour him with all the pompous parade of war."[7] It was these Trenton women who were responsible for the design of the arch, the composition of the ode, and all other aspects of the ceremony: in their use of rites and symbols these women showed themselves to be thinking along the same lines as their male counterparts and drawing on similar monarchical traditions, in this

Figure 5. View of the Triumphal Arch, and the manner of receiving General Washington at Trenton, on his route to New York. *Columbian Magazine* (Philadelphia), May 1789. Library of the American Philosophical Society. Less well known than a more elaborate and almost entirely fictional illustration of the mid-nineteenth century, this contemporary engraving shows one of the most remarkable female rites of the late eighteenth century. Traveling to his inauguration in New York City, George Washington rides toward a triumphal arch designed by the women of Trenton. When he passed under the arch the women and their daughters sang an ode to him and threw flowers before him.

case that of the triumphal arches employed by the English to welcome new monarchs into London and other cities.[8] The thirteen pillars supporting the arch and the laurel employed in its construction were common elements in contemporary male ritual.

But in other ways this women's celebration differed considerably from normative male ceremonies. A mid-nineteenth-century print of the scene by James Baillie (1848) reconstructed it along entirely more male and martial lines, displaying four large American flags and an American eagle with its wings outstretched atop the arch. None of these symbols of the white male polity were actually used by the women of Trenton, who had in fact placed a large sunflower at the summit of their arch. Their use of large numbers of flowers in place of the martial motifs employed by men had considerably softened the image of the triumphal arch, an impression compounded by the ode the women sang and by the flowers strewn in Washington's path by young girls wearing flowing white dresses. The women thus commemorated Washington's victory over the Hessians in their own style, while simultaneously articulating their expectation that "The Defender of the Mothers Will Also Protect their Daughters."[9]

The women of Trenton made clear their high expectations of Washington's presidency, and they were not simply deferring to those men in their community who defended the new Constitution and supported Washington. They had taken control of the rites and symbols of a major festive occasion and had thus moved into the popular political process, directing it to meet their own requirements and purposes, and to voice their own, gendered expectation of the nation's new leader.

New York City hosted both the inauguration and the grandest celebrations of Washington's accession to power. Ships flew decorative flags, bells rang, cannon roared, militia men marched, and thousands watched what they could of the inauguration itself. With night fall came a general illumination of the city and a superb display of fireworks. Several weeks later the elite enjoyed a celebratory ball similar to those staged a decade or two earlier in New York, Philadelphia, and Richmond in honor of the monarch's birthday: every woman who attended the ball was presented with a small fan, made in Paris, the ivory handle of which featured a portrait of Washington. If Washington was in some ways treated in the manner of a British king, his consort Martha was received as a queen. When she passed through Philadelphia on her way to join the president in New York City she was met by two companies of dragoons: they escorted her into the city, where she was greeted by the ringing of church bells and a fiery salute by a city artillery company.[10]

Thus from the very beginning of George Washington's presidency many of the traditional rites and symbols of monarchical rule were employed in his honor. Throughout his presidency his dignified and almost regal bearing together with his refusal to speak out against the use of these and other monarchical traditions showed Washington to be actively involved in the creation and enhancement of a quasi-royal political culture around his person and his leadership. This was particularly evident in the president's creation of what he and Alexander Hamilton considered appropriate forms of presidential etiquette. Washington agreed with and adopted Hamilton's recommendation that he should avoid a populist style of leadership and stress the dignity of his office, even "at the risk of partial or momentary dissatisfaction." The risk was a real one, for despite Washington's overwhelming popularity the ideological heritage of the American Revolution was strong: monarchy, aristocracy, and perhaps even deference were things of the past, while republicanism, liberty, and equality were the new political touchstones. Hamilton noted that "Men's mind's are prepared for a pretty high tone in the demeanor of the Executive; but I doubt whether for so high a tone as might in the abstract be desirable. The notions of equality are as yet in my opinion too general and too strong." [11]

As a result, in his official capacity as president Washington accepted no private invitations. Instead he held a levee once every week at which he conversed for half an hour with people admitted "by introduction through particular officers." [12] When Washington hosted these levees on Tuesday afternoons, guests found him standing before the fireplace in the rear dining room of his home, from which all chairs had been removed so that nobody could sit down in the presence of the president. Dressed in black silk velvet, his hair powdered and gathered behind him, and holding a cocked hat in his hand, Washington would formally bow to each visitor, a gesture that enabled the president to avoid the egalitarian shaking of hands.[13] These highly formal affairs served to further distance Washington from *all* other Americans, and they bore a clear resemblance to European court receptions. Many years later Lady Henrietta Liston, the wife of the British minister to the United States during Washington's presidency, remembered with the surprise of an English aristocrat that Washington had possessed "a perfect good breeding, & a correct knowledge of even the Etiquette of a Court." [14]

The levees immediately drew political criticism. William Maclay recorded attending one in December 1790.

> The practice, however, considered as a feature of royalty, is certainly antirepublican. This certainly escapes nobody. The royalists glory in it as a point gained. Republicans are borne down by fashion and a fear of being charged with a want of respect to General Washington. If there is treason in the wish I retract it, but would to God this same General Washington were in heaven! We would not then have him brought forward as the constant cover to every unconstitutional and irrepublican act.[15]

Maclay recognized that Washington's enormous popularity made it difficult to separate attacks on presidential practices and institutions from criticisms of the hero himself. But by the beginning of Washington's second term the partisan press of the Democratic Republican party was rather more assertive in its attacks on the policies of the Washington administration, and resentment of Washington's court began to surface. One satirical piece advertised for a courtly "Poet laureat," and was addressed "To the Noblesse and Courtiers of the United States." The advertisement required of the successful applicant's poetry that "certain *monarchical prettinesses* must be highly extolled, such as LEVIES, DRAWING ROOMS, STATELY NODS INSTEAD OF SHAKING HANDS, TITLES OF OFFICE, SECLUSION FROM THE PEOPLE, &c. &c."[16]

It was the anti-republican nature and intent of the levees that drew the fire of most correspondents. Assuming the pseudonym of the republican martyr "Sidney," one correspondent asserted that, however trifling the levees might appear in and of themselves, they remained "a deviation from the principles and spirit of our political institutions." If allowed to continue, Washington's courtly receptions would create "a distinction between the public servant and his visitors, a distinction incompatible with a republican constitution."[17] As Benjamin Franklin Bache observed in a letter to his father, the levees of President Washington "of whom no one six months ago would have thought disrespectfully . . . are [now] generally censured."[18]

While the levees were largely private affairs, more public presentations of Washington in regal fashion proved even more controversial. In a pointed if perhaps apocryphal letter to the editor of the Philadelphia *Aurora*, "A Farmer" reported that his neighbor had recently seen a magnificent coach on the streets of the American capital, and had returned with tales of having seen Prince Edward. Rumor had it that George III's son was visiting Canada, giving the story some plausibility, so the intrigued farmer had gone to Philadelphia to see the coach and its royal occupant for himself. French in design, the cream-colored coach was painted with decorative motifs protected by thin sheets of glass, and it was drawn by four white horses driven by a liveried German servant. Traveling along the Frankford road the farmer met the largest ceremonial coach then in existence in the United States, but to his "utter surprize and disappointment, who should it be but the President of the United States!—Ah thought I to myself the times are changed, and have changed with them the *plain and republican General Washington* into a being, which my neighbour Tribble took to be a Prince." Another correspondent attacked Washington's coach as one of those "baubles [which] are an insult to the understanding of a free people." [19]

Despite serious ideological rifts within the Federalist party, the leading members of Washington's administration were deeply involved in the construction of this presidential culture of and around Washington. Hamilton may have believed in an almost monarchical and aristocratic society while Adams may have been a true republican, but they shared a belief in the necessity of a rigidly hierarchical society. With Washington at the summit of this society, Federalists hoped that popular support for their leader would make the enactment of policies they favored easier. Support for the development of this partisan cult came from white men and women of all social ranks, but especially from the residents of port towns and cities who constructed many of the most elaborate festivals and celebrations in honor of Washington. Opposition to both the culture of Washington and the policies advanced under its auspices also came from all ranks, from the elite Southern slaveholders who employed the rhetoric of republican liberty to galvanize opposition to Federalist policies, to the ordinary men and women who were perhaps a little less calculating in their employment of such rhetoric.

The result was that struggles over and within the culture of Washington generally assumed a strongly partisan tone: those who defended the presidential culture appeared as Federalists, those who attacked it as Democratic Republicans. Much of the time the issue was not Washington himself, for most white Americans had enormous respect and even love for the man. The issue was more the partisan deployment of the man and the symbol, so a Continental veteran laboring in the streets of New York

City might revere the man but despise the construction of a partisan cult around him.

The drawing of partisan lines was clearly visible in the congressional battles over whether the president should enjoy a formal title, and whether his head should appear on the national coinage, contests that informed the larger popular debate over the cult of Washington. During the late 1780s Washington had occasionally been referred to as "His Excellency," but no formal title came with the office of the Presidency, and the Constitution had been clear in its directive that "No Title of Nobility shall be granted by the United States." As a consequence, when Vice-President John Adams began referring, during Senate discussions of Washington's first inaugural address, to *"His most gracious speech,"* the indomitable William Maclay rose to his feet and warned Adams that during the recent struggle "against kingly authority" Americans had learned to hate such terms: they were, he concluded, "odious to the People" and would "give offense."[20]

Adams made no secret of his belief in the need for rule by the natural elite, by means of a balanced constitution in which the best and the brightest of the white male American elite would rule with rank, titles and privilege. Maclay disagreed, arguing that

there had been a revolution in the sentiments of the people respecting government, equally as great as that which had happened in the government itself. That even the modes of it [monarchical government] were now abhorred. The enemies of the Constitution had objected to it the facility there would be of transition from it to kingly government, and all the trappings and splendor of royalty. That if such a thing as this appeared on our minutes, they would not fail to represent it as the first step of the ladder in the ascent to royalty.[21]

The debate over a title for Washington spread beyond Philadelphia, and Washington's supporters soon realized that their campaign could do Washington and his administration more harm than good. The president's friend David Stuart wrote from Virginia that nothing "could equal the ferment and disquietude, occasioned by the proposition regarding titles."[22] He added that Adams was widely regarded as the instigator of the plan and that Washington's name remained unsullied, but in a quiet and tactful manner Stuart warned Washington that his popularity would suffer should he actively seek a title for himself.

As a result Maclay won the day, and a writer in the *New-York Journal* commended the Congress for "their good sense and independence of monarchical and European habits."[23] But many citizens, worried by the conservative, counter-revolutionary tendencies they saw in the fiscal programs and foreign policies of the Federalists, remained concerned about the attempts by the Federalist ruling elite to enhance their power and prestige. They feared that "the name of federalist had been assumed by men who approve the constitution, merely as 'a promising essay towards a well ordered government,' that is to say, as a step towards a government of kings, lords and commons."[24] The planters and yeoman farmers who comprised the Democratic Republican Society of Pinckneyville, South Carolina were typical in their contention "that men, by appointments to public offices, are not rendered honourable. . . . We, therefore, consider all honourable titles of office, all affectations of etiquette . . . not only frivolous, but beneath the dignity of republicans, and subversive of equal liberty."[25] Members of the Democratic Society of Pennsylvania, a more urban group composed primarily of middling craftsmen and artisans with a few members from both the working poor and the local Democratic Republican elite, unanimously passed a similar resolution in which they expressly condemned "courtly forms, etiquettes and manners" and "the mimicry of . . . [this] absurd pomp by the citizens of a free commonwealth."[26]

Citizens formed Democratic Republican societies in every state of the union because of their concern about "the amazing want of Republicanism, which now forms a conspicuous trait in the characters composing the highest offices in the federal government,"[27] and these groups censored "the measures of our general government" with "the vigilance of a faithful centinel."[28] The Sons of Liberty and the various committees set up to coordinate resistance and revolution provided indigenous models for these societies while the Jacobin club in Paris furnished contemporary inspiration, and the first of well over forty Democratic Republican societies was formed in Philadelphia during the spring of 1793. The members of this Democratic Society of Pennsylvania were typical in their practice of addressing each other as "citizen" and their absolute refusal to use titles of any kind.[29] The farmers, craftsmen, and planters who organized Democratic Republican societies based them on "the celebrated declaration of American Independence"[30] and sought "to revive the republican spirit of '76."[31] These men were angered by the attempts of leading Federalists to construct a partisan cult of Washington that would temper American republicanism with a hierarchical government and society, and the partisan use of Washington's popularity as a shield for policies that favored the interests of the mercantile elite: in these societies they organized feasts and festivals, they composed, circulated, and published manifestoes and resolutions, and they petitioned the federal government and published addresses to the American people in order to organize resistance to what they interpreted as counter-revolution in both the style and the substance of national government.[32]

One of the clearest examples of what its enemies labeled "the spirit of Aristocracy in America"[33] came toward the end of Washington's first term as president, with the creation of the United States Mint, an integral part of Secretary of the Treasury Hamilton's controversial economic program. Most of the European coins circulating in the United States followed traditional iconographic patterns, with an emblem or coat of arms on one side and a portrait or bust on the other. Various representations of "Liberty" had appeared on state coins since the late 1770s, as had the increasingly popular new national emblem, the eagle. But during the later 1780s pressure grew to follow tradition and the example of several states by featuring a representation of Washington on the first coins to be produced by the federal government. Hamilton's lengthy "Report on the Establishment of a Mint" touched on the significance of the emblems to be placed on the national coinage. "The devices of the Coins are far from being matters of indifference," he mused, for "they may be made the vehicles ["instruments" in Hamilton's first draft] of useful impression."[34]

The bill resulting from Hamilton's plan reached the House of Representatives on March 24, 1792, and it specified that Washington's head, his first initial, and his full last name would appear on the coins of the United States. Along with the bill came sample patterns for the one cent coin, which were distributed among the congressmen.[35] (See Figure 6.) There followed an acrimonious congressional debate over the significance of various political symbols. John Page of Virginia argued that the practice of placing heads on coins was clearly monarchical, and that "it will be more agreeable to the citizens of the United States to see the head of Liberty on their coin, than the heads of presidents." Samuel Livermore of New Hampshire responded by arguing that "the President was a very good emblem of Liberty . . . how the President's head being on our coins could effect the Liberty of the people, was incomprehensible to him."[36]

When the debate reopened two days later, John Francis Mercer of Maryland argued that stamping heads on coins had done nothing for the honor of Nero or Caligula, and William B. Giles of Virginia pointed out that whatever was placed on the coins of the United States would represent

Figure 6. Cent coin. 1792. Smithsonian Institution. A sample cent similar to many state-issued coins of the era. Alexander Hamilton and some Federalists hoped to enhance popular respect for the new Federal government by having Washington's bust impressed on the coins of the new republic. Only after long debate was the plan defeated by those who feared it savored too much of monarchy.

the nation to the rest of the world. Egbert Benson of New York put up a last ditch defense of the Federalist position; he "ridiculed the idea of the people's being enslaved by their presidents, much less by his image on their coin."[37] Page finished the business, and ensured that Washington would never live to see his image on the nation's coins, by warning his "constituents of the danger . . . of imitating the flattery and almost idolatrous practice of Monarchies, with respect to the honor paid to their Kings, by impressing their images and names on their coins. . . . We are under obligations to the great man now our President, but a lover of Liberty and friend to the Rights of Man, would be cautious how he showed his sense of that obligation." Page concluded that were he the President, "I would cut off my hand rather than it should sign the act as it now stands." By a vote of 32 to 24, the House refused to recede from its amendment.[38]

Once Congress had defeated his plan, Hamilton lost all control of the process. The United States Mint was controlled by Jefferson in the Department of State, and he gave control of the mint and coinage to the ardent Democratic Republican David Rittenhouse.[39] With the control of iconography securely in republican hands, the American coins produced during the 1790s bore impressive emblems of liberty. Moreover, as the contagion of French Revolutionary radicalism spread, these female representations of liberty came to bear a striking resemblance to the French figure of Marianne, "mild yet resolute . . . firm, but femenine," with long hair billowing out from under a liberty cap.[40] (See Figure 9 below.) But after Jefferson's retirement and Rittenhouse's death these Democratic Republicans were replaced by the Federalists Timothy Pickering and Elias Boudinot, who lost little time in removing liberty caps from several American coins and recasting the figure of liberty in more stately and less revolutionary terms: clearly both sides agreed with Hamilton that these symbols were "instruments of useful impression."[41] It was a battle won by the Democratic Republicans, however, for after Jefferson's election his supporters and appointees were able to reestablish liberty poles and caps on the coinage.

It is difficult to gauge the popular significance of this battle, but it is surely no exaggeration to say that the symbols of popular liberty rather than adulatory images of Washington impressed on coins handled by journeymen and merchants, and seamstresses and farmers, must have had some impact on popular mentalités. The actual battles over levees, titles, the coinage, and other monarchical rites and symbols of Washington's presidential rule were generally elite affairs, fought out by the partisan members of the ruling class. Occasional newspaper commentaries and the resolutions of Democratic Republican societies show that white men below the ranks of the elite were well aware of these issues and thought them significant, but more than anywhere else it was in the public realm of festive culture—in what went on in the streets and in the public places of the republic—that ordinary Americans were best able to participate in or challenge the developing cult of Washington.

Popular celebrations honoring Washington and the anniversary of his birthday developed quickly during the early 1790s. The president visited both the northern and southern states during his first term, allowing men and women of all races and social ranks an opportunity to see their national leader and greet him as they saw fit. In Congregational New England the rites varied from a simple militia escort and tour of local "woolen manufactures" in Hartford to more elaborate celebrations in Salem.[42] The diarist William Bentley recorded that many of "the Inhabitants" of the Massachusetts port town congregated to greet Washington in the fall of 1789: militia men, local officials, clergy, merchants, mechanics, and school children assembled in well ordered ranks, while a large number of women, laborers, mariners, and perhaps some of the town's black population gathered as spectators. Washington passed through the assembled masses, who then formed in procession behind him and marched to the Court House for a welcoming ode and speech followed by a few words from the president. The day concluded with a display of fireworks and an elite feast.[43]

In the south the rites of welcome were particularly extravagant, drawing on the regional traditions of elite-dominated receptions for new governors and celebrations of the British monarch's birthday. When the president arrived in Charleston aboard a small boat handled by thirteen masters of American ships, he was serenaded by musicians of the American society and the choir of St. Philip's Church, who sang such pieces as the triumphal ode "He Comes, the Hero Comes." Once in the city proper Washington was greeted at the Exchange by a cannon salute, a militia parade, and a large gathering of the citizenry.[44]

From there Washington went on to Savannah, where he was welcomed by a committee of prominent citizens and militia officers "who were dressed in light blue silk jackets, black sattin breeches, white silk stockings, and round hats with black ribbons having the words Long Live the President, in letters of gold." Artillery companies fired welcoming salutes, a band and singers performed the familiar "He Comes, the Hero Comes," ships flew their decorative flags, and a procession assembled to escort Washington to his hotel.[45] Even before Washington was halfway through his first term, a good many Americans had seen the new president and witnessed or even participated in the rites of welcome staged by members of the local elite, even in such small rural communities as Edenton and Salisbury in North Carolina.[46] In addition to the residents of these communities, Americans who could not see their president were able to read about these elaborate welcomes in their local newspapers.

It was the annual celebrations of Washington's birthday, however, that allowed ordinary folk all over the country to take part in the festive culture developing around the first president, and thus to participate in the political battles fought out within this aspect of early national festive culture.

For although the earliest commemoration of Washington's birthday had been restricted to Virginia, by the early 1790s the practice had spread throughout the new republic, and had become an important component of early national popular political culture. (See Map 1.)

Perhaps the celebration of the birthday of an elected president appeared logical to citizens who had some small familiarity with the celebration of royal birthdays, just as English men and women had substituted celebrations of Cromwell's birthday for their celebrations of Charles I's birthday in the mid-seventeenth century.[47] There is still something quite surprising about the nature of Washington's birthday celebrations, however, for celebrations of royal birthdays had been rare outside the great seaports of colonial America and yet celebrations of Washington's birthday quickly spread all over the new republic and were reported on the pages of most newspapers. Perhaps the collective memory of royal birthdays had remained strong, or perhaps detailed newspaper reports helped establish a stock ritual, for the new republican celebrations rapidly assumed a standard form. In many communities the dawn of the twenty-second of February was greeted with the firing of cannon or perhaps the ringing of church bells, rites that were repeated at regular intervals throughout the day. The usual rhythms of work were interrupted in the middle of the day by a militia or civic parade, culminating in an assembly of the citizenry at some central location. Following this, members of the white male community gathered at local inns, taverns, and even private homes for civic feasts and toasting ceremonies, although in larger urban locations these groups were often further subdivided along class, trade, and partisan lines.

In locations from coastal Maine to Charleston, South Carolina, from Morristown, New Jersey to Savannah, Georgia, and from Bristol, Rhode Island to Lexington, Kentucky and Rutland, Vermont, one can find a high degree of conformity within the festive structure of Washington's birthday celebrations.[48] In these public events there remained, however, a space wherein participants and onlookers could give some measure of ideological shape and meaning to relatively standardized festive rites. Despite their veneer of ritual conformity, Washington's birthday celebrations were often contested events, with different groups jostling for a voice within local observance of one of the new nation's most important festive occasions.

At the heart of this contest lay partisan politics and the battle between the rival policies and ideologies of the Federalists and the Democratic Republicans. This political struggle was complicated by issues of class: Washington enjoyed considerable popularity among military veterans, urban

Map 1. Communities that celebrated George Washington's birthday, 1789–1801.

workers, and many yeoman farmers and planters, but during the 1790s more and more of these men reacted angrily against the members of the Federalist elite who were actively constructing a cult of Washington, and striving to employ the president's birthday to further strengthen their position. Sectionalism, too, came into play: by the latter end of the 1790s, the most adulatory rites celebrating the Virginian president were concentrated not in the Democratic Republican South where they had originated but instead in the rather more Federalist northern states, especially those in New England.

Throughout the decade Federalist leaders showed themselves to be particularly able in their organization of rites of celebration. At Worcester, Massachusetts in 1796, for example, Washington's birthday was ushered in with the ringing of church bells, and at the town's civic feast the first toast to the President was greeted with nine cheers and a stirring rendition of the song "God Save Great Washington."[49] The rites in Boston a year later were particularly elaborate: several theaters displayed illuminations and transparencies honoring Washington, and one featured both a large portrait and a fifteen-foot-high bronze equestrian statue of the President, a common symbol of military prowess and statesmanship, which was surrounded by several small illuminated transparencies.[50]

The celebration in Albany in that year resembled nothing so much as a party political event. Some "150 gentlemen" raised their glasses to "The illustrious Washington," to his successor "JOHN ADAMS" and the hope that the people would respect "his virtues and talents," to the "uncorrupted statesman" Alexander Hamilton, and to John Jay, partisan toasts that were published in the local press as a statement of partisan and ideological unity. Governor Jay and the other Federalists dining with him in Albany saw Washington's birthday as a useful occasion on which to bring their community together in celebration of "The illustrious WASHINGTON," while at the same time uniting party stalwarts behind the leaders, policies and ideals of the Federalists.[51]

In addition to celebrating their champions, Federalists did not hesitate to slight their opponents. A group of Philadelphia "gentlemen" drank a Washington's birthday toast wishing "Tom Paine to the Devil,"[52] while a group in western Massachusetts wished "The prison in Paris where Tom Paine got so terribly frightened" to "all Gallo-American 'patriots'."[53] The partisan nature of these Federalist events was obvious to their political opponents, as illustrated by one Democratic Republican's snide commendation of the *"federalism"* of Boston's celebrations of Washington's birthday in 1798.[54]

The Federalists' attempts to make partisan use of celebrations and festivals honoring Washington were contested by those who interpreted Federalist ideology and policies as counter-revolutionary. As early as 1790, a writer in the *New-York Journal* pointed out that "RESPECT to rulers is the virtue of a patriot, but it ought to have its limits. If it degenerates into a blind servility, and extravagant flattery," he concluded, "it injures the sickly cause of liberty, and degrades the character of freemen."[55] In the same year, while members of the Boston elite feasted in honor of Washington's birthday, citizens at the Coffee House struck a different note with their toast to "The 4th of July, 1776," a symbolic date that expressed allegiance to the radical republicanism of revolution, rather than fealty to the man who had commanded American armies.[56]

A year later a correspondent in the *Aurora* complained that the elaborate rites of welcome staged in every town and city Washington visited "savors too much of Monarchy to be used by Republicans."[57] In an article entitled "Forerunners of Monarchy and Aristocracy in the United States," "Mirabeau" argued that republicanism in the United States was threatened by a combination of titles, levees, *"Keeping the birth days of the Servants of the public," "Establishing a ceremonial distance between the officers of the government and the people,"* and *"Parade of every kind in the officers of government,* such as pompous carriages, splendid feasts and *tawdry gowns."*[58]

"A Democrat" wrote in a similar vein to the editor of the *Aurora*, commending the members of the New City Dancing Assembly, who in 1793, although "sensible of the President's virtues and merits," had decided not to honor his birthday with a ball because "they considered a celebration of this sort as incompatible with their republican character."[59] A year later another correspondent asserted that "Birth-day celebrations are inconsonant with republicanism, and as such ought to be proscribed by every man who wished to preserve the purity of the principle," while "A MILITIA MAN" expressed his resentment that the Philadelphia militia were being "converted into a *pretorian band,* to offer up incense of adulation to the first servant of the people."[60]

The Federalists enjoyed the upper hand in manipulation of the symbolic Washington for partisan purposes, but the Democratic Republicans proved to be quite ingenious in their responses within this festive culture. When Democratic Republicans were able to exercise some control over feasts and festivals, their toasts paid less and less attention to the man him-self. Instead they focused on the republican principles for which Washington had fought and which they believed themselves to be struggling to uphold, often in opposition to Washington's administration. In 1793 some of the white male citizens of Warren, Bristol, and Barrington in Rhode Island drank a cursory toast to "The PRESIDENT of the United States," and then quickly moved to more lavish tributes to the French republic, the Franco-American alliance, and the "patriots of *seventy-five*." [61] These latter-day "patriots" were clearly unhappy with Washington and his administration's reluctance to commit the United States to support of revolutionary republican France. The same was true a year later in Annapolis, where militia men virtually ignored Washington, preferring to tie past and present American patriots to the French republicans with a toast expressing their hope "May the Sons of Liberty triumph over their enemies." [62]

In 1792 in Richmond a simple first toast to "GEORGE WASHING-TON" was followed by others that hoped "the government of the United States [would] obey, and not pervert the principles of the Constitution," and one to "JAMES MADISON, the congressional defender of the rights and happiness of the people." [63] Two years later Virginia militia men gathered on the anniversary of Washington's birthday but they scarcely mentioned or in any way celebrated the president, choosing instead to pass several resolutions commending the "patriotic efforts" of James Madison, the steadfast leader of the opposition to the Federalists in the House of Representatives. [64]

Washington's support of the Jay Treaty between the United States and Great Britain so angered Democratic Republicans in Roxbury, Massachusetts that on the night of February 21, 1796 they spiked the town's cannon to prevent its being fired the following morning to celebrate the dawn of Washington's birthday. [65] This kind of activity was unusual, however, and it was far more common for the Democratic Republicans either to work within festive culture to change its tone or to work without it by creating alternative rites and symbols of celebration. Thus residents of New Hanover, Pennsylvania assembled on February 22, 1799, and erected a "TREE as the classic symbol of liberty," bearing a flag with the motto "Our LIB-ERTY and CONSTITUTION," which sentiment clearly meant more to them than the man whose birthday provided the occasion for their gathering. There were no pictures, statues, or transparencies of Washington in evidence, and in their place stood the popular republican symbol of the liberty tree. Although those present at the civic feast toasted Washington, they commemorated only his achievements in the Revolutionary War, drawing a critical veil of silence over his actions as president.[66]

The Democratic Republicans' assertion that principles and not men were the proper objects of celebration attracted the criticism of Federalists, who worried that it would soon be "uncomely for republican mouths to praise such men as Washington, or for the public to toast them, when convened to celebrate events, which they had been greatly instrumental, under providence, in bringing about."[67] Playing the popularity of Washington for all it was worth, Federalists sought to place the man himself at the center of their festive culture: thus criticism of the cult of Washington and the rites employed to laud the man (and by implication express support for his government and its policies) became criticism of the man himself, a criticism that precious few Democratic Republicans were willing to articulate. In New York City Noah Webster argued in the *American Minerva* that "The whiggism of 1776, was to rally round the *Venerable Statesmen and patriots* of our country," prompting an angry response in Philadelphia by the editor of the *Aurora* who asserted that "The whiggism of 1776 was to rally round the standard of independence, that was the prize contended for, and therefore the true point of rallying."[68]

Federalists continued to center their political festivals around celebrations of Washington, hoping that they could continue to employ rites derived from earlier monarchical forms of political culture grounded in the as yet considerable popularity of the president, and that this activity would promote and protect the administration and its policies. But by the middle of the decade the unpopular fiscal and foreign policies of the Federalists spurred Democratic Republicans to move beyond attacks on the festive culture surrounding Washington and on to assaults on Washington himself, his administration, and its policies. Members of the Democratic Society of Washington County, Pennsylvania met in Pittsburgh and resolved that they were "persuaded that no man but a Washington, fenced round as he is by the unapproachable splendor of public favor, would have dared, in the very prime and vigor of liberty to have insulted the majesty of the people by such a departure from any principle of republican equality, and regard for the great charter of the constitution."[69] A letter from "Pittachus" published in the *Aurora* on October 1, 1795 described with anger how the Federalists were employing popular gratitude for Washington's past services to exact "a silence and passiveness under every act of his administration, however wrong in itself, however hostile to our constitution, however repugnant to the principles of Republicanism."[70]

A month earlier a correspondent had noted that when the President had visited Charleston during his southern tour, the letters "V.W." had been displayed on a ship in the harbor to honor Washington's virtues and victories, and to wish him long life. But the letter "V" had fallen off, leading the correspondent to wonder whether this was "prophetic of his declining virtue."[71] When Governor John Jay proclaimed a day of thanksgiving in New York in the same year, one Republican dismissed it as "a party production," and complained that it was totally inappropriate for Jay to "enjoin us to pray for the valuable and useful life of the president at the very moment 9 persons in 10 are exasperated at his conduct."[72] Noah Webster's declaration in his *American Minerva* that it was treacherous to object to toasting Washington, prompted Bache to respond in the *Aurora* that "if want of respect for Mr. WASHINGTON is to constitute *treason*, the United States will be found to contain very many *traitors*."[73]

Throughout Washington's presidency, then, the partisan contest between Federalists and Democratic Republicans dominated public celebrations of George Washington and his birthday. This contest created an arena in which poorer white men and white women could participate, for the rival celebratory rites shared a degree of dependence on popular participation and support for their success. Thus it was not elite partisan leaders but rather the mechanics and artisans who comprised the thirteen tribes of New York City's Tammany Society who drafted and then drank the Washington's birthday toasts to "the RIGHTS of MAN" and "Wisdom in the cabinet." [74]

Similarly, while Boston's elite celebrated Washington's birthday in 1793 with a civic feast at Concert Hall, a mixed race group of mariners, laborers, and artisans held their own celebration in the streets. Calling themselves "the citizens of Liberty-square," they made celebration of popular crowd action in the American revolution and in favor of the French Revolution central to their festivities. A month earlier these citizens had celebrated the French republic's victory at Valmy by renaming Oliver's Dock (the site of Andrew Oliver's supposed stamp office in 1765) as Liberty Square and planting a new liberty pole there. On Washington's birthday these citizens drank but one toast: "May the citizens of the spot which in 1765 witnessed the destruction of an infamous Stamp Office, be ever famous for celebrating events propitious to the Equal Liberty of all

Mankind."[75] This was a defiantly non-deferential popular celebration that smacked more of radical inversion than of respectful commemoration.

It is likely that members of the lower sorts often held such celebrations on the streets and in taverns and dram shops, but only on rare occasions do these events appear in contemporary newspapers, correspondence, and diaries, and it is often difficult to decode their significance to those who took part. In Salem, for example, the diarist William Bentley recorded in February 1796 that the standard rites honoring Washington's birthday were supplemented by the actions of "seamen [who] in jolly sort went up & down the street with Flags, Drums, [and] fifes."[76] In Philadelphia, two years later, Elizabeth Drinker recorded that "a Croud with lighted candles" and a "Drum and Fife" went by her house in the evening. For her and for many middling and elite Americans this was—as she put it—"a little mob fashion."[77] Drinker was not alone in dismissing these gatherings as mindless and inappropriate crowd actions, void of legitimate political and ideological content. It is only in rare instances like the published account of Boston's "citizens of Liberty-square" that we see any indication of the inner meanings of these events.

Women were almost certainly involved in these more truly popular festivities, but the full range and tenor of their participation are all but lost to us. However, there is some evidence of the nature and significance of female spectatorship of or participation in the parades, militia maneuvers, and feasts commemorating Washington. Newspaper accounts throughout the country contained many pat references to the socially, racially, and sexually diverse crowds who witnessed the ritual behavior of white men "with every demonstration of public joy."[78] Occasionally women's presence at more formal events was noted by male commentators, as in a passing reference to the "four & five hundred ladies and gentlemen" who attended a ball hosted by Philadelphia's City Dancing Assembly on February 22, 1793. The women present joined the men in drinking a relatively conservative series of Federalist toasts, and their political activity was reported in the *Aurora*.[79]

But most accounts describe only the activities of white men, and Federalist rites were focused on the doings of "the Principal Gentlemen."[80] Their stylized toasts to "the virtuous fair," or their praise of the "brilliant company of ladies" who attended their feasts or balls illustrate that these men expected women to play a supporting role in this political ritual.[81] Washington's birthday was a largely white male rite, a day for "marks of manly joy and decent festivity,"[82] and some male citizens went so far as to commend women whose "correctness of manners" kept them out of the public political sphere.[83] When one hundred and fifty Philadelphia women attended a ball to celebrate Washington's birthday in 1795, the *Aurora* reported that "nearly twice the number of citizens were present": women, according to these men, were not citizens and consequently had no political identity independent of their fathers and husbands.[84]

Throughout the 1790s the politicization of white women disconcerted the male leaders and supporters of both the Federalists and the Democratic Republicans. In some ways the Federalists showed themselves to be far more open to female displays of political identity and partisan allegiance than did the Democratic Republicans. With their hierarchical conceptions of republican society, Federalists applauded the actions of their wives and daughters who went beyond simple spectatorship in such events as the reception of Washington into Trenton on the way to his inauguration. For the Federalists saw these women as virtuous republican mothers and daughters who were articulating support for the governments of Washington and then Adams: far from transcending their subordinate position in society, these women were affirming it.

The Democratic Republicans developed as a coalition of urban working men, planters, and yeoman farmers, a coalition that made little allowance for public political activities by either women or African Americans. Having said that, in their opposition to Federalist ritual and in their creation of an alternative festive culture—most notably in their celebrations of the French Revolution—the Democratic Republicans craved the fervent participation of women and youths, for the success of their oppositional festive culture was contingent on enthusiastic expressions of community support.

Thus Democratic Republicans and Federalists shared a willingness to countenance the limited politicization of women who supported them— albeit in what these men saw as an appropriate manner—and opposition to the public activities of women who opposed them. One Democratic Republican observed that female participation in partisan celebrations of Washington's birthday was "inconsonant with republicanism," and he condemned "ladies and beaux [who] take pleasure in keeping up this farce."[85] But even this angry reaction against Federalist manipulation of the cult of Washington contained, at least implicitly, an acknowledgment that women did enjoy some form of political identity in the public sphere. For rather than criticizing women for presuming to take a political stand, he was actually condemning them for displaying what he considered to be the wrong political decisions and allegiances.

On rare occasions, as in Trenton in 1789, women did seize the initiative and arrange their own celebrations of Washington and his birthday. Seven years later, in a Newburyport, Massachusetts celebration of Washington's birthday a group of women organized their own feast and then drank several very revealing "highly republican toasts." After a cursory toast to "our beloved president," the women moved on to salute Martha Washington by name and to drink to their hope that "the fair patriots of America never fail their independence which nature equally dispenses." Their most interesting toast was to Marie-Charlotte Corday, the French woman executed for the assassination of Jean-Paul Marat: "May every Columbian daughter," these women hoped, emulate Corday and "be ready to sacrifice their life to liberty." This is far more than republican motherhood, and far more than a desire to serve the republic by raising virtuous male citizens. These women articulated a vision of themselves as political actors, with rights and obligations that were entirely independent of their relationships with men.[86]

*   *   *

It was not the president's retirement in 1796 but rather his death in 1799 that brought the contest over and within the political culture of Washington to a climax. The commemorative rites that filled turn-of-the-century American newspapers were played out in the context of intense partisan politicking: supporters of the Federalists were divided into the followers of Adams and Hamilton, while the Democratic Republicans were suffering under Alien and Sedition laws designed to stifle their political rhetoric and culture and weaken its base of support. The latter party were set to take control of Pennsylvania, and both parties were preparing for the following year's presidential election.

Despite the criticisms of Washington, his policies, and the political culture around him, as the most visible hero of the war for independence Washington remained very popular, and almost all white Americans participated in the rites of mourning. In Salem William Bentley recorded that the "sentiments of respect to G. W. are general," while in Philadelphia Elizabeth Drinker was somewhat more astute in her observation that "many will join in ye form that car'd little about him."[87] Federalists hoped to capitalize on all the mourning that resulted, and many of their reports of the commemorative rites emphasized the solidarity of the community in its respect for and allegiance to the departed hero and all that he represented. As the party of Washington, the Federalists expected to organize the rites of mourning, and hoped to retain power in the new republic under the mantle of their departed leader.

With this in mind they created commemorative rites intended to encompass entire communities. Few Americans can have been left unaware of these rites: muffled church bells, booming cannon, flags flying at half mast, and black ribbons of mourning pervaded the public sphere. Women's participation was particularly important, and many middling and upper class women found themselves with more room in the public realm than they had ever been accorded when the great man was alive.

Abigail Adams set the stage within a couple of days of Washington's death by taking the unprecedented step of publicizing her private levees in the public prints. In the pages of the *Gazette of the United States* she postponed her "Drawing room," and directed that in future female visitors and the "Ladies of the officers of the general government" wear appropriate clothes of mourning.[88] Those who did not mourn in an acceptable fashion were not welcomed by the First Lady, and around the nation women who chose to wear mourning, from the elaborate outfits of the wealthy to the simple black ribbons of those with fewer resources, found their actions encouraged and even appropriated by the Federalists. Thus the "young Ladies" of Salem who wore badges on their arms bearing the initials G. W.,[89] and the women of New York City who wore "A crape around the arm with black gloves and ribands" became, whatever their beliefs or ideologies, public members of the Federalist community.[90]

Many white women attended the formal rites of commemoration: Elizabeth Drinker believed that some 4,000 people attended a memorial service in Philadelphia, among whom were her daughters Ann, Mary, and Sarah.[91] In New York City Margaret Bayard Smith clearly saw herself and other women as an important part of the community of mourners, and she wrote that she would "be very much disappointed if I do not hear" Gouverneur Morris's oration, although she admitted that it would be "almost an impossibility for ladies to be present, as the crowd will be so large."[92] In Hallowell, Maine Martha Ballard was one of many local women who attended a commemorative service, while others participated in a parade "clad in white, with black hats & cloaks, & white scarfs."[93] Far to the south a "large assemblage of ladies, dressed in mourning"[94] attended a funeral oration in Louisville, Georgia, and there and elsewhere one can well imagine a great many women and perhaps a good many black Americans joining the "numerous assemblage of citizens"[95] who gathered together to witness the symbolic funeral processions staged all over the country.

For white men of all ranks, the opportunities for participation were more varied. Many towns and villages held their own symbolic funerals, and from Waynesborough, Georgia to Salem, Massachusetts large funeral processions incorporated white men of all classes.[96] It was here that partisan politics became most apparent, as those who took part struggled against each other within these commemorative rites. In New York City, for example, the Corporation and "several Societies" met on Christmas Day to plan a funeral procession for New Year's Eve.[97] Federalist leaders hoped that the grand procession in honor of "the Great Deceased" Federalist leader would unite the citizens on the eve of the presidential election.[98] But the lengthy account of the procession that appeared in *The Weekly Museum* showed a divided rather than a united white male community. Major General Hamilton, still in command of the Federal army raised ostensibly for a possible war against France but clearly intended to intimidate the Democratic Republicans, marched with military officers and militia behind cannon captured from the British during the revolutionary war. This was a powerful acknowledgement of the late Federalist leader's role in securing American independence, and—Federalist leaders hoped— a timely reminder to citizens that they would do well to remain loyal to Washington's policies and party. The pall bearers were attended by members of the elite and generally pro-Federalist Society of the Cincinnati, and they and the members of the committee of arrangements all wore "the badges of the Cincinnati," a black cockade that during the late 1790s had become the badge of the Federalist party.[99]

Gouverneur Morris's funeral oration at St. Paul's Church rounded out the partisan rites, but the event was far from an unqualified Federalist success, for not all participants had been motivated by or acted in accordance with Federalist intentions. Almost half of one printed account of the procession described the members of the Tammany Society and the Free Masons, groups of working and middling white male New Yorkers who were more likely to identify themselves with and support the Democratic Republicans. At the head of the Tammany Society a member bore one of the great republican symbols, "the Cap of Liberty veiled in crape." The message was obvious to those versed in the symbolic language of the day:

the Tammany Society mourned Washington but refused to applaud the policies and creed of Federalism, preferring to salute their own political ideals and partisan beliefs, which they purposefully identified with the departed Virginian.[100]

Behind the Tammany Society marched the Mechanic Society, who in previous feasts, toasts, and processions had shown themselves to be firm opponents of the Federalists, and they were followed in turn by members of the "Masonic Lodges," which as John Brooke has shown had become ever more Democratic Republican in sympathy by the time of Washington's death. Marching behind General Hamilton could be interpreted as nothing so much as a silent rebuke of his Anglophilic and Francophobic policies and a striking call for peaceful resolution of the Franco-American conflict. What the men and women who watched New York City's procession would have seen was that a good half of those taking part, all marching together, were Democratic Republican in sympathy. In short, Federalist attempts to capitalize on their rites in mourning of Washington's death had failed in the nation's largest city.[101]

Much the same happened in Philadelphia. On December 23, 1799 Philadelphia newspapers published Hamilton's instructions for the memorial procession and service to be held in Philadelphia on the day after Christmas.[102] Both Federalist and Democratic Republican newspapers reported the funeral procession in great detail, but they focused on different aspects of this event. For the Federalist correspondent in the *Gazette of the United States*, the central image in the whole procession was the classic and time-honored image of the dead soldier-statesman, a splendid, riderless white horse, which he described in great detail: The "General's horse, with his saddle, holsters and pistols—boots in the stirrups, reversed; led by two serjeants, with black scarf—The horse trimmed with black—the head festooned, with elegant black and white feathers—the American Eagle displayed in a rose upon the breast, and in a feather upon the head." Although Washington was already dead and buried in Virginia, the Federalists still made him, or more specifically, popular reverence for him, the central focus of the largest parade staged in Philadelphia since the ratification of the Federal Constitution. The various militia and army units in the procession were simply described as "Military," while the officers of the Federalist government were described in some detail.[103] (See Figure 7.)

The account in the Republican *Aurora* was quite different. For editor William Duane the lower and middling men who comprised the militia companies embodied the republicanism Washington had initially fought

Figure 7. High Street, From the Country Market-Place Philadelphia. With the procession in commemoration of the Death of General George Washington, December 26th 1799. William Birch and Son, Philadelphia, 1800. The Library Company of Philadelphia. At the center of Philadelphia's funeral parade honoring George Washington was the riderless horse, but the militia men who marched before it were separated by political allegiance, with Democratic Republican units leading off and Federalists following them. The weeping man in the foreground would be removed from later prints, but the republican mother holding the hand of her young son remained, cementing the connection between the virtue of Washington and that of the generations of citizens to come. This woman was almost certainly a symbolic creation by Birch: most women can

for, and they were central to his account of the event. It is more than likely that many of these men still revered Washington the man but opposed the party he had led, its policies, and its use of him as a symbol in attempts to retain control of the national government.

In his dutiful and respectful account of the proceedings, Duane was able to show readers that Federalist control of this ceremonial event had been sharply contested. Virtually ignoring the riderless horse, Duane informed his readers that the Republican and Federalist militia groups had not been united in their mourning: he listed every one of the twenty-two militia units, together with their political affiliation, "Republican" or "federal." Even a cursory glance at the long article gave readers an impression of disunity, for Republicans marched and mourned with fellow Republicans, while Federalists marched with their own. To those present at the event, the differences between the generally more elite Federalist militia corps, many of whom had bought their own expensive uniforms, firearms, and horses, and the rather more motley crew of Democratic Republicans who constituted the local militia groups would have been very obvious. But Duane was communicating this Democratic Republican act of defiance to readers elsewhere, who, had they relied on Federalist newspapers, would have thought the rites of mourning in the nation's capital to have been an entirely Federalist affair.[104]

While many of the funeral and memorial parades may have been contested, Washington's death furnished Federalists with other opportunities to revitalize their cult of the departed general and thereby strengthen their hold on the federal government. Clergymen all over the nation, but especially in New England, delivered and published eulogies for Washington, comparing him to all the great classical and biblical heroes and praising his every act. Over three hundred such eulogies were published within a few months of Washington's death. For many of these Federalists it was easy to make the transition from a defense of Washington to an attack on the Democratic Republicans, as was made clear in a New England broadside entitled *The Death of General Washington, With Some remarks on Jeffersonian Policy*.[105]

But the Federalists failed in their attempt to translate commemoration of Washington into uncontested partisan demonstrations of support for their party, for many Americans were able to mold their participation in these rites in such a way as to memorialize the departed leader while simultaneously pronouncing their partisan objections to the Federalists and their policies. As a result Washington was in many ways less central to these rites than the Federalists had hoped, and the battle between the two emerging parties was focused more on confrontations between the living than on respect for the dead. With Adams as president and his rival Jefferson preparing for the election of 1800, white men and women found themselves with yet more opportunities to enter the political fray as both parties campaigned in the public sphere for popular support of these leaders.

The Federalist party were at something of a disadvantage here. For all of his commendable record of public service, John Adams was a poor successor to Washington, a man who evoked little in the way of passionate loyalty and who did not enjoy the complete support of members of his party. Thus it is hardly surprising that little in the way of a celebratory political culture developed around the nation's second president. Whereas celebrations of Washington's birthday had spread out from his native Virginia to encompass the entire nation, festivities in honor of Adams's birthday never moved out from central New England, and even there it was only celebrated with any real enthusiasm during the crisis of the Quasi-War.[106]

Elsewhere citizens were often quite pointed in their opposition to the development of celebrations in honor of Adams. When Adams traveled from New England to Philadelphia in the fall of 1797, local authorities published instructions to local militia units to prepare for his reception, very much in the manner that they had always fêted Washington on his return to the seat of government.[107] "An Old Solider" indicated in the *Aurora* that this was unacceptable to some of the lower and middling white men who served in these units, and he complained that such receptions should be voluntary in a free republic. "When the farce of monarchy was first acted here, as an apology for it we were told that Washington fought our battles, that he saved his country, and therefore extraordinary honours were due to him, and that it was to the man and not to the magistrate, such distinctions were intended. What is now to be the excuse?"[108] The powerfully angry letter concluded with the promise that the author would never "degrade the character of a man by the servility of a slave, the uniform of a soldier by making it the livery of a servant, or the dignity of a citizen by an idolatry to a Magistrate."[109] The Editor of the *Aurora* was far more personal in his attack on Adams and the preparations for the reception of "his Rotundity"[110] into Philadelphia, and his sarcastic account of the event was entitled "TRIUMPHAL ENTRY OF HIS SERENE HIGHNESS OF BRAINTREE INTO THE CAPITAL."[111]

Midway during his presidency, however, Adams surprised himself and everybody else by becoming popular. His strong stand against the growing number of French attacks on American shipping, followed by his handling of the ill-advised attempts of French agents to garner bribes from American emissaries and the ensuing Quasi-War, were both effective and popular, and to Adams's great pleasure his popularity soared and lavish receptions were staged for the president wherever he went. In August 1797, for example, Adams was collected from his Quincy home by a Boston troop of cavalry whose members then escorted him to their city where he was received by local dignitaries, the ringing of bells, and an artillery salute. At an elaborate dinner in Fanueil Hall, attended by many local dignitaries and members of the state government, Adams's and Washington's portraits were hung side by side.[112] A similar reception was given to Adams in New York in October 1797. The interior of the New City Assembly Room was decorated with a "bower of trees" along the dining tables, and on top of a column of golden sugar was a representation of "Wisdom," who held a bust of Adams in one hand and a garland of sixteen roses in the other, thus symbolically uniting all the states in the union under Adams's Federalist administration. At both celebrations Washington, the Federal Constitution, and the current Congress were toasted in clearly partisan terms.[113]

Despite Democratic Republican objections, the French crisis encouraged Federalists in Philadelphia to give Adams something approaching a royal welcome into the national capital. On the outskirts of the city he was met by three troops of cavalry from the city and one from the county. Within Philadelphia itself the citizenry assembled with the heads of the government departments, and Adams was "welcomed by the huzzas" of the crowd when he alighted from his carriage.[114] Even such a good Quaker as Elizabeth Drinker, who was generally "not for parade of any sort," recorded the city's celebration of the return of Adams to the capital with evident pleasure. With her Federalist sympathies shining through, she confided in her diary that "every thing considered I would have been pleased to have seen a little more of it." [115]

Many citizens, particularly those who identified with the Democratic Republicans, criticized these events as "rather in *the style regal*." With rites and symbols that were "truly *high federal*, and foam[ing] with diplomacy, George Washington, *Federalism*, [and] Timothy Pickering," they were clearly engineered to foster support for the Federalist administration and its combative attitude toward France.[116] When a Federalist militia company which escorted Adams through Boston during the summer of 1799 later wished in a toast that "the pernicious doctrine of modern liberty and equality may be discarded," a writer in the *Aurora* seized the opportunity to attack Federalist principles and their celebrations of Adams. What "does this wish amount to," he pointed out, "but that republican government may be discarded and *monarchy* substituted in its stead?"[117] For citizens weaned on Paine and Jefferson, the celebrations of a president who was renowned for his support of aristocracy, a monarchical form of government and the British constitution were at best in bad taste and at worse downright counter-revolutionary.

Despite these criticisms Adams and his policies were the focal point of a large number of popular demonstrations of support. During 1798 communities all across the country sent messages, resolutions, and petitions to the president, supporting and congratulating him on his stand against France. Adams handled his unexpected popularity quite magnificently, spending long hours replying to each and every message that he received. Supporters of the Federalists seized on this, and William Cobbett published over fifty petitions and many of Adams's responses in the partisan Philadelphia newspaper *Porcupine's Gazette*. Almost half of these petitions came from what were described as groups of "citizens" who had assembled for the purpose, and one-eighth came from groups of young men or students who were volunteering their services for the defense of the nation. Another eighth came from militia companies, while just over one-fifth were sent by merchants, judicial or governmental officials, and militia officers.[118]

At the end of the year the Boston editor William Austin published *A Selection of the Patriotic Addresses, To the President of the United States. Together With the President's Answers*. Every state except Kentucky was represented in the volume, which included 39 addresses from New England, 33 from the middle states, and 34 from the south. The Federalist party reveled in their rediscovered popularity among many ordinary Americans. For perhaps the first and only time since Washington's first term, Americans across the country had agreed to unite in order to articulate and demonstrate their support of a Federalist administration.[119]

The content and significance of these petitions were publicized in open meetings and in the Federalist press, and signatures were often collected at a variety of locations. A petition in Albany was signed by over eight hundred citizens,[120] one in Newport, Rhode Island by another three hundred,[121] while one "breathing the *true American spirit*" garnered over fifteen hundred signatures in the first week of its circulation in Boston.[122] Copies of the latter were available in five Boston stores, and details of "this honorable and patriotic transaction" were reported in the Federalist press as far away as Philadelphia.[123] Apparently every single inhabitant of Sandgate in southern Vermont signed their petition, although it is not unreasonable to assume that "Inhabitants" referred to adult white males alone.[124]

Although these petitions were employed for distinctly partisan purposes, they usually contained relatively apolitical statements of support for the Adams administration together with promises to defend America against any attacks by the French. Many began with a statement of the signers' understanding of the dangers the United States faced. The "inhabitants and citizens of Gloucester," Massachusetts believed themselves to be living through "a crisis in which the dignity and independence of the United States is at stake," and they recognized the need to express a "union of sentiment."[125] Given that the language of these petitions stressed the need for national defense against a growing French threat, many Democratic Republicans were hardly opposed to them, and it is highly probable that some even signed them. But the partisan use of these petitions by supporters of the Adams administration ensured that the Democratic Republican press did not report them with much enthusiasm, and on rare occasions citizens assembled to voice their opposition to Adams and his policies, as happened in Albermarle, Virginia, and in six different counties in Kentucky.[126]

Coming some fifteen years after the conclusion of the war of independence, these patriotic rites were the self-acknowledged work of—as in the case of "The YOUTH of New-Brunswick and its vicinity"—the white sons of fathers who had "ever been ready at the call of their country."[127] The gendered and generational aspect of these displays of patriotism and martial vigor is quite striking, and in a very real way it transcended partisan political bickering. For young white men who had grown up in the shadow of their fathers' exploits during the war that had brought the nation into being, the urge to display in public their own commitment to the republic must have been irresistible.

Just as young men sought to affirm their patriotism in rites supporting the Federalist government, so too did young women who created flags and colors that they presented to militia groups. In Shelburne, Massachusetts, for example, "a large number of ladies" presented "a set of American colors" to Colonel Long's Volunteer Company, after the militia company had been engaged in some practice maneuvers.[128] These proceedings appear to have had colonial precedents: in 1747, for example, Philadelphia women, "by Subscriptions among themselves, provided Silk Colours" for the militia companies organized by Benjamin Franklin during the war with Spain.[129] The Quasi-War presentations often ended with the women and men singing "Adams and Liberty" or other patriotic Federalist tunes, and these rites provided women with the means to publicly condone the patriotic stance of their menfolk, to express their approbation of Federalist foreign policy, and to articulate their support of the administration of John Adams.

Supporters of Adams seized on these expressions of community support for the president and labored to incorporate them into a partisan political culture. On April 28 and 30, "upward of 800 young men" assembled in Philadelphia to prepare an address in support of the Adams administration, and they voted to present the document to the president on May 7.[130] During the intervening week preparations were made for the event, with Federalist newspapers providing a fanfare of publicity. When some twelve hundred young men processed from the City Tavern to the president's house, they were watched by several thousand spectators, many of them wearing the black cockades of the Continental Army and, more recently, the Federalist party. Working on the partisan assumption that female politicization was a good thing if acted out in an appropriate way and in support of the right side, Cobbett reported that "Every female in the city, whose face is worth looking at, gladdened the way with her smiles." The Federalists were ardent in their belief that all members of the community, male and female, rich, middling, and poor, should support the administration. When Adams emerged from his house to receive the address he was wearing a full dress military uniform and a black cockade: he was the man at the top of the Federalist hierarchy, and he reveled in this display of community support.[131]

Despite Adams's popularity during the Quasi-War, there was never any real possibility that public rites in his honor would emerge as a political cult similar in form to the one that had been constructed around Washington. The enmity between Adams, on the one hand, and Hamilton and many members of Adams's cabinet, on the other, helped create a major rift within the Federalist party, making it quite difficult for party supporters to mount enthusiastic celebrations of a controversial leader. In many ways Adams was more moderate than Hamilton, yet Democratic Republicans did not hesitate to portray the president as a rather too conservative supporter of the values of American republicanism, so neither Federalists nor Democratic Republicans were enthusiastic about celebrating John Adams. In large areas of the country many men and women never even saw, let alone participated in, celebrations of Adams and his presidency.

This situation stands in stark contrast to that of his opponent Thomas Jefferson, the clear leader of the emerging Democratic Republican party. During the later 1790s Democratic Republicans of all ranks who opposed Federalist rule began to stage a variety of public rites in honor of the ideologies they and Jefferson espoused, although these were carefully constructed so as to avoid the monarchical forms favored by their opponents. Jefferson had his own part to play in this process of reinventing the rites of leadership. While Lady Henrietta Liston had commended Washington's courtly etiquette and rituals, Sir Augustus John Foster complained that Jefferson, once he became president, studiously ignored "all our received notions of propriety and etiquette." As Secretary of the British Legation between 1804 and 1808, Foster was well positioned to evaluate Jefferson's presidency. He correctly noted "the sudden alteration in the etiquette heretofore practiced by General Washington and Mr. Adams," attributing it to Jefferson's desire to flatter "the low passions of a mere newspaper-taught rabble." [132]

What Foster did not realize was that Jefferson's enormous popularity was, at least in part, required of him by Americans who rejected the cult of Washington and its trappings. Jefferson chose not to use an elegant European coach, and he rode around the capital on horseback. Unlike Washington's courtly procedures of a decade earlier, Jefferson's "Memorandum on the Rules of Etiquette" was remarkable in its adherence to "the principle of equality." [133] When he received visitors his clothing was informal to say the least, and he often appeared wearing an old threadbare blue coat and "ragged slippers, with his toes out." [134] In this context Jefferson's "decision to submit his first annual message to Congress in writing rather than deliver it in person was a calculated political act designed to underline the return to sound republican simplicity." [135]

Jefferson may well have been opposed to rites and ceremonies that honored him rather than the democratic republican principles he ostensibly held, but this does not mean that party supporters were simply honoring a man in the manner he chose. The political culture of the Democratic Republican ascendancy was very much the product of negotiation between those who constructed and participated in it, and those like Jefferson who benefited from it. Many Democratic Republicans had opposed Federalist policies and the cult of Washington, and for much of the preceding decade they had pointedly drunk to the sentiment "Principles and Not Men": these citizens demanded a political culture that honored particular political values and ideals. When a Philadelphia artillery company welcomed Jefferson into Philadelphia as the new vice president on March 2, 1797, their flag bore the motif "Jefferson the Friend of the People," and it was usually "the People" who were central to these political celebrations.[136] At a civic feast for Jefferson held at Fredricksburg, Virginia in July of 1798, the first toast was to "The people of the United States—May those principles which produced their emancipation, never cease to operate."[137] Jefferson himself was not even toasted.

Perhaps it was inevitable, however, that the news of both Jefferson's election to the presidency and his inauguration on March 4, 1801 prompted a large number of Republican civic festivals all across the country. Jefferson and his Vice-President Aaron Burr were toasted thousands of times, yet rarely did participants lose sight of their political principles. Usually the toasts given at these meetings honored the people, the revolutionary spirit and principles of 1776, and the Constitution. When Jefferson was toasted, it was rarely as an individual per se, but rather as a faithful servant of the people, who adhered to the Constitution and the Spirit of '76. On New Year's day, 1801, "the democratic republicans of this state at the seat of government, celebrated the success of the republican cause" in Lancaster, Pennsylvania, drinking toasts "in the true spirit of liberty." The first toast celebrated "The PEOPLE—and the Constitution, which *they* have ordained." When Jefferson and Burr were toasted, it was because they had been "placed by the *People* on the Pillars of the Constitution."[138]

In Easton, Pennsylvania a band celebrated Jefferson's inauguration by climbing to the top of the tallest building in town on the evening of March 3, where they played the "Dead March," "as a requiem to expiring Federalism." At precisely midnight, "they struck up Jefferson's March, and played various other appropriate tunes." Many houses were illuminated, and apparently most of the citizens were out on the streets, although whether they were all celebrating is unclear. In Philadelphia the victuallers roasted an ox and a sheep for the celebrating citizens, some two thousand of whom dined under a liberty pole erected for the occasion.[139]

The liberty pole was a central feature of many such celebrations, including the small western Pennsylvania village of Brady's Run, where it was erected by people "commonly called democrats."[140] In Newport, Rhode Island the celebrations of Jefferson's inauguration ended under a liberty tree that was "splendidly illuminated" for the occasion.[141] But it was in their toasts, always central to the festive celebrations, that these citizens proclaimed what was important to them about Jefferson's victory. In East Windsor, Connecticut Democratic Republicans toasted the day and then stated their principles: "May monarchy nor aristocracy never prevail over the genuine principles of elective democracy in the United States of America." [142] Jubilant Democratic Republicans in Murfreesboro, North Carolina toasted "The 4th of July, 1776," [143] and quite often the spirit of '76 and the day of celebration were explicitly united, as when the Republican Greens militia company of Philadelphia gave as their first toast, "The Day we celebrate, being the completion of the revolution of 1776, and the commencement of the happy æra of true liberty." [144] An editorial in a Rhode Island newspaper shamelessly predicted that "THE FOURTH OF MARCH 1801, will become as celebrated in history as the 4th of July, 1776." [145]

The late Washington was sometimes ignored by the revelers, and when he was toasted it was usually with qualifications. Often he was referred to as only one of a number of departed heroes of the war of independence, with no mention of his actions since that date, as in the thirteenth toast at Germantown's celebration, which hailed "The memory of Franklin, Washington, and all other patriots and heroes, who served their country in the day of tribulation." [146] Rhode Island militia men drank heartily to the sentiment "Never may a candidate for a crown'd head obtain a place in Presidency," a none too subtle criticism of the cult of Washington and the supposed monarchical sympathies of Adams. [147]

Given the ideology of members and supporters of the Democratic Republican party, it is hardly surprising that they actively resisted creating a cult of Jefferson to rival the Federalists' partisan cult of Washington. But these contests within and over celebration of popular leaders had created a space where poorer men and occasionally women could enjoy some small role in politics, helping by their very presence to mold the discourse that constructed a national political culture. Black Americans were very much on the margins of these events, yet their role had some significance as each party eagerly sought out the support of the entire community for its celebrations. But once the Democratic Republican alliance assumed power its members took as much control of the public sphere as possible, parading, toasting, and affirming liberty as part of the framework of rights and freedoms of white men.

This is not to say that there had not been real and significant change in this aspect of American political culture. Washington, hardly a great intellect but far from a fool, had done nothing to prevent his supporters from making partisan use of his person as a symbol in their celebrations in the public sphere, and it had been readily apparent to many Americans that he was deeply and consciously involved in the Federalist political culture molded around himself, with a view to achieving, augmenting and retaining power. The Federalists' use of traditional ceremonies, symbols, and festivals to strengthen the government around Washington had proved very effective during the early 1790s, forcing citizens to contest the ideological content and interpretation of the celebrations of Washington's birthday, rather than attacking the event itself.

But with Washington's death and Jefferson's election this kind of political behavior effectively ended. Although some citizens continued to view the Federalist political culture of Washington with some distrust, they recognized that the late president's image no longer threatened them. Cincinnatus, the hero of the revolution, could now be recognized and applauded in relative safety, without appearing to endorse Federalist policies. Slowly celebrations of the anniversary of Washington's birthday began to evolve into artisan festivals, the work of white yeoman farmers and urban workers. The cult of the living Washington, as men and women of the 1790s had known it, was dead. A new and less political one, full of virtue and cherry trees, was just beginning.

3

The Popular Politics
of Independence Day

BY THE DAWN OF THE NINETEENTH CENTURY the annual commemoration of George Washington's birthday had become a leading celebration in the early national festive calendar, but it was the Fourth of July that had developed into the nation's principal commemorative festival.[1] The size, number, and popularity of annual celebrations of the anniversary of independence all soared during the decade following Washington's inauguration, and throughout the country Americans took part in grand and spirited celebrations in which "Cannons were thundering, bells ringing in all quarters of the City, the shops generally shut, [and] the streets alive with military parades & citizens driving to and fro."[2]

However, these displays of patriotic ardor and civic festivity could not conceal the fact that independence day celebrations had been as politically divisive and as bitterly contested as commemoration of Washington and his birthday. During the earliest years of Washington's presidency the friends and supporters of his administration had attempted to fashion the Fourth into a patriotic civic rite of national unity under the enlightened administration of Cincinnatus. The Federalists felt quite justified in employing the Fourth in this manner: they reasoned that Washington's government had been duly elected under the new frame of government and was working in the best interests of the nation as a whole, and they expected "the People at large [to] have the Wisdom to support and sustain it."[3]

Many of the white male citizens who were increasingly dissatisfied with the policies of Washington's government began to see in these Independence Day festivals a disingenuous use of patriotism for partisan purposes. They reacted by contesting celebrations of the Fourth: sometimes opponents of the Federalists employed oppositional language, rites, and symbols on the margins of ostensibly pro-Federalist celebrations of the

Map 2. Communities that celebrated Independence Day, 1789–1801.

Fourth; on other occasions they held completely separate, alternative Independence Day rites; elsewhere they struggled against supporters of Washington and Adams for control of civic feasts and festivals in their communities.[4] (See Map 2.)

Ritual celebration of the anniversary of American independence played an important role in the construction of the Democratic Republican party, for it was part of the process by which the elite leaders of the nascent Democratic Republican party allied themselves with white farmers and urban craftsmen and workers, and formed the coalition that won control of the national government in the election of 1800. It was in their carefully constructed July Fourth festivals that these men proclaimed and promoted their alliance, and in a very real sense created some facets of the national Democratic Republican party. Throughout the 1790s they molded Independence Day into a thoroughly partisan event populated by the supporters of Jefferson, thereby transforming the Fourth into a kind of festive annual meeting of the Democratic Republican party. So complete was their victory that by the early nineteenth century many Federalists refused to participate in these festive rites, either staying at home or creating their own small-scale alternative celebrations.

The conquest of the Fourth by the Democratic Republicans is not altogether surprising, given their commitment to the Declaration of Independence's exalted rhetoric of liberty and equality. These were men who extolled the revolutionary overthrow of traditional conceptions of the relationship between king and subject, and who remained vehement in their defense of the rights of the citizen. But their victorious assertion of equality was predicated on the continuance of inequality within the discourse of domestic relations, and thus the republican assertion of the rights of white men was premised upon their continued rule over white women and black Americans. All this found expression in their Independence Day celebrations, for while the Fourth of July acclaimed the revolution in white male rights and privileges, a corresponding celebration by or of female and African American was seldom justified nor countenanced by the white men who created and populated these events.

Among Democratic Republicans celebrations of Independence Day became festive occasions on which white women could do little more than applaud the pomp of their fathers, brothers, and sons, and from which free and enslaved black Americans were generally excluded. The festive culture of the Fourth was vital in the development of early national political parties, with rites and rhetoric imbued with the Painite and Jeffersonian republicanism of 1776, but it reveals much of the exclusionary nature of an American republicanism that defined political activity in entirely white male terms. As the Democratic Republican alliance assumed power at the turn of the nineteenth century, its members showed themselves to be less interested in the continued spread of liberty and equality than in securing and then consolidating their hold on political power, and keeping their fragile alliance intact.

*   *   *

Celebrations of the anniversary of independence during the early years of Washington's presidency differed little from those of the late-1770s and the 1780s. Small in size and local in character, they centered on demonstrations of patriotic ardor and military prowess by companies of militia or chapters of the Society of the Cincinnati. The latter were a generally elite group of former Continental army officers: many had been enthusiastic supporters of the Federal Constitution, and most of them felt strong personal ties to Washington.[5] Often state branches of the Cincinnati gathered together for their annual meetings on the Fourth, and then united with local militia companies for a parade that recalled the military achievement of winning the war for independence, while simultaneously acclaiming the new nation's government and its leader.

At a typical celebration held at Trenton in 1790, a contingent of local militia paraded to Polhemus's tavern where the state's branch of the Cincinnati were holding their annual meeting. Together with students and teachers from a local school, the entire group then marched to the Presbyterian church to hear an oration by James Armstrong, after which the Cincinnati returned to the tavern for a civic feast. Their toasts, each of which was accompanied by an artillery salute, hailed such sentiments as "The President," "The Congress," and "The Day."[6]

During the first two or three years of Washington's presidency these celebrations were somewhat political in their support of the new federal constitution, but they were not particularly partisan. Until Washington's government began pursuing controversial domestic and foreign policies, fairly bland affirmations of allegiance to the president and the new federal government were hardly controversial. Rites similar in tone and style to those staged in Trenton could be found throughout the country, in Albany, New York and Carlisle, Pennsylvania in 1789, in Boston, Elizabethtown, New Jersey, and Newbern, North Carolina in 1790, in Blandensburg,

Maryland and Lexington, Kentucky in 1791, and in Camden, South Carolina in 1792.[7] Usually the dawn of the Fourth was announced by cannon or the ringing of church bells, and in the port towns both foreign and domestic shipping was decorated in honor of the day. After small-scale parades the companies of militia, local chapters of the Cincinnati, and groups of military officers and citizens of high social standing dined at inns, public houses, and private homes.

Relatively few Americans enjoyed a direct role in these civic rites. The meetings of the Cincinnati and the civic feasts were the terrain of community leaders, and although the local militia—embracing as it did white men from all walks of life—performed military maneuvers or participated in parades, their primary purpose was to salute the new nation and its government. Thus many white men could do little more than march in formation or watch these Independence Day celebrations, and black and female Americans were allowed no direct role at all. One July Fourth in Boston in 1790 Nathan Webb recorded "high parade in the common with the negroes &c.," but in all likelihood he was referring to their own revelry on the Common, for virtually all contemporary accounts make absolutely no mention of black participation in celebrations of the Fourth. The attendance of white women as spectators was more readily acknowledged by male citizens, but generally in terms of a role no larger than the one enjoyed by the "thronged circles" of Trenton women who "beamed approbation" on their community's militia and Cincinnati parade.[8]

For many Americans, then, the Fourth of July in the early 1790s was hardly a major public festival. Harrison Gray Otis, visiting New York City in July 1792, wrote to Elizabeth Otis and told her that a "noisy peal of most infamous bells, and the firing [of] a few cannon, alone distinguished . . . [Independence Day] from other days," and in Philadelphia a year later Moreau de St. Mery observed that over "three fourths of the stores remained open" on the Fourth.[9] For those at the bottom of society, celebrations of the anniversary of independence may have consisted of little more than merry toasts in taverns, "rioteous doings," and "breaking of windows."[10] While many different Americans may have felt the anniversary of independence to be worthy of note, their exclusion from direct participation in small-scale and relatively staid community celebrations left them with little option but to mold their own alternatives to the civic festivals conducted with "decency and order"[11] by "respectable citizens."[12] There was meaning in their alternative rites: wealthier citizens commonly celebrated on the evening of the Fourth by placing candles and lamps in every window, but a good many one-time Loyalists, lukewarm Patriots, and Quakers were unwilling to illuminate their homes in this manner. Darkened windows became political targets, and by breaking windows these ordinary folk could strike a blow against those with wealth and power who had been less than enthusiastic in their support of a struggle for independence that had been hard and costly for many at the bottom of society.

Such riotous activity contrasted sharply with celebrations of the Fourth in the national capital, for by the middle of Washington's first term federal and local officials had begun to revive the practices of the Second Continental Congress by orchestrating semi-official celebrations designed to foster popular allegiance to the new government and recognition of its authority. Building on the development of Washington's birthday celebrations, delegations of congressmen respectfully attended President Washington and presented him with the good wishes of their constituents. For the larger, public rites of celebration, state and city authorities published "Orders" in which they detailed the militia rites planned in honor of the day. The centerpiece of the capital's large militia parade, watched by members of the government and much of the city's populace, was the deferential parade past Washington's official residence.[13]

As the policies of the Washington administration began to arouse opposition, however, the "orders" published by Pennsylvania militia officials, including Thomas Proctor, Lewis Nicolas, Josiah Harmar, and John Shee, became increasingly controversial. In 1793 Philadelphia newspaper editors who were unhappy with the Federalist leadership of George Washington began distancing themselves from these July Fourth rites, for they appeared to be celebrating a partisan Federalist administration as much as a patriotic anniversary. One welcomed the "anniversary of the day from which we date our existence," and contrasted the noble day with celebrations of Washington's birthday. "Let slaves toast the birth-days of their masters," he wrote, for "freemen will celebrate that of liberty," recalling "those sentiments which dictated the solemn declaration of 1776."[14] The contest over and within Philadelphia's Independence Day rites was a particularly significant one. Philadelphia was both the birthplace of independence and the current seat of the national government, with the result that Philadelphia's July Fourth rites were reported in great detail in newspapers all over the country, thereby informing the development of Independence Day celebrations throughout the nation.

By the end of Washington's first term the enthusiasm of many Philadelphia laborers, artisans, and mechanics for the "merry" celebrations of

the party of Washington was much diminished, and these ordinary Philadelphians began developing their own forms of celebration.[15] By 1794, as
partisan newspaper editors were quick to point out, the civic unity expressed in the formal militia parade and review was fractured when the
marchers began separating according to partisan sympathies and identities,
with "Select parties" going on to enjoy their own feasts and drink their
own toasts at different locations.[16] Divided into partisan groups, the supporters and opponents of the government were able to enjoy civic feasts in
the company of politically like-minded people.

It is all but impossible to determine who organized most of these civic
feasts, but what little evidence there is suggests that militia companies and
other groups and societies elected committees to organize the events and
to prepare the toasts to be given at the meal's end. While Blair McClenachan, Michael Leib, Hugh Ferguson, Jr., and other leaders of the emerging
Democratic Republican party were members of the Democratic Society of
Pennsylvania's Committee of Arrangements, it is clear that quite a wide
range of men—from the occasional mariner and laborer, to varying levels
of artisans and mechanics, all the way to merchants—joined them on this
and other committees, where they enjoyed considerable influence over the
style and the content of their July Fourth celebrations.[17]

As the ritual of separate July Fourth feasts developed in Philadelphia,
some significant social differences between the supporters and opponents
of the Federalist administration became apparent. Over three-quarters of
the Federalist civic feasts took place at expensive hotels and inns. These
institutions had become, during the late eighteenth century, bastions of
the Philadelphia elite where gentlemen were unlikely to encounter the
lower sorts. In contrast, over half of the oppositional Independence Day
feasts were staged in the open air, a cheaper, more democratic, and certainly more public alternative to the rites of Philadelphia's high society.
Another third took place in smaller taverns and in private homes, while less
than one tenth were held in either inns or hotels.[18]

Rites highlighting social hierarchy and support of the government
were central to these Federalist events. Thus on Independence Day in 1794
the Federalist members of the Pennsylvania Society of the Cincinnati feasted
at Richardett's Hotel, where they toasted the President and then in good
Federalist fashion "waited on the governor with their congratulations."[19]
Oppositional groups were increasingly uncomfortable with these deferential performances, and in 1794 most of the militia groups that had taken
part in the morning procession feasted in private homes or taverns and did

not wait on the governor. Volunteer companies of artillery and cavalry hoped in one toast that "principles and not men [will] ever be the object of republican attachment," [20] while members of the Second Regiment of the Philadelphia Militia raised their glasses to similar sentiments at the Swan Tavern, honoring "American Independence—May the principles that dictated the act, ever be supported by the people." [21]

This partisan sniping was rooted in growing popular disapprobation of Federalist ideals and policies. Citizens who opposed the aristocratic and even monarchical tone of Washington's administration, his support of fiscal policies that appeared to benefit elite monied interests, and his approval of a neutrality policy that benefited counter-revolutionary Great Britain far more than revolutionary France combined to challenge the Federalist deployment of the Fourth as an uncritical display of loyalty to Washington's government. At first in Philadelphia and then all across the nation, citizens contested the orchestration of July Fourth celebrations by the Federalists, and worked to transform these rites into celebrations of all the ideals and values that they believed the young American republic represented. As Federalist policies became increasingly controversial in 1793 and 1794, the number of Independence Day celebrations rose dramatically. In stark contrast to the small-scale public celebrations and private feasts of the social elite that had dominated Washington's first term, these festivities featured a far broader range of white male participants and markedly more democratic and oppositional language and rites.

The growth of and the changes in American celebrations of Independence between 1793 and 1795 were truly remarkable. By 1795 detailed accounts of dozens of celebrations—large and small, and from near and from afar—were appearing in newspapers all over the country. [22] It was unusual for published accounts to give any sense of how many people took part in these Independence Day parades and festivals. However, the occasional estimates of the number of participants that did appear in printed accounts confirm that from the end of Washington's first term, more and more Americans were participating in ever more oppositional celebrations of the Fourth. In 1793 just over 100 citizens enjoyed Newark's open-air feast, following an Independence Day militia parade: this represented approximately 84 percent of the adult white male population of Newark, or approximately 38 percent of the entire adult white population if—which would have been very unusual—women had taken part in the feast. [23] Two years later some 900 New York City residents took part in their city's July Fourth parade, close to 8 percent of the city's adult white male population;[24] "several hundred citizens"[25] gathered around Newark's liberty pole, and 200 Wilmington residents—over one-quarter of the town's adult white male population—took part in a parade, after which eighty of them enjoyed a civic feast.[26]

These larger celebrations of Independence Day gave ritual shape and significance to a surge of popular opposition to some aspects of Federalist policy, as farmers and urban residents sought "to assert and defend the Rights and Privileges of the People."[27] During the middle years of Washington's presidency the small-scale, patriotic festivals of the early 1790s were replaced by larger and more socially inclusive political parades, which were populated by white men of the lower and middling orders, and in which the iconography of democratic republicanism usurped displays of allegiance to Washington and his government. In 1793, for example, citizens in Alexandria, Chestertown, Fayetteville, Hudson, Newark, and Philadelphia gave the liberty cap pride of place in their processions and feasts, affirming their support of the ideals and principles of democratic republicanism with its most popular symbol, newly energized by the French revolutionaries.[28] This trend continued in 1794 and 1795, as these ordinary Americans fashioned the liberty and equality then being championed by the French into partisan symbols and language that were central to their celebrations of American nationhood.[29]

Newark's celebration of 1793 exemplifies this development. The day started with an artillery salute from beneath a tall flag pole topped by "the red cap of liberty, with a gilded tuft and border." At the head of a parade of the "citizens and militia" was another Liberty Cap, and those who assembled listened to a reading of the Declaration of Independence. During the afternoon male citizens sat down to an open-air feast, and they placed the liberty cap used in the militia procession at the center of their table. Made "of scarlett sattin," the cap bore the gilded motto "Rights of Man, Liberty and Equality."[30]

With over one hundred men at this civic feast, either a large majority of Newark's adult white men were present or a good number of like-minded residents of the town and the surrounding area had joined together to celebrate something of considerable importance to them.[31] Given the contemporary political situation this was a decidedly partisan festival, replete with such symbols of support for revolutionary republicanism as the Declaration of Independence and the liberty cap. In the context of Washington's proclamation of American neutrality and his cool reception of French ambassador Citizen Edmond Genet, the ritual use of these symbols represented an affirmation of loyalty to the republican values of liberty and equality, and opposition to the ostensibly counter-revolutionary tendencies of Washington's administration. As yet a well organized oppositional political party did not exist, and many present may not have enjoyed the franchise. But in this, the largest political festival of their year, the farmers, craftsmen, artisans, and merchants of Newark proclaimed their political principles and said something about the policies they favored and those they opposed.

The residents of Newark and other communities were able to invest their Independence Day rites with a defiantly oppositional tone, but in Philadelphia and elsewhere supporters of the Federalists struggled hard to retain control over the civic celebrations. In the capital it was only after the civic parades and militia maneuvers organized by Federalist authorities had ended that participants were able to break off into smaller groups for feasting and toasts in which they voiced their antipathy toward the underlying ideology of the official pro-government rites. Philadelphia's Democratic Republican Society spent weeks preparing for their Independence Day feast in 1794. Their toasts, written by a small committee and then approved by the society's members, were typical of those to which glasses were raised across the country.[32] One toast saluted the "representatives of the people," with the injunction that they should "never forget the source of their power," while others struck out against the Federalist administration with toasts condemning "Governmental secrecy," the "Excise," and the "Public debt." With toasts saluting "the Sans-Culottes of France" and "the Jacobin Clubs of America," it was abundantly clear that this large and powerful group of Philadelphians believed their government to be slipping away from its republican moorings.[33]

All around the nation men were raising their glasses to equally partisan sentiments. In Baltimore on July Fourth, 1794, a group of militia volunteers toasted the people as the "fountain of power," and the government as merely the "trustees of the people," while in Morristown militia men and "a large assembly of private citizens" drank to Washington as no more than their "fellow-citizen."[34] The men who populated these increasingly partisan Independence Day feasts were not slow to hail as a virtuous republican opposition those in Congress and the Cabinet who stood firm against Washington's foreign and domestic policies. At a civic feast in Freehold, New Jersey those present drank to the "virtuous republicans in congress,"[35] citizens standing beneath a liberty tree in Newport, Rhode Island toasted "every true Republican" and "all the Democratic Societies in the United

States,"[36] while in Portsmouth, New Hampshire "a very respectable part of the inhabitants" drank to "*Republican* firmness" in Congress, a sentiment echoed in the Wilmington toast to "The Republican members of Congress."[37]

Even more revealing, perhaps, were toasts to the "great and honest man—Thomas Jefferson,"[38] and to "the virtuous"[39] Jefferson and Madison, drunk with enthusiasm at Lynchburg, Virginia and Portsmouth, New Hampshire respectively. By the end of the decade such toasts to the leaders and heroes of the Democratic Republican party would play a central role in Independence Day feasts. But in 1794 these were the first such toasts to appear, further evidence of the transformation of these celebrations from small-scale patriotic festivals into a day when white men of lower and middling status took to the streets in support of the newly forming Democratic Republican party.

Gone, then, were the relatively bland and innocuous sentiments of earlier years, replaced during Washington's second term by enthusiastic toasts to France, the rights of man, liberty and equality, and the people. Over 70 percent of the sets of July Fourth toasts drunk in 1793, 1794, and 1795 featured sentiments that made clear the commitment of those present to their partisan vision of the principles of the American Revolution, and their opposition to various policies and ideals of the Federalist administration that appeared to be threatening that vision. In contrast, under 5 percent of these sets of toasts were enthusiastic in their support of the personnel and policies of the Federalist government, and can thus be described as Federalist.[40]

Published and republished in newspapers all over the country, Independence Day rites were created and recreated many times over, and the slates of toasts printed in early national newspapers constituted powerfully partisan manifestoes of political sentiment. The citizens of Annapolis—who had held open public meetings to arrange their celebration—toasted the "Friends of the French Revolution—of Liberty and Equality—throughout the world."[41] Further to the north, Elizabethtown residents wished for "Perpetuity to the principles" of the American Revolution, while the "Sons of Freedom" in Schenectady drank a toast to Thomas Paine that was echoed around the country.[42] Salutations to both the French and the American Revolutions were standard fare in these celebrations: the citizens of Carlisle, Pennsylvania and Sussex, New Jersey were far from alone in raising their glasses to "The 4th of July 1776,"[43] while in Lynchburg, Virginia citizens toasted the "spirit of 1776," affirming the ideological link between the participants and the revolutionary republican ideology of Paine, Jefferson, and the Pennsylvania Constitution of 1776.[44]

These toasts provide valuable information about the political beliefs of participants, since—as one contemporary observed of July Fourth toasts— they "may justly be denominated the criterions of sentiment and truth."[45] Toasts were written well in advance so that the sentiments they expressed could be carefully controlled: custom ordained that nobody would drink to a toast if he disagreed with the sentiment it expressed, so it was vital that the toasts offered were acceptable to all present. But this ritual unity around the festive table did not result in politically shallow sentiments; rather, different groups of the politically like-minded seized these opportunities to articulate and affirm their political beliefs publicly, and partisan politics permeated their toasts. These "verbal broadsides" were published in local newspapers and often were republished further afield, sending the strongly worded political messages of ordinary citizens out across the country.[46]

The rhetoric correspondents used to describe these festivities and their participants confirms the increasingly partisan tone of many July Fourth celebrations. On July Fourth, 1794 it was the "republican citizens" of Hackensack who participated in Independence Day rites, while the most radical toasts drank in New York City were those given at a "democratic festival."[47] In Newport, Rhode Island it was "staunch Democratic Republicans" who, following their community's militia parade, enjoyed a civic feast beneath and in honor of the liberty tree.[48] A year later it was the "pure republicans" of Elkton, Maryland who celebrated, while militia men and citizens of Delaware enjoyed "a republican repast."[49]

It is clear that these celebrations were mounted and populated by men who were identifying themselves in and through these events as opponents of the conservative policies of the Washington administration. The president's refusal, in the middle years of the decade, to take a firm stand against the British and their attacks on American commerce and seafarers resulted in an even greater increase in the number of oppositional Independence Day celebrations and a heightening of their partisanship. By the middle of the decade the Federalists were on the defensive not only within the government itself but also in July Fourth celebrations across the nation. They struggled as and where they could to reestablish a paradigm of the Fourth as a civic rite of communal reverence of the constituted authorities. In New York City Federalist merchants assembled at the Tontine Coffee House, where they toasted John Jay and "Washington our President."[50] The members of the Cincinnati in Philadelphia deferentially waited on the governor and toasted President Washington, while deep in the heart of Federalist New England Salem's "only celebration consisted in firing guns at noon, sundown & the evening upon North Field bridge with a few huzzas of such as were assembled."[51]

There were places where Federalists and their supporters were able to retain control of the Fourth. The Society of the Cincinnati dominated the celebration of Independence Day in Trenton, for example, where in 1794 they focused the event on "their attachment to the constitution and government of their country." This was a celebration that continued in the tradition of those that had taken place at the beginning of Washington's presidency, in which an austere and dignified militia and Cincinnati parade dominated the festivities, witnessed and applauded by "the social circles of the fair."[52]

Mention of female attendance and participation was far more common in the newspaper reports of Federalist celebrations. For the friends and supporters of Washington's administration these parades and feasts were truly "civic" celebrations, which highlighted the new republic and its elected government and affirmed the need for all members of society— including women—to salute and support that government. The Federalists recognized the importance of these civic affirmations of support for the government, and following the celebrations of Independence Day in 1794 a correspondent in the *Gazette of the United States* declared his pleasure at the size and number of appropriate festivals, and "the spirit of federalism" in the toasts drunk at all but "a few party clubs" on the day.[53]

By the mid-1790s the large majority of July Fourth celebrations were not, however, the civic and quasi-official parades and private feasts preferred by the Federalists, but were instead much larger, more partisan, and popular oppositional celebrations. In their rites as well as in the language of their toasts, these were ever more radical events that often united the French and American revolutions. In New York City in 1794 a large parade organized by the ever more Democratic Republican members of the Tammany, Democratic Republican, and mechanic societies, marched behind the liberty cap to the tune of the "Marseillaise," and members of the three societies listened respectfully to the Declaration of Independence.[54] The Federalists were becoming increasingly suspicious of revolutionary France and were anxiously promoting a treaty with Great Britain, but this did not prevent the citizens of Hackensack, New Jersey from making a symbolic affirmation of the ideological unity between themselves and the people of

France. An American flag topped by a liberty cap enjoyed pride of place in their celebration, and at an open air feast the participants in a militia parade toasted "Our Sister the Republic of France" and "Citizen Thomas Paine," toasts that could be heard or read all over the nation.[55]

But while the French Revolution informed the style and content of the Democratic Republican celebrations, it was American politics that determined much of their style and content. During the final two years of Washington's presidency the toasts drank at July Fourth festivals were often quite pointed in their attacks on Washington's government and their defense of Democratic Republican favorites. The sentiments of Lynchburg citizens were typical: a toast wishing for "Equal laws & a Republican executive" was followed by one to the new American ambassador to France, James Monroe, expecting that he would "abhor the vile Aristocratic conduct" of his predecessor, the arch-Federalist Gouvernour Morris. Their less than enthusiastic fourteenth toast to Washington hoped that he would "remember that he is but a man; the servant of the people and not their Master," and they all drank to the desire that "the pride of Aristocrats, and luke warm Patriots be soon humbled." [56]

Such toasts were vehemently partisan, and no supporter of Washington and his government would have raised his glass to such sentiments: thus it is extremely unlikely that any Federalists were present for these or similar toasts. In this simple rite, repeated in town and countryside alike, one can trace the contours of a popular opposition that was taking shape in the new republic. As an organized opposition and then later as a full-fledged political party the Democratic Republicans were dependent on this groundswell of organized and coherent popular opposition to the Federalists. The significance of the rapidly growing number of partisan oppositional July Fourth rites and sentiments was readily apparent to those who attended or read about them: even in rural Vermont, for example, citizens read numerous accounts of oppositional celebrations and toasts, together with an editor's acknowledgement "that the *similarity* of them is so striking." [57] An opposition was developing, in part in the parades, feasts, and toasts of ordinary Americans all across the nation.

The celebrations of Independence Day in 1795 took place only days after publication of the enormously unpopular Jay Treaty between the United States and Great Britain. While politicians debated the merits of Washington's foreign policy, the American citizenry expressed fury at their government in an unprecedented number of angrily partisan July Fourth festivals. Many Americans, bitter with memories of the hardships and sacrifices they had endured in the long and bloody struggle against Britain, had no desire for a treaty with Britain that appeared to betray American interests and independence. Coming from an administration that appeared elitist if not monarchical in tone, and following in the wake of Hamilton's financial program, the Jay Treaty appeared to be a rank betrayal of the independence, the republicanism, and the liberty and equality that many citizens held so dear, and they expressed their anger at this betrayal in some of the angriest toasts and rites of the decade.

Democratic Republican editors made much of this popular reaction: one commented that "from one end of the United States to the other," these toasts included "one common sentiment of the most pointed disapprobation of the treaty,"[58] while another reprinted many of the toasts drunk in opposition to the treaty by various groups and organizations in New York City.[59] Senator Stevens Mason, who had only days earlier leaked the treaty to a Philadelphia newspaper, was lauded in many toasts,[60] and a group of "pure republicans" in the village of Elkton in Maryland drank to the minority of senators who had voted against the Jay Treaty.[61] This "Patriotic"[62] or "virtuous"[63] senate minority were similarly applauded in New York City by the Tammany Society and Colonel Snowden's artillery company, in Philadelphia by a group of militia officers, and in Princeton by the members of Morford's Light Infantry Company.[64]

Toasts condemning the Jay Treaty were given and drunk with enthusiasm all across the country, and even in the heart of Federalist Connecticut Benjamin Franklin Bache observed the erection of liberty poles in "most of the small towns" in preparation for oppositional celebrations of the Fourth of July.[65] Affirmations of the republican ideology that undergirded popular opposition to the Jay Treaty were central features of most of these celebrations. In Fairhaven, Vermont members of the local Democratic Republican society hailed the rights of man,[66] while the citizens of Harrisburg, Pennsylvania—who had gathered ahead of time to organize their "public entertainment"—drank to the "Cap of Liberty."[67] At Schraalenburg, New Jersey a group of self-proclaimed "patriotic citizens" toasted the fact that "supreme power is lodged in the people,"[68] the inhabitants of Queens, New York raised their glasses to "the tree of liberty,"[69] and the "Sons of Independence" in Steuben extolled "Liberty and Equality."[70]

Pointed statements of partisan identity and affiliation usually accompanied these ideological pronouncements, as in the toast of "a large company" at Middletown-Point, New Jersey to "The Republican Interest" and a similar toast in Centreville, Maryland to "The Democrats."[71] Around the nation partisans echoed the toast to Thomas Jefferson given by militia men in Wilmington, Delaware and by the "patriotic gentlemen" of Queen Ann's County, Maryland.[72] Jefferson's recent retirement from government office prompted the officers of the Philadelphia County Brigade to raise their glasses to the hope that he might soon "be called from his retirement."[73]

In these angry and yet celebratory July Fourth festivals the self-conscious development of an oppositional party is ever more clear, as revealed in the Republican Society of Baltimore's toast to the nation's "democratic republicans."[74] After holding their annual meeting the Democratic Society of Rutland County, Vermont feasted and toasted both "Republicanism" and "The united Democrats this day assembled in free America."[75] More and more of the men celebrating the Fourth believed it to be a day on which, as a group of diners in Dover, Delaware put it, only "genuine" republicans would gather to celebrate the "Republican principles" saluted by artillery officers in New York City.[76] In short, not only were the Democratic Republicans winning control of the Fourth of July, but they were beginning to claim it for their own, exclusive use.

At the center of the nation's factious celebrations of Independence Day in 1795 was the particularly fierce battle in Philadelphia, where opponents of the Jay treaty were enraged by Federalist attempts to employ the city's celebrations to bring some peace and order to a very angry populace. Federalist authorities issued their usual "General Orders" for the militia parade, probably hoping that the familiar rite would furnish a welcome demonstration of popular support for Washington, his government, and its policies.[77] But popular disillusion with Washington and the Jay Treaty was such that for the first time these orders were completely denounced in the city's Democratic Republican press. After challenging their legality one writer asked his fellow citizen soldiers if they were no better than "*a pretorian band*," who were "called upon on government gala days" to "rejoice at the establishment of *British politics* in our country, and exhibit the countenances of joy, when their hearts must be overwhelmed with sorrow."[78]

Others called for a boycott of the usual militia parade, and for elaborate rites of mourning rather than celebration. Thus partisans of the Democratic Republicans articulated their protest in terms of civic ritual: joyful participation in the Federalist-organized festivities could only be interpreted as support of the administration and policies of Washington, whereas protest against these could best be expressed in a series of contrary rites. In the end the militia procession did take place, and few of the regular participants appear to have actually boycotted the event. But the tenor of their participation was muted, and the day "was celebrated in this City with a funeral solemnity." [79]

Then, for the first time since 1778, Philadelphia's citizens organized their own counter-procession on the evening of July Fourth, an event which Federalists denounced as an "unwarrantable procedure," and which Elizabeth Drinker believed to have had the "appearance of a riot, or mob." [80] What took place was neither a standard Independence day procession nor a common riot: "Never was a procession more peaceably conducted," enthused its defenders, who proudly claimed that those who participated "seemed to vie with each other in decorus behaviour." The event was organized and populated by ordinary citizens rather than organized militia groups, and it coalesced around an effigy of John Jay, who was represented as selling "American liberty and independence" for "British gold." The procession was silent, with wagon wheels muffled and participants seldom talking, giving local officials no excuse to break up the event: when an elite volunteer militia company attempted to break up the procession they were driven off by spectators bearing stones and clubs. The event did not, however, turn into a riotous demonstration against either people or property, and after driving off the militia the march continued through the major streets of Philadelphia and on to Kensington, where the participants burned the effigy "amid the acclamations of hundreds of citizens." [81]

This rite owed much to the mock funeral marches and popular protests mounted by anti-British crowds during the pre-revolutionary period, and it was revived by Philadelphia citizens as a powerful and evocative means of demonstrating their opposition to Washington's government, and their unhappiness with formal rites organized by and for the Federalist rulers of city, state and nation. It is more than likely that some of the men who marched in the anti-Jay evening parade had also marched in the official militia parade earlier in the day, as had the elite volunteer militia group who challenged the evening parade. Celebration itself had become a venue for popular political conflict.

By the mid-1790s, then, white male citizens in Philadelphia and all over the country were vying with the Federalists for control over the commemoration of independence, and were transforming celebrations of the Fourth into well organized, well populated party political events. Resisting the Federalist rites of deferential allegiance to government, many white male citizens were constructing, participating in, and witnessing alternative celebrations that made icons of liberty trees and liberty caps and employed the language of liberty, equality, and the rights of man. Their increasing use of the labels "Democrat" and "Republican" to describe themselves, their celebrations, and their political favorites underlined the relationship between democratic republican ideology and partisan politics in these events.

A year later, in 1796, the fact that Washington's enduring albeit battered reputation had secured both ratification and funding of the Jay Treaty continued to inform Democratic Republican attitudes toward the Fourth. In one Philadelphia newspaper an "Old Soldier" was relentless in his criticisms of official celebrations, and he hoped that "the Republicans of the United States" would take no part in Federalist festivities: "Washington alone may rejoice," he concluded, for the President had "triumphed over the *constitution* of his country." [82] Philadelphians who described themselves as "firm friends to the cause of Republicanism" ended their feast with a toast to "The 4th of July 1776: May the vices of Government never change our festival into a day of mourning." [83] The suggestion that Washington's government was betraying basic republican principles deeply offended Federalists who rejected these toasts as "pure defecated Jacobin politics," implying that Republican positions were hardly patriotic but in fact alien in origin and anarchic in their consequences. The Federalist *Gazette of the United States* listed one set of Republican toasts, complete with a critical commentary that attributed the Republican sentiments to "*the vices of faction.*" [84]

But the Federalists were losing more and more control over the celebrations of the anniversary of American Independence. Since at least the beginning of the decade it had been customary for the Governor to give the orders for the firing of all Philadelphia's official artillery salutes, and for one artillery company to honor the Society of the Cincinnati by following their toasts with yet more cannon salutes. In 1796 the Second Company of Philadelphia Volunteer Artillery was awarded these honors, but the men and officers of the Second Company ignored tradition. Despite a "strenuous request," the militia men refused to time their salutes to coincide with the toasts of the Federalist members of the Cincinnati, replying that "as freemen and soldiers, [they] were not bound to wait on any description of men." Moreover, they declined to wait for orders from the Governor, and "with a truly republican spirit" they fired salutes as and when they pleased. At their own feast later in the day these men toasted "The day, and all those who honour it," who were identified in the third and fourth toasts as "The patriots of '76," and "The independent patriots of '96," among whom they presumably included themselves.[85] These citizens identified themselves as the heirs of the revolutionary tradition forged by the Patriots who had declared and secured independence, and in their celebratory rites they very effectively excluded the Federalists from America's revolutionary republican tradition.

The partisan opponents of Washington's government in Philadelphia recognized that they were playing a leading role in the transformation of Independence Day throughout the nation. In the columns of the Philadelphia *Aurora* "Toby Swig" hoped that citizens around the nation would employ their July Fourth toasts to "oblivionize the funding system, our British treaty, ministers of state &c.," and so they did.[86] On the Kentucky frontier "a large number of citizens" paraded behind a flag bearing a representation of liberty, and drank toasts to "The people" and the "virtuous and humane Thomas Jefferson." In Morristown, New Jersey residents enjoyed a celebratory feast and then drank toasts celebrating "The day," "Our Sister Republics," "THE VIRTUOUS MINORITY" in the House of Representatives, "Our liberty tree," and "The Rights of Man." Even more striking was their toast against "The President," in which they demanded that "the virtues which inspired him in '76 [would] ever direct his future conduct."[87]

Federalist frustration at the refusal of many citizens to countenance rites that appeared to support the government, and anger at their creation of alternative oppositional rites and rhetoric, was neatly summarized in an account of a fictional Independence Day ritual held at "Whigstown." Attended by "all the Whigs of the year '76," the celebrations included an oration by the Reverend Lexington against banks, funding, and assumption, and toasts that condemned Washington, the Jay Treaty, and Congress. In short, this Federalist author could think of no better vehicle for his partisan attack on the Democratic Republicans than a satirical assault on their Independence Day celebrations: in poking fun at these rites he acknowledged their political importance.[88]

In a rapidly declining handful of towns and villages including Bristol, Rhode Island, Albany, New York, Hanover, New Hampshire, and York, Pennsylvania, the Federalists and supporters of government struggled to stem the Democratic Republican tide. Drinking toasts to America's "ornament and savior, GEORGE WASHINGTON,"[89] to "Alexander Hamilton,"[90] to "Mr. *Jay*,"[91] and to Fisher "Ames and the Members of the House of Representatives who virtuously opposed a daring Faction, and eventually caused the Law and Constitution to triumph,"[92] these were celebrations of the friends of order. The Federalists who organized the celebratory rituals in York continued to represent their festival as an inclusive, civic event celebrated "with much cheerfulness and satisfaction" by "the Inhabitants of the Borough and Neighborhood." Some of the town's women arranged their own feast, and in good Federalist form they toasted "The Day," Washington, and "The Constituted Authorities," although they perhaps went farther than their Federalist fathers and husbands might have liked by adding their own salute to "The Rights of Women."[93]

It was their desperate attempt to retain sovereignty over the Fourth that encouraged the Federalists to fashion the day into a public show of civic unity in support of a duly elected republican government. In these kinds of Independence Day festivities the Federalists were far more likely than their opponents to encourage and even celebrate the participation of women, who as fairly passive spectators, as guests at celebratory balls, or even as the organizers of their own rites made public show of the support of their section of the body politic for the duly constituted governing authorities. The toast of "a Number of Ladies" in York, Pennsylvania to "The Rights of Women" suggests that some of these women made use of this opportunity to express a level of political self awareness and a consciousness of the possible extension of the rights that inhered within republican rhetoric.[94] In acknowledging the political existence of subordinate members of the polity, the Federalists risked admitting women's agency and even their independence.

While the Federalists struggled to maintain the illusion of civic unity in support and celebration of government, the opposition made no such claims. Predicated on a partisan opposition to the party in power that was firmly rooted in the rhetoric of republicanism, Democratic Republican celebrations were consistently more exclusive than those of their Federalist opponents. If women were in fact welcome as spectators, from Massachusetts to Georgia there was little if any mention of them in newspaper accounts. Thus, although women were able to wear the colors, attend the parades, and sing the songs of their party of choice, it seems as if the middling and elite white women who thus participated in Federalist celebrations enjoyed a larger political role than did women who sympathized more with the Democratic Republicans. Neither party welcomed the participation of women from the lower sorts, and the Democratic Republicans' exuberant July Fourth celebrations of liberty and equality, with their denunciations of Federalist counter-revolution and their celebration of the rights of man, all served to display the limitations of democratic republicanism as much as its blessings.

Black Americans enjoyed an even smaller degree of participation in these partisan celebrations. The Fourth of July commemorated the republican rights and freedoms secured by American white men in a long and bloody revolutionary war between king and subjects. When black revolution erupted in Haiti in 1791, white Americans feared that the contagion of liberty and violent revolution might spread to the subordinate black peoples of the United States. As a result of these white fears, the dramatic expansion of Independence Day during the 1790s was accompanied by a systematic exclusion of black Americans from celebrations of the Fourth. Writing in the early nineteenth century, James Forten complained "that black people, upon certain days of public jubilee, dare not be seen after twelve o'clock in the day." Angrily he concluded "I allude particularly to the *Fourth of July!*"[95]

On one Fourth of July free blacks assembled alongside white Philadelphians outside Independence Hall, only to be beaten off under a stream of abuse.[96] Bitter resentment at their exclusion from the festival of freedom encouraged other black Philadelphians to take to the streets on the evening of another July Fourth. After forming themselves into unofficial military units, parodying the white militia parades seen earlier in the day, they marched through the city, beating white citizens who crossed their paths, and "damning the whites and saying they would shew them St. Domingo."[97] Largely excluded from white political culture, many black Americans devoted their energies to the development of a rich festive culture of their own. By the end of the first decade of the nineteenth century, they had fashioned an explicitly black alternative to the Fourth of July, and every January first the black Americans of northern urban centers could be found celebrating the anniversary of the end of the slave trade and Haitian independence day.[98]

In a sense, however, it was their very exclusivity that gave Democratic Republican celebrations of the Fourth much of their popular political power, for these were occasions on which large numbers of the white male political nation were able to gather together in order to reaffirm their allegiance to a partisan platform and ideology. It was in the streets, in celebrations of the French Revolution and the Fourth of July that members of the political nation mobilized with dramatic efficiency against the Federalist administrations of first Washington and then Adams. This was abundantly clear to many Federalists, not least the younger generation highlighted by David Hackett Fischer, who realized that in order to compete with the Democratic Republicans the Federalists needed to build their own political party within this context of popular politics.[99]

As a result, the Federalists moved quickly when in the wake of the Jay Treaty, a dramatic and violent decline in Franco-American relations and a subsequent war scare momentarily increased their popularity, and they worked hard to regain control over celebrations of the Fourth as part of their endeavor to maintain dominion over the polity. The battle began slowly in 1797, as Franco-American relations began to sour and French attacks on American shipping increased. Democratic Republicans who had championed the French and maligned their British enemies drank nervous toasts wishing that France and the United States would "happily terminate their mutual and just complaints."[100] By 1797 relatively few Americans supported revolutionary French republicanism with the enthusiasm they had shown in 1793, but their opposition to counter-revolutionary Britain remained strong. The Jay Treaty had placed a wedge between the sister republics and forced the United States closer to Great Britain: this, together with the policies of the Federalist government, was interpreted by many American citizens as a betrayal of American republicanism.

But the more radical and partisan affirmations of liberty and equality that had characterized the Democratic Republican celebrations of earlier years were largely absent from the oppositional festivals of 1797. With relatively few toasts to the spirit of 1776, the people, liberty and equality, and the rights of man, and with no toasts to Paine or the liberty cap, it was declarations of partisan identity that dominated these events. Toasts to Jefferson were again common, as were salutes to emerging Democratic Republican leaders, including James Monroe and William Giles. The Second Artillery Company feasted at the Buck Tavern in Philadelphia, where they condemned the Federalists as "apostate whigs, old tories, and British hirelings" in one toast, while celebrating "real republicans" in another,[101] while on the banks of the Schuylkill local fishermen toasted "the republican members in the senate."[102] Elsewhere partisans drank to such sentiments as "all true republicans,"[103] "Republicanism,"[104] and the "spirit of Republicanism."[105]

In these events supporters of the Democratic Republicans were more on the defensive than they had been in preceding years, and they were forced to adopt the Federalist strategy of molding their partisan and oppositional celebrations of the anniversary of independence in order to give them the appearance of community demonstrations in support of the Democratic Republicans. As such they became somewhat more likely than usual to encourage and even celebrate the supportive participation of women. On July Fourth, 1797, "a large number of gentlemen" were joined by almost two hundred women at a Democratic Republican open-air feast in Elizabethtown, New Jersey, a community whose total population— men, women, and children—stood at about seven hundred and fifty.[106] By 1798 the confidence of the Democratic Republicans was deteriorating, as the French government's seizure of American ships and goods brought the two nations to the brink of war. Americans rallied around Adams's administration in its stand against the French, and in the national capital Federalists moved with a vengeance to reassert their control over Fourth of July celebrations. The militia parade of 1798 was the largest seen in Philadelphia since the early years of the decade, and Federalists reveled in "the universal glow of patriotism" that surrounded their rites. Every "real American," they believed, would demonstrate support of the nation and its government by watching or participating in the Federalist rituals.[107]

Early in the morning, Adams "received the congratulations of the members of both houses of Congress, the Heads of departments, Militia officers, the Cincinnati, Clergy, and other citizens."[108] But the militia parade was the highlight of the day, including representatives from many of the city's militia companies and the new volunteer corps raised in preparation for a possible war with France. Thousands of Philadelphians watched the parade, encouraging Federalists to describe it as "a day of national joy and enthusiasm."[109] The Republicans had worked hard to identify their party with the Patriots of 1776, but now the Federalists raised their glasses to "Seventy-six and Ninety-eight, two rival æras in the age of glory." Toasts to Adams and Washington linked the Federalist leaders with American honor, suggesting that infidelity to these leaders was unpatriotic and unrepublican.[110]

Federalists around the country struggled to take advantage of their new-found popularity. Fisher Ames found the young men of Dedham, Massachusetts to be "unexpectedly well prepared"—a telling admission by a hardened Federalist that the Fourth had already become a Democratic Republican festival—when he suggested that they mount an explicitly Federalist celebration of the Fourth of July. The "proposition took exceedingly well," and about sixty men—approximately 10 percent of the town's adult white males—attended an Independence Day feast, encouraging Ames to conclude that the event would "rally the friends of government."[111] In Augusta, Georgia the rites, feasts, and toasts were unmistakably Federalist in tone, as confirmed by toasts to "The *Federal* Officers of our Government," to the "federal government," and to the constitution.[112] Far away in the district of Maine, "truly Federal and Patriotic" toasts to the government, to the President, and to Washington climaxed with the sentiment "Federalism Triumphant."[113] All around the country toasts to popular respect for government and the laws, to the constitution, to government officials, and to Hamilton, Sedgwick, Pickering, Jay, and other leading Federalists filled these Federalist celebrations.

Elsewhere Federalists sought to enhance their control over the premier national holiday with the introduction of new rites. In Hackensack, in what William Cobbett gleefully described as the "Funeral of Jacobinism," Federalists ceremonially removed the liberty cap "of '93" from their liberty pole and then buried it. They replaced it with "an *elegant* EAGLE," as a symbol of a strong government, firm in its stand against the "Gallic despots."[114] A ceremony in Newport, Rhode Island naming a new defensive fort in honor of President Adams was the highlight of the Federalist Independence day celebrations, while in Schenectady the friends of order organized a parade with three militia companies, local officials and magistrates, local college students, and the citizens taking part.[115]

The crisis of 1798 provided the supporters of the Federalists with their best opportunity to regain ascendancy in early national popular political culture. In celebrations of Washington's birthday, the Fourth of July, and in a variety of new rites they struggled to reclaim the public sphere on the nation's greatest public holidays and demonstrate that all Americans supported the Adams administration and its policies. Women played a significant role in this effort, furnishing further evidence of the ways in which Federalist women were able to negotiate a public role for themselves, and articulate their partisan beliefs and affiliations in a manner that was far less common in Democratic Republican celebrations of the Fourth.

These female rites were relatively standardized: while militia companies paraded and performed military maneuvers, Federalist women united to present new military colors to the men of local militia companies. In Philadelphia two Federalist women presented an emblematical painting to MacPherson's Blues, while in Lancaster three groups of women presented colors to other cavalry and infantry companies. One woman spoke for each group, and in their short speeches they asserted that these colors were "an emblem of their affection to the cause you have engaged to defend."[116]

Similar rites were performed throughout the northern and Middle Atlantic states. Women in Middleton, Connecticut joined for a feast and toasts to Martha Washington, Abigail Adams, and the "daughters of America," ending with a procession to the town's liberty tree.[117] Another group of women in Princeton saluted the Federalist parade and rites by wearing "the American cockade" before a feast in which approximately 40 percent of the town's adult white male population took part.[118] In York, Pennsylvania, young women dressed in white presented new colors to a local militia company, an event that "drew tears from the eyes of assembled thousands."[119] In these events women were able to speak out in public on a major American festival and voice their faith in the principles Adams's administration was defending. But this new form of female involvement in Federalist celebrations of American independence, built on the precedents of female support of the militia and Continental Army during the war for independence, was limited to the height of the Quasi-War frenzy in 1798, and women enjoyed no comparable role or power in the festivals of the following years.

For all its enthusiasm and innovation, the festive renaissance of the Federalists was an incomplete and ultimately unsuccessful effort. Of almost fifty complete sets of toasts appearing in newspapers all over the country in 1798, over thirty appear to have been drawn up and drunk by Democratic Republican opponents of the government. Moreover, the Democratic Republicans were not slow to respond to the new July Fourth rites of the Federalists. In North Springfield and South Orange, New Jersey "the citizens" met to rename their home Jefferson's Village, and to pass resolutions condemning the Federalist "gentlemen of the *high order*," defending their rights to free speech and a free press, and calling for divine vengeance against their opponents before they succeeded "in royalizing America."[120] In Newburgh, New York "a respectable number of citizens" raised a liberty pole bearing the inscription "*Liberty or Death, a Constitution inviolate*," while in Winchester, Kentucky citizens paraded behind a flag bearing an emblem of liberty.[121]

Yet the unexpected popularity of Adams in his stand against France and his political opponents at home had forced the Democratic Republicans onto the defensive. The toasts of the Republican Society in Bennington to the militia and to "freedom of speech and of the press"[122] were echoed around the nation, from the frontier town in Kentucky to the Louisa Court House in Virginia.[123] With the Adams administration equipping a large standing army against the extremely unlikely event of a French invasion, and the Federalist-dominated Congress debating the alien and sedition bills that would make criticism of the government a criminal offense, it was only logical that opponents of the government used the Fourth to draw attention to their vulnerable position and to the pending attack on rights and liberties that would render oppositional politics all but illegal.

Thus many Democratic Republican toasts focused on the preservation of the Constitution against "*further* encroachments."[124] In Montgomery, New York a group of citizens hoped that their "Representatives in Congress" would "continue firm in defence of the liberty of their constituents," thereby checking the power of the president, while in Philadelphia the Southwark Light Infantry attacked "*Domestic Tyranny*."[125] In Duchess County, New York the attack was more forceful, with a condemnation of the "deficient wisdom" of John Adams, while in Vermont others drank to the wish that the president would "reverence the majesty of the people."[126]

But it was the numerous toasts to party leaders, and especially to Jefferson, that dominated the Independence Day feasts of the Democratic Republicans. Toasts to local leaders—Edward Livingston in New York and Albert Gallatin and Thomas McKean in Pennsylvania—were common, but almost everywhere Jefferson was hailed as party leader. In Easton, Pennsylvania two militia companies saluted Jefferson and hoped that "his calumniators be bro't to shame"; in Sagharbour, New York citizens applauded Jefferson as "the friend of the people"; while in Dover, Delaware residents extolled the "virtues and patriotism" of the Vice President.[127]

The undeclared Franco-American naval war, together with the Alien and Sedition acts, prompted an even more bitter struggle over Independence Day in 1799, as the friends of order redoubled their efforts to rally the populace behind the Federalist administration in time of war. The Connecticut branch of the Cincinnati held their annual meeting in New Haven on the Fourth, and at their civic feast they raged against the opponents of the government with toasts to "True Federalism Triumphant," "Anarchy in Mourning," and "The Triumph of Law."[128] The Pennsylvania Cincinnati echoed these sentiments in Philadelphia, drinking to Adams, Washington, the "Constitution and government," and the "friends of law and social happiness."[129]

In Warren, New Hampshire Federalists ushered in the day with a Federal discharge of sixteen cannon, and then staged a procession of two militia companies, the clergy, and "a number of the CITIZENS." One of the militia companies, the Federal Blues, toasted "THE FEDERAL CONSTI-

TUTION," wished long life and continuance in office to President Adams, and gave thanks to the navy and standing army.[130] In Williamstown, Massachusetts students at the local college angrily burned Ezekiel Bacon's oppositional July Fourth oration. In Congress the Federalists were using the Sedition Act to make Democratic Republican political culture illegal, while in the country as a whole their supporters were working to drive Democratic Republicanism out of all celebrations of Independence Day.[131]

William Duane, newly ensconced as the editor of the Philadelphia *Aurora*, recognized this. He responded with a fictional account of an Independence Day celebration of "*staunch federalists*" several hundred miles "east of Trenton." These men, who had always "held in detestation revolutionary principles," enjoyed an oration "upon the blessings" of monarchical government and standing armies. They ceremonially burned the Declaration of Independence, and then toasted "General Arnold," wished "Confusion to all republics," and celebrated the "inflexible loyalists of '76." With other toasts condemning independence, the "rebels who were shot in the revolution," and the "Old Whigs," it is clear that Duane was presenting the Federalists as enemies of everything that the Fourth of July represented to truly patriotic Americans.[132]

Just as in 1797 and 1798, the Federalists maintained or secured control of celebrations of the Fourth in some villages, towns, and cities, but the Democratic Republican slates of toasts published in newspapers all over the country continued to outnumber those of the Federalists by more than two to one. Moreover, large numbers of people participated in these oppositional festivals, at the height of what Democratic Republicans would later refer to as the Federalist "age of terror." Approximately 400 "Republicans" gathered in Centreville, Maryland for an open-air celebration, militia—"the proper and natural defence of a free government"—maneuvers, and open-air feast. With enthusiastic toasts to the "virtuous, and enlightened citizen Thomas Jefferson," to Gallatin, Livingston, the spirit of 1776, and "virtuous Republicans," this was no Federalist celebration. Since the total population of Centreville, including men, women, and children, free persons and slaves amounted to about 200 in 1807, many people must have traveled in from the surrounding countryside for this celebration.[133]

Much the same was true in Scott County, Kentucky, where some "600 people convened" for Independence Day orations and a large barbecue. This constituted approximately 23 percent of the entire county's adult white population, and close to 45 percent of the adult white male population. With toasts to Jefferson "and the patriotic minority in congress," and celebrations of the freedom of speech and of the press, this day belonged to the community's self-proclaimed Democratic Republican "sons of liberty."[134]

Thus, at a time when Democratic Republican congressmen and editors suffered under the Sedition Act and trembled at the standing army, and while President Adams enjoyed a popularity that neither he nor his supporters had ever dreamed possible, hundreds and thousands of citizens continued to gather on the Fourth of July to celebrate their Democratic Republican ideology and articulate their opposition to Adams's Federalist administration. From the "Republicans and sons of Freedom"[135] who gathered in Carlisle, Pennsylvania, to the "real friends of America"[136] in Paterson, New Jersey, to the fifty-odd "old fashioned citizens of 1776"[137] who assembled at Frankford near Philadelphia, to the "lovers of Liberty, Equality, and the Rights of Man"[138] in Newark, New Jersey, opponents of the Federalist government continued to regard Independence Day as their own.

The Declaration of Independence played an ever more important role in these Independence Day festivities: the Declaration was read aloud at Newark and under a new liberty pole at Jefferson's Village in New Jersey, before several companies of militia in New London, Connecticut, before the Tammany and mechanic societies in New York City, and all around Philadelphia.[139] In Lancaster, Pennsylvania residents drank to the wish that "every American who loves not above all the Declaration of Independence," may "become the subject of a tyrant," and many men raised their glasses to the Declaration.[140] The toast of the Republican Blues and the Republican Greens in Philadelphia to the "author of the Declaration of Independence" was echoed by opponents of the government nationwide.[141]

There were good reasons for these Democratic Republicans to privilege the Declaration in their celebrations. Toasts to the more radical expressions of liberty, equality, and the rights of man, symbolized during the heady early years of the French Revolution by the liberty tree and cap, had been of declining significance in July Fourth festivities as the day steadily evolved from a memorial of revolutionary democratic republicanism into a partisan celebration of the Democratic Republican party and its leaders and policies. But the Federalist attack on political expression clearly worried the thousands of Americans who attended oppositional Independence Day celebrations in the final years of the decade. By focusing on the Declaration as the embodiment of everything America had fought for in the war for independence, and by lauding Jefferson as its creator and embodiment, white male Democratic Republicans were able to unite their party firmly with the spirit of 1776, their hope for "a free elective representative, democratic government,"[142] and their wish that Jefferson might become "the next president."[143]

In Philadelphia, despite the large and well-organized Federalist rites in honor of the Fourth during the closing years of the decade, Democratic Republican militia men adamantly refused to surrender Independence Day to their political enemies. In 1798 the Southwark Light Infantry took part in Philadelphia's military parade and review, but at their feast later in the day they toasted "Republican governments—May they be so not only in name but in the action of its genuine principles." This implicit criticism of Adams and his government was made explicit when the diners did not toast the president, preferring to salute Vice President Jefferson, hoping that "his republican virtues [would] ever be remembered with gratitude."[144] The Republican Blues militia company also marched in the morning parade, but they left Federalist rituals far behind when they settled down to a feast in the ruins of a British redoubt, symbolically uniting themselves with the Patriots who had fought Britain two decades earlier. After listening to the Declaration of Independence, they toasted the document, and then— with thirteen cheers—lauded Jefferson as "the friend of his country, the framer of the declaration of Independence."[145]

By 1799 at least eleven of the fifteen militia companies taking part in Philadelphia's Independence Day parade appear to have contained a majority of men who supported the Democratic Republicans, effectively nullifying Federalist control of an event Federalists ostensibly organized. In Philadelphia the number of volunteer militia companies grew rapidly during the 1790s, and for the lower and middling sorts of men who filled their ranks these institutions represented a viable avenue into the political process. For it was through their organization into militia companies and other partisan groups and societies that these citizen soldiers were able to claim Independence Day as their own, and three-quarters of all July Fourth civic feasts held in Philadelphia and reported in local newspapers between 1793 and 1801 were organized and attended by citizens whose toasts voiced opposition to the Federalists. It was these men, marching in the morning and feasting in the afternoon, who had won Independence Day for the Democratic Republicans.[146]

Few muster rolls survive for militia companies active in Philadelphia during the 1790s, making it difficult to gain an accurate sense of who these men were. The background of members of elite volunteer units like the ardently Federalist First City Troop of Cavalry is somewhat easy to surmise: these men wore ornate blue uniforms and rode matching bay horses with silver trimmings on the harnesses, all of which wealthy members paid for out of their own pockets. The Volunteer Light Infantry Company, a Democratic Republican unit, provided a very striking contrast to the Federalist horsemen. With no common uniform and often without their own firearms, it was the plane-maker John Bartley, the cordwainer Charles Hollick, the china-mender John Thomas, and dozens of similar men who comprised the bulk of the company. Many of the members of this particular company hailed from homes in the northern section of the city, an increasingly working class area. In both its membership and its politics the Volunteer Light Infantry Company was typical of many of the city's militia companies, and it seems likely that a good many of the Democratic Republican militia men who took control of Philadelphia's Independence Day celebrations came from similar occupations and neighborhoods.[147]

Bartley, Hollick, and Thomas, and ordinary mechanics and artisans like them, played a crucial role in the transformation of Philadelphia's July Fourth festivities. Interpreting the Federalist policies and ideology of the 1790s as a betrayal of the policies and principles they favored, and choosing to support and help create an oppositional Democratic Republican party, they refused to accept explicitly Federalist celebratory rites. Instead, they elected committees to organize their own festivals, which were imbued with the ideals and rhetoric of democratic republicanism. During these years partisan leaders including Alexander Dallas and Thomas McKean began construction of a Democratic Republican party machine in Pennsylvania and indeed all around the nation. But although these leaders benefited from the Democratic Republican conquest of Independence Day in Philadelphia, there is little evidence to suggest that they completely orchestrated or controlled it. The plane-makers, the cordwainers, the chandlers, the tailors, and the china-menders played a vital role in wresting control of the Fourth of July from the Federalists, and this festive day belonged to them as much as to the party leadership.

These men finally secured a complete victory in Philadelphia in 1800, when Democratic Republican newspapers announced that "there was no *federal* procession or parade" in the capital. The Fourth of July, 1800, "WAS CELEBRATED BY REPUBLICANS—AND BY THEM ONLY." Independence Day had become a thoroughly Democratic Republican event, and the party's supporters reveled in the fact that having recently won the governorship from the Federalists, they had secured almost complete control over the celebration of what they viewed as the most important festival in the American calendar. Church bells were silent because Federalists refused to ring them, and there was "no joy, seen among those who *call themselves* Federalists." The friends and supporters of the Democratic Republicans took part in the militia parade with "conviviality and gladness," as they celebrated "the happy return of the nation from the delusion under which it has so long labored."[148] The very rhetoric of these partisan newspaper accounts confirm the significance these men attributed to control of the celebration of Independence Day.

Once again Jefferson's Declaration of Independence was at the forefront of many Republican celebrations. Two infantry companies from the outlying Northern Liberties and Frankford were typical in beginning their feast with a reading of the Declaration, followed by cannon and musket fire, and the cheers that greeted the Philadelphia Blues' toast to the Declaration and its author were echoed in similar celebrations throughout the city and the entire nation.[149] A professor at the University of Pennsylvania who objected to the Declaration being read aloud on the grounds that "it might offend some [Britons] who were present" was castigated in the city's Democratic Republican press.[150] The lone Federalist celebration of the day that found its way into the newspapers of either party was the annual feast of the Cincinnati. Their toasts to President Adams and the memory of Washington, together with others to the Federalist leaders Alexander Hamilton and Thomas Pinckney, were hollow clarion calls, heard by few and heeded by even fewer.[151]

The Declaration of Independence assumed the symbolic place in these rites once occupied by the somewhat more radical liberty pole and liberty cap. The preamble to the Declaration, far more than any other single document, encapsulated and symbolized the republican ideology that was at the core of Democratic Republican political thought. For many white male Americans, the preamble to the Declaration confirmed that the American Revolution had been fought on their behalf and to secure their political rights. A group of Pennsylvania Democratic Republicans, celebrating their successes in the state elections of 1799, effectively summarized this ideology in their toasts. Having drunk to "The sovereignty of the people—The foundation of democratic republics," they raised their glasses to the sentiment: "Thomas Jefferson . . . May the spirit which dictated the declaration of independence—preside in the union."[152] A year later, following their party's success in the presidential election, Democratic Republicans in Easton, Pennsylvania drank to the day of Jefferson's election: "The third

of December 1800—the legitimate offspring of the Fourth of July, 1776,"
while in Lancaster others saluted his inauguration with the toast "The
principles of the 4th July, 1776, confirmed the 4th March, 1801." To these
citizens, Jefferson better represented the spirit of 1776 than any other man
living, and his Declaration of Independence was their manifesto.[153]

On the Fourth of July, 1801, with the Democratic Republicans firmly
in control of the national government, Elizabeth Drinker lamented that
the "sensible part of ye community, have more reason to lament than rejoice," and her opinion was shared by many Federalists.[154] The *Gazette of
the United States* gave only a passing salute to the Fourth of July with a
one-line comment noting that "the Anniversary of AMERICAN INDE-
PENDENCE" had been celebrated in the city.[155] The "special interference
of the governor was necessary to compel" Federalists to ring the bells of
churches throughout the city: the Fourth of July had become the sole
property of the Democratic Republican party, and a day of mourning for
the Federalists.[156]

Philadelphia's militia procession took on a new partisan vitality in
1801: more companies took part "than on any former occasion; and several
new companies joined for the first time." Bands played the Democratic Republican anthems "Yankee Doodle," "Jefferson's March," and the "Marseillaise" throughout the day, while people sang "Jefferson and Liberty"
in the streets. The toast of a group of citizens dining at Francis's Hotel
summarized the sentiments of many Democratic Republicans: those present drank to "Thomas Jefferson—The patriot chosen to maintain in 1801
the principles which he declared in 1776."[157] These partisans believed that
the ideology that had motivated the American Revolution had been vin-
dicated and protected by Jefferson's election, or more precisely, by the
expulsion of counter-revolutionary Federalists from office. While the Philadelphia Blues acknowledged the Fourth of July, 1776 as "the first jubilee
in the calendar of liberty," their next toast was to "*The Year* 1801—The
Political Millenium—The most glorious of jubilees, destined to restore
and perpetuate liberty, peace, and happiness."[158] The Federalists remained
a potent—and in some parts of the nation a dominant—force on the political scene. But by 1801 they had lost control of Philadelphia's July Fourth
festivities, and had thus been defeated on one of the early republic's most
important political battlefields.

Throughout the nation the story was much the same, with Democratic Republicans monopolizing commemoration of the Fourth in the
years immediately before and after Jefferson's election. Even in their New

England strongholds Federalists often retired from the festive scene and generally refused to mount celebrations of a day that they could no longer control. Virtually no Federalist rites and only a handful of Federalist toasts found their way into the newspapers of either party, but thousands of Americans continued to participate in and witness Democratic Republican celebrations of Independence. In 1800 some 400 citizens, including the Republican Light Infantry company, a musical band, and "a number of their fellow citizens" attended an open-air feast in Germantown, Pennsylvania. If all of these were men, over 45 percent of the adult white male population was present to hear the Declaration of Independence read and to drink toasts to Jefferson, McKean, and all "true republicans." [159] In Lewistown in far western Pennsylvania the Declaration was also read aloud to around 200 "citizens," who constituted over 75 percent of the adult white male population. Their Democratic Republican sympathies were made abundantly clear in a toast to the "Author of the Declaration of Independence," in which they hoped that he would be "placed in the Presidential chair at our next election." [160]

The political significance of the alleged differences in scale between Federalist and Democratic Republican celebrations was made abundantly clear a year later in a Democratic Republican account of the celebration of the Fourth of July in Newport, Rhode Island. Making fun of Federalist claims that their rites had "engrossed the adoration and wonderment of every Citizen," the writer claimed that the citizenry of Newport had actually ignored the "federal group," except when it was forced to give way to a far larger Democratic Republican parade, previously organized by the "Republicans" at a town meeting. He reported that only 158 "Old Tories, Refugees, and British agents and hirelings, ex-government officers, disappointed demagogues, and their satellites" participated in the Federalist parade, and argued that this showing of just over 10 percent of Newport's adult white male population had been dwarfed by the "extended lines of the Republican procession." [161]

Toasts to Jefferson could be heard everywhere. Many joined the men of the Artillery Company who feasted in an Augusta, Georgia tavern in 1800 by exalting Jefferson as "the drafter of the declaration of our independence," while others echoed the "true republicans" in Mifflin-Town, Pennsylvania who drank to the wish that the author of the Declaration of Independence would "be acknowledged and rewarded by the suffrages of all republicans at the next presidential election." [162] In other toasts William Duane and those editors who had suffered under the Sedition Act were heralded as heroes, while the Alien and Sedition laws and the Federalist standing army were condemned as unconstitutional and unrepublican. But more than anything else, the Independence Day celebrations in 1800 were rallies of the members and the supporters of a political party preparing for a national election. Thousands drank to such sentiments as those toasted by the citizens in Baltimore who hoped that "all *honest* Republicans" would "*turn out* Rogues," and the militia men in Philadelphia who drank to the hope that "the pure flame of republicanism" might destroy "aristocracy throughout the union." [163]

A year later, just as in Philadelphia, it was the euphoria of victory that colored Democratic Republican celebrations of the Fourth. One newspaper editor claimed that the day was celebrated in every town, village, and hamlet with "a greater display of patriotic enthusiasm" than ever before. [164] In New York City the young Thomas Cope recorded in his diary that the Battery "was crowded with military & other citizens," that the streets were "alive" with people, and that "the whole City wore the appearance of festivity." [165]

Toasts to Jefferson, the "patriot who penned the Declaration" [166] and who was the embodiment of "republican patriotism," [167] dominated many of these festivals. But with the Democratic Republicans now in control of the national government, the oppositional rhetoric of radical republican beliefs and values that had characterized popular celebrations of the Fourth during the early to mid-1790s were quickly forgotten. Thomas Paine and the rights of man were virtually ignored, as were liberty and equality and the familiar rites involving the liberty pole and liberty cap.

The white men who had made Independence Day their own had spent years assailing the Federalists for their misuse of power and their abrogation of the rights of American citizens, while simultaneously celebrating the liberty and equality they championed. Yet once their party was in power these men began celebrating sentiments that—a decade earlier—had belonged to the Federalists. Salutes to the constitution, the "political bible of Republicans," [168] were common, as Democratic Republicans congratulated themselves for having "saved it from destruction," [169] and they now voiced joyful allegiance to the new "Republican Administration." [170] In Philadelphia a group of citizens drank to "Consistent Patriotism," which translated into their belief that "the revolutionary whig on the 4th of July, 1776" was "a democratic republican on the 4th of July, 1801." [171]

By 1801, then, little of the radical rites and language of 1776 remained, and the Fourth of July was controlled and largely populated by the urban and rural adult white men who supported the emergent Democratic Republican party. These men supported an elite-controlled political party whose leadership shared many of their favored policies and objectives and recognized their citizenship and political identity. In Lancaster, Pennsylvania the Republican Blues were presented with a new standard by "the ladies of the borough" in a rite closely modeled on those employed by the Federalists in 1798.[172] It was very rare, however, for Democratic Republicans to stage this kind of event. With their hierarchical conception of society many Federalists had been able to acknowledge a limited political role for unequal and dependent members of the polity, which allowed virtuous mothers, wives, and daughters to express support for the legitimate government of the republic. In contrast, the egalitarian rhetoric of the Democratic Republicans was premised on an equality limited to white men. The absence of women and black Americans from the vast majority of Democratic Republican rites and celebrations suggests that these men were uncomfortable affording any kind of public political role to dependent members of the polity.

With few Federalists willing to attend or participate in celebrations of the new political status quo, many Democratic Republicans began to criticize their opponents as enemies of the ideology that had inspired the American Revolution. Church bells that had rung "sweetly to the sound of monarchy and prelacy," but were now "dumb, muffled and silent at the voice of republicanism" told a story of Federalist dissent.[173] Democratic Republicans were chagrined at an 1804 article that appeared in the Federalist *New York Evening Post*, which reprobated "the practice of reading the *declaration*" of independence, on the grounds that America and Britain were now allies.[174] A writer in a Philadelphia Republican newspaper noted that the practice of reading Jefferson's Declaration had "been discontinued" by New England Federalists, and four years later the same newspaper recorded that the "federalists of Boston" had actually "abandoned their original plan of celebration," and had refused to celebrate the day at all.[175]

The birth of this new American tradition, the celebration of the anniversary of national independence, was thus a profoundly partisan contest. For a decade the supporters and creators of the nation's first political parties had struggled for control over the public symbols and rites that comprised these popular celebrations, but by 1801 the supporters of the Democratic Republicans had won the most important battle in the popular political culture of the early republic, and the Fourth of July had been developed into America's premier political festival, on very much their own terms. The public space where these rites were staged was a significant political battlefield, one dominated by the mechanics, artisans, and yeoman farmers who comprised the coalition that empowered the Democratic Republican party. Many Americans participated in or chose to watch the Independence Day festivities, and it was in these and similar rites that they took part in the partisan politics of the early republic.

The Federalists and their supporters were far less successful than the Democratic Republicans in the establishment of an effective political culture of Independence Day. Unsympathetic to the politicization and radicalization of large numbers of common folk, they were loath to allow the genie of popular politics out of the jar. When a Federalist leader was pursuing popular policies, as when President Adams took a firm stand against France during the Quasi-War, the Federalists were able to use civic feasts, military processions and ceremonies, and songs in quite effective ways, for they were more than happy to encourage shows of support by dependent members of the polity. They were not, however, inclined to accord any agency to these people who watched or participated in July Fourth festivities in subordinate roles.

Federalist political culture was thus most effective when the Federalists were pursuing popular policies and when they were willing to countenance and even encourage popular demonstrations of support. But when Federalist leaders were promoting less popular policies, Federalist popular political culture was generally weak and ineffective. Given these shortcomings of the Federalists and the far more democratic and populist tenor of the Democratic Republicans, it is perhaps not surprising that the Fourth of July had become a Democratic Republican festival by 1801, or even that their leader had been elected president. But the role and the significance of Independence Day rites in the Democratic Republican victory have often been overlooked. As the focal points of their expanding commercial empire, the Federalists had anticipated that they would dominate the politics of the towns and cities of the young republic. But an enormously successful oppositional political culture denied the Federalists their expected primacy in these key places: it eroded their power, as Theodore Dwight argued in an angry July Fourth oration before the die-hard Connecticut Cincinnati, "in toasts, in orations . . . in secret cabals, and in civic thanksgivings."[176] While Democratic Republican leaders may have occasionally organized and taken part in this popular political culture, it was the ordinary white male Americans who objected to Federalist policies and ideology and responded by creating a new style and perhaps even a new kind of politics. Men wearing tri-colored cockades, cheering and taking part in the Independence Day parades and celebrations of plane-makers and shoe-makers, burning effigies of their opponents, and drinking partisan toasts at their feasts, had transformed politics and indeed the entire political process.

4

Celebrating the
French Revolution

DURING THE LATTER HALF OF WASHINGTON's presidency, celebrations of
the French Revolution engulfed the festive calendar of the early American
republic, overwhelming the annual rites commemorating the anniversaries
of Independence Day and the president's birthday. (See Map 3.) These
French Revolutionary feasts, festivals, and parades were, however, pecu-
liarly partisan in character, for while white men from both political parties
came together each year to contest the form and content of celebrations
of Washington's birthday and the Fourth of July, virtually all those who
identified themselves as members or supporters of the evolving Federalist
party refused to participate in rites commemorating the French Revolution. From the outset, then, the lavish celebrations of the French Revolution that enriched early national festive culture were distinctly partisan
affairs, and Democratic Republicans did not have to contend with their
Federalist opponents for control over these festive rites and symbols.

However, this lack of participation by the members and supporters of
a democratically elected Federalist government created significant problems for Democratic Republicans in the northern states, where the large
majority of French Revolutionary celebrations took place. These festivals
lacked the legitimacy conferred by the participation of the party in power,
and given the absence of a clear sense of the nature and role of a legitimate
opposition, the white male Democratic Republicans who supported and
staged many of the events honoring France were forced to foster alternative ways of validating celebrations that were often explicitly oppositional.[1]
The festive rites themselves and the thick descriptions of them that appeared in partisan newspapers illustrate that the Democratic Republicans
strove to legitimate their partisan French Revolutionary festivals by assert-
ing that the entire community—rather than merely those members of the
white male citizenry who supported the Democratic Republicans—was

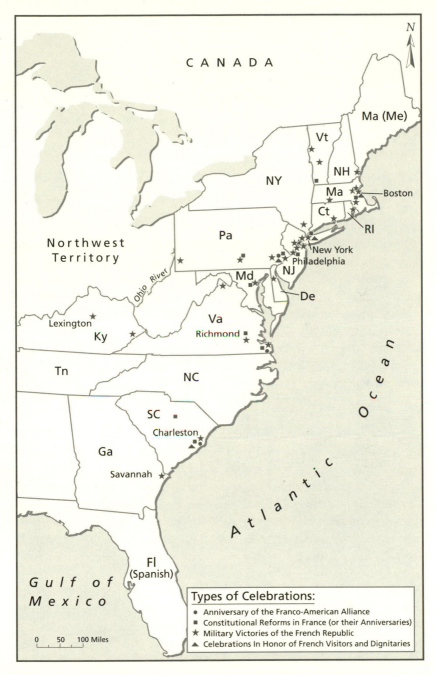

Map 3. Communities that celebrated the French Revolution, 1789–1801.

united in its desire to honor the French and all that the French Revolution represented. During most of Washington's presidency this tactic was so successful as to make it all but impossible for the Federalists to criticize these rites.

The result of the Democratic Republican stratagem was that members of subordinate groups—including women, the poor, and black Americans, all of whom were excluded from or had strictly circumscribed roles in the white male contests over July Fourth and Washington's birthday celebrations—found a larger role for themselves in French Revolutionary celebrations than in any of the other rites and festivals of the early American republic. The opposition needed community sanction, and to a limited yet significant degree this empowered the community. Those who were often on the margins of the politics of the street were able to enjoy an uncommonly active role in the proceedings, and to exercise some small yet significant role in the popular construction of the Democratic Republican party, its agenda and its leadership in these festive events. It was white men of lower social rank who benefited the most, and throughout the nation, but especially in the northern states, such men were able to work within French Revolutionary festive culture to register their particular opposition to Federalist policies and personnel.

*   *   *

Boston's celebration of the French victory at the Battle of Valmy was the largest and the most elaborate French revolutionary celebration ever staged in the United States, and it exemplifies the partisan nature of these festive rites, the lack of participation by Federalists who kept their criticism to themselves, and the unusually high degree of participation by members of subordinate groups. Americans well understood the significance of Valmy: by the fall of 1792 internal dissension and foreign invasion impended a disastrous end to the new French republic, but at the end of September French troops defeated a Prussian invasion at Valmy and thereby eliminated a serious foreign threat to the new French republic and secured the position of the revolutionaries. Their victory generated widespread celebration throughout France, and in the United States, in communities as far apart as Charleston, New York City, Princeton, Providence, Savannah, Lexington, and Boston, Americans organized and participated in their own civic festivals in honor of Valmy, in which they extolled all that the French Revolution meant to them.[2]

In Boston the festivities began at dawn on January 24, 1793, when militia men stationed at the fort fired an artillery salute. Several hours later about 800 of the city's school children paraded along State Street, and were then presented with small cakes bearing the words "LIBERTY and EQUALITY."[3] These "words of the day"[4] were central motifs of the celebration. Later in the morning citizens took up positions around a large carriage bearing the ox that had been roasted for the occasion. It was decorated with tri-colored ribbons, and its horns were draped with the French and American flags, and a gilded sign that read "PEACE OFFERING TO LIBERTY AND EQUALITY."[5]

An elaborate procession followed the roasted ox, including citizens carrying the French and American flags, the grand marshal and the committee of organization, men bearing the flags and colors of the various trades and crafts of the city, a musical band, all twelve of the butchers wearing clean white robes, a cart drawn by six decorated horses carrying 800 loaves of bread, another cart loaded with two hogsheads of punch, and several hundred male citizens marching in formation.[6]

As the procession moved through Boston, white and black men, women, and children first watched it pass and then joined the rear. The participants halted three times, to salute with three cheers the French Consul, to pay homage at the stump of the Liberty Tree, and to conduct a ceremony renaming Oliver's Dock as Liberty Square. The dock had borne the name of the hated stamp collector of 1765, and this rearrangement of urban space affirmed symbolically the unity of the American and French revolutions, and the power of the crowds who had destroyed Oliver's office and who now marched in celebration of the French Revolution. This was an entirely new processional route, which had passed through both the northern and southern sections of Boston, uniting the traditionally antagonistic areas populated by artisans, craftsmen and journeymen—the town's workers. Employing familiar motifs including the liberty pole and the flags and colors of craftsmen, the Valmy procession and festival was intended to unite residents in an entirely new kind of political celebration, aimed against the Federalist government in Philadelphia and against the mercantile Federalist elite in Boston itself.[7]

A great many Bostonians participated in this rich and multi-faceted festival, and when the parade concluded on State Street in the large area around the State House, many thousands of the town's residents were present. The twelve uniformed butchers set about carving up the ox on the "Altar of Democracy" and distributing the meat, bread and punch to those present, while a band in the balcony of the State House played a familiar French Revolutionary anthem, the "Ça Ira." As the citizenry feasted, two large balloons were raised from nearby Market Square: from one hung the American flag, while the other trailed the motto "Liberty and Equality." [8]

Then, while the populace feasted, a second procession set out from the State House led by Lieutenant Governor Adams and the French Consul Citizen Letombe. The city's Democratic Republican elite, politicians, merchants, lawyers, and other dignitaries marched to Faneuil Hall, which was beautifully decorated for the occasion. At one end of the hall stood an obelisk topped by a statue of liberty, her outstretched right hand bearing the emblem "The Rights of Man." Beneath her feet lay the shattered remnants "of Civil and Ecclesiastical Despotism," and on either side of the obelisk hung the French and American flags. At the other end of the hall allegorical statues of Fame, Justice, and Peace held aloft a banner proclaiming "LIBERTY & EQUALITY." [9] After their civic feast concluded those present drank toasts to such sentiments as "The American and French Revolutions," "Democratic organs to express American sentiments," and "The fraternity of Freemen." [10]

But the Democratic Republican party leadership, safely ensconced in Faneuil Hall, did not enjoy exclusive control over the form and the ideological content of this celebration of Valmy by the people of Boston. Citizens, "whether common or military, whether in the Hall or Street," [11] celebrated on their own terms, and militia companies and groups of artisans and mechanics held their own civic feasts, while on the streets many people fashioned their own celebrations. The "citizen soldiers of the independent fusiliers" [12] dined at Bryant's Liberty Hall, Citizen Bradlee's company of artillery" [13] feasted at Concert Hall, a company of "citizen Mechanicks" [14] feasted at a local tavern, and an interracial and sexually mixed assembly of the lower sort enjoyed their own "entertainment" at the stump of the Liberty Tree. [15]

Thus many different Bostonians created the town's biggest public political event of the 1790s: according to one spectator, "even the chimneytops were covered" with spectators, and one "would have thought the very windows spoke," so many people were watching and cheering. [16] As darkness fell people retired home in good order, enjoying the spectacular illuminations of the State House and the home of the French consul and a large bonfire and fireworks on Copps Hill. Never before had there been a festival of this kind or on this scale in the United States. Thomas Greenleaf, partisan editor of the *New York Journal*, justified devoting almost an entire issue of his newspaper to an account of the Bostonians' festivities as "an additional feather in their cap, and that posterity might recognize their *zeal* in the cause of the RIGHTS of MAN." [17]

In its symbols, rites and ideology this festival was planned and presented in local and more distant newspapers as a thoroughly partisan Democratic Republican event. When one correspondent wished naively for the "pen of a Burke" [18] to describe the Valmy celebration he was roundly castigated for associating such a name with this event: the "venal and corrupt" pen of the counter-revolutionary Briton Burke, for all his popularity among several leading Federalists, was ill-suited to "describe the pleasing scene of 'Liberty and Equality.'" [19]

From the time of the first American celebrations of the French Revolution in late 1791 and early 1792, the Federalists and their supporters seldom participated in or countenanced these festivities. [20] Boston's civic festival was no exception, but so great was its popularity among many different townsmen and -women that Federalists anxious for good relations between Great Britain and the United States and extremely wary of the radical democratic impulses of the French revolution, were forced to keep their "hints, shrugs . . . [and] sneers" to themselves. [21] By early 1793 events in France frightened more conservative Americans: John Adams wrote that he was disappointed that his cousin Samuel had taken part in the Valmy celebration, and his son John Quincy described the event as "anarchical." [22] William Bentley proudly recorded in his diary that his friends and neighbors in Salem had mounted no comparable celebration, and thus the lower sorts were not "diverted a moment from their employments." He had heard reports that Boston's roasted ox had fallen "prey to the fury of the rabble," and was clearly grateful that no partisan crowd actions of this kind had occurred in Salem. [23] The Federalist lawyer Joseph Dennie told his parents that he had always admired the "old whigs of 1775," but that the shortcomings of their ideology had become apparent now that "they gave Tars and Tailors a civic feast and taught the rabble that they were viceroys." [24]

Dennie had a point, for the "rabble" had indeed enjoyed an active role in the proceedings. After the great public feast had ended, "a number of citizen seamen" had taken up the charred remains of the ox's horns and marched with them to the liberty pole, followed by a large group of their fellow citizens. They deposited the skull and horns at the foot of the liberty pole, and announced that they would pay to have the horns gilded and then mounted on the top of the pole, as a lasting tribute to the day's ceremonies and the event they commemorated. These black and white seafarers were at the bottom of early national urban society, but in this rite they affirmed their interest in the success of revolutionary democratic republicanism, both abroad and at home. Moreover, in the context of growing wealth inequality and the class-based partisan politics of the old Puritan town, these men and those who supported their actions were adding their own voices and expectations to the partisan agenda of the Democratic Republican elite who had sponsored the Valmy festival.[25]

Boston's celebration assumed shape and significance in a crucible of national and local political and economic battles, and it is in the context of the political, social and economic controversies that engulfed the town during the late 1780s and early 1790s that the full meaning and the significance of the festival begins to become apparent. Boston was a deeply troubled community during the last quarter of the eighteenth century, in which the "*Mercury* in the *political Thermometer*" stood "but a few degrees below the *boiling water mark*."[26] Rapidly increasing wealth inequality, combined with the devastating impact of cheap British imports on domestic manufacturing, served to increase the hardships faced by many lower sort Bostonians, and economic hardships exacerbated class tension and fueled the development of partisan politics. As a result intense political warfare, exacerbated by these class issues, plagued Boston throughout the closing decades of the eighteenth century.[27]

In 1784 and again in 1792, for example, a proposal to abolish the town meeting and replace it with an incorporated city government had caused uproar in Boston. For one and one-half centuries the town meeting had allowed much of Boston's white male population to participate in politics and government, and these men resented an attempt to disable this generally democratic form of government. Against the national backdrop of the new Federal Constitution and the politicized cult of Washington they censured the innovators as "*a formidable combination of aristocracy*"[28] who sought to take government out of the hands of poorer and propertyless men, and vest power in elected officials drawn from the ranks of the propertied elite. Over 1,200 townsmen, close to 30 percent of Boston's adult white men, entered Faneuil Hall in January of 1792 to defeat this assault on their "liberties and privileges."[29]

A heated debate over the reform of the legal profession further illustrated the depth of political bellicosity in early national Boston. Under the pseudonym "Honestus," Benjamin Austin, Jr. argued that the current legal system was part of an aristocratic conspiracy designed to rob the people of their liberty, their rights, and their property. In a series of newspaper essays, later republished as a pamphlet, "Honestus" proposed the exclusion of lawyers from civil suits, and the representation of defendants in criminal suits by an "advocate general." Boston's mercantile and professional elite were horrified by these proposals, which they believed would inevitably result in anarchy and the destruction of republicanism, and a furious newspaper debate erupted.[30]

The rapid development of national partisan politics intensified this political conflict. Its rhetoric and ideology permeated local political discourse, from newspaper attacks on the "Demon of Aristocracy" raised by Washington's administration, to defenses of the use of titles.[31] Inevitably national partisan politics spilled over into local politics, provoking a series of highly contentious local elections that heightened partisan tensions. The congressional elections of 1788, 1790, and 1792 were all won by Fisher Ames, an ardent supporter of Washington's administration and the Federalist policies championed by Hamilton. In these elections Ames was challenged by either Samuel Adams or Benjamin Austin, both of whom were leading figures in the state's emerging Democratic Republican party. The town's newspapers were filled with partisan electioneering rhetoric: when Austin was defeated in 1790, for example, the *Boston Gazette* printed an obituary for free elections. Suggesting that Ames had won by less than fair means, the author described how "Liberty & Independence . . . Patriotism . . . [and] The Genius of Mechanick arts" had been buried, but he hoped for their "glorious Resurrection" in time for the next congressional election.[32] On the other hand, a gubernatorial election between Samuel Adams and Thomas Cushing inspired the Federalist *Mercury* to warn Boston voters that their "COUNTRY IS IN DANGER from the intrigues of Jacobins," and that only the election of Cushing could prevent the anarchy of a Democratic Republican government.[33]

This, then, formed the backdrop for the participation of Boston's ordinary folk in the Valmy celebration. The success of this event as a show of support for Democratic Republican leaders was contingent on their securing the participation and support of the townspeople as a whole, but there were clear risks involved in enlisting "all classes and persons without discrimination" in this celebration of radical democratic revolution.[34] The town's Democratic Republicans had welcomed the participation of "every class of Citizen patriots" in their partisan celebration, promising that social rank would be "abolished by the title of Citizens," and hoping to draw a large enough crowd to cow their Federalist opponents.[35] These partisan leaders envisioned a large celebration of Valmy, premised on the rhetoric of liberty and equality, that would give them temporary control of public space and demonstrate the depth and extent of popular support for their pro-French and—by implication—anti-Federalist sentiments.

Some white townswomen were not slow to employ the logic of this Democratic Republican rhetoric in order to assume a meaningful role in the proceedings for themselves. Throughout the 1790s it was unusual for Democratic Republican leaders to seek or recognize more than the enthusiastic spectatorship of women. But after decades of war and out-migration Boston was a city in which adult women outnumbered adult men, and the fierce politicking of partisan leaders and their desperate search for communal support and sanction involved the participation of thousands of women, many of whom wore tri-colored cockades to indicate publicly their support for the French Revolution and its ideals as they interpreted them.[36] To a significant degree, the success of Boston's Valmy festival was contingent on both the passive and active participation of "bevies of our amiable and beautiful women,"[37] and newspapers as far away as Pennsylvania reported how some Boston women took advantage of this to demand equal title with male citizens participating in political culture, with the appropriate label "citess."[38]

Federalists were quick to seize on these female incursions into the male realm of politics in order to condemn their partisan opponents who had made such actions possible by their sponsorship of the inclusive Valmy festival. After complaining about Boston's celebration, John Adams protested that "Cit and Citess is to come instead of Goffer and Gammer, Gooder and Gooden, Mr. and Mrs."[39] Other criticisms of female politicization were of far greater consequence. The rites, symbols, and language of Boston's Valmy celebration implied a very real leveling within the political community, an equality that did not sit well with Federalist conceptions of deferential female activities within an orderly and hierarchical polity. One satirical poem that appeared in the *Connecticut Courant* attacked "every *Citizen* and *Citess*" who had worshiped the stump of the liberty tree "like heathen folks," with seemingly savage "*Indian talk*."[40] Another Federalist, also from Connecticut, derisively dismissed the "citesses in Boston" by applauding a local woman who had just given birth to "FOUR equality citizens," and by condemning another who had taken the rhetoric of liberty and equality to heart and decided "that her husband ought not to be the sole occupant of her; that all men have an equal right—and that she is determined to keep open hours."[41]

This was a clear condemnation of women who transcended the domestic and subservient role of wife and mother ordained by men. Such criticism was taken a stage farther in a poem that made explicit the criticism that women who ventured too far into the male domain of the public sphere were no better than prostitutes:

No citess to my name I'll have, says Kate,
Tho' Boston lads about it so much prate,
I've asked its meaning and our Tom, the clown,
Says, darn it, 't means a woman of the Town.[42]

All around the country Federalist men sought to exploit the discomfort of Democratic Republican men over this kind of inappropriate female political activity. In Philadelphia, for example, one public official carefully crossed out the words "a Citizen" when women signed as witnesses for seafarers applying for seamen's protection certificates. Citizenship, and the role in popular political culture that it implied, was no place for women, and this gave Federalists one more weapon with which to attack oppositional French Revolutionary festive culture.[43]

By suggesting that the "revolutionary usage" of citizenship might be carried to the ridiculous length of according "citizen Pompey" and other slaves the rights and titles of full and equal participants in the polity, Federalists went even farther in trying to rend asunder the festive coalition carefully constructed by Democratic Republicans.[44] The partisan success of Boston's celebration of Valmy and similar festivals depended on the appearance of communal unity in the streets, and if this unity could be undermined then the whole oppositional endeavor might fall apart.

Nor were the friends of order slow to challenge the participation of Boston's lowly white and black seafarers in Boston's Valmy festival, although they voiced this criticism in a rather different manner. When news of Louis XVI's execution reached America, the seamen's liberty pole and gilded horns were taken down. A writer in a Democratic Republican newspaper congratulated his "fellow-citizens and all *true-republicans*" on the defeat "of a few *monarchy-men*" in Boston who mourned the death of Louis. He reported that when these "*mourners of Louis*" arrived at Liberty Square, a large number of citizens broke down the pole and horns, and cheerfully consigned them to the grave with Louis XVI, accompanied by "a *liberty*-discharge of cannon and three equal huzzas."[45] But the city's Federalists interpreted this rite as a renunciation of the entire Valmy celebration and the values that it had endorsed. They claimed that the committee that had arranged the procession agreed to cut down the Liberty Tree and horns, and then bury them as evidence *"that the news of ... [Louis XVI's] execution has given them great pain."* [46]

The struggle for control over the interpretation of the political activities of lowly seafarers illustrates their significance to the elite, and confirms that subordinate groups had secured a voice in the political proceedings of their rulers. The liberty pole represented all that was most radical about popular participation in Boston's Valmy celebration: boasting a long and radical heritage, with ties to the rites of social inversion associated with the popular erection of maypoles, the symbolic power of the liberty pole had been re-energized by its more recent association with the political inversion of revolution in the United States and then France. [47] Therefore this liberty pole, erected by a mixed race group of men near the bottom of society, symbolized their politicization in the age of the French Revolution, and their demands for a greater role within the American polity. With a patriotism fueled by a burning hatred of British impressment, seafarers were enthusiastic in their promotion and support of the leveling ideals of the French Revolution. [48]

Well over a year after this remarkable festival had taken place, a New Hampshire newspaper published an attack on the partisan politics of Governor Samuel Adams. The assault demonstrated how French revolutionary festivals were energizing American popular political culture, and how their language, rites, and symbols infused the rhetoric of partisan politics. Attacking Adams for "gubernatorial insanity," the author complained that Adams was ready to "mount some *Jacobin Jack ass*" and ride to Philadelphia in order to demand that George Washington change his political stripes and "metamorphose himself into a 'Citizen of Oliver's Dock.'" The black and white sailors and laborers and the women who had celebrated Valmy at Liberty Square were thus the point of reference for an attack on Adams for excessive partisan zeal and radicalism: their very actions had become part of the rhetoric of early national popular political culture. [49]

*   *   *

Notwithstanding the unusually grand scale and sophistication of Boston's wintery celebration of Valmy, it was typical of many hundreds of French Revolutionary civic festivals held in the United States during Washington's presidency. The inclusive language employed by Democratic Republican organizers; the ways in which domestic partisan politics informed participants' vision of the French Revolution and the French republic that were the ostensible objects of celebration; the creation of a festive venue that was unusually accessible to white men of all classes and to members of subordinate groups; the barely stifled Federalist attacks on the French Revolution and those who celebrated it in America, attacks that became ever more strident as the decade wore on; and the growing uneasiness of Democratic Republican leaders, who worried about both the increasing radicalism of the French Revolution, and the radicalism of celebrations in American that they had created but could not fully control—all these were played out in feasts, festivals, and processions across the nation.

French Revolutionary celebrations pervaded public space during Washington's presidency, energizing popular politics by fueling oppositional politicking of an unprecedented intensity, and by furnishing impoverished white men, white women of all classes, and black men and women with far greater opportunities for participation in popular politics than were afforded by domestic festive occasions. Benjamin Tappan, a young apprentice in the "mechanic trades," was one of many for whom the French Revolution provided both inspiration and opportunity for entry into the public world of popular politics, and he first took "his stand on the democratic side" at a festival honoring "the recapture of Toulon from the British & Spanish."[50]

This kind of ritual enjoyed a prominent role in American popular politics because the French Revolution had so completely captivated Americans.[51] Throughout the closing years of the eighteenth century many joined Elizabeth Drinker in devouring "Very Important intelligence" from France in each "days paper," for American newspapers sustained popular enthusiasm for the French Revolution by filling their pages with reports from France of constitutional debates, arguments over the monarchy, wars between the French republic and foreign aggressors, and a host of related issues.[52] However, given that these press accounts were generally drawn from unsympathetic British newspapers, it was often quite hard for Americans to follow the complicated train of events in France.[53] Many found the intricacies of revolutionary French politics somewhat confusing, and it was the fall of the Bastille, major military victories, and significant constitutional developments that captured popular attention. But this confusion did not prevent Americans from enthusiastically applauding the progress of the French Revolution, and for five years they participated in French Revolutionary festive culture by wearing French tri-colored cock-

ades, singing French Revolutionary songs, and participating in the many
parades, feasts, and festivals staged in honor of the French.

American reactions to and celebrations of the French Revolution
were, in the vein of Boston's celebration of Valmy, shaped and informed
by domestic politics. In the eyes of many opponents of the administrations
of Washington and Adams, the Federalists were moving the government
and people of the United States farther and farther away from republicanism and liberty. Their somewhat Anglophilic foreign policies and their
hierarchical vision of a decidedly undemocratic American republic all combined to threaten some white male Americans with the loss of rights and
powers secured in the recent struggle with Great Britain. Moreover, in
towns and cities throughout the nation many lower and middling sorts of
men and women were beginning to suffer as a result of British attacks on
neutral American shipping, and British impressment of American sailors.
These Americans started identifying the Federalists as a party of elite monied interests, dominated by merchants with more interest in commercial
alliance with counter-revolutionary Britain than in the ideals of the American and French revolutions.

Such a response was hardly accurate, given that many merchants became Democratic Republicans and that Federalists were far from counter-
revolutionary.[54] Nevertheless, in response to policies that appeared to
privilege the interests of the nation's mercantile and professional elite,
Democratic Republicans around the nation employed the French Revolution to ignite public demonstrations of the scale and the extent of popular
allegiance to their versions of republicanism and liberalism, and opposition
to Federalist policies at odds with these values. For leading Democratic
Republicans, and for many of those who participated in the French Revolutionary political culture promoted by these leaders, the new French republic furnished the language, symbols and rites with which to articulate
their political beliefs, and a whole new set of occasions on which to do so.

Given the extremely partisan nature of Americans celebrations of the
French Revolution, it is far from surprising that the large majority of those
who identified with the administrations of Washington and Adams refused to attend or participate in any French Revolutionary festivals, sport
tri-colored cockades, sing or cheer French revolutionary songs, or toast the
success of the French republic. As far as many Federalists were concerned,
republican revolution did not and indeed should not entail the radical social revolution and assaults on persons and property that they saw occur-
ring in France and being applauded in the United States. As a result, those

members of the American ruling elite who identified with a Federalist ideology of order and hierarchy were quick to condemn what they interpreted as the unjustifiable excesses of the revolutionaries in France. William Cobbett thought it "a sarcasm on republicanism" to describe France as a republic, adding a year later that if indeed one described France in that way, then the definition of a republic must include "all that is ruinous, tyrannical, blasphemous and bloody."[55] The bloody violence of the lower sorts in the French Revolution clearly worried the Federalists. Noah Webster agreed, noting that the French people had destroyed all who appeared to stand in their path. "Now in reality," he added, "where the people have the power of doing this, there is *no* liberty." In their search for "*liberty* & *equality*" the French had "run into despotism" through which the crowds and their chosen rulers had destroyed those very values.[56]

Events in far distant France, however, can scarcely explain the rapid coherence of a uniformly hostile Federalist reaction against American celebrations of the French Revolution. By 1795 misgivings about the course of events in France would have been more than understandable, but the friends of order were uneasy about French festive culture in the United States well before such events as the execution of Louis XVI, the Terror and the Vendee tore French society apart. From the very beginning it was the rhetoric and ideology of the French Revolution in an American context that concerned them, particularly when this rhetoric of "Liberty and Equality" was articulated by impoverished white men, women, and even, on occasion, black Americans, and was then appropriated by the Democratic Republican opposition in their partisan war against the Federalists.[57]

This kind of reaction to the politicization of the American lower sorts found expression in the actions of one Charleston resident who, on the night preceding that city's celebrations of the anniversary of the storming of the Bastille in 1793, affixed a large poster on the door of the Exchange condemning the day and all who celebrated it. He hoped that "the detested day be ever Curs'd," complaining that the "detested Villains" who had executed Louis XVI had taught "the Ignorant Rabbell" in America to think of their actions as "LIBERTY."[58] Farther to the North a Philadelphian who revealingly signed himself as a "respectable citizen" complained that he had never before seen "so shabby and mongrel" an "assortment of whites, mulattoes and negroes" as those who celebrated the French military victories in Italy during 1797.[59] When two men convicted of murder were hanged in Harrisburg, Pennsylvania on Bastille Day in 1798, William Cobbett described the event in terms of an American celebration of French

Revolutionary ideals. Beneath the satire was a clear warning: Americans who celebrated the French Revolution were in fact applauding social dislocation, anarchy, and murder.[60]

Federalists associated the ideology of those Americans who celebrated the French Revolution with the actions and beliefs of those in France they commemorated, and many went on to equate the worst crowd violence of the French Revolution with oppositional activities in the United States. A typical Federalist condemnation of the "cruel and unjust *assassination*" of Louis XVI slid with ease into an assault on the "unprincipled slanderers" in America who were undermining Washington's administration.[61] Fear of social and political revolution pervaded Federalist thinking, and the friends of order conjured up images of Democratic Republican "highfliers [who] use every means to make the people abhor the laws, the constitution, Congress, and the executive officers."[62] "A Farmer" worried that America had a "corps of officers to lead" the rabble, and "bring about a state of what the Jacobins term *sovereign insurrection* and *permanent revolution*."[63] Two decades later John Adams wrote to Thomas Jefferson recalling "the terrorism excited by Genet, in 1793, when ten thousand people in the streets of Philadelphia, day after day, threatened to drag Washington out of his house, and effect a revolution in the government, or compel it to declare war in favor of the French revolution and against England."[64]

Adams was far from alone in seeing conspiracy within American celebrations of the French Revolution: conspiracy against the Federalists and their beliefs and interests, and conspiracy against republican government as they understood and defended it. Thus he and other Federalists refused to participate in American celebrations of France, and they felt strongly the political and ideological necessity of attacking the principles of those Americans who actively supported the French Revolution.[65]

Thus partisan opposition to the personnel and the policies of the Federal government was intrinsic to these French revolutionary festivals, yet Democratic Republicans employed a language of civic unity and inclusion in their promotion of these events. Partisans in Philadelphia appealed to all "who, feeling an interest in the glorious cause of liberty, wish to commemorate the establishment of the French Constitution,"[66] and later invited all "friends of the French Republic" to participate in a celebration of the anniversary of the creation of the French republic.[67] In Carlisle, Pennsylvania Democratic Republicans invited citizens to a public meeting "to fix on some plan to express their joy" at a major French military victory,[68] while in Charleston they welcomed residents to join in a celebration of the victory of a French naval vessel over its British opponent off the American coast.[69] Local partisans in New London, Connecticut hired the town crier to broadcast an invitation "To *all* citizens" to a public celebration of French victories in Holland, and to preface this cry with a rousing chorus of "Liberty" and "Equality."[70] Throughout the nation Democratic Republicans insisted that these were *civic* festivals, and thus that it was "the *people*" as a whole who were "the celebrators of this [French] revolution."[71]

These tactics were enormously successful, and tens of thousands of Americans took part in hundreds of French Revolutionary festivals. Federalist commentator William Cobbett estimated, for example, that during 1795 over twenty thousand Democratic Republican partisans (and many, many more spectators) celebrated the French conquest of Amsterdam with "twenty two grand civic festivals, fifty one of an inferior order, and one hundred and ninety three public dinners." Moreover, during that same year Americans organized, participated in, and witnessed many more celebrations honoring other French victories, the Franco-American alliance, and the anniversary of major constitutional events and achievements in the French Revolution.[72]

The French Revolution thus dominated the politics of the street during Washington's presidency, and newspapers were filled with accounts of French revolutionary political culture in the United States: it was from his survey of such newspapers that Cobbett was able to calculate the numbers of American celebrations of French victories in Holland.[73] In general terms these American celebrations fell into four main categories: commemoration of the anniversary of the Franco-American alliance of 1778, the achievement of major constitutional reforms in France, the battlefield victories of the French republic, and the arrival in the United States of Citizen Edmond Genet and other representatives of the new French Republic.

*   *   *

Celebrations of the anniversary of the French alliance had begun in 1779, and throughout the war for independence members of the elite had marked the day with small-scale civic feasts. In the aftermath of the fall of the Bastille, however, commemoration of the day assumed a new form and significance.[74] The majority of subsequent celebrations of the alliance— and certainly all the more elaborate ones—took place in Philadelphia and Charleston, cities that hosted many visiting French sailors and were home to the largest French emigre populations in the United States. The French men and women who lived in these port cities were surely a constant reminder to American residents of the debt the American republic owed to the people of France: moreover, in the partisan atmosphere of the 1790s, French men and women who supported their nation's revolutionary progress provided additional support for the Democratic Republicans who sought to organize and profit from celebrations of France and the French Revolution.[75]

The most popular of the French constitutional anniversaries was July 14, and it was celebrated throughout almost the entire 1790s: only the deterioration of Franco-American relations into the Quasi-War brought American festivities in commemoration of the fall of the Bastille to an end. In comparison, August 10 was commemorated somewhat less widely in 1793 and 1794, while September 22 was celebrated in 1794 and 1795 in no more than a handful of towns.[76] The significance of the assault on the Bastille as an opening salvo in a popular revolution was readily apparent, and it appeared to many Americans as a relatively uncomplicated milestone, a simple yet powerfully symbolic event whose significance Americans familiar with Lexington and Concord could easily grasp. The popularity of visiting veterans of the assault on the Bastille, and of plays or even puppet and firework shows that recreated the historic event, underscore the significance of the outbreak of the French Revolution and the excitement that it generated within the United States.[77]

But by far the most popular French revolutionary festivals and celebrations were those that commemorated French military victories, and these outnumbered all other celebrations of France combined. The size and scale of these myriad celebrations suggests that for many ordinary Americans the complexities of constitutional development and the endless political infighting within France were less important and less interesting than the easily comprehensible battlefield victories of America's new sister republic against the enemies of republicanism. In civic feasts and festivals, in parades and processions, and with songs and badges and flags, Americans celebrated Valmy during the winter of 1792–93, the victory at Toulon in the spring of 1794, the "liberation" of Holland in 1795, and that of Italy in 1796 and again in 1800. From Savannah, Georgia to Lexington, Kentucky to Hackensack, New Jersey to Burlington, Vermont, Americans united with enthusiasm in order to celebrate the successes of French arms.[78]

In fact it was with their commemoration of the French victory at

Valmy that Americans began large-scale celebrations of the French Revolution. Most of the celebrations of Valmy were constructed around existing festive traditions. In New York City in 1792, for example, the Tammany Society successfully petitioned the Mayor to set aside a Thursday "as a *Day of Jubilee*" for the French victory at Valmy, to be ushered in "by the ringing of bells" and closed by a Federal salute from the Battery.[79] That evening the members of the Tammany Society drank toasts in their "elegantly illuminated"[80] Great Wigwam, while the Society of Mechanics met for their own celebrations and toasts in Mechanics Hall.[81]

A similar ringing of bells took place in New Brunswick, New Jersey, where a "large and respectable" group of citizens assembled at the White Hall Tavern. Beneath the flags of the United States and the French republic the company dined and drank toasts.[82] The inhabitants of the small town of Washington in western Pennsylvania had "neither bells to ring nor cannon to fire," but the local Mechanical Society met at the home of one of their number and they too drank celebratory toasts.[83] In Petersburgh, Virginia it was the "friends of liberty" who dined and toasted at Brewer's Tavern in honor of "the late glorious triumph of liberty."[84]

Yet for all their familiarity, these rites differed significantly from the evolving national traditions of political celebration on Washington's birthday and the Fourth of July. The profoundly partisan nature of French Revolutionary festivals meant that it was mechanics, artisans, and "citizens" who populated many of these celebrations, and in their toasts these white men showed something of what they understood the French victory at Valmy to represent. Beyond their customary nods toward the people and governments of France and the United States, they regularly lifted their glasses to such sentiments as "Thomas Paine"[85] and "The Rights of Man,"[86] or to more elaborate formulations in the manner of "WE THE PEOPLE: may we always have understanding to know our rights, moderation to use them, and courage to defend them."[87]

In the language of these toasts participants self-consciously united the French and American Revolutions, a ritual act that had much to do with the domestic political situation. The "friends of equality and of the French revolution" who dined in celebration of Valmy at Oeller's Hotel in Philadelphia toasted President Washington, but only "because he is a friend to the rights of man," and they went on to drink to "The undisguised political principles of 1776."[88] The citizens of Montgomery, who referred to themselves as "the sons of Liberty," arranged a celebration at which they drank toasts to liberty and equality (the touchstones of celebration in Boston and all over the nation), to Paine, and to the hope that the citizens of both America and France would "preserve the blessings of liberty."[89]

In other places these partisan sentiments informed the creation of somewhat more elaborate new forms of festive occasion. Thus in Carlisle, Pennsylvania and Providence, Rhode Island the citizenry held public meetings to plan an extraordinary celebration. In Carlisle the bells rang for six hours, and large transparencies on the Court House displayed the messages—"LEGIBLE AT A GREAT DISTANCE"—"LET MAN BE FREE" and "TYRANNY IS ABOUT TO CEASE."[90] The people of Providence enjoyed a parade that included French citizens and dignitaries along with local militia men, dignitaries, and citizens, and a large civic feast ending with a Federal cannonade and the illumination of the Court House.[91]

In Lexington, on the Kentucky frontier, male and female citizens attended a ball and celebratory dinner honoring Valmy: just as in Boston, this gathering represented a united community. The table's centerpiece featured a flag "supporting the cap of liberty," on either side of which were the American and the new French flags, "which were connected with each other and with that of the cap of liberty by a blue ribbon." At the head of the table flew the National flag of France, while at the foot of the table stood the American flag, bearing the words "Independence declared July 4th, 1776."[92]

In the partisan milieu of these Valmy celebrations, with Democratic Republicans eagerly seeking the support and sanction of many different members of their communities, the women who chose to participate were occasionally able to take their own political stands. In Menotomy, Massachusetts some fifty women assembled at the home of Mrs. Willington to mount their own celebration "of liberty and equality" and "to fecilitate their sisters in France upon the happy revolution in their nation."[93] They and the women of Portsmouth, New Hampshire "wore upon their caps the national cockade," and a woman among the latter group made clear her "patriotic disposition" by calling for "the democratic dance Ça Ira."[94]

It was in the wake of these celebrations of Valmy that Americans in the port towns and cities first encountered enthusiastic representatives of the French republic, including the ambassador, consular officials, the officers and crews of French ships, and the French citizens who streamed into coastal towns and cities, especially Charleston, Philadelphia and New York.[95] As they encountered these French republicans, the enthusiasm of Americans for public celebration of the French Revolution grew quickly.

Throughout 1793 ordinary citizens regularly formed crowds on the streets and wharves of American ports in order to express publicly their jubilation at the rise and success of the French republic, and to articulate exactly what this meant to them.

The reactions of the townsfolk of New York City, Boston, and Philadelphia were typical. Following the arrival in Philadelphia of a French frigate and the British ship it had captured in the spring of 1793, "thousands & thousands of the *yeomanry* of the city crowded the wharves." Their mood was jubilant, "and when the British colours were seen *reversed*, & the French flying above them they burst into peals of exultation."[96] Three months later, when a fleet of seventeen French ships arrived in New York City, such was popular enthusiasm that "the people assembled were at a loss how to express their joy."[97] One observer wrote to a friend in Philadelphia that "ten thousand of the citizens" of New York were present, and that they greeted the mighty *Embuscade* "with shouts of joy."[98] A week later the frigate *Concorde* docked in Boston, and the "hills, wharves, and many of the houses commanding a view of the scene were covered with the citizens," who greeted the French with "loud acclamations and huzzas."[99]

Citizen Edmond Genet, the Girondin ambassador posted to the United States, encountered similarly enthusiastic receptions as he traveled from Charleston up to Philadelphia and eventually on to New York City. The excitement in Philadelphia was tremendous: several popular meetings were held at the State House to plan welcoming ceremonies, and those present elected a committee to draft "an address congratulating Citizen GENET . . . on his arrival in America."[100] Genet confounded their plans by arriving unannounced, but following an ad hoc public meeting the citizens marched to the City Tavern and presented the address to the French minister. Genet, "evidently affected with the warmth of the public attachment," responded with a short but enormously successful impromptu speech of thanks. "Shouts and salutations" filled the streets, and all who had taken part then departed with "virtuous and patriotic satisfaction."[101]

Leading Democratic Republicans often organized civic feasts for Genet and other honored French guests, but it was these truly popular welcomes that encouraged Genet to virtually ignore the administration's neutrality in the war between France and Britain. The French ambassador was so heartened by his reception that he felt empowered to threaten the administration that he would go over Washington's head to the American people, a threat that underlined the significance of all this popular political activity. The men, women, and children, black and white, and young and old who filled the public places of the American republic to celebrate the French Revolution, wearing tri-colored cockades, attending civic festivals and parades, and singing revolutionary songs, dominated public political culture during Washington's second term. To Genet in his dreams and to the Federalists in their nightmares, it was these people who seemed the one and only legitimate source of political authority.

Given the large number of French Revolutionary festivals, celebrations, and civic feasts that Americans staged during 1793, it is far from surprising that Genet reached such a conclusion. For in addition to all the Valmy celebrations and the crowd actions welcoming the French into American towns and cities, the citizens of such communities as Boston, Princeton, Philadelphia, and Richmond celebrated the anniversaries of the Franco-American alliance, the fall of the Bastille, and August 10.[102] The majority of these celebrations were relatively small scale, involving civic feasts and partisan toasts to such sentiments as "Liberty and Equality"[103] and "The real Friends to the rights of man."[104]

But celebration was by no means restricted to the more elite Americans who attended exclusive feasts. In Richmond, on August 10, 1793, common militia men paraded in the name of "RIGHT, LIBERTY and EQUALITY!"[105] and citizens used the occasion to plan a meeting "in order to draft an address to the President" in order to raise their objections to his Neutrality Proclamation.[106] In New York City the celebrations of Bastille Day in 1793 were extensive enough to prompt the cancellation of classes at Columbia College on Monday July 15, while on Sunday July 14 the Presbyterians of Princeton feasted and drank toasts, held a celebratory ball at which both men and women gave toasts and sang the "Marseillaise," and enjoyed the illumination of Nassau Hall replete with a large transparency of the French and American flags and the motto "Liberty Throughout the World."[107] For such a small community this was a remarkably large-scale celebration, and was one which would have commanded the attention of most if not all of the community's residents.

But it was the victories of French armies that most excited Americans, and when the French recaptured Toulon in early 1794 Americans were quick to initiate a new round of celebrations. However, changes in the domestic political context transformed both the ritual content and the symbolic significance of these events. During Washington's second term his administration was increasingly inclined to adopt a hard line against any who opposed federal power and policies, particularly those in the back country from Pennsylvania to North Carolina who were resisting the government's Whiskey Tax. At the same time, British attacks on American shipping and impressment of American sailors threatened Washington's precarious neutrality, and the Federalists and their supporters prepared for the arrival and defense of John Jay's enormously unpopular Anglo-American treaty.

In this context, the participation of many Americans in celebrations of the French victory at Toulon became ever more oppositional and vehemently Democratic Republican. Yet citizens continued to participate very much on their own terms, promoting their own particular beliefs and agendas. When, for example, a premature report of the liberation of Toulon reached New York City, the "lower class of citizens" celebrated by invading the Tontine Coffee House and ejecting "for the night the Tories from the House." These mechanics, laborers, and mariners, "almost to a man," were enthusiastic supporters of the French, but their delight in French victories was informed by their own concerns and problems.[108]

Those Federalist merchants who peopled the Tontine Coffee House actively supported the continuation of trade with Britain, and their sympathy for Hamiltonian policies was all too clear. But members of the lower sort were struggling against British impressment and coping with the interruptions in trade and work occasioned by British attacks on American shipping, which combined to make life all the harder for seafarers and their families. That these New Yorkers celebrated a victory by the French republic in its battle to preserve liberty, equality, and fraternity by attacking a bastion of elite Federalist merchants who were profiting from ostensibly Francophobic policies that hurt these men was far from surprising.

The economic situation in Boston had become so dire that the committee elected by townsmen to organize the city's celebration of Toulon "recommended temporary suspension of all festive appearances." In a city whose "citizens in general are deprived of their daily employments, and are suffering under the severe depredations of the British," such celebration could actually hinder the cause of those who sought a change in government policy by presenting an inaccurate image of the "flourishing situation" of the town.[109] As a result, there was no organized celebration of Toulon in the town that had commemorated Valmy with the nation's largest French revolutionary festival.

Elsewhere, however, Americans followed the example of New Yorkers and appropriated the French victory to fashion their own political statements in similar form. In rural Vermont, for example, celebrations in Burlington, Rutland, and Vergennes all expressed the anger of yeoman farmers against Federal government policies and personnel, and support of the ideals of the French Revolution in an American context.[110] In all three locations Washington was toasted by those present, but with more reproof than praise. While citizens at Burlington hoped that the president's "well earn'd fame" might "never be tarnished by an inconsistent, or pusillanimous act,"[111] those of Vergennes wanted death to "close his eyes before his heart shall be enchained or contaminated, by tyranny or despotism."[112]

Celebrations of France that included attacks on Washington and his government's policies constituted a popular political reaction against the Federalists: the toast of yeoman farmers expressing the wish "May the American Congress ever continue the true guardians of the people's liberty" was as much a statement of political defiance as one of celebration of constitutional liberty.[113] These statements were important to the citizens who made them. When the *Farmer's Library* in Rutland printed an incomplete and incorrect version of the toasts drunk by Burlington citizens in celebration of Toulon, the committee that had drafted the toasts reprimanded the editor who was quick to print an apology.[114]

Residents of Baltimore enjoyed a feast, toasts, and French revolutionary songs, all under the entwined French and American flags and a liberty cap, which "gave a lively recollection of 76."[115] In western Massachusetts the citizens of Springfield exhibited "Republican demonstrations of joy," which were republican both in the sense of the ideological content of the event and the fact that few if any Federalists participated in this implicitly Democratic Republican celebration.[116] Around the nation, heightened partisan tensions, strong local support for the ever more radical ideology symbolized by the French Revolution, and deepening antipathy toward the British encouraged those who celebrated Toulon to do so in new ways. In Virginia the "Democratic Citizens of Norfolk and Portsmouth" combined for a celebration that included as honored guests the French consul and the captains and some of the crew of two French frigates and several French merchant vessels. The day of celebration began in traditional fashion with the firing of cannon and the display of colors by shipping, but then moved on to an entirely new set of rites. Late in the morning the company assembled at the point in Portsmouth, where they sang the "Marseillaise" while the French ships fired Federal salutes of fifteen guns. After drinking the health of the two republics, the citizens and their guests formed a procession led by citizens bearing an American flag and a presumably small "tree of Liberty." They marched to the wharf and were then ferried in decorated boats across the Elizabeth River to Norfolk, where they were greeted by "Crowds of citizens." The company once again sang the "Marseillaise," and all present "testified their joy and admiration by enthusiastic acclamations." In this ritual activity the citizens of two communities united to take a partisan political stand, developing new rites to affirm their unity and commitment to the ideals held holy by "every *patriotic* French and American citizen," by which they clearly excluded those at home and abroad who were by definition unpatriotic.[117]

In Philadelphia, too, different groups united to celebrate Toulon when the Democratic Republican Society of Pennsylvania and the German Democratic Republican Society organized a civic festival and feast attended by "about 800 citizens," which constituted at least 10 percent of the adult white males resident in the city in 1790.[118] Following the feast Blair McClenachan, the president of the Democratic Republican Society, "gave the fraternal embrace" to Citizen Edmond Genet, after which those present were escorted to the minister's residence "by music and the colours of the Republicans" and "one of the companies of volunteer infantry," thus allowing even more Philadelphians to participate in and watch the proceedings.[119]

This and another celebratory feast staged by Philadelphia citizens at Dally's Tavern proved too much for supporters of the Federal government. A volunteer toast at the latter event to "The Mountain its summit the heavens, its base the whole earth"[120] was characterized by one Federalist critic as being "stamped with that diabolical spirit of intolerance, faction and persecution, so common to the Democrats of the present day."[121] In the eyes of the Federalists and their supporters, the implicit oppositional tone of Valmy celebrations had one year later been replaced by the explicitly adversarial partisanship of the Toulon festivities. When citizens of Woodbridge, Perth, and South Amboy celebrated Toulon with a toast to "Mr. Madison and the republican members of both Houses of Congress—Confusion to all anti-republicans," these farmers were criticizing the Federalist administration in popular festive forums from which Federalists had excluded themselves.[122]

It was in this increasingly embittered partisan context that Americans continued to construct and interpret French Revolutionary celebrations. Celebrations of the sixteenth anniversary of the French alliance in Philadelphia and Charleston were typical in the way they combined symbols and rites that affirmed their continued support of revolutionary France with partisan celebrations of radical republicanism and assaults on the Federalist government at home. Both used liberty caps as focal points of their festivals, and their celebrations of liberty, equality, and the French alliance included scathing attacks on Washington's government. The Philadelphia celebration was held at Richardet's Tavern, and French sailors and officials arrived as honored guests preceded by a small band and the French and American flags topped by a scarlet liberty cap. The "democratic citizens" united in a series of toasts markedly more radical than those proposed on this occasion a year earlier. The first toast applauded France's revolutionary triad of "Liberty, Equality and Fraternity," while others indicted Washington's government for abandoning the French alliance, applauded the "persecuted Citizen Genet," defended America's Democratic Republican Societies as "watchful guardians of liberty," and lauded "the Republican majority in Congress." [123]

In Charleston the members of the Democratic Republican Society assembled wearing tri-colored cockades, and then marched with their French guests to Harris's Hotel, preceded by a person holding a liberty cap suspended on a long pole, and a band of drummers and pipers playing the "Ça Ira." Their toasts were similarly vehement in their attacks on the policies of Washington's Federalist government. They drank to "The firm patriot and true Republican" Genet and to "Citizen Madison and the Republican party in Congress," and then drank against "those miscreant Americans" who favored royalty and aristocracy, hoping that the enemies of Republican France would perish "in whatever clime they may be found." [124]

After the toasting ceremony was over, those present set the Cap of Liberty on the president's head, and then on the head of each member present. Every time the hat was placed on another republican head the assembly cheered three times and sang a few lines from the "Ça Ira." [125] The ritualistic sharing of the liberty cap, even more than the toasting ceremonies, affirmed that every member of the company publicly identified with a united French and American democratic republican cause, as expressed in their toasts. It also united all present—the silver smith Enos Reeves, the planter James Kennedy, the brick maker George Parker, the merchant Andrew Kerr, and the tanner George Dener—in a rite that not only strengthened the emerging Democratic Republican party, but also gave a political voice and significance to white men regardless of their station.[126]

The oppositional nature of these events was all too apparent to the Federalists. Three years later William Cobbett recalled the celebration of the "republican tribe" in Charleston, commenting on the "state of infatuation, of stupidity, of debasement and ferocity a city must be sunk to, that could suffer itself to be amused with such exhibitions as this."[127] Cobbett's anger is more than understandable, for the celebration had taken place during the epochal year of the Whiskey Rebellion, when Federalists were forced to contend with armed resistance to the policies of the Federal government, with democratic republican societies throughout the union that were focal points for inter-class and inter-regional opposition to the government, and with a precipitous decline in Anglo-American relations. Washington, whose stature and popularity had been tarnished but by no means destroyed, responded by effectively doing away with the Democratic Republican societies by condemning them for illegitimate interference in the governing of the republic, which included the organization of French revolutionary partisan oppositional activities.

During this violent year American citizens participated in more celebrations of the French Revolution than ever before or after. In addition to festivals for the Franco-American alliance and Toulon, in 1794 Americans celebrated the anniversaries of July 14, August 10, and September 22, the only year in which all three constitutional anniversaries were widely commemorated. Small wonder, then, that the friends and supporters of the Federalist government looked with such fear and loathing at French Revolutionary festivals in February, March, April, May, July, August, and September, a long succession of rites that united Americans in defiant opposition to their government.[128]

Of all these festivals, the largest and perhaps the most frightening to Federalists was Philadelphia's "Feast of Reason," held on Monday August 11. More like a Parisian festival than anything else ever staged in America, this festival united a broad cross section of Philadelphians in a celebration of radical revolution and popular liberty that took place a stone's throw away from the homes and work spaces of the members of the Washington administration. The *Aurora* advertised a public meeting at Oeller's Hotel, open to all "friends of the French republic,"[129] at which detailed arrangements for this extraordinary event were worked out and then published in advance.[130]

The day began in traditional fashion, with a cannonade: however, rather than the usual Federal salute, twenty-two cannon were fired in honor of the date "so dear to all true friends" of France. At eight o'clock another salute "called the citizens to meet at the center square." No estimate of the number of participants survives, but the fact that it took two hours to organize those who took part in the ensuing parade suggests the large scale of this event, particularly when one considers that many of those who watched the parade pass by then joined it.[131]

It was a grand but unusual procession, given that the organizers strove for the dignity of a Parisian festival by demanding that the "dignity of the people" be expressed by "the strictest order and a most profound silence."[132] This was no rabble-rousing demonstration in the nation's capital, but rather a powerful demonstration of popular support for the French Revolution and the Democratic Republicans. Two cannon with French and American crews led the way, followed by drummers, long rows of American and French citizens, four men bearing a large obelisk surrounded by young girls dressed in white, a member of the French National Guard in full uniform, local and visiting dignitaries, with "an immense number of citizens of both nations arm in arm" bringing up the rear. Such a large procession was certainly witnessed by many more Philadelphians, with white men of all ranks, black men, and women of the lower orders participating as spectators along the sides of the streets, while other women watched from the windows and balconies of buildings en route.[133]

The obelisk that formed the centerpiece of the parade was carried by four American and French citizens, each wearing militia or military uniform and liberty caps. The obelisk itself was "surmounted by a Liberty cap," and on its four sides were written mottos commemorating "*immortality*," the French republic, "*liberty, equality and fraternity*," and a warning to "*tyrants*." The young girls in white who skipped and danced around this monument wore tri-colored ribbons and carried baskets full of flowers. The procession wended its way through the streets of the American capital before ending in the gardens of Jean Antoine Joseph Fauchet, the French minister who had succeeded Citizen Genet. In the center of the garden "was erected an altar to liberty, with an elegant statue of the goddess of liberty on it." Perhaps this melding of Catholic and radical republican symbols surprised the American participants and spectators who crowded into the garden as the young girls and the musicians took up positions around the altar. After a short speech by citizen Dubois Chotard and a response by Fauchet, the band struck up the "Marseillois and other patriotic hymns" while the girls cast their flowers on and around the altar and Fauchet and the French citizens present "swore to uphold the republic, to live free or die."[134]

Having watched these ceremonies with great interest, the assembled spectators then began their own celebration, dancing to the "Carmagnole" and other patriotic airs performed by the band, enjoying refreshments, and then crowding out onto Market Street a few blocks west of both Congress and Washington's residence in order to burn the British flag. While these ordinary folk thus celebrated the French republic, "about 500" more elite partisans feasted at Richardet's Tavern, drinking toasts that reflected the sentiments of the day, which ended with "a beautiful exhibition of fire works."[135] The French orations meant little to many present, but the monuments to liberty, the tri-colored ribbons and liberty caps, the young women dressed in white, the secular altar, and the affirmations of devotion to liberty were rites and symbols that were readily accessible to those American men and women present. Thus when thousands danced to the "Carmagnole" in the gardens of the French minister, they were taking part in a ritual affirmation of the goals and the ideology of the French Revolution, and their opposition to the policies of Washington's government which were steering the nation away from France and toward the counter-revolutionary nation of Great Britain. Moreover, all this took place in the nation's capital, a few blocks from the Pennsylvania State House and the homes of the President and Vice-President.

Bastille Day, August 10, and September 22 were celebrated with equal partisan vehemence from Boston to Baltimore and from New York City to Camden, South Carolina.[136] These constitutional festivals were, however, somewhat less widespread than celebrations of French military victories and were usually held in the larger seaport towns and cities. With militia parades, cannon fire and church bells, and civic feasts and partisan toasts, the citizens of these communities who favored the ideals of the French Revolution and opposed many of the ideals and policies of the Federalists united publicly. From lower sort shipwrights and mariners in Philadelphia to "citizens of both sexes" in Boston, these were a diverse group of Americans, who were steadily increasing the range of oppositional political activity in the streets and public places of the American republic.[137]

The following year brought the arrival, publication, and eventual ratification of the controversial Jay Treaty, which infused French Revolutionary celebrations with an even higher degree of partisan style and content. A commentator in Philadelphia's *Aurora* proclaimed the "general joy . . . among the citizens of Philadelphia" at the news from Holland, pointedly contrasting "the disposition of the citizens" toward the "misconduct of our administration" in ignoring the French republic while treating with the counter-revolutionary British.[138] When Benjamin Franklin Bache—the partisan editor of the *Aurora*—somewhat facetiously invited President

Washington to a civic feast in celebration of the French victories, the justly renowned master of etiquette refused even to reply to what he interpreted "*as an Insult.*"[139]

The unpopularity of Washington's policies was ever more central to many of these celebrations. In Boston, amid the usual bell-ringing and cannon fire, those who attended a civic feast pointedly drank no toast to Washington,[140] an unusual omission by these "bigotted democrats" that drew the wrath of Federalists as far away as Charleston.[141] In Portsmouth, New Hampshire "a large number" did drink a cursory toast to "The President of the United States," but they made their partisan sympathies clear with lavish tributes to "The mighty Republic of France," "genuine republicanism," "All American friends to the French revolution," "Thomas Jefferson the American Statesman, Philosopher and Patriot," and "James Madison, the distinguished patriot of America."[142]

Even in the heart of Federalist Connecticut, partisans gathered to celebrate the French conquest of Holland. In New London "all the Democratic Citizens" were invited to celebrate by a town crier, who was employed to broadcast information about the celebration, prefacing his public invitation with a salute to "liberty" and "Equality." This message commanded attention in the small town, capturing a significant element of public space for opponents of the government. These partisans worked hard to maintain this victory: following the celebratory feast a small group of mariners, laborers, mechanics, and apprentices, all invigorated "with the true spirit of patriotism," marched around the city with drums and fifes playing the great songs of the French Revolution.[143]

All around the nation partisans continued to mount what William Cobbett would later recall as "rascally *civic feasts*" in honor of the French victories.[144] Over 500 citizens dined in celebration in New York City, after which they marched to the home of the French Consul bearing a liberty cap and a live liberty tree, which they then planted on the pedestal on the Bowling Green that had once supported a statue of George III.[145] With men and women of different classes and races supporting and thereby participating in this rite as spectators, the partisan opponents of Washington's government symbolically united themselves with the ideals of the American Revolution in a rite that commemorated the radical destruction of order and government on two continents.

Celebrations of the fourteenth of July, the tenth of August, and the twenty-second of September were preempted by the furor caused by the publication of John Jay's Anglo-American Treaty, and by the yellow fever epidemic that gripped the capital's population throughout the late summer of 1795. In the port towns of Charleston, Baltimore, Norfolk, Philadelphia, and Boston, domestic issues and partisan concerns often overwhelmed the French Revolutionary events that were the ostensible objects of celebration.[146] In Charleston, for example, the celebration of Bastille Day by "the American sons of Freedom" appeared to one observer to be no more than an extension of "the late extreme agitation" over the Jay Treaty, and the celebration ended with "The British flag being disgraced to the dirt."[147]

Anger at Federalists—both local and national—was expressed in the toasts of "a large number of American citizens" who gathered in Boston to celebrate September 22. Drinking to such sentiments as "The Town of Boston, and its citizens who are friends to liberty," and then to Washington and their hope and expectation that he might "never forget his friends and the Principles which led him to glory," these events were ever more deeply rooted in domestic partisan politics.[148] In Philadelphia there was no public celebration of August 10: "having reflected on the present political situation of the United States of America," French officials and citizens published a request that celebrations by both Americans and French citizens be held in private.[149]

*   *   *

Throughout 1793, 1794, and 1795 the French Revolution provided partisans of the Democratic Republican party with some of their most effective weapons in the battle against the Federalists, and many ordinary folk gave both life and political power to these events, expressing their displeasure at Federalist policies and ideals that seemed rooted in counter-revolutionary ideology, and which were destined to hurt their material interests. While white Americans continued to invoke their own revolutionary heritage and the exceptionalism inherent to that invocation, this partisan adoption and employment of the French Revolution—an event with far greater significance for the shaping of modern nations and democracies than the American war for independence—suggests that on this one point Americans who celebrated the French Revolution shared a more worldly viewpoint than was shared by those who condemned it.[150]

But from 1796 on, the increasing belligerence of the French Revolution and the rising tide of condemnation by American clergymen, together with the ensuing decline of Franco-American relations that continued until the turn of the century, combined to encourage Democratic Republican leaders to distance themselves from the French Revolution.[151] As French armies conquered more and more of Europe, Jefferson and his allies began to recognize the threat that French power posed to American interests, and they distanced themselves from the French. Yet many ordinary Americans took far longer to move away from France, and celebrations of French victories continued until the end of the century. In Boston, for example, the sailors on board the ship *Eagle* celebrated Bastille Day in 1796 with "distinguished conviviality."[152] The following spring "between two and three hundred citizens assembled at Kensington" outside Philadelphia, in order to celebrate French victories in Italy. In a toast to "The ship-carpenters of Kensington—May the next treaty made by our government give them bread instead of a stone," these mechanics and artisans articulated their informed opposition to Federalist policies. Another toast to "The patriots of 1776" and "the spirit which animated them in that crisis" says something of their radical ideology, as did one to the American Republic, which hoped that "the glory of her revolution [may] never be tarnished by base ingratitude, or by a coalition with tyrants."[153] Cobbett dismissed these "ship-carpenters" as "seditious persons," who thus had no legitimate place or role in national politics.[154]

Although these events were far more rare than the celebrations of the early to mid-1790s, they were kept alive by such ordinary folk as these and the pioneering yeoman farmers of Fayette County in Kentucky who celebrated French victories in Italy in 1800. This suggests that popular creation of and participation in French Revolutionary festive culture was by no means contingent on the enthusiasm of the Democratic Republican leadership. Ordinary citizens exercised more control than ever over the shape and content of these celebrations, expressing ideals that in some sense held Democratic Republican leaders to account: in one toast Kentucky citizens saluted Thomas McKean, the newly elected Democratic Republican governor of Pennsylvania, as an "old fashioned republican of 1776, who acknowledges no sovereign but the people."[155] To the Federalist *Gazette of the United States* these feasts were "associations of Traitors," while to Elizabeth Drinker they seemed like "a mob gathering," but to the working men and farmers who constructed and populated them these were valuable opportunities to unite publicly and articulate dearly held political beliefs and ideals.[156]

By the closing years of the decade Democratic Republican leaders no longer organized or participated in French Revolutionary festivals, and by the time of Jefferson's inauguration they had disappeared altogether. Yet this aspect of early national festive culture had been given power, and its demise had been delayed, by the participation of white men of all classes and by members of subordinate groups. In the hands of these men and women many elements of this festive culture endured, in other festivals, in tri-colored cockades, in song and sentiment, and in language and ideology. Although these French Revolutionary festivals were a relatively short-lived phenomenon, their large number and geographic range gave them a tremendously important role in the evolution of partisan politics in the early republic.

If these events provided important building blocks for the construction of the Democratic Republican party, they did so in a markedly sectional manner. For while the rural South provided the nascent Democratic Republican party with its most important power base, relatively few French Revolutionary festivals took place in the South outside of Charleston. Not only were these celebrations rare in the sectional home of the Democratic Republican party and its best-known leaders, but they were in fact most common in the large port cities from Charleston to Boston, places that served as crucial power bases of the Federalist party.

It seems likely that, for all their opposition to Federalist domestic and foreign policies, the application of the French Revolution to local contexts was too frightening a prospect for rural white southerners, particularly after the French Revolution had spread to Haiti and shown what the French Revolution could mean for enslaved Africans.[157] While French Revolutionary festive culture was clearly important in the evolution of partisan politics, its greatest impact was in the north, where white men of lower and middling classes and some white women and black men and women were able to witness and participate in oppositional celebrations that were dependent on large-scale participation for both legitimacy and success.

While encouraged and promoted by Democratic Republican leaders, in a very real sense these events had belonged as much to the lower sort as they had to the elite. For a brief moment even boys "that dressed flax in the barn," as Lyman Beecher recalled, "read Tom Paine and believed him."[158] These men and women participated in French Revolutionary festivals and thus helped mold the language and topics of political discourse, the rise of a legitimate opposition in the Democratic Republican party, and the slowly forming national political culture itself.

5

Songs, Signs, and Symbols:
The Everyday Discourse
of Popular Politics

FOR MANY EARLY NATIONAL AMERICANS the periodic battles between and within various rites, festivals, and parades were enhanced by a diverse and colorful array of emblems, songs, and symbols. Not only did they give life and color to organized celebrations, they allowed ordinary Americans to participate in the politics of the street on a day-to-day basis. The French Revolution played a vital role in this process, magnifying the power and the popularity of this kind of everyday politics by furnishing new songs and symbols, and by investing more familiar ones with new significance. The tri-colored cockade a woman wore pinned to her hat, the "Marseillaise" sung by laborers and seafarers in a dockside tavern, and the powerful and assertive Marianne-like figure of liberty that graced American coins were all a common or garden part of everyday life throughout the 1790s, providing further evidence of the ways politics permeated the lives of all manner of Americans.

When people expressed opposition to the personnel and the policies of the duly constituted federal government, the songs they sang, and the badges and colored ribbons they wore on their hats and coats became a cause of real concern to the Federalists. As a result the Federalists and their supporters became quite adept at fostering their own songs, signs, and symbols, and popular politics in the 1790s was in large part a battle between these rival expressions of partisan allegiance.

It was impossible, however, completely to eliminate popular agency in the use and interpretation of these base elements of partisan popular politics, and neither party was able to prevent the appropriation and interpretation of these signs and symbols by ordinary Americans. Throughout the 1790s, this particular political discourse belonged to and in the streets, where rural and urban Americans of different classes, sexes, and races were able to express a variety of opinions by employing badges, songs, and symbols in different ways and to different effects. Inevitably the songs, signs, and symbols of the 1790s retained some of the power and meanings ordinary Americans had invested in them: it would be a *reductio ad absurdum* to label as a Democratic Republican or a Federalist the freed slave who wore a badge depicting a liberty cap, or the white woman who read Mary Wollstonecraft and wore a tri-colored cockade, or the rural laborer or seafarer who sang the "Marseillaise" in a tavern named The Liberty Tree.

The partisan battle for control over the use and meaning of simple songs, signs, and symbols underscores the vitality of the popular political culture that comprised such a vital part of the politics of the street. Over the course of the 1790s the white male partisans of the Democratic Republican party worked hard to gain control of the symbolic language of the American and French Revolutions, and to ensure that their versions triumphed over those of the Federalists. They assumed the tri-colored cockade as a party emblem and the "Marseillaise" as a party anthem, and gave the liberty cap and liberty pole a new prominence in the party's ritual culture.

In the process, however, the Democratic Republicans sanitized and de-radicalized many of the most popular rites and symbols, rejecting some and turning others into an everyday part of the political activity and identity of white male American citizens, shorn of much of their revolutionary significance. But it was not until the end of the century that the Democratic Republicans were able to take control of the songs, badges, and symbols of the streets, and throughout the 1790s their meaning within early national political culture had been deeply contested by all manner of Americans. These ordinary folk played a vital role in the development of a symbolic language of popular political culture, a language of songs, signs, and symbols that was crucial to the creation of a national popular political culture.

*   *   *

Men, women, and children colored the streets of the early republic with the cockades and ribbons that they wore; from theaters, taverns, private homes, and the streets came the sound of Americans singing the songs of the French Revolution; in urban and rural communities alike, new and refurbished liberty poles and trees occupied central places; and images and representations of liberty abounded on coins, on large illuminated transparencies, on newspaper mastheads, and on tavern signs. All around Americans were the sights and sounds of early national popular political culture, enlivened by the interplay between the French Revolution and American partisan politics.

The tri-colored cockades of the French Revolution were a vital part of this everyday political culture. Americans citizens were already familiar with cockades, which were simple rosettes fashioned out of silk or some cheaper fabric, for in the years after the Battle of Yorktown the soldiers and officers of the Continental Army had continued proudly to sport as emblems of their patriotic service the black cockades they had worn during the War for Independence.[1] Later, during the early years of the French Revolution, Americans read in their newspapers about the French patriots who stormed the Bastille wearing "the cockade of Union, white rose, and blue,"[2] and about the subsequent symbolic battles between royalists wearing white cockades and republicans wearing the tri-colored "national" cockade.[3]

Shortly thereafter republican French sailors and privateers first introduced the simple yet striking tri-colored cockades into American port communities. American men and women who favored the cause of the revolutionaries took to making and wearing these badges themselves, and soon the red, white, and blue ribbons were in evidence all over the nation, "the men with it in their hats, the women on their breasts."[4] Almost "all the little boys" in Morristown, New Jersey had "a tri-colored French ribbon on their hats,"[5] many Philadelphians chose to "put on the national cockade,"[6] the "tri-colored cockade was generally worn"[7] in Charleston, and women in Boston wore "upon their caps the national cockade."[8]

While the tri-colored cockade grew in popularity, many of the men who had served under Washington as officers in the Continental Army continued to wear their black cockades. Since a good many of these men were sympathetic to the Federalists, the black cockade soon evolved into a badge of support for both Washington and his Federalist administration. In contrast, as the Democratic Republicans in Congress began to criticize Washington's neutrality policy—a policy that appeared to favor mercantile connections with counter-revolutionary Britain while abandoning America's wartime ally France to the tender mercies of her enemies—they seized on the popularity of the tri-colored cockade as evidence of popular support for France and for their own partisan position. Well before organized political parties came into existence, ordinary Americans were already wearing partisan political badges.

Tri-colored cockades, however, could have meanings and significance to those who wore them that transcended mere partisan affiliation. To women who had taken an active role in the American Revolution, and who had read in their newspapers about French women's activities in their own revolution, these cockades may have represented a good deal more than unquestioning support of the rights and freedoms of the white male citizenry. Many educated women were familiar with and somewhat sympathetic to Mary Wollstonecraft's *A Vindication of the Rights of Woman*. The book was so popular in Annis Boudinot Stockton's "neighborhood" that she had trouble locating a copy, but having finally secured one she spent two days "reading the rights of women."[9] The conservative Quaker Federalist Elizabeth Drinker wrote that Wollstonecraft "speaks my mind," while Federalist president John Adams ruefully recorded that his spouse Abigail was a "Wollstonecraft disciple."[10]

Such women might have read with interest the accounts of female politicization in France, as when "4,000 citizen wives" assembled in Bordeaux "with the national cockade in their breasts," in order to affirm publicly their intention to "bring up their children in the principles of the new constitution."[11] This was republican motherhood, of a sort, but it was rather more public and decidedly more assertive than anything to be found in contemporary America. This is not to say, however, that American women were unable to grasp the implications of the extension of revolutionary republicanism to their own situation. Employing the familiar model of female discussion of political issues in a *salon*, a woman who signed herself "C" published a "conversation" in which Roxana longed for "the glorious day . . . when our sex shall be delivered from an ignominious slavery of 6000 years," and Thalestris answered that there must be "100,000 sisters in the United States" who supported this proposition and anticipated "the glorious day when American ladies shall be Commanders, Presidents of Congress, Ambassadors, Governors, Secretaries of State, Professors, Judges, Preachers."[12]

Adams and Drinker were typical of many elite and well-educated women, in that they sympathized with the political conservatism of their husbands. Both John Adams and Henry Drinker were committed to a Federalist conception of an ordered and structured society led by the "better sort," and Abigail Adams and Elizabeth Drinker joined their husbands in condemning the leveling radicalism of the French Revolution. Yet these and other well-educated elite women were beginning to develop their own ideas about women's political rights, and the signs, songs, and symbols of French revolutionary political culture played a role in their evolving ideas of women's right to discuss and participate in politics.

It was rather more common, however, for non-elite women and girls actually to wear the National Cockade, and hundreds of lower and middling sort women in Boston thus exhibited "their patriotic enthusiasm"[13] during one French Revolutionary festival, just as a group of young Philadelphia women wore white dresses and tri-colored cockades when they escorted French mariners to the home of the French consul.[14] The impoverished women of Philadelphia's Northern Liberties who warned their neighbor that her windows would be broken if she did not remove the English flag that hung from her house understood well the power of symbols, and their actions recalled those of women during the early stages of the war for independence, when the "Daughters of Liberty" often played as large a role as men in enforcing resistance through non-importation and non-consumption.[15]

It is difficult to gauge the meaning of the red, white, and blue to those white women of the lower orders who adopted the tri-colored cockade. Many were illiterate and most were impoverished, and Wollstonecraft's ideas were surely nearly inaccessible and all but irrelevant to their day-to-day struggle for survival. Most were unable to secure a sufficient income to survive independently, and they relied on the wages of husbands, fathers, and sons, many of whom worked as sailors or in the various industries that supported seafaring commerce. When the wars of the French Revolution broke out, the British government began a series of devastating attacks on American commerce and renewed the practice of impressing American sailors, policies which had a very real effect on the lives of tens of thousands of poor American women. The unwillingness of successive Federalist administrations to respond to these British affronts may well have encouraged many women of the lower orders to adopt the tri-colored cockade as an emblem of their opposition to government policies that they deeply resented, policies supported by merchants who were thriving while these women and their families suffered. Moreover, these cockades may have served as badges of their support for the French revolutionaries in their war against Britain and its counter-revolutionary assaults on American commerce.[16]

This kind of politics, informed as it was by class-based concerns, may have influenced the reactions of white working men to the French Revolution in a somewhat similar fashion. By wearing the National Cockade, these men would have joined women in making public show of their antipathy towards an American government that showed little interest in taking a stand against intolerable British policies. On the day before Philadelphia's elections in 1796, for example, a group of perhaps several hundred sailors took to the streets wearing tri-colored cockades, demanding protection against the attacks of foreign governments, and better pay and working conditions. Federalist authorities reacted violently, and a government supporter recorded that by the end of the day "near 40 of these Rioters are in Goal, & 2 or 3 of them much hurt." [17]

Tri-colored cockades allowed men of the lower sorts to articulate their support for the cause of revolution and republicanism in France, their sympathy with the struggle of the French people against foreign tyrants who sought to crush the revolution, and perhaps most significantly, their own allegiance to the ideals of liberty and equality in an American context. As both words and symbols, liberty and equality dominated American celebrations of the French Revolution, harkening back to the radical promise of the rhetoric espoused by Paine and Jefferson in 1776. Thus when the Democratic Republican leadership attempted to employ tri-colored cockades in their partisan war against the Federalists, they faced a real problem of maintaining control over and benefiting from the potentially radical leveling ideology these badges symbolized.

Black Americans were the one group of Americans who were often physically excluded from participation in the political culture of the early republic. With the exception of the black seafarers who appear to have participated on a regular basis in the crowds that formed in port towns and cities during the 1790s, there is little evidence to suggest that many black Americans were able to take an active part in French revolutionary political culture. Only for a brief, radical moment did French Revolutionary festive culture hold open the promise of a breach in the exclusive language of republicanism, and the extension of political rights and participation beyond the white male citizenry. Vermont citizens, all wearing "the national cockade in their hats," were not alone in toasting the cause of "Emancipation throughout the world" at their Bastille Day feast, but such sentiments were far from common. [18] The Democratic Republican party fast developed into a party committed to the defense of slavery, a party with many white members and supporters who were adamantly opposed to the extension of liberty, fraternity, and equality to black Americans.

This did not mean, however, that white Americans were completely successful in denying black Americans any kind of political voice or identity, but rather that the members of this subordinate group were forced to create a political existence outside of and apart from that of white Americans. Attempts by black men to take their own political stands within the larger political culture elicited much the same response as did the egalitarian political culture enjoined by women in French Revolutionary celebrations, namely immediate and complete censure. When two black male residents of Newark "decorated with the caps of liberty" danced around an American flag to celebrate French victories in Italy, Federalists did not hesitate to blame the men's "drunkenness and complexion" for what they interpreted as the prostitution of the American flag.[19] On another occasion several New York City Federalists ordered their slaves to erect a liberty pole "in order to burlesque" the white Democratic Republicans who were raising many such "sedition" poles in opposition to the administration of John Adams. These "impudent" black men proved, however, that they were more than simple pawns in the political battles of their white masters: the liberty pole held meaning for them, too, as they made clear when they appended a sign declaring "FREEDOM TO AFRICANS."[20]

More than anything else it was the spread of the French Revolution to Haiti that united white Americans across the political spectrum against the possible extension of the promise of the American and French Revolutions to black Americans. Although the Federalist administrations of Washington and Adams maintained full diplomatic and trade relations with the black Haitian republic, most Americans remained terrified that the contagion of liberty and race war would spread to the United States. Throughout the 1790s white Americans feared the outbreak of bloody black rebellion in towns and cities as far apart as Albany, Baltimore, New Haven and Charlotte. Even a woman as uncomfortable with slavery as Elizabeth Drinker filled her diary with such rumors, which sometimes so frightened her as to make sleep impossible.[21]

These fears illustrate that white Americans were well aware of the potential power and significance of French Revolutionary ideology and political culture amongst black Americans. When reports reached New York City that another slave "conspiracy" had been uncovered in a Spanish Caribbean colony, few white Americans were surprised that "French cockades" had been discovered in the "possession of the Ring-leaders." Within this context, almost any level of black participation in America's French Revolutionary political culture became all but impossible.[22]

But it was easier for white Americans to eliminate the rites and symbols of this political culture than the ideals and objectives that underlay them, as became clear in Richmond during the spring of 1800. The city was alive with partisan politics, with the presidential election providing a backdrop for crucial elections to the General Assembly. It was in this context that perhaps the greatest slave conspiracy in the history of the United States came to light, a conspiracy led by the free black artisan Gabriel Prosser and inspired by the language of liberty and equality that infused Democratic Republican political culture. In the most complete history of the rebellion, Douglas R. Egerton illustrates that Gabriel Prosser and his comrades made the fatal mistake of taking the revolutionary rhetoric of the Democratic Republicans at face value, and that they hoped for and even expected the support of urban white Democratic Republicans in a rebellion against the Federalist merchants who enjoyed both political and economic power in Richmond.[23]

White male Democratic Republicans were in a double bind. The very ideology they held holy could be used by women and African Americans to enlarge their own political rights, while their Federalist opponents would pounce on such moves and declare Democratic Republicanism to be a dangerous revolutionary ideology that threatened the United States with anarchy and destruction. Virginia Governor James Monroe was all too aware of the danger Gabriel's Rebellion posed for his party as its members prepared for the presidential election, for it showed that the ideals of the American and French Revolutions—appropriated and molded by the Democratic Republican party for their own partisan objectives—could be used by black Americans in ways that threatened the very existence of the white male polity as Monroe and others envisioned it. Monroe did his best to isolate the captured rebels from the media and he had almost all the records surrounding the uprising destroyed. By silencing the conspirators Monroe could present the outside world with an image of slave rebellion, rather than a deeply politicized urban rebellion of both enslaved and free men that was infused with the political ideology of the era.[24] The Richmond *Recorder* attempted to move attention away from Democratic Republican popular political culture by attributing responsibility for the rebellion to newspaper editors who had reprinted the Haitian constitution.[25]

The political ideology of Gabriel and his co-conspirators, the occasional records of black Americans employing tri-colored cockades and the songs and emblems of revolution, and the ways Haiti inspired slave rebellion and resistance in the United States for generations to come all suggest that black Americans were far from immune to the contagion of liberty.[26] Just as important was the way the French and Haitian Revolutions informed white American reactions to any degree of black politicization and political activity. Northern whites balked at the thought of black social and economic equality, while southern whites swore to themselves that they would avoid what had happened in Haiti by strengthening slavery and stripping free blacks of what few rights they possessed.

As a result the 1790s and early 1800s saw white Americans systematically excluding black Americans from the mainstream of white popular political culture. Black communities in many northern cities responded by fashioning their own alternative political festivals, which often retained some muted shades of their profound interest in the radical possibilities of the French and Haitian revolutions. By the early nineteenth century, the free black American leader Absalom Jones was applauding the "pomp" and "ceremonies of a festive day" in honor of the anniversary of "the day of the abolition of the slave trade in our country," and—rather more surreptitiously—Haitian independence day.[27]

Thus, for all of the attempts of members and supporters of the Democratic Republican party to appropriate tri-colored cockades as weapons in their battle against the Federalists, it is clear that these French Revolutionary badges retained a variety of different meanings for the women, the impoverished white men, and the black Americans who wore them. To the supporters of the Washington and Adams administrations, these red, white, and blue ribbons thus represented a whole range of social, political, and racial oppositional sentiments, all of which implied some degree of public opposition to a duly elected republican government. For, despite Madison's arguments in *Federalist 10*, the very concept of a loyal opposition remained an apparent contradiction in terms in late eighteenth-century America. It was difficult for Federalists, who were all too aware of the violent radicalism of impoverished French men and women throughout the 1790s, to accept without question the public badges of opposition worn by men and women who were not full members of the polity. Their Democratic Republican opponents shared this concern that the rhetoric, rites, and symbols of radical revolution might allow the poorest of white men, white women, and black Americans to push towards meaningful inclusion in the American polity.

Tri-colored cockades may have played an important role within partisan political discourse, but they assumed an increasingly uncomfortable revolutionary significance in the eyes of both Federalists and Democratic Republicans. Few Federalists appear to have been surprised when those who did rebel against Federal authority sported the red, white, and blue ribbons of revolution. A French tricolor was flying above the court house in Harrisburg, Pennsylvania in 1794 when a Federal force took control of the town away from the Whiskey rebels. Five years later, during the trial of John Fries, Jacob Eyerly recalled how dozens of the "rebels" he had seen in Bethlehem, Pennsylvania wore "three coloured cockades," while many members of an even larger band that he spotted just outside Upper Milford "had French cockades in their hats, red, blue and white." [28]

But because of the enormous popularity of tri-colored cockades during the first half of the 1790s, it was not until the French cause lost popularity during the latter half of the decade that Federalists were able to mount a concerted attack against these badges of "*despotism*" and "anarchy." [29] They did not, however, try to appropriate the red, white, and blue emblems and invest them with new political meaning, but chose instead to respond with an organized revival of the black cockade. Their strategy proved remarkably successful, for the black cockade of Washington, Continental Army veterans, and the Society of the Cincinnati had an unmistakably patriotic and nationalistic air about it during the war-frenzied years that closed the decade.

This is not to say, however, that the Federalists adopted this badge as a bipartisan emblem: rather, they sought to appropriate the impeccably patriotic heritage of the black cockade to their own party, and the cockade thus functioned as a badge of partisan affiliation. Throughout the 1790s, therefore, to wear a black or a red, white, and blue cockade was to make a public statement of support for one or other political party. While the tri-colored cockade had symbolized the promise of a revolution in progress, the black cockade harkened back to a successfully completed patriotic war for independence, and represented allegiance to the elected government established under Washington. Often referred to by those who wore it as the "American Cockade," these black rosettes represented a "symbol of Independence and Freedom," and "a pledge of friendship among Federalists, and of attachment to our Constitution and Government." [30] Moreover, they were "emblematical of attachment and esteem for the President of the United States [Adams] and his eminently just and wise administration, [and were worn] as a mark of indignation towards French principles and all those who propagate them." [31]

By the end of the 1790s, events in Europe and the United States facilitated the spread of the partisan black cockade throughout the nation's white population. The increasing radicalism of the French Revolution (and the resulting uneasiness of Democratic Republicans who had enthusiastically championed the French), together with a decline in Franco-American relations that reached their nadir with the XYZ Affair and the Quasi-War, led many Americans to discard their tri-colored cockades. The members of one New Jersey militia company burned their tri-colored cockades and then replaced them with "American Black Cockade[s]" while a band played "Hail Columbia": a good many white American men and women followed this course, albeit with a good deal less pomp and circumstance.[32]

The Federalists were elated when they saw that they were succeeding in their attempt to rid themselves of what they interpreted as an emblem of social disorder and illegitimate opposition to their government and its policies. A Republican who angrily tore a black cockade from the hat of a New York Federalist was fined $30,[33] while in Boston those who refused to wear the black cockade "were exposed to every insult . . . [and] treated with the greatest indignity" by the Federalists.[34] In Raynham, Massachusetts a singularly foolhardy young Republican ventured into a Congregational Sunday service "wearing a '*French Cockade*' in his hat." Fuming Federalist church-goers waited until the end of the service before jumping upon the young man; during the ensuing scuffle he dropped his hat, and members of the congregation clambered around the pews to retrieve it. They tore off the cockade and then threw the Republican and his hat into the street.[35]

By the summer of 1798 the Federalists were at the peak of their popularity, making it extremely difficult for any citizens to wear the tri-colored cockade. In contrast, the black cockade was everywhere to be seen and "*all* the Federalists wore this badge, the men in their hat and the women in their bosom." Even "John Adams while President . . . [commonly wore] the black cockade," and the "black cockade gentry" insulted and attacked "those who would not wear the badge." Benjamin Tappan recalled that he and other New England Democratic Republicans who refused to adopt the Federalist badge were forced to procure "stiff hickory canes" in order to protect themselves.[36] Tappan was surely right, for when Philadelphia butcher boys appeared outside the State House wearing tri-colored cockades in the spring of 1798, "order was restored" by throwing several of them into jail.[37] All around the country, Federalists castigated the few "villains" who persisted in wearing tri-colored cockades, announcing that "They will skulk through the streets, marks of public scorn, they will be hooted by the boys, and will finally be obliged to flee to their beloved France, or meet the doom which traitors deserve, and will e'er long experience."[38]

Armed with their patriotic badges, the supporters of the Adams administration were not slow to brand those who wore the "French" cockade as traitors, and one correspondent went so far as to suggest that newspaper editors should publish the names of any who wore "that emblem of treason," so that they could "be avoided by all Federalists, as if infected with the leprocy or plague."[39] Thus were partisanship and nationalism neatly conjoined, and the Federalists were delighted when many white men and women assumed the black cockade as a patriotic badge during the wartime crisis. Almost all the residents of rural Greenville, Tennessee, for example, wore black cockades when they assembled to celebrate Independence Day in 1798.[40] Philadelphia newspaper advertisements suggest that many more citizens may have purchased "the Cincinnati eagle," a small silver eagle pinned in the center of their black cockades by members of the Cincinnati.[41] The leaders of the Federalist party interpreted the rout of the tri-colored cockade by the black cockade as evidence of a rise in the popularity of their government, a development that they viewed as entirely right and fitting.

But while the Federalists chose to interpret the popularity of their American Cockade as proof of widespread popular support for their party and its policies, it seems likely that many citizens adopted the badge as evidence of their patriotism during a time of crisis. With the end of the Quasi-War, the popularity of the black cockade faded rapidly. In the fall of 1800 Pennsylvania Governor Thomas McKean refused to make the black cockade the official badge of the Pennsylvania militia, preferring a red and blue one that harkened back to the tri-color while ostensibly matching his soldiers' uniforms. Although this action enraged Federalists who argued McKean had abandoned the *"Patriotic Badge"* worn by American soldiers when they "fought [for] and gained our Independence," there was little that they could do to prevent the decline of the black cockade.[42] Lewis Miller sketched one rite in York, Pennsylvania in which Democratic Republicans mounted a funeral procession for the Federalist emblem and then, with cheering, adopted McKean's new red and blue cockade.[43] (See Figure 8.)

In the years following Jefferson's election to the presidency his supporters did not attempt to revive the tri-colored cockade. As the white male coalition enhanced their control of national and local governments, they were happy to adopt less controversial emblems, symbols, and colors,

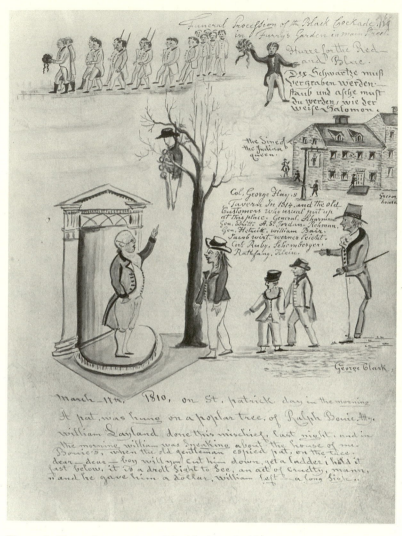

Figure 8. Funeral procession of the black cockade, York, Pennsylvania. Lewis Miller, 1800(?). The Historical Society of York County. The artist recorded a funeral procession for the Federalists' black cockade and the ensuing cheers for the red and blue colors of Pennsylvania Democratic Republicans. Similar rites took place all over the country, underlining the significance of the partisan battles over the symbols of popular political culture, and the political power of ordinary folk as expressed in actions such as these.

particularly the American flag, in place of the somewhat discredited badge of French republicanism. After all, the Democratic Republicans claimed that Jefferson's election had rescued the republic from disaster, that it heralded the fulfillment of the American Revolution, and that the government was now secure in the hands of the servants of the people. The tri-colored cockade had symbolized liberty and equality to all manner of Americans, and once the party of Jefferson had assumed power its members and supporters were less than enthusiastic about enslaved or free blacks, white women, angry unemployed laborers and mariners, or impoverished rural folk continuing to wear an emblem of revolution.

It was the simplicity and the immediate availability of cockades that gave them such power during the 1790s, and women and men from all walks of life assumed these badges in order to proclaim a wide variety of political beliefs and partisan allegiances. However, another vital element of French revolutionary political culture, the liberty cap, was never adopted as part of everyday clothing, and thus liberty caps were rather less accessible to ordinary Americans. Long a familiar symbol in the political iconography of Anglo-America, Americans and Europeans saw the liberty cap as a lineal descendant of the conical Phrygian caps worn by freed slaves in Rome. As a symbol of the struggle for liberty against oppression, the liberty cap had played an important role in the iconography of the American war for independence, and had functioned as a symbol of liberty that helped unite many different Americans under the Patriot banner.[44]

But whereas the liberty cap had united Americans during the 1770s and 1780s, following its adoption by the French revolutionaries in the early 1790s the familiar symbol became a rather more divisive emblem.[45] Throughout the 1790s the supporters of the Democratic Republicans commonly employed the liberty cap in their partisan feasts, parades, and processions, drawing on both American and French revolutionary traditions in their ritual display of political principles. Often, for example, these men used the liberty cap to display their allegiance to the ideology of liberty and equality, affirming their faith in the concept of political equality by passing it from one diner to the next at their civic feasts.[46]

This kind of symbolic association of the American and French revolutions meant that Federalists had little time for the liberty cap, and they reacted to the icon in the manner of William Hogarth and his depiction of John Wilkes as an ugly and dangerous rabble-rouser armed with a liberty cap.[47] Thus one friend of order dismissed Democratic Republican liberty caps as *"anarchy caps"* that were in fact *"destructive of liberty."*[48] But to the white men of the Democratic Republican party the liberty cap appeared a good deal less threatening than the tri-colored cockade, for it was far easier for members and supporters of the party to retain control of the relatively small number of these revolutionary icons. By the mid-1790s Democratic Republicans all across the country were making use of liberty caps or representations of liberty caps. The city of Newport, Rhode Island, for example, was one of many communities with a coffee house or tavern named "The Cap of Liberty," in which locals read reports from France published in the *Rhode Island Museum*, printed a few doors away. The newspaper's striking motif quickly drew the eye: a seated female representation of Liberty held a liberty pole topped by a liberty cap.[49]

These kinds of familiar images were everywhere, reinvigorated by the French Revolution and its popularity among many Americans. The coins created under the direction of the Democratic Republican David Rittenhouse (working under the direction of Secretary of State Jefferson) often featured similar representations of Liberty with a liberty pole and a liberty cap.[50] The seal of the newly founded Union College in Schenectady, New York featured a similar bust of Liberty wearing a striking liberty cap.[51] Perhaps most striking of all is the example of Charleston's Democratic Republican Society: when the French consul presented a relic of the Bastille to the members of the society, they voted to have engraved on its surface a liberty cap triumphant over the reversed arms of royalty and the church.[52]

However, the widespread use of partisan representations of liberty in civic rites and on engravings, coins, and newspapers, transparencies, and a variety of different media, meant that these emblems of liberty and liberty caps were available to and could be seen and interpreted by different Americans in quite different ways. Such was the case with representations of liberty as a female figure. The gendering of representations of liberty created during the 1790s, although ostensibly silent on contemporary gender roles, suggests important changes in contemporary perceptions of womanhood. Prints and engravings published during the struggle for independence had often portrayed America as a powerless and violated Native American woman, although once the war was brought to a successful conclusion these images gave way to portraits of a sedate and somewhat subdued white female liberty figure, as seen on some of the first coins minted by the federal government.[53]

French revolutionary iconography, however, was instrumental in changing these kinds of American representations of their nation and its sacred values. By 1795 the female figure on American coins had begun to

bear more than a marked resemblance to Marianne, the French personifi-
cation of liberty. With long hair streaming behind her and liberty poles
and caps prominently displayed, these American representations of liberty
began to show a markedly more assertive and martial woman. There was a
clear tension between this image and the passivity white men expected of
all women, a tension articulated by one New Jerseyan when he described
"the mild but resolute, the firm but femenine" features of "that divine
goddess" of liberty as she appeared on the newly issued gold half-eagle
coins.[54] (See Figure 9.)

These changes in American representations did not indicate that
American women were being empowered by events in France or America.
Yet the Democratic Republicans who used these images on coins, transparencies, and statues all across the country often imagined and presented
their young republic just as the French did, as a proud, militant, and strong
woman. In an era when white men of the middling and upper classes
sought to restrict white women to a domestic sphere of private virtue,
these female representations of public civic values pushed in the opposite
direction, and these powerful images were universally accessible on coins
that found their way into every hand and pocket in the country, offering
Americans a symbolic image of women as powerful and political.

On the other hand, it is quite possible that female civic allegories
sometimes served a more base and prurient purpose. In the final toast following their festival in honor of French victories in 1793, Vermont Democratic Republicans professed their "passions for the Goddess of Liberty."[55]
Such sentiments, when taken with pictures and statues of loosely-clad female figures, suggest that on occasion these male-created images were created as much for the pleasure of men as for their edification. Moreover, the
evolving gender roles of the early republic and men's attempt to exclude
women from an active role in the public sphere was—in a sense—the exclusionary tactic that allowed for the use of female figures on pedestals.
White women, outside of and not a part of the male political world, were
reconstructed by white men as safe symbols for civic virtues.[56] The relationship between women as political symbols and women as real actors in
popular politics is extremely problematic.

*   *   *

In a very real sense the Federalists spoke from the vantage point of
eighteenth-century notions of paternalism and deference when it came

Figure 9. Eagle coin. 1795. Smithsonian Institution. In place of Washington's stately bust, representations of Liberty appeared on many American coins throughout the 1790s. The French Revolution, together with the iconography of domestic partisan politics, radicalized these images, produced by the Mint of the United States under the direction of David Rittenhouse and his superior, Secretary of State Thomas Jefferson. This particular image shows Liberty with long, flowing hair and wearing a liberty cap; she bears a marked resemblance to the French Revolutionary icon Marianne.

to female political activity. In contrast, the Democratic Republicans were informed by the more modern ideology of republicanism that fired the revolutionary transformations of the late eighteenth and early nineteenth centuries. Many Federalists began by envisioning themselves less as a party or faction and more as the duly elected government of the republic, a meritocratic elite who deserved the deferential allegiance of all members of the body politic, wherever they happened to stand in the social and political hierarchy. This created at least some space within popular political culture for the wives and daughters of Federalists to articulate their support of the Federalist administration, although oppositional political activity by any women and especially those of the lower sorts generally was condemned as inappropriate by Federalist editors.

When the Democratic Republicans first began fashioning a party in July Fourth and French Revolutionary celebrations, they desperately needed community sanction for their oppositional activities, with the result that they countenanced some female participation. For quite different reasons, then, both political parties recognized a certain degree of female political agency, an agency that women did not hesitate to use during the 1790s, sometimes with their own political agendas in mind. However, the Democratic Republicans moved much faster in fashioning something resembling a modern political party, an organization of those white males that they argued had a full and exclusive right to participate in the polity, and a right to voice their opposition to a Federalist government that was allegedly betraying the ideals and principles of the American republic.

Over the course of the decade the Democratic Republicans and their supporters systematically excluded white women and black Americans from more and more of their partisan rites and celebrations. Therein lies a striking paradox of Democratic Republican political culture. For, while the Democratic Republicans strove to take full advantage of female republican iconography, they simultaneously worked to exclude real women from an active role in their partisan political culture, and by the dawn of the nineteenth century women were allowed little or no place in July Fourth celebrations, Democratic Republican societies, and many of the formal and informal institutions of white male political life.

Only during the heady years of the early French Revolution—with its comparatively radical rites, language, and symbols, over which the Democratic Republicans were never able to exercise complete control—had the boundaries of the public political sphere expanded in such a way as to make women's participation somewhat more practical. Women wearing tri-colored cockades, women singing or applauding French revolutionary songs, women participating in French Revolutionary feasts and festivals, and women as symbols of liberty all worked together to make limited changes in the gendered dynamics of political culture. Since white male Democratic Republicans sought to present French revolutionary festivals as expressions of community support for their partisan interpretation of the French cause, they in fact required women's "firm, but femenine" participation.[57]

When women chose to take advantage of this situation, Federalists seized on Democratic Republican uneasiness at such transgressions. William Cobbett pointedly blamed French Revolutionary political culture for the fact that women had begun "to talk about liberty and equality in a good masculine style," echoing the classical republican belief that political discourse was inherently and indeed by definition an exclusively male discourse. Federalists attacked the wearing of tri-colored cockades in explicitly gendered terms, as the mindlessly female fashionable desire to "attach ourselves to everything FOREIGN," led by "bold, daredevil, turban-headed females."[58]

The images of liberty and of liberty caps and liberty poles could thus hold quite different meanings for women, for the Democratic Republicans who sought to use them, and for the friends and supporters of the government who attacked them. The same was true for impoverished white men of the lower sorts such as disenfranchised mariners, a group who appropriated and used these symbols in unique fashion. The illiterate New Jerseyan John Alexander, for example, had a female liberty figure tattooed on his arm; twenty-seven-year-old John Peterson of New Orleans, also illiterate, had "the tree of liberty" on his left arm; Abraham Carson had "the mark of the Cap of Liberty" inscribed on his left arm.[59] All these men came of age during the 1790s, and their tattoos were a significant part of the popular political culture of that era: at the bottom of white male society, these men interpreted and employed the symbols of popular politics in their own unique ways. Other echoes of the politics of the lowly seafaring community can be heard in the defiantly Anglophobic and angrily democratic toasts of seafarers celebrating Bastille Day in 1794, or in the lives and actions of the mariners who chose to serve on ships with such striking names as the *Rights-of-Man*. These propertyless men did not enjoy the right to vote and were unable to hold office in the new republic, but they showed themselves to be acutely aware of the power of ritual and symbolic action in the public political world, announcing their political existence and identity with tattoos on their hands and arms, and thus assuring that their political identity and their political opinions could not be ignored.[60]

The lower sort's appropriation and display of emblems inspired or reinvigorated by the French Revolution can also be seen in the erection of a very controversial display of a liberty cap, liberty pole and French and

American flags in New York City's Tontine Coffee House on June 14, 1793.[61] Ostentatiously located within a public space of central importance to the Federalist mercantile elite, this display marked a symbolic victory for the crowd of mariners, laborers, and craftsmen who were responsible for its erection. Peter Livingston astutely recognized the significance of this kind of symbolic incursion into the heart of Federalist mercantile power in his observation that, following reports of a major French military victory, the "lower class of citizens . . . invaded the elite Tontine Coffee House" and banished "the Tories from the House."[62] Not surprisingly, the Federalists and their supporters were vexed by the display, and during the spring of 1795 the liberty cap was defaced and the French flag that flew below it stolen, causing "uproar" in the city.[63] Thousands of ordinary citizens assembled at the Coffee House, enraged by the violation of the city's best-known political symbol. The "attention of the whole town" was engaged by the incident, and "the peace and harmony of our citizens" disturbed by what partisans saw as an attack on "the Citizens at large."[64] The power of these symbols and the strength of popular affection for them was considerable.

This incident occurred during the early summer of 1795, while the British were attacking American commerce and impressing American seafarers, and while the Senate met in closed session to debate the already unpopular Anglo-American treaty. During the early 1790s white men of the lower sorts may have employed representations of liberty to articulate their own political and economic concerns, but by the middle of the decade many were employing them to identify themselves with the Democratic Republican party, whose leaders and organization appeared best suited to address their needs and concerns and oppose Federalist domestic and foreign policies. By the end of Washington's presidency a mechanic who attended a July Fourth feast at which the liberty cap was given pride of place, a seafarer who wore a tattoo of a female liberty figure and a working man who participated in the erection of the Tontine display were increasingly likely to identify themselves with the Democratic Republican party and its policies.

As Jefferson's party grew in popularity, its members worked hard to add the rites surrounding the erection of liberty trees and poles to their partisan arsenal. While images of these wooden totems could be found on coins, transparencies, and even the skin of some American men, liberty poles and trees were also a very real part of everyday life for many Americans. Just like the liberty cap, these trees and poles had been employed by the Patriots during the war for independence, and had then been reinvigorated by the French Revolution. In French Revolutionary festivals and in a variety of other rites and ceremonies, Americans revived liberty trees and poles as prominent and instantly recognizable symbols of liberty, equality, and republicanism. As such they proved extremely useful for Democratic Republican partisans who believed that the Federalist administrations of Washington and Adams were pursuing policies that undermined the rights and freedom of the citizens of the American republic, while the friends of order condemned these "sedition" poles as pernicious expressions of popular disloyalty to a duly elected republican government.

There were liberty poles in towns and cities throughout the union, and they were scattered across the countryside of the northern states. Theophile Cazenove was evidently surprised to find one, often decorated with a liberty cap, in almost every New Jersey town and village through which he passed.[65] During the war for independence the British had destroyed liberty poles and trees wherever they found them, and it was not until the early years of the French Revolution that the residents of many communities chose to replace them. The citizens of Boston employed a new liberty pole erected near the site of the original liberty tree in their celebrations of the French victory at Valmy, while two years later residents of New York City planted a liberty tree that they had used in the city's formal celebrations of French victories in Holland. The New Yorkers chose a vacant pedestal on the Bowling Green: two decades earlier this space had been occupied by a statue of George III that had been toppled by a Patriot crowd and then melted down to make musket balls.[66] (See Figure 3.)

As very real expressions of popular radicalism, liberty trees and poles could reveal a tension between Democratic Republican partisan politics and the objectives of different groups in the population as a whole. This tension between popular and Democratic Republican politics became particularly clear in central and western Pennsylvania during the mid-1790s, when angry farmers employed liberty poles as focal points in their rebellion against the Whiskey Tax that Hamilton intended to help finance his economic program. While Democratic Republican leaders benefited from liberty poles that expressed peaceable opposition to Federalist policy, popular rebellion around these familiar symbols did far more to hinder than help their partisan cause.

The actions of the whiskey rebels recalled the rites of Patriots who had gathered under liberty poles and trees during the 1760s and 1770s to organize and commemorate resistance against oppressive British taxes. By the fall of 1794 the rebels had erected at least thirteen new liberty poles in western Pennsylvania, clear tokens of "the disposition of the people." They functioned as symbols of the rights and liberties of the white male citizenry, and were clearly and consciously aimed against the Federalist administration of George Washington. In *Modern Chivalry* Hugh Henry Brackenridge described the gathering of a large crowd of whiskey rebels. While members of the crowd shouted "Liberty and no excise, down with all excise officers," others buried "the butt end of the sapling in the hole dug for it, and it stood erect with a flag displayed in the air, and was called a Liberty Pole." Federalists were quick to condemn these "*whiskey liberty poles*" as symbols of illegal dissent and disorder, and these poles, some bearing tri-colored French flags, were soon felled by the army sent to quell the rebellion.[67]

Alexander Graydon later recalled how the tearing down of a French flag flying above the Harrisburg court house gave "a momentary triumph to the poor handful of Harrisburgh federalists."[68] The Federalists refused to honor the American heritage of the liberty poles they destroyed, and they worked hard to identify them as invalid and inappropriate French icons that challenged the legitimate power of a representative republican government. The friends of order were all too well aware that liberty trees and poles recalled the republican stand of Patriots against illegitimate British taxes, and that many of these poles had been destroyed by an oppressive British standing army.

Democratic Republican partisans, too, were troubled by the fact that the liberty pole represented inversion and even revolution. For while they and their supporters were more than happy to draw on the Patriot heritage of liberty poles and trees in their struggle against the Federalists, when Americans who rebelled against the Federal government made explicit use of these symbols they succeeded in tarnishing both the symbols of liberty and the Democratic Republican party with the unwelcome stain of treason. As a result almost all Democratic Republicans disavowed the actions of the Whiskey rebels, and for the remainder of Washington's presidency accounts of rites celebrating the erection of liberty poles all but disappeared from American newspapers.

Toward the end of the decade, however, when the Adams administration passed the Alien and Sedition acts and introduced the nation's first Direct Tax, popular opposition and rebellion once again coalesced around liberty poles. Ordinary Americans reappropriated liberty poles and French Revolutionary colors in order to fashion their own political protests, and from Pennsylvania to New Hampshire white men gathered to articulate their opposition to the Direct Tax.[69] But again this opposition swelled into a rebellion of sorts, thus embarrassing Democratic Republicans who presented themselves as an entirely legitimate and law-abiding opposition. Many of those who participated in the fiercest resistance to the federal tax were relatively recent German immigrants to the United States, and their adoption of tri-colored cockades and liberty poles in opposition to the Adams administration underlines the trans-Atlantic nature of this symbolic and ritual culture. More important, however, the actions of Jacob Fries and the other rebels illustrate how these new Americans recognized that in order to take part in American political culture and make their voices heard, they needed to employ the media of that culture.[70]

Far more common, however, were the liberty poles erected in opposition to the Sedition Act, a law which was in part designed to stifle oppositional popular political culture. Banking on their unusual popularity during the XYZ Affair and the Quasi-War with France, the Federalists seized on their "glorious opportunity to destroy faction" and passed legislation designed to undermine Democratic Republican domination of the politics of the street by stamping out oppositional rites and symbols.[71] The Whiskey Tax of 1794 and the Direct Tax of 1798 had incited rebels to draw on the heritage of the liberty tree in their forceful opposition to the economic policies of the central government, and most of the Democratic Republicans and their supporters had condemned the unlawful actions of the rebels. The Sedition Act, however, posed a substantial threat to the most basic political liberties enjoyed by Democratic Republicans who were angered by the Federalist attempt to render illegal any criticism of the personnel and policies of the government.

As a result, the partisans of the Democratic Republican party once again employed the liberty pole in their public displays of opposition to government policies that threatened the liberties white men had secured for themselves in the war for independence. In New York alone, citizens raised liberty poles in Newburgh, Blooming Grove, Montgomery, Goshen, Fishkill, Southwold, Southampton, and Bridgehampton.[72] In the southern states liberty poles had always been less common, and the Haitian revolution may have helped dampen partisan enthusiasm for rites that proclaimed liberty and recalled revolution. As a result, southern Democratic Republicans appear to have erected few if any new liberty poles, and their newspapers carried very few accounts of the raising of oppositional liberty poles in the northern states.

Throughout the rest of the country, however, Democratic Republican partisans created new rites to add patriotic luster to the erection of these familiar and impressive symbols of resistance against an oppressive government. When a Federalist stole the decorated liberty cap from the top of a liberty pole in Newark, New Jersey, residents gathered together in force to replace it. Two veterans of the war for independence carried the new liberty cap, thus allowing the Democratic Republicans to proclaim the patriotic lineage of the liberty cap and pole and the message their party carried. While a band played "American tunes" under an American flag, a discharge of cannon saluted the occasion, and the new cap was hoisted into place. An inscription on the new liberty cap made clear their opposition to the Federalist "friends of order": "May the friends of Liberty increase In Freedom, Unity and Peace."[73]

Elsewhere the opponents of the Adams administration were less subtle. In Newburgh a new liberty pole bore the brazen inscription "1776 LIBERTY. JUSTICE. THE CONSTITUTION INVIOLATE. NO BRITISH ALLIANCE. NO SEDITION BILL," thereby enunciating several planks of the Democratic Republican platform.[74] Here, perhaps, the opponents of the government were informed by a longstanding English tradition of affixing seditious or libelous notices on maypoles.[75] Residents of Vassalborough, Maine christened their new liberty pole by burning copies of the Alien and Sedition acts at its base and then drinking toasts to such sentiments as "Freedom of speech, trial by jury, and liberty of the press," and "May Americans ever remember that the power is in the people."[76]

The "citizens" of New Windsor, Connecticut were joined by others from New Cornwall, Bethlehem, and Little Britain in their raising of a liberty pole "as an emblem of their true republicanism." Following a short ceremony they adjourned to Morrel's tavern, sang "several excellent songs, suitable to the occasion," and raised their glasses to a series of extremely partisan toasts. Beginning with the sentiment "May the tree of liberty never want supporters," they drank to "the spirit of 1776," the Constitution "as the pillar of civil and religious liberty," "the rights of man inviolate," and "Liberty of speech."[77] In Bridgehampton, New York "a large concourse of people" erected a seventy-six-foot-high liberty pole, sang "the celebrated song of the 'Liberty Tree,'" and then raised their glasses to such sentiments as "The Tree of Liberty," "The People of the United States," and "Thomas Jefferson."[78] In the context of the crisis in Franco-

American relations and the passage of the Alien and Sedition acts, these rites and toasts constituted enthusiastically partisan attacks on the policies of the Adams administration.

In 1798 and 1799 Democratic Republicans raised liberty poles in towns and villages across the northern states, and sometimes even on the farms of individuals, including Isaac Wetzstein of Berks County, Pennsylvania.[79] Even in German Pennsylvania, an area that was home to people who had brought their own language and traditions to the United States, the rites and symbols of the new national popular political culture were gaining widespread currency. This was the very oppositional political culture that the Federalists had hoped would be destroyed by their Sedition Act, and the supporters of the Adams administration were quick to react against "so strong an opposition to the measures of the general government."[80] Often they took the direct approach by banding together and cutting down the poles. Some "federal young men of Dedham"[81] in Massachusetts cut down their town's pole, while in Vassalborough a company of volunteers hacked down their community's "disgraceful Signal of Opposition to the Federal Government."[82] In an inversion of the rites of those who had erected the latter liberty pole, it's destroyers then gathered to raise their glasses and salute such sentiments as "Our Federal Government," "Ever staunch may the Federalists stand," and "May all Sedition Poles fall like Lucifer, never to rise again."[83] Recognizing the symbolic power of the rites used by those who erected liberty poles, and the ways in which this power was amplified by the publication of accounts of these rites in Democratic Republican newspapers all over the country, the Federalists apparently sought to create a ritual alternative that presented their destruction of liberty trees as the patriotic act of defenders of the federal government and constitution.

On occasion the Federalists went beyond this kind of ritual destruction. In Dedham, Massachusetts they invoked the Sedition Act and indicted the itinerant preacher David Brown for his role in the erection of Dedham's liberty pole.[84] The pole had born the motto "No Stamp Act, No Sedition Act, No Alien Bills; No Land Tax; downfall to the tyrants of America, peace and retirement to the President, Long Live the Vice-President and the Minority; May moral virtue be the basis of civil government."[85] Brown was convicted, fined $480, and sentenced to eighteen months imprisonment, but repression of this kind did little to advance the Federalist cause.

*　*　*

Political songs and music were both as prevalent and as deeply contested as cockades and liberty poles and caps. They could be learned and sung by almost all Americans, who were thereby enabled to participate in the transmission of information, the construction of idealized versions of truth, and the articulation of beliefs.[86] Quickened by events in France, political songs were ubiquitous in early national America, and their sounds filled the public and private spaces of the American republic.

The songs of the French Revolution were enormously popular during the first half of the 1790s. Thus both John Francis and Alexander Anderson remembered male and female New Yorkers singing and dancing the "Carmagnole,"[87] while in Philadelphia John Watson was only one of many Americans who "had caught many national airs, and the streets by day and night, resounded with the songs of boys, such as these: "Allons, enfans de la partie, le jour de glorie est arrive!" &c.—"Dansons le carmagnole, vive le sang! vive le sang! &c.—"A ç'ira, ç'ira," &c. Several verses of each of these and others were thus sung."[88]

Throughout 1793 and 1794 American newspapers printed translations of the leading French revolutionary songs including the "Ça Ira," the "Marseillaise," and the "Carmagnole," and Americans were as quick to learn French songs as they were to assume French cockades. Contemporaries often identified French songs with patriotic American songs, as when one correspondent described the French armies singing the "Ça Ira" after the battle of Valmy, and then explained that the "tune of Ca ira in France, answers to Yankee-doodle in America."[89] Once again these French imports were favored by Democratic Republican partisans: while "Yankee Doodle" was a patriotic air favored by Federalists and Democratic Republicans alike, only the members of the latter party adopted the imported "Ça Ira" or the "Marseillaise" as political anthems. The "Marseillaise" was the most popular of the French anthems, and the power and emotion of this simple song touched many Americans: Charles Biddle was far from unusual in his observation, after hearing the crew of the French frigate *L'Embuscade* perform this stirring refrain, that "there never was a more animating song composed."[90]

While on one level French tunes served to delight and entertain, it was all but impossible for contemporaries to ignore their political nature. Popular in the truest sense of the word, they allowed all of those Americans who so desired to learn, articulate and perhaps even rework a variety of political sentiments. Within the context of domestic partisan politics, either singing or applauding the singing of French Revolutionary songs generally indicated support for the Democratic Republicans and opposition to the ostensibly pro-British policy of neutrality maintained by Washington's administration. But these songs could say and mean much more, including support for the cause of the French Revolution, outrage at British attacks on American shipping and their impressment of American sailors, and protest against what some Americans perceived as the counter-revolutionary policies and personnel of the Federalist government. Perhaps songs of revolution had even deeper resonance among those for whom the American Revolution had done little, including black Americans, white women, and the urban and rural poor. Thus a poor washer woman, a tattooed mariner, or a free black laborer singing or whistling the "Marseillaise" while walking through the streets was able to voice an unmistakably political comment with a variety of possible meanings: once again the political culture of the French Revolution had enabled the voiceless to find a new voice.[91]

This politicization of music also inspired the creation of new songs in the United States. One "Young Lady" of New York City, published "The Rights of Woman," to be sung to the tune of "God Save the King." Firmly critical of the fact that "Man boasts the noble cause" while women lay "In base obscurity," this songwriter championed women's "equal rights" and "Wolstoncraft," beginning and ending with the rousing chorus "Woman is Free!" Although the song may never have enjoyed a public performance, it was reprinted in newspapers around the country, thus reaching a wide audience of both men and women.[92] When Sarah Bache wrote to her son Benjamin Franklin Bache and requested "the music and words" of several of the popular political songs of the early 1790s, she illustrated that such material was as much within women's as men's domain, and that politics could be performed in the parlor as well as out in the street.[93]

Other new songs included "God Save the Rights of Man,"[94] "On the Revolution in France"[95] by one Mrs. Marriot, and Joel Barlow's light-hearted "God Save the Guillotine," in which he hoped that England's royalty would lose their heads along with "all the sceptre'd crew," after which all people "O'er tyrants graves shall dance."[96] This satirical image of social dislocation so enraged Federalists who were combatting a rising tide of popular dissatisfaction with their foreign and domestic policies, that one of their number responded with another version of "THE GUILLOTINE," in which he condemned the "wild, unruly crew" of Democratic Republican partisans by singing

GOD save all Guillotines,
Till all *our* Jacobines;
Their power shall prove.[97]

The partisan political ramifications of French revolutionary songs transformed theaters into popular political forums, in which audiences of men and women of different social ranks and sometimes black Americans could make public political statements in their demands that orchestras perform certain political songs. In Philadelphia's New Theater, early in 1794, the orchestra responded to "repeated calls from the *mountain*" and assuaged "the audience with [the] *Ça Ira*."[98] Later that same year French sailors joined a New York City theater audience on Evacuation Day. No sooner had the first members of the orchestra appeared than "there was a general call of '*ça ira*.'" Everyone present stood for the song, which was followed by the "Marseillaise," sung by the French sailors while the Americans "applauded by gestures and clapping of hands." Only when the curtain was finally raised did the cries of "Vivent les Francois" and "Vivent les Américains" fade away.[99] In the spring of 1794 a correspondent wrote to the *Boston Gazette* requesting that two "pieces of *loyal* music" be played in the Boston theater, namely "Yankee Doodle" and the "Ça Ira."[100]

During Washington's presidency theater audiences were far more inclined to support republican France than monarchical Britain. A performance of *The Poor Soldier* in Boston in 1796 was interrupted by an enraged audience who thought the character Bagatelle constituted "a libel on the character of the whole French nation." The audience proceeded to tear the theater apart, breaking windows, chairs, and benches. This Francophilia and Anglophobia continued to plague English actors well into the nineteenth century.[101] A performance of *Henry V* in Philadelphia in 1808 caused uproar when Shakespeare's King Harry maligned the French once too often, provoking "a strong dissent from many of the audience, and of such continuance as threatened an abrupt conclusion of the play."[102] Theater audiences were enormously diverse, containing rich, middling, and poor, men and women, and whites and blacks. Their calls for French Revolutionary songs represented a rare expression of some level of solidarity between classes, races, and sexes, and in the face of this display of partisan unity the Federalists and their supporters had little choice but to congregate in more sedate sections of the theaters or avoid these performances altogether.

There were ways, however, for opponents to drive wedges between the members of this popular coalition. At least one theatre company performed a revised version of *The Poor Soldier* in which the French fool Bagatelle was replaced by a black servant, also a fool, named Domingo. This was an astute transformation that can hardly have been unconscious, for—at least in terms of this one character—it changed an interracial and intersexual alliance of audience members in support of revolutionary France into a white alliance whose members laughed at the spectacle of a black fool named Domingo, a clear lampoon of the extension of the liberty and equality of the French Revolution to the enslaved inhabitants of "St. Domingo," or Haiti. Once again, black Americans were carefully and consciously excluded from active and meaningful participation in political discourse.[103]

This was only one example of the many ways in which the Federalists and their supporters strove to subvert the musical politics of the coalition of men and women who publicly supported the French Revolution and all that it represented to them in an American context. In 1794 English-born Benjamin Carr produced a new musical arrangement entitled the "Federal Overture," which integrated popular French revolutionary tunes into a medley of American and English tunes. Carr's was an orchestral piece without lyrics, which immediately eliminated the radical language of the "Marseillaise" and thus significantly lessened audience participation and bonding during these musical performances. But more than that, Carr was able gently to poke fun at the French songs and their enthusiasts, with grave and melodramatic musical introductions to the "Ça Ira" and the "Marseillaise" that hinted at menace and foreboding. With wry humor he then followed these anthems with the popular contemporary song "O Dear, What Can the Matter Be." In contrast, Carr presented patriotic American songs such as "Yankee Doodle" and the "President's March" with grace, enthusiasm, and far more subtlety. Carr's strategy was remarkably successful, and his "Federal Overture" played well in theaters in Boston, New York City, Baltimore, Hartford, Annapolis, Norfolk, Charleston, and elsewhere.[104]

The popularity of French songs dwindled as Franco-American relations deteriorated during the later years of the 1790s. Philadelphia's *Gazette of the United States* printed a letter in April 1798 addressed to the Managers of the Theater, hoping that they would no longer "grate and torture the public ear with those shouts for *Ca Ira* and the *Marseilles Hymn*," and would instead play the Federalist favorite, "The President's March."[105] When a theater orchestra in Baltimore began playing the "Marseillaise" a "violent hissing and hooting . . . immediately ensued,"[106] while a performance of the "Ça Ira" in Augusta resulted in "a hissing and cry of '*stop the music,* [and] *stop that tune.*'"[107]

With the aid of performers and song writers such as Benjamin Carr and Joseph Hopkinson, Federalists moved quickly to take advantage of the situation, and "Hail Columbia," "Adams and Liberty," and "God Save Great Washington" were performed with great success in theaters throughout the nation. "Hail Columbia," set to the tune of "The President's March," was written by the Philadelphia lawyer Joseph Hopkinson. By the spring of 1798 both pieces inspired an "enthusiastic clamor and applause" among the members of a Philadelphia theater audience who clearly supported the stand President Adams was taking against France. The last verse was a paean to "the CHIEF WHO NOW COMMANDS," and when it was performed for the sixth and final time "the house shook to its very centre . . . [and] the song and the whole were drowned in the enthusiastic peals of applause."[108]

Adams made dramatic and effective use of this surge in his popularity when, a few days later, he attended the same Philadelphia theater with Abigail Adams and several leading members of his administration, an event publicized ahead of time in the Federalist press. The audience rose and cheered the president when he entered his box, and "The President's March" was "repeatedly sung" by the entire audience.[109] In a Baltimore theater the same piece of music was "received with unbounded claps of approbation from near 1000 spectators,"[110] while in a theater in Augusta, Georgia armed and uniformed militia men stood at attention on stage while the "President's march" was performed, presenting "a truly elegant and pleasing appearance."[111]

Hopkinson's "Hail Columbia" was usually performed to the tune of the 'President's March,' and the Federalists made liberal use of both titles in their attempt to identify the policies of the current administration with patriotic verve. According to one observer who witnessed the debut of "Hail Columbia" at the Philadelphia theater on April 25, 1798,

The unbounded and repeated plaudits which accompanied the new National song set to the President's march last evening, exceeded any thing of the kind ever witnessed in a public place; not even at France at the commencement of the revolution when fired with enthusiastic zeal the performers sung a favourite air, was it encored with such fervor, such unanimous approbations as was bestowed on this "applicable air to that tune" by a most numerous and respectable audience.[112]

The article ended with the hope that "the ladies will practice the music and accompany the words at its next repetition."[113]

Farther north, Boston Federalists celebrated the dissolution of the Franco-American alliance in 1798 with a martial procession that ended at the Old Brick Meeting House, which was "almost completely occupied by the patriotic, enquiring and judicious of the fair sex," who joined the men in singing partisan anthems such as "Adams and Liberty."[114] In the public singing of political songs and anthems, women were able to enjoy a relatively high degree of political activity; given the relatively safe themes of patriotism and preparedness propounded by these pieces, Federalist men were quite comfortable in enjoining this kind of female participation.

Patriotism, valor and military preparedness were common themes in these Federalist songs, as seen in Boston editor Thomas Paine's "Adams and Liberty," which like "Hail Columbia" was set to the familiar tune of the "President's March." Should the French invade the United States, Paine pronounced, "Let your cannon declare the free charter of trade." The oppositional Democratic Republicans were explicitly referred to as "traitors," and one verse began

> Let our Patriots destroy Anarch's pestilent worm,
> Lest our Liberty's growth should be check'd by corrosion.[115]

Despite their considerable popularity in American theaters in the closing years of the century, the performance of these Federalist anthems on occasion prompted angry and even violent reactions among Democratic Republicans. During President Adams's visit to New York city in July of 1798, a group of young Federalists walked past the Battery singing "Hail Columbia." They were challenged by a group of Democratic Republicans, probably dominated by laborers and mariners, who taunted them by singing the "Ça Ira." The confrontation degenerated into a brawl, and the larger group of Republicans "beat and bruised" their opponents.[116] On the following evening a much larger group of about four hundred Federalists appeared at the Battery, all wearing black cockades and singing "Hail Columbia." On this occasion they met no resistance, and they then proceeded to the house of one of the young men who had been seriously injured by the Republicans the previous night, gave three cheers, and dispersed. For once a Federalist crowd had taken control of the streets of New York City, a comparatively rare event.[117]

*   *   *

Political songs, signs, and symbols thus permeated early national political culture, invigorated by popular interest in events in France, and given new significance by the actions and attitudes of the many different American who appropriated them. Elite partisan leaders were not slow to realize the power of these simples rites and symbols, and they fought to control and benefit from popular badges, images and songs. Through the middle of the 1790s Democratic Republicans were happy to employ various components of French revolutionary political culture in their attacks on the Federalists, until the decline in Franco-American relations led partisans to drop those elements that were too radical and politically costly, while subsuming sanitized versions of the rest into their arsenal of partisan weaponry. At the same time the Federalist "black cockade gentry" sought to take full advantage of the declining popularity of the French by striving to eliminate the songs and badges of the French Revolution, and replacing them with their own.[118]

Thus badges, songs, and symbols were key components of partisan conflict during the 1790s, which gradually evolved into a regularized part of the political process: by the early nineteenth century, badges, songs, and other related emblems had become part of the discourse of partisan political activity. However, while white male partisans competed with one another for control over the use and interpretation of this stuff of popular politics, they could never hope to achieve complete control over these emblems, rites, and songs. For Americans were still free to make what they would of these badges, songs, and representations, whatever they might mean to partisan leaders. Thus, for example, members of the free black population of early nineteenth-century Charleston wore badges that proudly proclaimed the freedom of their bearer with an image of a liberty cap. (See Figure 10.) Given the heritage of this symbol and its connections to the French (and indirectly the Haitian) Revolution, it is far from unreasonable to assume that the symbol was defined quite differently by those free blacks who wore it and by the white Democratic Republicans who ordained its use. Ordinary Americans continued to exert varying degrees

Figure 10. "Free" badge. Charleston, South Carolina. The Charleston Museum. During the 1790s the authorities in Charleston, South Carolina began requiring slaves and free black men to wear badges identifying their status. This badge, probably dating from the early nineteenth century, belonged to a free man. It showed a liberty cap and pole, two of the most radical symbols of the 1790s. The badge shows that the symbols of popular political culture were malleable and could be appropriated and interpreted by all manner of Americans, even those the larger society sought to control and subordinate.

of influence over the language, rites, and symbols that had played such an important role in the popular politics of the 1790s. Politics and political society had expanded in such a way that a complete disavowal of this kind of political activity was all but impossible, and the rhetoric and images of rights, freedom, and liberty continued to be contested both by political partisans and by those on the margins of the evolving political process.

6

Conclusion:
The Regularization of
Popular Political Culture

A NEW NATIONAL POPULAR POLITICAL culture emerged in the United States during the waning years of the eighteenth century. Although the popular politics of the early republic drew on colonial and revolutionary era precedents, what developed between 1789 and 1801 was new in several important ways. With remarkable rapidity, ordinary Americans developed a shared symbolic and ritual language of political expression, and celebrations of Washington's birthday, Independence Day, and the French Revolution assumed common forms throughout the nation. By participating in the rites and symbols of these festivals, many ordinary Americans collaborated in the creation of a new way of practicing politics and inventing new political parties.[1] While on the one hand this new, shared language of political activity bound Americans together, on the other it furnished them with the means to wage partisan political warfare against one another in the streets and public places of the new republic.

The process whereby public ritual and festive culture became part of a new, national discourse of political activity might best be described as the regularization of popular political culture. During the final quarter of the eighteenth century the "People *without doors*" had assumed a new role and significance in American political life.[2] Popular action had been vital to the success of protests against British policies in the 1760s and 1770s, and when combined with the heady rhetoric of liberty and equality and with a series of crises in authority at both local and national levels it had resulted in ordinary Americans gaining a heightened awareness of their right to participate in political life. The disparate regional rites and symbols of the colonial era melded, during the 1790s, into a unified language of national politics, furnishing Americans with a principal arena wherein they saw, participated in, and influenced the politics of their nation.

Symbolic violence, including the burning in effigy of John Jay following the publication of the Anglo-American Treaty of 1795, occupied an important place in the politics of the streets. It is quite remarkable, however, how successful Americans were in excluding real violence from the mainstream of their political culture. Violence was a regular feature of the political culture of both the American and French Revolutions, but popular political culture in the United States during the 1790s was focused on the creation of political parties and partisan conflict carried out peaceably within the polity. Real violence worked outside of and against the political process, and during the 1790s it was avoided by most Americans for most of the time. Those who, for example, attacked a tax collector in western Pennsylvania or rebelled against slavery in Richmond were members of truly violent groups who moved beyond peaceable participation in the polity to an attack on its very foundations.

Newspapers played a vital role in the transformation of the rites and symbols of festive culture into part of the currency of political exchange. A well-to-do merchant's wife in Delaware could have read of a Federalist celebration of Washington's birthday in Albany; on the Kentucky frontier a settler could read about the popular protests against the Jay Treaty in Charleston; while in the national capital a government minister could read about the actions of black and white seafarers in a celebration of the French Revolution in Boston. Accounts of these kinds of rites and festivals filled the pages of early national newspapers, vying with and often usurping the traditional polemical essays and editorials that had long been the staples of elite politics: for many Americans this popular political culture became the stuff of politics.

Political festivals and celebrations from all over the nation were continually created and re-created in the newspapers of cities, towns and rural hamlets alike. Thus a succession of essentially non-literary political activities assumed a textual existence in the early national press, creating a nexus of old and new, urban and rural, and northern and southern forms of politics. A national popular political culture was created simultaneously on the streets in the actions of ordinary Americans, and on the pages of the newspapers that reported them. While some of the local color and meaning of Boston's Pope's Day celebrations in the late colonial period would have been lost to a resident of the Chesapeake, by the end of the century the ritual form and symbolic content of popular political culture had developed into a common, national language of politics and political activity. Consequently a Virginian could read of July Fourth celebrations in Boston and understand the form, content, and meaning of what was going on, including the political agenda and ideology of the ordinary Americans who were supporting the event as participants and spectators.

Thus the popular political culture that had taken form by the turn of the nineteenth century was national both in the way its rites and symbols were replicated throughout the sixteen states of the republic and through their reproduction in both local and more distant newspapers. Large-scale festivals, parades, and so forth were rather less common in the rural south, perhaps because of the relative lack of easily recognizable community centers, and because of the potential dangers of acting out a relatively democratic form of political activity in the midst of an enslaved population. In many important ways the Democratic Republican party drew much of its power and many of its leaders from these southern states. But this study has illustrated the vital role of the popular politics of the streets in the towns, cities and rural centers of the northern states in the Democratic Republican victory. Many Federalists had expected to enjoy success in the northern towns and cities that were bastions of mercantile power and influence, but their rule had been contested in the parades, festivals, and crowd actions chronicled in this book.

It was ordinary citizens who had populated these events. The regularization of popular politics had enhanced the political power of these ordinary Americans, including those who were on the margins of the established political process, thereby expanding the arena of exchange between rulers and ruled.[3] The tumultuous politics of the 1790s furnished black and white, male and female, rural and urban, and poor, middling, and wealthy Americans with different opportunities to participate in the political process. Employing different features of parades, feasts, crowd actions, and so forth, members of these different groups all enjoyed some access to popular politics and a limited ability to articulate their own political positions. However, the large-scale inequality between these groups meant that they enjoyed very different levels of access to and power within the rites and symbols of popular political culture. Thus, while rural folk, white men and women of the lower and middling sorts, people of color, and elite white men and women all participated in popular politics, they did so on grossly uneven terms. The politics of the streets was an arena comprised of a complex and often contradictory mix of competing interests and values.

During the 1790s the rites and symbols of popular political culture developed into essential components of political power itself, and the supporters of the Federalists and the Democratic Republicans struggled to take the fullest advantage of the songs, parades and festivals that filled the early national public sphere. However, those Federalists who believed in deferential respect for and obedience to the duly constituted authorities were somewhat hampered by their own ideology, and they sought a more conservative and less dynamic political culture. Emphasizing the importance of obedience to elected authorities, those Americans who supported the administrations and policies of Washington and Adams rarely captured the limelight of popular political culture, for they were loath to engage in public political activity that did anything but deferentially hail and salute those who governed.[4]

In stark contrast, many of those within the broad national coalition that comprised the Democratic Republican party were far more comfortable with popular politics, and party members and supporters soon realized the full potential of the politics of the street. While the Federalist elite disparaged the very notion of popular politics, out in the public sphere a broad array of ordinary men and women participated in a popular political culture that was often explicit in its opposition to Federalist ideology, policies and leaders. It is in the rites of Boston sailors who erected a liberty pole in honor of revolutionary France, of women who read Mary Wollstonecraft or wore tri-colored cockades, and of free black Americans who celebrated Haitian independence day, that we see the full potential of the age of democratic revolution, and the excitement and commitment it generated among the whole population.

Far more than did the Federalist party, the Democratic Republican coalition took form in the crucible of popular political culture. By working through and within the rites and symbols of popular politics, the Democratic Republicans secured dominance in the public sphere, and were thereby fortified in their struggle to win control of the polity itself. The rulers of the Democratic Republican party were a socially diverse group, including everyone from the wealthy southern planter Thomas Jefferson to the Vermont congressman Matthew Lyon, who had emigrated from Ireland in 1765 as a penniless indentured servant. One thing shared by these party leaders was an awareness of the importance of popular political culture in securing the support of the diverse folk who participated in its parades, festivals and other rites, from southern planters to northern yeoman farmers, from westerners to urban craftsmen and workers.

Thus the Democratic Republicans learned how to use and benefit from many different aspects of popular political culture. By the time of Jefferson's inauguration, July Fourth celebrations and even Washington's birthday celebrations had become, in many areas of the United States, Democratic Republican events. While some of the fluidity and vitality of the parades and festivals of the early and mid-1790s was lost as these evolved into partisan political events, many different Americans had participated in the creation and molding of these events, and thus in the creation of the political parties themselves.[5]

In fact the turmoil of popular politics between 1789 and 1801 had allowed members of marginal groups, including, for example, white women, free African Americans, and impoverished laborers and seafarers, to enjoy varying degrees of access to and participation in the politics of public ritual and festive culture. But while the Democratic Republicans sought to promote popular politics, they were constantly seeking to limit or prohibit the participation in popular politics of women and black Americans. By the time Jefferson entered the White House, many of the feasts, festivals, and parades of popular political culture had become partisan events staged by the white male supporters of the Democratic Republican party. But however much such events as July Fourth processions and celebrations of Washington's birthday might have resembled the more authentically popular events of the 1790s, their gradual incorporation into the Democratic Republican mainstream substantially altered their meaning and significance. The radical rhetoric and form of many of the rites and symbols of the 1790s was thus seriously undermined by the exclusion of their radical substance. As a result, when in 1801 a working man toasted newly-elected President Jefferson as a "man of the people" he was paradoxically articulating the rhetoric of popular rule while confirming and even supporting the "natural" right to rule of a wealthy Southern planter who traded in human flesh.[6] Much of the power of ideology lay in its blunting of the reality of subordination and the consequent public acceptance of hegemony. The continued use of rites and symbols that boasted a radical heritage obscured the reinvigorated power relationship between rulers and ruled, often fostering an illusion of meaningful change and concrete achievement. Moreover these rites rapidly acquired the force of custom, binding participants and observers to an emerging social order marked by increasing inequalities of wealth, status and power.[7]

These popular political victories were part of a larger process of exclusion by which the Democratic Republican coalition distinguished between the legitimate political culture of the party's members and supporters, and what they dismissed as the illegitimate political culture of their Federalist opponents and of the different groups of women and people of color who had participated in the popular politics of the 1790s. Jefferson's election in 1800 was accompanied by the crushing of Gabriel's Rebellion and the subsequent strengthening of slavery and defenses of slavery by Democratic Republicans in the southern states; by the end of legal voting for propertied women and black men enacted by the Democratic Republicans of New Jersey; and by the revision of revolutionary era state constitutions, and their replacement with more conservative documents, many of which were produced by Democratic Republicans.[8]

Early national popular political culture was thus redefined by the exclusion of female and black Americans from many aspects of the large majority of partisan rites and festivals. African American innovations, especially the early nineteenth-century celebrations of the anniversary of Haitian Independence Day and the end of the slave trade, were marginalized by the Democratic Republican coalition in an attempt to exclude them from the discourse of early national popular political culture. Such a development was, perhaps, all but inevitable. For although free black Americans, elite and poorer white women, farming families, craftsmen, and the laboring poor had all to varying degrees been able to participate in the heady street politics of the 1790s, their conflicting class, racial, and sexual identities made the finding of common ground almost impossible. There was an enormous gulf between the politics of such groups as the elite white women who read Mary Wollstonecraft and the laboring black American men who celebrated Haitian Independence Day, despite the fact that both groups suffered from the attempts of the Democratic Republicans to marginalize and exclude them from almost any kind of meaningful participation in popular politics.

Thus while the hegemony of those who saw themselves as the natural rulers of eighteenth-century America had been challenged by and in the politics of the streets, the Democratic Republicanization of many of the rites and symbols of popular politics, and the party's subsequent electoral victories all demonstrated the formation of a new, partisan hegemony. This is not to say that the Democratic Republicans enjoyed complete and absolute power, or that Federalists and others outside of the Democratic Republican coalition had no political power: rather, it is to say that in many parts of the new nation the rites and festivities that filled public places were distinctly and deliberately Democratic Republican events, giving the party and its supporters enormous power in the public sphere.

What had made popular political culture so very important in the 1790s was the way in which ordinary Americans propelled the politics of the street into the mainstream of American politics, thereby renegotiating the political relationship between rulers and ruled by forever changing the very way in which Americans experienced and participated in politics. Much of the fervor of those exhilarating days was lost when the Democratic Republican coalition appropriated many of the rites and symbols of popular politics and attempted to exclude all but their white male supporters from meaningful participation in popular politics.

But the very act of appropriation had entailed recognition of the political legitimacy of the politics of the street, over which the shaky Democratic Republican coalition could never hope to exercise complete control.[9] Throughout the nineteenth century many very different groups of Americans would participate in politics by taking to the streets and mounting parades, festivals and crowd actions, and by wearing political badges and singing political songs. The ideology of impoverished and disenfranchised white men who were absorbed into the Jeffersonian polity pushed forward to Jacksonian democracy; middle and upper class white women negotiated Republican Motherhood into moral reform and eventually into the women's movement; and black and white Americans took egalitarian discourse forward to create abolitionism. The politics of those on the margins endured temporary defeats and setbacks but was never completely destroyed. Popular political culture had come of age.

Abbreviations

APS	American Philosophical Society
BPL	Boston Public Library
CU	Columbia University
HSP	Historical Society of Pennsylvania
HU	Houghton Library, Harvard University
MHS	Massachusetts Historical Society
NA	National Archives
NYHS	New York Historical Society
NYPL	New York Public Library
PSA	Pennsylvania State Archives
Rosenbach	Rosenbach Museum and Library
SCHS	South Carolina Historical Society

Notes

Preface

1. An emphasis on "high" political thought and ideology has dominated the political history of revolutionary and early national America. See, for example, Charles A. Beard, *An Economic Interpretation of the Constitution of the United States* (New York, 1913); Noble Cunningham, Jr., *The Jeffersonian Republicans: The Formation of Party Organization, 1789–1801* (Chapel Hill, 1957); Paul Goodman, *The Democratic-Republicans of Massachusetts: Politics in a Young Republic* (Cambridge, 1964); David Hackett Fischer, *The Revolution of American Conservatism: The Federalist Party in the Age of Jefferson* (New York, 1965); Bernard Bailyn, *The Ideological Origins of the American Revolution* (Cambridge, 1967); Richard Hofstadter, *The Idea of a Party System: The Rise of Legitimate Opposition in the United States, 1780–1840* (Berkeley, 1969); Gordon S. Wood, *The Creation of the American Republic, 1776–1787* (Chapel Hill, 1969); James M. Banner, *To the Hartford Convention: The Federalists and the Origins of Party Politics in Massachusetts, 1789–1815* (New York, 1970); Richard Buel, Jr., *Securing the Revolution: Ideology in American Politics, 1789–1815* (Ithaca, 1972); Lance Banning, *The Jeffersonian Persuasion: Evolution of a Party Ideology* (Ithaca, 1978); James H. Broussard, *The Southern Federalists, 1800–1816* (Baton Rouge, 1978); John M. Murrin, "The Great Inversion, or Court versus Country: A Comparison of the Revolution Settlements in England (1688–1721) and America (1776–1816)," in *Three British Revolutions: 1641, 1688, 1776*, ed. J.G.A. Pocock (Princeton, 1980), 368–453; Joyce Appleby, *Capitalism and a New Social Order: The Republican Vision of the 1790s* (New York, 1984); Gordon S. Wood, *The Radicalism of the American Revolution* (New York, 1992); James Roger Sharp, *American Politics in the Early Republic: The New Nation in Crisis* (New Haven, 1993); Stanley M. Elkins and Eric L. McKitrick, *The Age of Federalism: The Early American Republic, 1788–1800* (New York, 1993).

2. Alfred F. Young has been one of the leading pioneers here, beginning with *The Democratic Republicans of New York: The Origins, 1763–1797* (Chapel Hill, 1967), and continuing with "The Crowd and the Coming of the American Revolution: From Ritual to Rebellion in Boston," unpublished paper presented to the Shelby Cullom Davis Center for Historical Studies, Princeton University, 23 January 1976; "George Robert Twelves Hewes (1742–1840): A Boston Shoemaker and the Memory of the American Revolution," *William and Mary Quarterly* 3d ser. 38 (1981): 561–623; "The Women of Boston: 'Persons of Consequence' in the Making

of the American Revolution," in *Women and Politics in the Age of Democratic Revolution*, ed. Harriet B. Applewhite and Darline G. Levy (Ann Arbor, 1990), 181–226.

See also Jesse Lemisch, "Jack Tar in the Streets: Merchant Seamen in the Politics of Revolutionary America," *William and Mary Quarterly* 3d ser. 25 (1968): 371–407, and "Listening to the 'Inarticulate': William Widger's Dream and the Loyalties of American Revolutionary Seamen in British Prisons," *Journal of Social History* 3 (1969): 1–29; Gary B. Nash, *The Urban Crucible: Social Change, Political Consciousness, and the Origins of the American Revolution* (Cambridge, 1979); Mary Beth Norton, *Liberty's Daughters: The Revolutionary Experience of American Women, 1750–1800* (Boston, 1980); Linda K. Kerber, *Women of the Republic: Intellect and Ideology in Revolutionary America* (Chapel Hill, 1980); Rhys Isaac, *The Transformation of Virginia, 1740–1790* (Chapel Hill, 1982); Sean Wilentz, *Chants Democratic: New York City and the Rise of the American Working Class, 1788–1850* (New York, 1984); Gary B. Nash, *Forging Freedom: The Formation of Philadelphia's Black Community, 1720–1840* (Cambridge, 1988); Susan Branson, *Women and Public Space: Gender, Politics, and Society in the 1790s* (forthcoming); Douglas R. Egerton, *Gabriel's Rebellion: The Virginia Slave Conspiracies of 1800 and 1802* (Chapel Hill, 1993); Susan Stabile, "'By a Female Hand': Letters, Belles Lettres, and the Philadelphia Culture of Performance, 1760–1820" (Ph.D. diss., University of Delaware, 1996).

3. Recent examples include Sharp, *American Politics in the Early Republic* and Elkins and McKitrick, *The Age of Federalism*.

4. A new generation of historians are beginning to work through these records, examining the ways in which gender, nationalism, and fraternity were worked out in festive culture. See David Waldstreicher, "Rites of Rebellion, Rites of Assent: Celebrations, Print Culture, and the Origins of American Nationalism," *Journal of American History* 82 (1995): 37–61, and *The Making of American Nationalism: Celebrations and Political Culture, 1776–1820* (Chapel Hill, forthcoming); Branson, *Women and Public Space*; Len Travers, "'The Brightest Day in Our Calendar': Independence Day in Boston and Philadelphia, 1776–1826" (Ph.D. diss., Boston University, 1992); Shane White, "'It Was a Proud Day': African Americans, Festivals, and Parades in the North, 1741–1834," *Journal of American History* 81 (1994): 13–50. However, these historians have focused on subjects other than the role of public display and festive culture in early national political life.

5. See, for example, Christopher Hill, *The World Turned Upside Down* (Harmondsworth, 1972); Tim Harris, *London Crowds in the Reign of Charles II: Propaganda and Politics From the Restoration Until the Exclusion Crisis* (New York, 1987); E. P. Thompson, *The Making of the English Working Class* (London, 1963), *Whigs and Hunters: The Origin of the Black Act* (New York, 1975), and *Customs in Common: Studies in Traditional Popular Culture* (London, 1991); George E. Rudé, *Wilkes and Liberty: A Social Study of 1763 to 1774* (Oxford, 1962), *The Crowd in History: A Study of Popular Disturbances in France and England, 1730–1848* (New York, 1964), and *The Face of the Crowd: Studies in Revolution, Ideology, and Popular Protest. Selected Essays of George Rudé*, ed. Harvey J. Kaye (Atlantic Highlands, 1988); John Brewer, *Party Ideology and Popular Politics at the Accession of George III* (New York, 1976), and *The Common People and Politics, 1750s–1790s* (Cambridge, 1986);

Frederick Krantz, ed., *History from Below: Studies in Popular Protest and Popular Ideology in Honor of George Rudé* (Montreal, 1985); Mark Harrison, *Crowds and History: Mass Phenomena in English Towns, 1790–1835* (New York, 1988); Nicholas Rogers, *Whigs and Cities: Popular Politics in the Age of Walpole and Pitt* (Oxford, 1989).

Although he is more interested in religious—rather than political—ritual, Ronald Hutton has made a valuable contribution to the field with his *The Rise and Fall of Merry England: The Ritual Year, 1400–1700* (Oxford, 1994).

6. E. P. Thompson, "The Moral Economy of the English Crowd in the Eighteenth Century," in *Customs in Common*, 76. For further analysis of Thompson's contributions to the field, see Harvey K. Kaye and Keith McClelland, eds., *E. P. Thompson: Critical Perspectives* (Philadelphia, 1990).

7. Brewer, *Party Ideology*, 188, and "The Number 45: A Wilkite Political Symbol," in *England's Rise to Greatness*, ed. Stephen B. Baxter (Berkeley, 1983), 349–80.

8. Rudé, *The Crowd in History*, 7–11.

9. Harris, *London Crowds*, 5.

10. Harrison, *Crowds and History*, 190–91.

11. Rogers, *Whigs and Cities*, 356–57, 371, 366–67.

12. Ibid., 375, 386, 362–63. An explicitly Marxist and implicitly Gramscian interpretive framework has informed the work of several of these historians, particularly those interested in the development of an English working class. They have uncovered a history of popular political ideas, encompassing such as the Levellers, Wilkes and the London crowd, the Luddites, and the Chartists, which stands in dialogical relationship to the history of politics and ideas.

The contest between the power elites and the nascent working class below them has fascinated these historians. James Epstein described the rituals, festivals, and feasts of early nineteenth-century Lancashire as "an arena of contested meanings" in which a political culture was defined, while Rogers has suggested that a political culture evolved in which the lower sorts could no longer be ignored by an elite who had lost much of their control. As a result, he concluded, popular politics became the "site of struggle between contending groups." Gerald Jordan and Nicholas Rogers have noted that our notion of "popular" should include "the complex interplay of all groups that had a stake in the extraparliamentary terrain," and that our definition of the "political" has now moved out to encompass "the theater of the street, and the marketplace with their ballading, pageantry, and iconography." And Thompson too described culture as "an arena of conflictual elements," characterized by "fractures and oppositions within the whole." See James Epstein, "Radical Dining, Toasting, and Symbolic Expression in Early Nineteenth-Century Lancashire: Rituals of Solidarity," *Albion* 20 (1988): 290; Rogers, *Whigs and Cities*, 372, 367, 388; Gerald Jordan and Nicholas Rogers, "Admirals as Heroes: Patriotism and Liberty in Hanoverian England," *Journal of British Studies* 28 (1989): 201; Thompson, *Customs in Common*, 6.

Introduction

1. This description is based on the following accounts: "Celebration of the FEAST of LIBERTY and EQUALITY," *Independent Chronicle*, 31 January 1793; *Massachusetts Mercury*, 26 January 1793; *Gazette US*, 6 February 1793; "CIVIC FESTIVAL," *Columbian Centinel*, 26 January 1793; "CIVIC FESTIVALS," *Columbian Centinel*, 30 January 1793; *New-York Journal*, 6 February 1793.

A more detailed examination and analysis of this festival appears below in Chapter Four.

2. For previous work on parades, festivals, and civic feasts in late eighteenth- and early nineteenth-century America, see Whitfield J. Bell, Jr., "The Federal Processions of 1788," *New-York Historical Society Quarterly* 46 (1962): 5–39; Sean Wilentz, "Artisan Republican Festivals and the Rise of Class Conflict in New York City, 1788–1837," in *Working-Class America: Essays on Labor, Community, and American Society*, ed. Michael H. Frisch and Daniel J. Walkowitz (Urbana, 1983), 37–77; Susan G. Davis, *Parades and Power: Street Theatre in Nineteenth Century Philadelphia* (Philadelphia, 1986); Len Travers, "'The Brightest Day in Our Calendar': Independence Day in Boston and Philadelphia, 1776–1826" (Ph.D. diss., Boston University, 1992); Shane White, "'It Was a Proud Day': African Americans, Festivals, and Parades in the North, 1741–1834," *Journal of American History* 81 (1994): 13–50; Albrecht Koschnik, "Political Conflict and Public Contest: Rituals of National Celebration in Philadelphia, 1788–1815," *Pennsylvania Magazine of History and Biography* 98 (1994): 209–48; David Waldstreicher, "Rites of Rebellion, Rites of Assent: Celebrations, Print Culture, and the Origins of American Nationalism," *Journal of American History* 82 (1995): 37–61, and *The Making of American Nationalism: Celebrations and Political Culture, 1776–1820* (Chapel Hill, forthcoming); Diana Kater Appelbaum, *The Glorious Fourth: An American Holiday* (New York, 1989); Robert Pettus Hay, "Freedom's Jubilee: One Hundred Years of the Fourth of July, 1776 to 1876" (Ph.D. diss., University of Kentucky, 1967).

More general studies of ritual culture during these years include Ann Fairfax Withington, *Toward a More Perfect Union: Virtue and the Formation of American Republics* (New York, 1991); Catherine L. Albanese, *Sons of the Fathers: The Civil Religion of the American Revolution* (Philadelphia, 1976); Peter Shaw, *American Patriots and the Rituals of Revolution* (Cambridge, 1981); Richard J. Hooker, "The American Revolution Seen Through a Wine Glass," *William and Mary Quarterly* 3d ser. 11 (1954): 52–77; Robert Middlekauf, "The Ritualization of the American Revolution," in *The Development of an American Culture*, ed. Stanley Coben and Lorman Ratner (Englewood Cliffs, 1970), 31–43.

3. By no means all the people living in the United States were able to participate in or even watch these rites and festivals, for boundaries of both race and gender effectively limited full access. Native Americans, for example, seldom participated, while enslaved African Americans in the southern states were rarely able to watch, let alone take part in, these celebrations, and white women throughout the nation could rarely do more than watch the parades and festivals of their menfolk. Yet those who did take part in these exclusive events regularly employed the

inclusive term "Americans" to describe themselves and their fellow participants, and it is in this contemporary sense that I employ the label. It suggests, among many things, an awareness that participation in local festive culture and public ritual provided a voice and a role in the development of a national political culture.

4. James D. Tagg, *Benjamin Franklin Bache and the Philadelphia "Aurora"* (Philadelphia, 1991), 90–97; Donald H. Stewart, *The Opposition Press of the Federalist Period* (Albany, 1969), 16; Arthur Schlesinger, Sr., *Prelude to Independence: The American Newspaper War on Britain, 1764–1776* (New York, 1958); Charles E. Clark, *The Public Prints: The Newspaper in Anglo-American Culture, 1665–1740* (New York, 1994); David Paul Nord, "Newspapers and American Nationhood," in *Three Hundred Years of the American Newspaper*, ed. John B. Hench (Worcester, 1991), 391–405.

5. I am following Ronald L. Grimes in using the word "rite" rather than "ritual." According to Grimes, the term "rite" "denotes specific enactments located in concrete times and places. It refers to a set of actions widely recognized by members of a culture. Rites are differentiated (compartmentalized, segregated) from ordinary behavior. A rite is often part of some larger whole, a ritual system or ritual tradition that includes other rites as well." Ronald L. Grimes, *Ritual Criticism: Case Studies in Its Practice, Essays on Its Theory* (Columbia, 1990), 9–10. Thus July Fourth parades, Washington's birthday celebrations, civic feasts and toasts, and so forth are all rites, which when combined (in the eyes and minds of scholars) constitute ritual.

6. Simon Schama makes a similar point in *The Embarrassment of Riches* (Berkeley, 1988), 221–22.

7. On the changing relationship between print media and popular consciousness see Richard D. Brown, *Knowledge Is Power: The Diffusion of Information in Early America, 1700–1865* (New York, 1989), and Michael Warner, *The Letters of the Republic: Publication and the Public Sphere in Eighteenth-Century America* (Cambridge, 1990).

8. My use of the term "ordinary" is linked to but not restricted by socioeconomic class. For while parades and festivals may well have constituted the primary form of political participation for many "lower sort" Americans, this ritual activity was open to people across the social spectrum, and more middling and even elite Americans might take part in a large civic feast, march in a parade, or watch a festive celebration.

9. Raymond Williams makes note of the difficulties in defining and applying the term "elite": see Williams, *Keywords: A Vocabulary of Culture and Society*, revised edition (New York, 1983), 114–15.

10. Williams, *Keywords*, 91.

11. David E. Procter, *Enacting Political Culture: Rhetorical Transformations of Liberty Weekend 1986* (New York, 1991), 3–4.

12. Natalie Zemon Davis, "Toward Mixtures and Margins," *American Historical Review* 97 (1992): 1411.

13. Paula Baker, "The Domestication of Politics: Women and American Political Society, 1780–1920," *American Historical Review* 89 (1984): 622. Also useful

when considering political behavior is Frank McGlynn and Arthur Tuden, "Introduction," in *Anthropological Approaches to Political Behavior*, ed. McGlynn and Tuden (Pittsburgh, 1991), 17, 26.

14. Frank E. Manning, "Cosmos and Chaos: Celebration in the Modern World," in *The Celebration of Society: Perspectives on Contemporary Cultural Performance*, ed. Manning (Bowling Green, 1983), 16.

15. Carl Becker, *The History of Political Parties in the Province of New York, 1760–1776* (Madison, 1909), 5.

16. I refer here to Washington's pronouncement in 1794 that the Democratic Republican Societies were responsible for the Whiskey Rebellion, and the attacks on tri-colored cockades and liberty trees that were part and parcel of the suppression of the rebellion. See George Washington, Sixth Annual Address to Congress, 19 November 1794, *The Writings of George Washington*, ed. John C. Fitzpatrick (Washington, 1931), XXXIV: 28–37.

Later in the decade John Adams and others followed a similar line, associating the popular political culture of their opponents with the Fries Rebellion, and employing the Sedition Act to prohibit various rites associated with the erection of liberty trees. See chapter six for further discussion of these forms of opposition to popular political culture.

17. I am here indebted to Paul A. Gilje. In our numerous conversations in Boston during the summer of 1987 and in his study of crowd actions in New York City, Gilje makes a rather different yet related argument about the transformation of crowd actions between the 1760s and the 1830s. In essence Gilje argues that earlier riots were sanctioned by the community, whose needs and desires were articulated by crowd members who seldom attacked persons and property. By the beginning of the Jacksonian period, however, Gilje contends that communal unity had broken down, and that interest politics inspired violent and bloody crowd actions. See Gilje, *The Road to Mobocracy: Popular Disorder in New York City, 1763–1834* (Chapel Hill, 1987), vii–viii.

18. Here, in particular, I follow the lead of the English historians cited above, especially Hill and Thompson, as well as E. J. Hobsbawm, *Primitive Rebels: Studies in Archaic Forms of Social Movements in the Nineteenth and Twentieth Centuries* (Manchester, 1959). And I have relied on Foucault's analysis of the negotiation of power between rulers and ruled: see Michel Foucault, *Power/Knowledge: Selected Interviews and Other Writings, 1972–1977*, ed. Colin Gordon, trans. Colin Gordon, Leo Marshall, John Mepham, Kate Soper (New York, 1980), 98.

19. This concept of a multiplicity of voices creating one discourse has been best articulated by Mikhail Bakhtin in *The Dialogic Imagination: Four Essays by M. M. Bakhtin*, ed. Michael Holquist, trans. Caryl Emerson and Michael Holquist (Austin, 1981), 261–62, 276, 288, 302, 333, 338.

20. For discussion of the ways in which men used various forms of associations in the public sphere see, for example, Mary Ann Clawson, *Constructing Brotherhood: Class, Gender, and Fraternalism* (Princeton, 1989), and Margaret C. Jacob, *Living the Enlightenment: Freemasonry and Politics in Eighteenth-Century Europe* (New York, 1991).

21. Donald J. Ratcliffe, "The Autobiography of Benjamin Tappan," *Ohio History* 85 (1976): 115.

22. I understand the public sphere to be a place of mediation, accessible to all. See Jürgen Habermas, "The Public Sphere: An Encyclopedia Article (1964)," *New German Critique* 5 (1974): 49–55.

Chapter One

1. David Hackett Fischer, *Albion's Seed: Four British Folkways in America* (New York, 1989); A. G. Roeber, *Palatines, Liberty, and Property: German Lutherans in Colonial British America* (Baltimore, 1993). Fischer has made the argument that four distinct "folkways" came from regions of Great Britain to different parts of mainland British North America, where they informed the creation of regional societies and cultures; Fischer's is an appealingly neat formula, but the reality was rather more complicated. More recently Roeber has made a compelling argument that German settlers brought with them a variety of ideas about liberty and property that informed their acceptance of the English rites and symbols that dominated the popular political culture of British North America. His well crafted case study illustrates the persistence of ethnic and racial political beliefs and practices under the increasingly hegemonic sway of English political culture.

2. Examples of accounts of royal celebrations or commemorative events can be found in *Boston Gazette*, 25 January 1731 and 24 October 1737, *South-Carolina Gazette*, 25 May 1734, and *Virginia Gazette* (Parks), 11 February 1736 and 30 December 1737. London's Whig celebrations of Guy Fawkes Day and the Landing of William at Torbay were reported in *Virginia Gazette* (Parks), 11 February 1736, and descriptions of the Liberty Cap and emblems of liberty appeared in *Virginia Gazette* (Parks), 15 May 1746. The loyal crowd celebrations of the English victory over the Jacobites, together with angry crowd violence after a Lord Mayor's Parade in London also appeared in *Virginia Gazette* (Parks), on 18 July 1746 and 22 January 1767 respectively. The best study of what he describes as "monarchical culture" in colonial America is Richard L. Bushman, *King and People in Provincial Massachusetts* (Chapel Hill, 1985).

3. This process is best described in John M. Murrin, "Anglicizing An American Colony: The Transformation of Provincial Massachusetts" (Ph.D. diss., Yale University, 1966).

4. The incident in Wallis's tavern is recounted by David W. Conroy in his essay "Puritans in Taverns: Law and Popular Culture in Colonial Massachusetts, 1630–1720," in *Drinking: Behavior and Belief in Modern History*, ed. Susanna Barrows and Robin Room (Berkeley, 1991), 29. See also David D. Hall, *Days of Wonder, Days of Judgement: Popular Religious Belief in Early New England* (New York, 1989), 4–5, 9–10.

5. See, for example, "Boston March 1," *Boston Gazette*, 5 March 1733; "BOSTON," *Boston Gazette*, 16 October 1738; "Boston," *Boston Gazette*, 3 November

1741; "BOSTON, June 5," *Boston News Letter*, 5 June 1766; "NEWPORT, June 9," *Newport Mercury*, 9 June 1766.

6. "NEW-YORK, NOVEMBER 17," *New-York Mercury*, 22 October 1759.

7. "NEW-YORK, November 11," *Pennsylvania Gazette*, 21 November 1754. These celebrations continued, in similar form, throughout the British occupation of the city during the Revolutionary War. See, for example, "NEW-YORK, June 9," *New-York Gazette*, 9 June 1777, "NEW-YORK, June 5," *New-York Gazette*, 5 June 1780, and "NEW-YORK, June 7," *New-York Gazette*, 9 June 1783.

8. John Fanning Watson, *Annals of Philadelphia, and Pennsylvania, in the Olden Time* (Philadelphia, 1905), II: 274.

9. See, for example, "PHILADELPHIA, November 16," *Pennsylvania Gazette*, 16 November 1752, and "PHILADELPHIA, November 14," *Pennsylvania Gazette*, 14 November 1754

10. See "CHARLESTOWN, March 4," *South Carolina Gazette*, 4 March 1732; "Annapolis, (in Maryland) Mar. 2," *South Carolina Gazette*, 30 June 1733; CHARLESTOWN, March 6," *South Carolina Gazette*, 6 March 1736; "Williamsburg, January 21," *Virginia Gazette*, (Parks) 21 January 1736; "CHARLES-TOWN, April 20," *South Carolina Gazette*, 20 April 1747; "ANNAPOLIS," *Maryland Gazette*, 5 June 1755; "ANNAPOLIS, December 1," *Maryland Gazette*, 1 December 1757.

11. These celebrations are described in "CHARLESTOWN, Novemb. 4," *South Carolina Gazette* 4 November 1732; "CHARLESTOWN, Nov. 1," *South Carolina Gazette*, 2 November 1734; "CHARLESTOWN, November 6," *South Carolina Gazette*, 6 November 1736.

12. "CHARLES-TOWN, November 5," *South Carolina Gazette*, 5 November 1744. See also "CHARLES-TOWN, Oct. 27," *South Carolina Gazette*, 4 November 1739; "CHARLES-TOWN," *South Carolina Gazette*, 6 November 1740; "CHARLES-TOWN, November 12," *South Carolina Gazette*, 16 November 1753; "CHARLES-TOWN, November 13," *South Carolina Gazette*, 13 November 1755; "CHARLES-TOWN, Nov. 15," *South Carolina Gazette*, 15 November 1760; "CHARLES-TOWN, JUNE 11, 1763," *South Carolina Gazette*, 11 June 1763.

13. "Williamsburg, Nov. 3," *Virginia Gazette* (Parks), 3 November 1738. See also "Williamsburg, November 4," *Virginia Gazette* (Parks), 4 November 1737; "WILLIAMSBURG, Novem. 2," *Virginia Gazette* (Parks), 2 November 1739; William Byrd, *Another Secret Diary of William Byrd of Westover, 1739–1741: With Letters and Literary Exercises, 1696–1726*, ed. Maude H. Woodfin and Marion Tinling (Richmond, 1942), 107; "WILLIAMSBURG, Nov. 7," *Virginia Gazette* (Parks), 7 November 1745; "WILLIAMSBURG," *Virginia Gazette* (Hunter), 14 November 1755.

14. "ANNAPOLIS, November 18," *Maryland Gazette*, 18 November 1756. For further examples see "ANNAPOLIS, November 17," *Maryland Gazette*, 17 November 1757; ANNAPOLIS, November 13," *Maryland Gazette*, 13 November 1760; "ANNAPOLIS, June 10," *Maryland Gazette*, 10 June 1762.

15. "NEW-YORK, October 8," *New-York Mercury*, 8 October 1753; "BOS-TON," *Boston News-Letter*, 3 July 1746.

16. "WILLIAMSBURG, October 27," *Virginia Gazette* (Purdie), 27 Octo-

ber 1768. For an account of a similar reception for Governor Alexander Spotswood in 1710, see William Byrd, *The Secret Diary of William Byrd of Westover, 1709–1712*, ed. Louis B. Wright and Marion Tinling (Richmond, 1941), 195.

Comparable rites were staged in other colonies. See the account of Governor Wright's arrival in Savannah in *South Carolina Gazette*, 20 February 1762, that of Governor Tryon's arrival in North Carolina in "WILMINGTON, (N. CAROLINA) Dec. 18," *Maryland Gazette*, 20 February 1766, and the descriptions of Governor Lyttleton's arrival in South Carolina in "CHARLES-TOWN, June 3," *South Carolina Gazette*, 5 June 1756.

17. "CHARLES-TOWN, May 3," *South Carolina Gazette*, 3 May 1740.

18. Robert Dinwiddie, "A PROCLAMATION," *Virginia Gazette* (Hunter), 12 September 1755.

19. Hall, *Days of Wonder*, 166–167. See also William D. Love, *The Fast and Thanksgiving Days of New England* (Boston, 1895), and Richard P. Gildrie, "The Ceremonial Puritan: Days of Humiliation and Thanksgiving," *New England Historical and Genealogical Register* 136 (1982): 3–16.

20. "CHARLES-TOWN, October 13," *South Carolina Gazette*, 13 October 1758.

21. "ANNAPOLIS, November 1," *Maryland Gazette*, 1 November 1759. For other enthusiastic celebrations of the capture of Quebec, see "Newport, October 23," *Newport Mercury*, 29 October 1759; "BOSTON, October 18," *Boston News-Letter*, 18 October 1759; "NEW-BRUNSWICK, in New Jersey," *New-York Mercury*, 22 October 1759.

22. "NEW LONDON, SEPTEMBER 26," *New-London Summary*, 26 September 1760.

23. "PHILADELPHIA, January 22," *Pennsylvania Gazette*, 22 January 1761.

24. For more on Bacon's Rebellion see Edmund S. Morgan, *American Slavery, American Freedom: The Ordeal of Colonial Virginia* (New York, 1975), 215–292; Wilcomb E. Washburn, *The Governor and the Rebel: A History of Bacon's Rebellion in Virginia* (Chapel Hill, 1957); Stephen Saunders Webb, *1676: The End of American Independence* (Cambridge, 1985), 3–163; John Harold Sprinkle, Jr., "Loyalists and Baconians: The Participants in Bacon's Rebellion in Virginia, 1676–1677" (Ph.D. diss., College of William and Mary, 1992).

The Regulators have received far too little attention. The better studies include Marvin L. Michael Kay, "The North Carolina Regulation, 1766–1776," in *The American Revolution: Explorations in the History of American Radicalism* ed. Alfred F. Young (DeKalb, 1976), 71–123; Richard M. Brown, *The South Carolina Regulators: The Story of the First American Vigilante Movement* (Cambridge, 1963); Paul David Nelson, *William Tryon and the Course of Empire: A Life in British Imperial Service* (Chapel Hill, 1990). For the Paxton Boys' march on Philadelphia, see Brook Hindle, "The March of the Paxton Boys," *William and Mary Quarterly* 3d ser. 3 (1946): 461–86; Wilbur R. Jacobs, ed., *The Paxton Riots and the Frontier Theory* (Chicago, 1967).

25. Rhys Isaac, *The Transformation of Virginia, 1740–1790* (Chapel Hill, 1982), 98–101.

26. Byrd, *The Secret Diary*, 416–17.

27. "WILLIAMSBURG, November 26," *Virginia Gazette* (Parks), 26 November 1736; "ANNAPOLIS," *Maryland Gazette*, 4 October 1749.

28. Isaac, *The Transformation of Virginia*, 88, 249.

29. Ibid., 114.

30. Edmund S. Morgan, *Inventing the People: The Rise of Popular Sovereignty in England and America* (New York, 1988), 207–8.

31. Gary B. Nash, *The Urban Crucible: Social Change, Political Consciousness, and the Origins of the American Revolution* (Cambridge, 1979), 198.

32. Joseph P. Reidy, " 'Negro Election Day' & Black Community Life in New England, 1750–1860," *Marxist Perspectives* 1 (1978): 102–9; Shane White, " 'It Was A Proud Day': African American Festivals and Parades in the North, 1741–1834," *Journal of American History* 81 (1994): 13–50; Melvin C. Wade, " 'Shining in Borrowed Plumage': Affirmation of Community in Black Coronation Festivals of New England, ca. 1750–1850," in *Material Life in America*, ed. Robert Blair St. George (Boston, 1988), 171–81; William G. Piersen, *Black Yankees* (Amherst, 1988), 113–40.

33. Shane White, "Pinkster: Afro-Dutch Syncretization in New York City and the Hudson Valley," *Journal of American Folklore* 102 (1989): 68–75; A. J. Williams-Myers, "Pinkster Carnival: Africanisms in the Hudson River Valley," *Afro-Americanisms in New York Life and History* 9 (1985): 7–17; Alice Morse Earle, *Colonial Days in Old New York* (New York, 1912), 196–99.

34. Reidy, "Negro Election Day," 109.

35. Ronald Hutton, *The Rise and Fall of Merry England: The Ritual Year, 1400–1700* (Oxford, 1994), 186.

36. Ibid., 252.

37. *New-York Gazette*, 7 November 1737.

38. "NEW-YORK, November 10," *Maryland Gazette*, 4 December 1755. See also Paul A. Gilje, *The Road to Mobocracy: Popular Disorder in New York City, 1763–1834* (Chapel Hill, 1987), 26.

39. The information about the occupations of participants in Pope's Day celebrations in 1749, 1752 and 1764 is drawn from Francis D. Cogliano, "No King No Popery: Anti-Popery and Revolution in New England, 1745–1791" (Ph.D. diss., Boston University, 1993), 75.

40. Ibid., 69.

41. This information is drawn from Alfred F. Young, "The Crowd and the Coming of the American Revolution: From Ritual to Rebellion in Boston," unpublished paper presented at the Shelby Cullom Davis Center for Historical Studies, Princeton University, January 1976, 25 (cited with the permission of the author). The best surviving account of these rites appeared in *Boston Daily Advertiser*, 9 November 1821.

For more on the English background of these rites see Nicholas Rogers, *Whigs and Cities: Popular Politics in the Age of Walpole and Pitt* (Oxford, 1989), 362, 363–64; O. W. Furley, "The Pope-Burning Processions of the Late-Seventeenth Century" *History* n.s. 44 (1959): 16–23; Nash, *The Urban Crucible*, 261.

42. "NEW-YORK, November 10," *Maryland Gazette*, 4 December 1755.

43. The members of the Loyal Nine "came from the socially conservative and economically hurting middling interest, were small merchants, distillers, part owners of ships, and master craftsmen." Dirk Hoerder, "Boston Leaders and Boston Crowds, 1765–1776" in *The American Revolution: Explorations in the History of American Radicalism*, ed. Alfred F. Young (DeKalb, 1976), 241.

44. Young, "The Crowd and the Coming of the American Revolution," 9.

45. Nash, *Urban Crucible*, 296–97.

46. Samuel Adams, as cited in Nash, *Urban Crucible*, 352. See also Young, "The Crowd and the Coming of the American Revolution," 17–18.

47. Nash, *Urban Crucible*, 293, 299–300.

48. Arthur Schlesinger, "Liberty Tree: A Genealogy" *The New England Quarterly* 25 (1952): 437–38; Peter Shaw, *American Patriots and the Rituals of Revolution* (Cambridge, 1981), 182–83. For further discussion of the trans-Atlantic development of the liberty tree, see J. David Harden, "Liberty Caps and Liberty Trees," *Past and Present* 146 (1995): 66–102.

49. For accounts of attacks on maypoles by the Puritan state in seventeenth-century England, see Hutton, *The Rise and Fall of Merry England*, 30, 87, 134, 158.

50. Young, "The Crowd and the Coming of the American Revolution," 5, 6–8. See also Edmund S. Morgan and Helen M. Morgan, *The Stamp Act Crisis: Prologue to Revolution* (1953) (New York, 1963), 161–63, 173.

51. Alfred F. Young, "The Women of Boston: 'Persons of Consequence' in the Making of the American Revolution," in *Women and Politics in the Age of the Democratic Revolution*, ed. Harriet B. Applewhite and Darline G. Levy (Ann Arbor, 1990), 188.

52. John M. Murrin, "Escaping Perfidious Albion: Federalism, Fear of Aristocracy, and the Democratization of Corruption in Postrevolutionary America," in *Virtue, Corruption, and Self-Interest: Political Values in the Eighteenth Century*, ed. Richard K. Matthews (Bethlehem, 1994), 113.

53. Shaw, *American Patriots*, 182.

54. "ANNAPOLIS (MARYLAND) August 29," *South Carolina Gazette*, 5 October 1765; "NEWPORT, August 26," *South Carolina Gazette*, 21 September 1765; "NEWPORT, September 2," *South Carolina Gazette*, 28 September 1765; "PHILADELPHIA, October 10," *South Carolina Gazetteer*, 17 December 1765; "New Brunswick, Oct. 29," *South Carolina Gazetteer*, 17 December 1765; "CHARLES-TOWN, OCTOBER 30," *South Carolina Gazette*, 31 October 1765; "NEW-YORK, November 4," *South Carolina Gazetteer*, 17 December 1765; "Portsmouth, (in New-Hampshire) November 4," *South Carolina Gazetteer*, 17 December 1765.
See also Morgan and Morgan, *The Stamp Act Crisis*, 159–79.

55. Descriptions and a list of New York City's liberty poles are collected together in the joint report of the New-York Historical Society and the Sons of the Revolution, "Minutes and Proceedings of the Joint Committee on the Removal of the Old Post Office Building, and the Erection of a LIBERTY POLE On The Site of the First LIBERTY POLE, erected June 4, 1776, in "the Commons," the Present City Hall Park, 1919–1921," Manuscript Collections, NYHS.

56. Peter W. Yates, "Opinion of the Justices at Schenectady—as to a number

of persons erecting a liberty pole in the public highway February 7, 1774," Manuscript Collections, NYHS.

57. "CHARLES-TOWN, OCTOBER 4," *South Carolina Gazetteer*, 4 October 1768.

58. *South Carolina Gazette*, 29 June 1769; "CHARLES-TOWN, SEPTEM-
BER 7," *South Carolina Gazette*, 7 September 1769.

59. "CHARLES-TOWN, MAY 17," *South Carolina Gazette*, 17 May 1770;
"CHARLES-TOWN, OCTOBER 25," *South Carolina Gazette*, 25 October 1770;
"CHARLES-TOWN, DECEMBER 15," *South Carolina Gazette*, 15 December
1770; "CHARLES-TOWN, DECEMBER 20," *South Carolina Gazette*, 20 December 1770.

60. "CHARLES-TOWN, MARCH 21," *South Carolina Gazette*, 21 March
1774.

61. "NORFOLK, MAY 24," *Virginia Gazette* (Purdie), 6 June 1766; "NEW
YORK, May 26," *Virginia Gazette* (Purdie), 20 June 1766; "ANNAPOLIS, June 12,"
Maryland Gazette, 12 June 1766; "PHILADELPHIA, May 29," *Virginia Gazette*
(Purdie), 20 June 1766; "CHARLES-TOWN, June 23, 1766," *South Carolina Ga-
zette*, 23 June 1766; "NEWBERN (in North-Carolina), June 27," *South Carolina
Gazetteer*, 5 August 1766; "Boston, May 26," *Boston Gazette*, 26 May 1766.

62. Samuel Wharton to Benjamin Franklin, Philadelphia, 13 October 1765,
The Papers of Benjamin Franklin, ed. Leonard W. Labaree (New Haven, 1968), XII:
315–16.

63. *Passages from the Remembrances of Christopher Marshall, Member of the
Committee of Observation and Inspection, Of the Provincial Conference, And of the
Council of Safety*, ed. William Duane (Philadelphia, 1839), 6–7.

64. Ibid.

65. Steven Rosswurm, *Arms, Country, and Class: The Philadelphia Militia
and the "Lower Sort" During the American Revolution, 1775–1783* (New Brunswick,
1987), 252, 265.

66. See, for example, Charles M. Andrews, "The Boston Merchants and the
Non-Importation Movement," *Transactions of the Colonial Society of Massachusetts*
19 (1916–1917): 159–259; Richard D. Brown, *Revolutionary Politics in Massachusetts: The Boston Committee of Correspondence and the Towns* (Cambridge, 1970);
Richard Alan Ryerson, *The Revolution Is Now Begun: The Radical Committees of
Philadelphia, 1765–1776* (Philadelphia, 1978); Pauline Maier, *From Resistance to Revolution: Colonial Radicals and the Development of American Opposition to Britain,
1765–1776* (New York, 1972); Albert H. Tillson, Jr., "The Militia and Popular Political
Culture in the Upper Valley of Virginia, 1740–1775," *Virginia Magazine of History
and Biography* 94 (1986): 285–306.

67. "VIRGINIA, March 1, 1766," *Maryland Gazette*, 27 March 1766.

68. "FROM THE SOUTH CAROLINA GAZETTE," *Virginia Gazette*
(Rind), 15 September 1774.

69. "CHARLES-TOWN, AUGUST 15," *South Carolina Gazette*, 19 September 1774.

70. *Boston Evening Post*, 12 February 1770.

71. See, for example, the appeal signed by "your affectionate countrywomen,

of Virginia" addressed "TO THE LADIES OF PENNSYLVANIA," *Virginia Gazette* (Rind), 15 September 1774. The wide and varied activities of women involved in the resistance movement have been described in Mary Beth Norton, *Liberty's Daughters: The Revolutionary Experience of American Women, 1750–1800* (Boston, 1980), 155–94; Linda Kerber, *Women of the Republic: Intellect and Ideology in Revolutionary America* (Chapel Hill, 1980), 35–67; Kerber, "'I Have Don . . . much to carrey on the Warr': Women and the Shaping of Republican Ideology after the American Revolution," in *Women and Politics in the Age of the Democratic Revolution*, ed. Harriet B. Applewhite and Darline G. Levy (Ann Arbor, 1990), 227–58; Kerber, "'History Can Do It No Justice': Women and the Reinterpretation of the American Revolution," in *Women in the Age of the American Revolution*, ed. Ronald Hoffman and Peter J. Albert (Charlottesville, 1989), 3–42; Young, "The Women of Boston," 181–226; Barbara Clark Smith, "Food Rioters and the American Revolution," *William and Mary Quarterly* 3d ser. 51 (1994): 3–38.

72. *Journal & Letters of Philip Vickers Fithian, 1773–1774: A Plantation Tutor of the Old Dominion*, ed. Hunter Dickinson Farish (Williamsburg, 1943), entry for 18 January 1774, 76.

73. John Adams, Diary, 3 September 1774, in *Diary and Autobiography of John Adams*, ed. L. H. Butterfield (Cambridge, 1961), II: 121.

74. *The Autobiography of Benjamin Rush: His "Travels Through Life" together with his Commonplace Book for 1789–1813*, ed. George W. Corner (Princeton, 1948), 112–13.

75. "OF TOASTS," *Columbian Herald*, 23 June 1791 (this essay was apparently reprinted from a Boston newspaper); "NEW-YORK, July 8," *Gazette US*, 10 July 1795. Some of the most explicit discussions of the political nature and significance of toasts took place in the 1790s, and therefore I have cited these in this discussion of the development of toasting as a vital element of popular political culture.

76. Minutes of the Committee of Amusement, Society of Tammany or Columbian Order, 25 November 1791, Manuscripts Collection, NYPL.

77. "TRIAL BY JURY," *Columbian Herald*, 12 February 1796.

78. Alexander Anderson, Diary entry for 4 May 1795, Manuscripts Collection, CU. I am indebted to the work of Peter Thompson for my analysis of the significance of toasts in the early republic. See Thompson, "'The Friendly Glass': Drink and Gentility in Colonial Philadelphia," *Pennsylvania Magazine of History and Biography* 113 (1989): 559, 560–61. See also Richard J. Hooker, "The American Revolution Seen Through a Wine Glass," *William and Mary Quarterly* 3d ser. 11 (1954): 52–77, and James Epstein, "Radical Dining, Toasting, and Symbolic Expression in Early Nineteenth-Century Lancashire: Rituals of Solidarity," *Albion* 20 (1988): 271–91.

79. "SAVANNAH, July 7," *Gazette of Georgia*, 7 July 1785.

80. For this use of the language of toasts see Epstein, "Radical Dining," 275. Thompson has described the publication of toasts in newspapers as "verbal broadsides," underlining their political content and significance. Thompson, "'The Friendly Glass,'" 560–61.

81. "NEWPORT, (in Rhode-Island) June 10," *Maryland Gazette*, 11 July 1765.

82. *Maryland Gazette*, 13 March 1766.

83. Ibid.

84. "BOSTON, Feb. 16," *Virginia Gazette* (Purdie), 5 April 1770; "Boston, March 12," *Boston Gazette*, 12 March 1770.

85. "WILLIAMSBURG, December 14," *Virginia Gazette* (W. Rind), 14 December 1769.

86. "BOSTON, December 14," *Virginia Gazette* (Purdie), 7 January 1768. This single article described the patriotic work of women in a dozen communities.

87. "NEW YORK, April 8," *Virginia Gazette* (Dixon), 20 April 1776. One hundred and seventy women of Stratford, Connecticut were described in this last article as a "petticoat army" prepared to tar and feather one Mr. Edwards who had named his newborn son Thomas Gage.

88. "By Letter from Boston," *Virginia Gazette* (Purdie), 27 January 1774.

89. The "political principles" of Mrs. M. Hutton of Calvert County, Maryland, caught the "attention of the public" when she refused to drink a toast to General George Washington, preferring to drink to "Peace and Quietness, for the hated spinning." "ANNAPOLIS, AUGUST 7, 1777," *Maryland Gazette*, 7 August 1777. On a more positive note, the "laudable example of public spirit" of five independent widow women who subscribed their names to the Association in Williamsburg was acknowledged by William Rind in "WILLIAMSBURG, July 27," *Virginia Gazette* (W. Rind), 27 July 1769.

90. "PHILADELPHIA, December 14," *Virginia Gazette* (Dixon), 29 December 1775.

91. Recent studies of black participation in and impact upon the revolutionary struggle include Peter H. Wood, "'Liberty is Sweet': African-American Freedom Struggles in the Years Before White Independence," in *Beyond the American Revolution: Explorations in the History of American Radicalism*, ed. Alfred F. Young (DeKalb, 1993), 149–84; Sylvia R. Frey, *Water from the Rock: Black Resistance in a Revolutionary Age* (Princeton, 1991); Graham Russell Hodges, "Black Revolt in New York City and the Neutral Zone: 1775–83," in *New York in the Age of the Constitution, 1775–1800*, ed. Paul A. Gilje and William Pencak (Rutherford, 1992), 20–47. Hodges demonstrates, far more than previous authors, the active role of black women in the struggle against slavery.

92. "BOSTON, July 25," *Maryland Gazette*, 15 August 1776.

93. "NEW YORK, July 8," *Virginia Gazette* (Dixon), 29 July 1776.

94. John Adams to Abigail Adams, 3 July 1776, in *Adams Family Correspondence. Volume 2. June 1776–March 1778*, ed. L. H. Butterfield (Cambridge, 1963), 30.

95. John Adams to Abigail Adams, Jr., 5 July 1777, *Adams Family Correspondence*, 274–75.

96. *Pennsylvania Packet*, 4 July 1778.

97. "ALBANY, THURSDAY, JULY 7," *Albany Gazette*, 7 July 1785.

98. "HARTFORD, July 9. ANNIVERSARY OF INDEPENDENCE," *Norwich Packet*, 12 July 1787; "BOSTON, July 9," *Newport Mercury*, 16 July 1787; "WILMINGTON (Delaware), July 4," *Maryland Gazette*, 24 July 1783; "CHARLES-TOWN, July 8," *Gazette of South Carolina* (Charleston), 8 July 1778; "ELIZABETH-TOWN, July 11," *New Jersey Journal*, 11 July 1787; "NEWPORT,

July 7," *Newport Mercury*, 7 July 1781; "Lexington, July 5," *Kentucky Gazette*, 5 July 1788.

99. Richard Henry Lee to Francis Lightfoot Lee, 5 July 1778, in *Letters of Delegates to Congress, 1774–1789*, ed. Paul H. Smith (Washington, 1983), X: 223–24. See also *Pennsylvania Packet*, 3 July 1778; Henrietta C. Ellery, "Diary of the Hon. William Ellery of Rhode Island, June 28-July 23, 1778," *Pennsylvania Magazine of History and Biography* 11 (1887): 478.

100. Elizabeth Drinker, 4 July 1777, *The Diary of Elizabeth Drinker*, ed. Elaine Forman Crane (Boston, 1991), I: 225.

101. Sarah Fisher, "'A Diary of Trifling Occurrences': Philadelphia, 1776–1778," ed. Nicholas B. Wainwright, *Pennsylvania Magazine of History and Biography* 82 (1958): 438.

102. The imprisoned sailors' July Fourth festivities in 1780 and 1781 were described by William Russell in his journal, cited in Ralph D. Paine, *The Ships and Sailors of Old Salem: The Record of a Brilliant Era of American Achievement* (New York, 1909), 129, 142. See also Jesse Lemisch, "Jack Tar in the Streets: Merchant Seamen in the Politics of Revolutionary America," *William and Mary Quarterly* 3d ser. 25 (1968): 401, 403, and "Listening to the 'Inarticulate': William Widger's Dream and the Loyalties of American Revolutionary Seamen in British Prisons," *Journal of Social History* 3 (1969): 3–4, 25–26.

103. Friederike Charlotte Luise Riedesel, *Letters and Journals Relating to the War of the American Revolution, And the Capture of the German Troops at Saratoga*, trans. William L. Stone (Albany, 1867), 165. See also Paul K. Longmore, *The Invention of George Washington* (Berkeley, 1988), 192, 210.

104. "ANNAPOLIS, November 29," *Maryland Gazette*, 29 November 1781; "Boston, October 26," *Boston Gazette and Country Journal*, 26 October 1788; *Pennsylvania Gazette*, 18 December 1783.

105. "PHILADELPHIA, December 10," *Pennsylvania Gazette*, 18 December 1783.

106. "WILLIAMSBURG, Feb. 19," *Virginia Gazette* (Nicholson), 19 February 1779, and "WILLIAMSBURG, February 26," *Virginia Gazette* (Nicholson), 26 February 1779.

107. "RICHMOND, Feb. 14," *Virginia Gazette, or the American Advertiser*, 14 February 1784.

108. "Lexington, July 5," *Kentucky Gazette*, 5 July 1788.

109. "NEWPORT, February 21," *Newport Mercury*, 21 February 1784.

110. The celebration in Bennington was described in detail in *Columbian Herald*, 18 September 1788.

111. "BOSTON, June 20," *New-York Daily Advertiser*, 26 June 1794.

112. "BOSTON, October 18," *Aurora*, 26 October 1792.

113. Early celebrations of the victory at Yorktown are mentioned in William C. Stinchcombe, "Americans Celebrate the Birth of the Dauphin," *Diplomacy and Revolution: The Franco-American Alliance of 1778*, ed. Ronald Hoffman and Peter J. Albert (Charlottesville, 1981), 53–57.

114. *American Minerva*, 27 November 1794.

115. *Aurora*, 29 November 1794.

116. *Aurora*, 1 December 1796. See also *Daily Advertiser*, 29 November 1796; *Aurora*, 1 December 1795; *Daily Advertiser*, 29 November 1796; *American Minerva*, 27 November 1794.

117. The best summary of this process can be found in Gordon S. Wood, *The Creation of the American Republic, 1776–1787* (New York, 1972), 519–24.

118. Excerpts of Francis Hopkinson's account of Philadelphia's Grand Federal Procession are reproduced in J. Thomas Scharf and Thompson Westcott, *History of Philadelphia, 1609–1884* (Philadelphia, 1884), I: 447–52; Charles Biddle, *Autobiography of Charles Biddle, Vice-President of the Supreme Executive Council of Pennsylvania, 1745–1821* (Philadelphia, 1883), 228.

119. Scharff and Westcott, *History of Philadelphia*, I: 448–51.

120. "CARLISLE (Penn.), January 2," *New-Jersey Journal*, 16 January 1788.

121. ONE of the PEOPLE, Letter to the Editor, *Carlisle Gazette*, 9 January 1788.

122. For an excellent account of the riot and the conditions surrounding it, see Saul Cornell, "Aristocracy Assailed: The Ideology of Backcountry Anti-Federalism," *Journal of American History* 76 (1990): 1148–72.

123. "Baltimore, May 6," *Gazette of Georgia*, 12 June 1788; *Boston Gazette and Country Journal*, 18 February 1788, and also "BOSTON, February 9," *Maryland Gazette*, 28 February 1788; "LAUS DEO," *State Gazette*, 3 December 1789; "NEW-BRUNSWICK, December 25," *New-Jersey Journal*, 2 January 1788; "Chelsea, July 5, 1788," *Norwich Packet*, 10 July 1788; "Charleston, May 28," *Gazette of Georgia*, 5 June 1788.

In his essay on the ratification parade in New York City, Paul A. Gilje concludes that this stage managed affair tells us less about ordinary people and their concerns than do the various riots and angry crowd actions of the late eighteenth century. If one treats the ratification parade in each town and city as an isolated event this may be true, but it is my contention that these ratification parades played a vital role in the formation of a national popular political culture, a lengthy creative process that was informed by the participation of ordinary Americans. See Gilje, "The Common People and the Constitution: Popular Culture in New York City in the Late Eighteenth Century," in *New York in the Age of the Constitution*, 48–73.

Chapter Two

1. For more on popular reverence for and mythologizing of Washington, see Gary Wills, *Cincinnatus: George Washington and the Enlightenment* (Garden City, 1984); Paul K. Longmore, *The Invention of George Washington* (Berkeley, 1988); Barry Schwartz, *George Washington: The Making of an American Symbol* (New York, 1987); Marcus Cunliffe, *George Washington: Man and Monument* (Boston, 1958); Daniel J. Boorstin, "The Mythologizing of George Washington," in *The Americans: The National Experience* (New York, 1965), 337–56; Bernard Mayo, *Myths and Men: Patrick Henry, George Washington, Thomas Jefferson* (Athens, 1959). In a recent review article, Longmore noted that "scholars, particularly Washing-

ton biographers, have never adequately analyzed him as a politician and political leader. . . . Scholars examining the Washington myth have given the most attention to its significance in the early nineteenth century. Those who have studied the late eighteenth-century legend, even those explaining it as part of the larger paradigm shift of the Revolution, have explicated primarily the eulogies of 1799–1800. Only a few writers have examined the image during Washington's lifetime. Little mention is made of Washington's own part in the creation of his myth, and then only in passing." Longmore, "The Enigma of George Washington: How Did the Man Become the Myth?" *Reviews in American History* 13 (1985): 185, 187.

2. *The Records of the Federal Convention of 1787* (1911), ed. Max Farrand (New Haven, 1966), 65.

3. Ronald Hutton, *The Rise and Fall of Merry England: The Ritual Year 1400–1700* (New York, 1994), 186.

4. Longmore, *Invention of Washington*, 210. For discussion of the ways in which Congress appropriated the power and authority of the monarchy, see Jerrilyn Greene Marston, *King and Congress: The Transfer of Political Legitimacy, 1774–1776* (Princeton, 1987).

5. See, for example, the reception of Washington at Wilmington, as reported in *Delaware Gazette*, 25 April 1789. For descriptions and analysis of the rites for English monarchs, see David M. Bergeron, *English Civic Pageantry, 1558–1642* (Columbia, 1971), 10, 75–86. Bergeron's account of the typical form for a royal progress and entry is strikingly similar to the forms used to welcome Washington as he traveled to his inauguration, and when he undertook "royal progresses" around the country during his presidency.

6. Jane Ewing to James Hunter, Jr., 23 April 1789, Manuscripts in Vault, New Jersey State Archives: I am very grateful to Dan Jones for bringing this document to my attention. A longer and more detailed narrative of this event is P.Q., "ACCOUNT of the Manner of receiving, at Trenton, his Excellency GEORGE WASHINGTON, President of the United States, on his Route to the Seat of Federal Government: Communicated in a Letter to the Editor," *Columbian Magazine* 3 (1789), 288–90. For descriptions of other receptions for Washington on his way to New York, see Mason L. Weems, *The Life of Washington* (1800), ed. Marcus Cunliffe (Cambridge, 1962), 132–34.

7. "ACCOUNT of the Manner of receiving . . . GEORGE WASHINGTON," 290. Washington acknowledged the unique nature of his reception by the women who "received him in so novel and graceful a manner" in a written note of thanks. Ibid., 289.

8. Bergeron, *English Civic Pageantry*, 75, 88–89.

9. James Baillie, "Washington's Reception by the Ladies on the Bridge" (New York, 1848).

10. Rufus Wilmot Griswold, *The Republican Court: Or, American Society in the Days of Washington* (New York, 1854), 145, 156, 161–62.

11. Alexander Hamilton to George Washington, 5 May 1789, *The Papers of Alexander Hamilton*, ed. Harold C. Syrett (New York, 1961–1979), V: 335–36. Hamilton was responding to a series of questions that Washington had sent to several advisors. See George Washington to John Adams, New York, 10 May 1789, *The*

Papers of George Washington: Presidential Series, ed. W. W. Abbot (Charlottesville, 1987), II: 245–47.

12. Hamilton to Washington, 5 May 1789, *Papers of Hamilton*, V: 335–36.

13. For descriptions of these levees see John Fanning Watson, *Annals of Philadelphia, and Pennsylvania, in the Olden Time . . .* (1844) (Philadelphia, 1905), I: 578–79. The "Lansdowne Portrait" of Washington shows him wearing the formal dress he assumed for the levees. See Richard G. Miller, "The Federal City, 1783–1800," in *Philadelphia: A 300-Year History*, ed. Russell F. Weigley (New York, 1982), 178.

14. "Lady Henrietta Liston's Journal of Washington's 'Resignation,' Retirement, and Death," ed. James C. Nicholls *Pennsylvania Magazine of History & Biography* 95 (1971): 514.

15. *The Diary of William Maclay and Other Notes on Senate Debates*, ed. Kenneth R. Bowling and Helen E. Veit (Baltimore, 1988), 342.

16. *Aurora*, 2 January 1793.

17. *Aurora*, 23 January 1793. The use of the pseudonym "Sydney" was common in the 1790s, just as it had been during the 1770s. Algernon Sydney's (1623–1683) writings, his reputation, and his martyrdom turned him into a "Rebel-Saint" in the years after his death. It was quite significant that an American correspondent would invoke his name in the 1790s, for it identified the author's target—in this case George Washington—as a tyrant. See Peter Karsten, *Patriot-Heroes in England and America: Political Symbolism and Changing Values over Three Centuries* (Madison, 1978), 18–20, 39–46, 59–64.

18. Benjamin Franklin Bache to Richard Bache, Philadelphia, 3 February 1793, Bache Papers—Castle Collection, APS.

19. *Aurora*, 29 January 1793, 7 December 1792. For more on Washington's ceremonial coach see Watson, *Annals of Philadelphia*, I: 581–82.

20. William Maclay, *Sketches of Debate in the First Senate of the United States in 1789–90–91* (1880) (New York, 1969), 1 May 1789, 20–21. For a discussion of Adams's position, see James H. Hutson, "John Adams' Title Campaign," *New England Quarterly* 41 (1968): 30–39.

21. Maclay, *Sketches of Debate*, 20–21.

22. David Stuart to George Washington, 14 July 1789, in *Papers of Washington: Presidential Series*, II: 199.

23. *New-York Journal*, 21 May 1789.

24. *New-York Journal*, 19 December 1792.

25. "PINCKNEYVILLE, (S.C.) APRIL 7," *Aurora*, 15 May 1794.

26. Minutes of the Democratic Society of Pennsylvania, 9 January 1794, HSP.

27. "Communication from the Society at Charleston," *Aurora*, 3 April 1794.

28. "Declaration of the Constitutional Society of Boston," *Aurora*, 6 February 1794. See also Eugene Perry Link, *Democratic-Republican Societies, 1790–1800* (New York, 1942), and Philip S. Foner, ed., *The Democratic-Republican Societies, 1790–1800: A Documentary Sourcebook of Constitutions, Declarations, Addresses, Resolutions, and Toasts* (Westport, 1976).

29. Minutes of the Democratic Society of Pennsylvania, 3 July 1793, 27 March 1794, HSP.

30. "An Address from the Massachusetts Constitutional Society . . . ," *Boston Gazette*, 5 January 1795.

31. "Introduction to the Constitution of the Norwalk Republican Society," *Bee*, 4 April 1798.

32. At least 30 printers and publishers were members of Democratic Republican societies, which helps explain why these organizations were able to use newspapers to such good effect. See Foner, *The Democratic-Republican Societies*, 9, and Michael Durey, "Thomas Paine's Apostles: Radical Emigres and the Triumph of Jeffersonian Republicanism," *William and Mary Quarterly* 3d ser. 44 (1987): 682–83.

33. *Boston Gazette*, 26 September 1791.

34. Hamilton, "Report on the Establishment of a Mint," *The Papers of Alexander Hamilton*, VII: 603–4, 567. For more on the emblems appearing on the coins of this era see Cornelius Vermeule, *Numismatic Art in America: Aesthetics of the United States Coinage* (Cambridge, 1971), 7–8, 9, 10–11; *Catalogue of Coins, Tokens, and Medals in the Numismatic Collection of the Mint of the United States at Philadelphia, PA* (Washington, 1912), 10; Charles T. Tatum, "The Beginnings of United States Coinage," *American Journal of Numismatic and Archaeological Societies* 29 (1895): 70–72; Schwartz, *George Washington*, 41–42.

35. Don Taxay, *The U.S. Mint and Coinage: An Illustrated History from 1776 to the Present* (New York, 1966), 58–59.

36. *The Debates and Proceedings in the Congress of the United States; With an Appendix, Containing Important State Papers And Public Documents, and All the Laws of a Public Nature; with a Copious Index* (Washington, 1849), III: 483, 485.

37. Ibid., 487–88.

38. Ibid., 488–89, 489.

39. Brooke Hindle, *David Rittenhouse* (Princeton, 1964), 331–32, 345–46, 355.

40. "GOLD COINAGE," *Jersey Chronicle*, 7 November 1795.

41. Hamilton, "Report on the Establishment of a Mint," 567.

42. "HARTFORD, October 26," *Norwich Packet*, 30 October 1789. See also *The Diaries of George Washington*, ed. Dorothy Twohig (Charlottesville, 1979), V: 445–97.

43. William Bentley, *The Diary of William Bentley, D.D. Pastor of the East Church, Salem, Massachusetts* (1905), (Gloucester, 1962), I: 130–31.

44. Robert Mills, "Description of George Washington's Visit to Charleston, S.C. 2–9 May, 1791," Manuscripts Collection, SCHS. See also *Diaries of Washington*, VI: 96–169, and Archibald Henderson, *George Washington's Southern Tour, 1791* (Boston, 1923).

45. *Aurora*, 1 June 1791.

46. "EDENTON, June 10," *State Gazette of North Carolina*, 10 June 1791.

47. One such celebration is described in Hutton, *The Rise and Fall of Merry England*, 222.

48. "GLOCESTER, (Cape Ann) FEB. 12," *Gazette of Maine*, 3 March 1791; "Charleston, Feb. 14," *Columbian Herald*, 14 February 1794; "Morristown, February 22, 1797," *New-Jersey Journal*, 1 March 1797; "SAVANNAH, February 24,"

Gazette US, 17 March 1797; "BRISTOL, Feb. 24th," *Herald US*, 1 March 1794; "Lexington, February 28," *Kentucky Gazette*, 28 February 1798; "GEORGE WASHINGTON'S BIRTH DAY," *Rutland Herald*, 26 February 1798.

49. *Gazette US*, 14 March 1796.

50. *Gazette US*, 7 March 1797.

51. "PRESIDENT's BIRTH-DAY," *Albany Gazette*, 24 February 1797.

52. "PHILADELPHIA, February 27," *Gazette US*, 27 February 1797.

53. "GENERAL WASHINGTON'S BIRTHDAY," *Porcupine's Gazette*, 8 March 1797.

54. *Aurora*, 14 March 1798.

55. *New-York Journal*, 15 October 1790.

56. "THE PRESIDENT'S BIRTHDAY," *Independent Chronicle*, 18 February 1790.

57. *Aurora*, 23 April 1791.

58. Mirabeau, "Forerunners of Monarchy and Aristocracy in the United States," *Aurora*, 7 December 1792.

59. A DEMOCRAT, "For the GENERAL ADVERTISER," *Aurora*, 18 February 1793.

60. *Aurora*, 14 February 1794; A MILITIA MAN, "For the GENERAL ADVERTISER," *Aurora*, 21 February 1794.

61. "WARREN, FEBRUARY 23," *Herald US*, 23 February 1793.

62. "ANNAPOLIS, February 27," *Maryland Gazette*, 27 February 1794.

63. *National Gazette*, 27 February 1792.

64. *Aurora*, 11 March 1794.

65. *Massachusetts Mercury*, 23 February 1796.

66. *Aurora*, 1 March 1799.

67. *Gazette US*, 28 February 1795.

68. *American Minerva*, 31 July 1795; *Aurora*, 5 August 1795.

69. *Aurora*, 25 July 1794.

70. *Aurora*, 1 October 1795.

71. *Aurora*, 30 September 1795.

72. *Aurora*, 20 November 1795.

73. "MORE TREASON!" *Aurora*, 12 May 1797.

74. "PRESIDENT'S BIRTH DAY," *The Weekly Museum*, 25 February 1792. The writing and organization of the toasts is recounted in the Society of Tammany or Columbia Order, Committee of Amusement Minutes, October 24, 1791—February 23, 1792, Manuscripts Collection, NYPL.

75. "BOSTON, Feb. 23," *Aurora*, 5 March 1793. The more elite rites of celebration were recorded in "Washington's Birth-day," *Massachusetts Mercury*, 23 February 1793.

76. Bentley, *The Diary of William Bentley*, II: 173.

77. Elizabeth Drinker, 22 February 1798, *The Diary of Elizabeth Drinker*, ed. Elaine Forman Crane (Boston, 1991), II: 1006.

78. "PHILADELPHIA, Feb. 23, 1791," *Gazette US*, 23 February 1791.

79. "PHILADELPHIA, THURSDAY, February 28," *Aurora*, 28 February 1793.

80. "GLOCESTER, (Cape Ann) FEB. 12," *Gazette of Maine*, 3 March 1791.

81. "EDENTON, Feb.13," *State Gazette*, 13 February 1790.

82. "PRESIDENT'S BIRTH DAY," *Aurora*, 22 February 1792.

83. This sentiment was expressed in the final toast at a Washington's birthday feast in Georgetown, reported in "GEORGETOWN, FEB. 27," *Aurora*, 7 March 1795. For an examination of this gendered "correctness of manners," see Susan Stabile, "'I Saw Great Fabius Come in State': Philadelphia Women's Court Poetry in the Age of Washington," unpublished paper presented at the annual meeting of the Society of Historians of the Early American Republic, Chapel Hill, N.C., July 1994.

84. "PHILADELPHIA, FEBRUARY 25," *Aurora*, 25 February 1795. The best examination of women's lack of legal and political identity during this period is Linda K. Kerber, "The Paradox of Women's Citizenship in the Early Republic: The Case of *Martin vs. Massachusetts*, 1805," *American Historical Review* 97 (1992): 349–78.

85. *Aurora*, 14 February 1794.

86. "Female Patriotism," *Maryland Gazette*, 17 March 1796. The concept of Republican Motherhood was first put forward by Linda K. Kerber in "The Republican Mother: Women and the Enlightenment—An American Perspective," *American Quarterly* 28 (1976): 187–205, and then again in her *Women of the Republic: Intellect and Ideology in Revolutionary America* (Chapel Hill, 1980), 269–88. For two decades the construct has enjoyed great popularity amongst women's and early national historians, for it allows for female agency within the domestic sphere. However, as Kerber makes very clear, this ideology was as restricting as it was liberating.

87. Bentley, *The Diary of William Bentley*, II, 325; Drinker, 25 December 1799, *Diary*, II, 1249.

88. *Gazette of the United States*, 20 December 1799.

89. Bentley, *The Diary of William Bentley*, II, 325.

90. Margaret Bayard Smith to Mary Ann Smith, New York City, 26 December 1799, Rebecca Gratz Collection, Library of Congress. I am grateful to Susan Branson for sharing her copy of this source.

91. Drinker, 27 December 1799, *Diary*, II: 1250–51.

92. Margaret Bayard Smith to Mary Ann Smith, New York City, 26 December 1799.

93. Henry Sewall, quoted in Laurel Thatcher Ulrich, *A Midwife's Tale: The Life of Martha Ballard, Based on Her Diary, 1785–1812* (New York, 1992), 32.

94. "Louisville, January 13, 1800," *Augusta Chronicle*, 18 January 1800.

95. "Lexington, January 30," *Kentucky Gazette*, 23 January 1800.

96. "AUGUSTA, Feb. 8," *Augusta Chronicle*, 8 February 1800; Bentley, *The Diary of William Bentley*, II: 325–26.

97. "FUNERAL PROCESSION," *Weekly Museum*, 28 December 1799.

98. "FUNERAL PROCESSION," *Weekly Museum*, 4 January 1800.

99. Ibid. See chapter five for further discussion of the black cockade.

100. Ibid.

101. Ibid. John L. Brooke, "Ancient Lodges and Self-Created Societies: Voluntary Associations and the Public Sphere in the Early Republic," unpublished

paper presented at the United States Capitol Historical Society Conference, 1990.

102. See, for example, *Gazette US*, 23 December 1799.

103. *Gazette US*, 27 December 1799.

104. *Aurora*, 27 December 1799. Benjamin Franklin Bache died during the yellow fever epidemic of 1798. His widow, Margaret Bache, continued publication of the *Aurora* with the assistance of the radical Irish emigre William Duane who had worked in the *Aurora* offices under Benjamin Franklin Bache. A year later Duane had married Margaret and assumed full editorial control, and he developed the *Aurora* into a national Republican daily. See Durey, "Thomas Paine's Apostles," 683, and James Tagg, *Benjamin Franklin Bache and the Philadelphia Aurora* (Philadelphia, 1991), 398–401. Duane himself led one of Philadelphia's Republican militia units during the funeral procession for Washington.

105. N[athaniel] Coverly, *The Death of General Washington, With Some Remarks on Jeffersonian Policy* (Boston, n.d.), Isaiah Thomas Collection of Ballads, American Antiquarian Society. Examples of these clerical eulogies abound: typical of the genre are, Joseph Dana, *A Discourse on the Character and Death of General George Washington . . . Delivered at Ipswich on the 22D. February, A.D. 1800 . . .* (Newburyport, 1800); John M. Brooks, *An Eulogy on General Washington: Delivered Before the Inhabitants of the Town of Medford, Agreeably to their Vote, and at the Request of their Committee. on the 13th of January, 1800 . . .* (Boston, 1800); Frederick W. Hotchkiss, *An Oration Delivered at Saybrook on Saturday February 22d, 1800: the Day Set Apart by the Recommendation of Congress for the People of the United States to Testify their Grief for the Death of General George Washington; Who Died December 14, 1799* (New London, 1800). See also David Hackett Fischer, *The Revolution of American Conservatism: The Federalist Party in the Age of Jefferson* (New York, 1965), 114–23; Mayo, *Myths and Men*, 27; Robert P. Hay, "George Washington: American Moses," *American Quarterly* 21 (1969): 780–91.

106. See, for example, "PRESIDENT'S BIRTH DAY," *Columbian Centinel*, 31 October 1798; "WARREN, SATURDAY, NOVEMBER 10," *Herald US*, 10 November 1798.

107. *Porcupine's Gazette*, 2 November 1797.

108. *Aurora*, 4 November 1797.

109. Ibid.

110. *Aurora*, 7 November 1797.

111. *Aurora*, 11 November 1797.

112. "BOSTON, August 18. REPUBLICAN GRATITUDE," *Gazette US*, 23 August 1797; "BOSTON, August 19," *Gazette US*, 25 August 1797.

113. "NEW YORK, OCT. 19," *Aurora*, 21 October 1797.

114. *Porcupine's Gazette*, 11 November 1797.

115. Elizabeth Drinker, 10 November 1797, *Diary*, II: 978.

116. "NEW-YORK, AUGUST 28. FROM A CORRESPONDENT," *Aurora*, 1 September 1797.

117. *Aurora*, 27 July 1799.

118. *Porcupine's Gazette*, 14 April to 31 December 1798. I found 56 addresses reprinted in Cobbett's paper during this period. 25 came from groups of citizens, 12 from merchants, judicial officials, militia officers, and government officials, 7 from

militia companies, 7 from young men and students, 2 each from masonic lodges and branches of the Cincinnati, and one from a group of British citizens resident in the United States.

119. [William Austin], *A Selection of the Patriotic Addresses, To the President of the United States. Together With The President's Answers. Presented in the Year One Thousand Seven Hundred and Ninety-Eight, and the Twenty-Second of the Independence of America* (Boston, 1798).

120. THE ADDRESS of the CITIZENS of ALBANY to the PRESIDENT of the UNITED STATES," *Albany Gazette*, 25 May 1798.

121. "To the President of the United States," *Companion*, 9 June 1798.

122. "Boston, April 24," *Gazette US*, 28 April 1798.

123. Ibid.

124. *Rutland Herald*, 25 June 1798.

125. Austin, *A Selection of the Patriotic Addresses*, 55.

126. "Address to Congress from Virginia," *Companion*, 9 June 1798; *Kentucky Gazette*, 1, 8, 15, 22, 29 August, 5 September 1798.

127. "NOTICE," *Guardian*, 5 May 1798.

128. *Porcupine's Gazette*, 22 October 1798. For a discussion of other such presentations, see Susan Branson, *Women and Public Space: Gender, Politics, and Society in the 1790s* (forthcoming), chapter six.

129. Benjamin Franklin, *The Autobiography* (New York, 1990), 107.

130. *Porcupine's Gazette*, 2 May 1798.

131. *Porcupine's Gazette*, 7 May 1798.

132. *Jeffersonian America: Notes on the United States of America Collected in the Years 1805–6–7 and 11–12 by Sir Augustus John Foster, Bart.*, ed. Richard Beale Davis (San Marino, 1954), 51, 52, 49–50.

133. These rules are reprinted in Jay Fliegelman, *Declaring Independence: Jefferson, Natural Language, and the Culture of Performance* (Stanford, 1993), 113–14.

134. William Plumer, quoted in Robert M. Johnstone, Jr., *Jefferson and the Presidency: Leadership in the Young Republic* (Ithaca, 1978), 58. The Federalist senator was as disgusted with Jefferson's informal dress as Sir Augustus John Foster, but he accurately conceded that Democratic Republicans would view it as suitable "court dress" for the "democratic" administration. Plumer, in Johnstone, *Jefferson and the Presidency*, 58.

135. Johnstone, *Jefferson and the Presidency*, 58–59.

136. *Gazette US*, 3 March 1797.

137. *Aurora*, 12 July 1798.

138. *Aurora*, 7 January 1801.

139. *Aurora*, 13, 7 March 1801.

140. "From a Correspondent at Beaver Town," *Pittsburgh Gazette*, 20 March 1801.

141. "REPUBLICAN FESTIVAL," *Guardian of Liberty*, 7 March 1801.

142. *Bee*, 3 April 1801.

143. "MURFREESBOROUGH, March 5," *Aurora*, 15 April 1801.

144. "TOASTS," *Aurora*, 9 March 1801.

145. *Guardian of Liberty*, 3 January 1801.

146. *Aurora*, 16 March 1801.

147. "NEWPORT, Saturday, March 21, 1801," *Guardian of Liberty*, 21 March 1801.

Chapter Three

1. Among the better studies of the early history of the commemoration of Independence Day are Robert Pettus Hay, "Freedom's Jubilee: One Hundred Years of the Fourth of July, 1776 to 1876" (Ph.D. diss., University of Kentucky, 1967); Susan G. Davis, *Parades and Power: Street Theatre in Nineteenth-Century Philadelphia* (Berkeley, 1988); Diana Karter Appelbaum, *The Glorious Fourth: An American Holiday* (New York, 1989); Len Travers, "Hurrah for the Fourth: Patriotism, Politics, and Independence Day in Federalist Boston, 1783–1818," *Essex Institute Historical Collections* 125 (1989): 129–61, and "'The Brightest Day in our Calendar': Independence Day in Boston and Philadelphia, 1776–1826" (Ph.D. diss., Boston University, 1992); Albrecht Koschnik, "Political Conflict and Public Contest: Rituals of National Celebration in Philadelphia, 1788–1815," *Pennsylvania Magazine of History and Biography* 118 (1994): 209–48; David Waldstreicher, "Rites of Rebellion, Rites of Assent: Celebrations, Print Culture, and the Origins of American Nationalism," *Journal of American History* 82 (1995): 37–61, and *The Making of American Nationalism: Celebrations and Political Culture, 1776–1820* (Chapel Hill, forthcoming).

2. Thomas P. Cope, *Philadelphia Merchant: The Diary of Thomas P. Cope, 1800–1851*, ed. Eliza Cope Harrison (South Bend, 1978), 67.

3. Francis Dana, manuscript entitled "Charge to the Grand Jury, 1791," Dana Family Papers, MHS. See also Stanley Elkins and Eric McKitrick, *The Age of Federalism* (New York, 1993); David Hackett Fischer, *The Revolution of American Conservatism: The Federalist Party in the Era of Jeffersonian Democracy* (New York, 1965); Linda K. Kerber, *Federalists in Dissent: Imagery and Ideology in Jeffersonian America* (Ithaca, 1970), and James Roger Sharp, *American Politics in the Early Republic: The New Nation in Crisis* (New Haven, 1993).

4. A few political historians such as Alfred F. Young have acknowledged the importance of popular politics in the history of the Democratic Republican party. See Young, *The Democratic Republicans of New York: The Origins, 1763–1797* (Chapel Hill, 1967). Richard Buel acknowledges the significance of popular politics, but is generally satisfied with discussion of what Federalist and Democratic Republican leaders thought of the phenomenon. See Buel, *Securing the Revolution: Ideology in American Politics, 1789–1815* (Ithaca, 1972). And indeed most of those who write about the Democratic Republican party tend to emphasize the thoughts and actions of its leaders, and all but ignore those below them. See, for example, Noble E. Cunningham, *The Jeffersonian Republicans: Formation of Party Organization* (Chapel Hill, 1957); Lance Banning, *The Jeffersonian Persuasion: Evolution of a Party Ideology* (Ithaca, 1978); Elkins and McKitrick, *The Age of Federalism*; and Sharp, *American Politics in the Early Republic*.

Recently historians interested in festive culture and public display have begun exploring the ways in which Independence Day celebrations figured in the development of American nationalism, but the significance of July Fourth rites and rhetoric in the construction of the Democratic Republican party and its policies remain largely unexplored. According to Len Travers, Boston's Independence Day festivals provided "an occasion for acting out the people's understanding of the Revolution, and reaffirming what it meant to be an American." Both Federalists and Democratic Republicans constructed alternative visions of national identity on each Fourth of July, and this was, Travers asserts, the basis of the partisan animosities that characterized the Fourth. Albrecht Koschnik has undertaken a similar study of Independence Day festivities in Philadelphia, concluding that citizens constructed and employed these rites "to legitimate the participants' aspirations to represent the nation by using a means that created an image of their own unity, and, ultimately, of national unity." For all their partisan differences, the goal here was an appearance of national unity. See Travers, "Hurrah for the Fourth," 159, 131, and Koschnik, "Political Conflict and Public Contest," 248.

While Susan Davis has agreed that political differences informed Independence Day celebrations in the early republic, she chose to focus on the fact that for all their political differences, Americans "shared common notions about the proper way to celebrate the anniversary." And in an extremely sophisticated study, David Waldstreicher has explored the larger significance of this sense of commonality, suggesting that "American nationalism emerged from the conjunction of local celebrations and their reproduction in the press." Newspaper descriptions of celebrations from both far and near furnished readers with examples of how patriotic citizens should behave, while simultaneously proving that such patriotic behavior was commonplace. The reality of an emerging American nationalism was situated less in any real social or ideological unity, he has argued, than in the rites and rhetoric of Americans gathered together at celebratory events such as Independence Day. See Davis, *Parades and Power*, 41, and Waldstreicher, "Rites of Rebellion, Rites of Assent," 37–38. See also his *The Making of American Nationalism*, chapter three.

5. Edwin G. Burrows, "Military Experience and the Origins of Federalism and Anti-Federalism," in *Aspects of Early New York Society and Politics*, ed. Jacob Judd and Irwin Polishook (Tarrytown, 1974), 83–92; Sidney Kaplan, "Veteran Officers and Politics in Massachusetts, 1783–1787," *William and Mary Quarterly* 3d ser. 9 (1952): 29–57.

6. "Extract of a letter from Trenton, dated July 6," *New-Jersey Journal*, 14 July 1790.

7. "Celebration of Independence," *Albany Gazette*, 6 July 1789; "Carlisle, July 8," *Carlisle Gazette*, 8 July 1789; "Fourth of July," *Independent Chronicle*, 8 July 1790; "Elizabeth Town, July 7," *New-Jersey Journal*, 7 July 1790; "Extract of a letter from Newbern, July 8," *State Gazette*, 16 July 1790; "Extract of a letter from Blandensburg, July 5," *Albany Gazette*, 28 July 1791; "LEXINGTON, July 9," *Kentucky Gazette*, 9 July 1791; "CAMDEN, July 4," *South Carolina Gazette*, 10 July 1792.

8. "Extract of a letter from Trenton, dated July 6," *New-Jersey Journal*, 14 July 1790.

9. Harrison Gray Otis to Elizabeth Otis, 5 July 1792, New York City, quoted in Travers, "Hurrah for the Fourth," 129; *Moreau de St. Mery's American Journey*, ed. Kenneth Roberts and Anna B. Roberts (Garden City, 1947), 336.

10. Elizabeth Drinker, 4 July 1791, *The Diary of Elizabeth Drinker*, ed. Elaine Forman Crane (Boston, 1991), I: 459.

11. "Elizabeth Town, July 7," *New-Jersey Journal*, 7 July 1790.

12. "CARLISLE, JULY 7," *Carlisle Gazette*, 7 July 1790.

13. For an account of the presentation of one such address to President Washington, see William Loughton Smith to Edward Rutledge, 4 July 1790, William Loughton Smith Papers, SCHS. A typical set of militia "ORDERS" was published in the *Aurora*, 4 July 1792.

14. *Aurora*, 4 July 1793. For examples of these "orders," see *Aurora*, 4 July 1792, 3 July 1795, and *Gazette US*, 1 July 1796.

15. *Aurora*, 6 July 1793.

16. *Aurora*, 7 July 1794.

17. The "Committee of Arrangements" elected by members of the Democratic Society of Pennsylvania in 1794 included McClenachan, Leib, Ferguson, and Benjamin Franklin Bache. See the Minutes of the Democratic Society of Pennsylvania, 26 June 1794, HSP. An example of an elected committee of the Tammany Society in New York City producing a slate of Independence Day toasts, which were then approved by the members of the society can be found in the Minutes of the Society of Tammany or Columbian Order, 3 July 1815, NYPL.

18. These figures are based on a survey of 38 July Fourth civic feasts that took place in Philadelphia between 1793 and 1801, which were reported in the *Aurora*, the *Gazette US*, and *Porcupine's Gazette*. Nine Federalist feasts were recorded, of which 7 (77.7%) took place in hotels and inns, while 2 (22.2%) were held outdoors. Of twenty-nine Republican feasts, 16 (55.2%) were staged outdoors, 11 (37.9%) took place in taverns and private homes, and 2 (6.9%) were in hotels or inns. For a discussion of the developing social differences between elite hotels and inns and all other eating and drinking establishments, see Peter Thompson, "A Social History of Philadelphia's Taverns, 1683–1800" (Ph.D. diss., University of Pennsylvania, 1989), 260–360, 441–527.

19. *Gazette US*, 7 July 1794.

20. *Aurora*, 9 July 1794.

21. *Aurora*, 8 July 1794.

22. I have surveyed thirty five newspapers covering the period 1789–1801, drawn from every state in the union, including Kentucky, Vermont and even the district of Maine. While some newspapers were not in print for this entire period, when taken together they provide a good sense of the dramatic rise in the number of Independence Day celebrations during this era.

23. "NEWARK, July 10," *Aurora*, 15 July 1793. My estimates of population are drawn from Riley Moffat, *Population History of Eastern U.S. Cities and Towns, 1790–1870* (Metuchen, 1992), 97.

24. *American Minerva*, 7 July 1795; Moffat, *Population History*, 127.

25. "NEWARK, July 8," *Gazette US*, 10 July 1795.

26. "WILMINGTON, JULY 8," *Aurora*, 13 July 1795; Moffat, *Population History*, 10.

27. "ANTI-ARISTOCRAT," *Boston Gazette*, 2 March 1789.

28. "ALEXANDRIA, July 6," *Aurora*, 12 July 1793; "CHESTERTOWN, JULY 9," *Aurora*, 13 July 1793; "AMERICAN INDEPENDENCE: FAYETTE-VILLE, July 9," *Aurora*, 20 July 1793; "HUDSON, July 11," *Aurora*, 17 July 1793; "NEWARK, July 10," *Aurora*, 15 July 1793; "PHILADELPHIA, SATURDAY JULY 6," *Aurora*, 6 July 1793.

29. On the liberty cap as a radical symbol in the age of the French Revolution see J. David Harden, "Liberty Caps and Liberty Trees," *Past and Present* 146 (1995): 66–102, and James Epstein, "Understanding the Cap of Liberty: Symbolic Practice and Social Conflict in Early Nineteenth-Century England," *Past and Present* 122 (1989): 75–118.

30. "NEWARK, July 10," *Aurora*, 15 July 1793.

31. "NEWARK, July 10," *Aurora*, 15 July 1793. There were approximately 500 people of all ages and races living in Newark in 1795. See Moffat, *Population History*, 97.

32. Minutes of the Democratic Society of Pennsylvania, 12, 19, 26 June, 1794, Manuscripts Collection, HSP.

33. *Aurora*, 5 July 1794.

34. "BALTIMORE, July 8," *Gazette US*, 11 July 1794; "MORRISTOWN, July 4, 1749 [sic]," *New-Jersey Journal*, 16 July 1794.

35. "From Monmouth, July 4," *Guardian*, 22 July 1794.

36. "NEWPORT, July 7," *Museum*, 7 July 1794.

37. "PORTSMOUTH, JULY 8," *Aurora*, 21 July 1794; *Delaware Gazette*, 12 July 1794.

38. "LYNCHBURG, Vir. July 19," *Gazette US*, 30 July 1794.

39. "PORTSMOUTH, JULY 8," *Aurora*, 21 July 1794.

40. I have examined eighty complete sets of July Fourth toasts for 1793, 1794 and 1795, drunk by groups in cities as large as Boston, New York, and Philadelphia, and in communities as small as Bristol, Rhode Island, Fayetteville, North Carolina, Rutland, Vermont, and Union, South Carolina.

41. "ANNAPOLIS, July 11," *Maryland Gazette*, 11 July 1793.

42. "ELIZABETH-TOWN, July 10," *Aurora*, 15 July 1793; "From a corre-spondent at Schenectady," *Albany Gazette*, 29 July 1793. For a detailed discussion of popular enthusiasm for Paine in the early 1790s, see Alfred F. Young, "*Common Sense* and *The Rights of Man* in America: The Celebration and Damnation of Tho-mas Paine," in *Science, Mind, and Art: Essays on Science and the Humanistic Under-standing in Art, Epistemology, Religion, and Ethics in Honor of Robert S. Cohen*, ed. Kostas Gavroglu et al. (Dordrecht, 1995), III: 418–28.

43. "Carlisle, July 9," *Carlisle Gazette*, 9 July 1794; "SUSSEX, July 4, 1794," *New-Jersey Journal*, 23 July 1794.

44. "LYNCHBURG, Vir. July 19," *Gazette US*, 30 July 1794.

45. "OF TOASTS," *Columbian Herald* 23 June 1791.

46. Peter Thompson, "'The Friendly Glass': Drink and Gentility in Colonial

Philadelphia," *Pennsylvania Magazine of History and Biography* 113 (1989): 560–61. See also Richard J. Hooker, "The American Revolution Seen Through the Bottom of a Wine Glass," *William and Mary Quarterly* 3d ser. 11 (1954): 53–58, and James Epstein, "Radical Dining, Toasting, and Symbolic Expression in Early Nineteenth-Century Lancashire: Rituals of Solidarity," *Albion* 20 (1988): 271–79.

47. "Bergen County, Hackensack, July 8, 1794," *New-Jersey Journal*, 23 July 1794; "NEW-YORK, July 8," *American Minerva*, 8 July 1794.

48. "NEWPORT, July 7," *Museum*, 7 July 1794.

49. "ELKTON, Cæcil County, State of Maryland, July 4," *Aurora*, 11 July 1795; "WILMINGTON, JULY 8," *Aurora*, 13 July 1795.

50. "NEW-YORK, July 5," *American Minerva*, 5 July 1794.

51. William Bentley, *The Diary of William Bentley, D.D. Pastor of the East Church Salem, Massachusetts* (Salem, 1907), II: 97. For details of the Cincinnati celebrations in Philadelphia see "PHILADELPHIA, MONDAY JULY 7," *Aurora*, 7 July 1794, and *Gazette US*, 7 July 1794.

52. *New-Jersey Journal*, 9 July 1794.

53. "HARTFORD, July 14," *Gazette US*, 18 July 1794.

54. See "NEW-YORK, July 5," *American Minerva*, 5 July 1794; *Moreau de St. Mery's American Journey*, 125; "HAIL! INDEPENDENCE HAIL!," *Weekly Museum*, 5 July 1794.

55. "Bergen County, Hackensack, July 8, 1794," *New-Jersey Journal*, 23 July 1794.

56. "LYNCHBURG, Vir. July 19," *Gazette US*, 30 July 1794.

57. *Farmer's Library*, 29 July 1794.

58. "MONMOUTH, SATURDAY, *August* 1," *Jersey Chronicle*, 1 August 1795.

59. *New-Jersey Journal*, 8 July 1795.

60. See, for example, "BALTIMORE, JULY 7," *Aurora*, 10 July 1795; "ANNIVERSARY OF AMERICAN INDEPENDENCE," *Aurora*, 7 July 1795; *Aurora*, 16 July 1795; "WILMINGTON, JULY 8," *Aurora*, 13 July 1795.

61. "ELKTON, Cæcil County, State of Maryland, July 4," *Aurora*, 11 July 1795.

62. "NEW-YORK, July 8," *Daily Advertiser*, 8 July 1795.

63. *Aurora*, 15 July 1795.

64. The celebrations of both the Tammany Society and Snowden's artillery company were featured in "NEW-YORK, July 8," *Daily Advertiser*, 8 July 1795; see "ANNIVERSARY OF AMERICAN INDEPENDENCE," *Aurora*, 7 July 1795 for an account of the Philadelphia celebration, and *Aurora*, 15 July 1795 for the rites in Princeton.

65. Benjamin Franklin Bache to Margaret Hartman Bache, Stanford, 3 July 1795, Bache Papers—Castle Collection, APS.

66. "Fairhaven, July 4th, 1795," *Rutland Herald*, 13 July 1795.

67. "HARRISBURGH, JULY 6," *Aurora*, 14 July 1795.

68. "NEW JERSEY," *Aurora*, 20 July 1795.

69. "NEW-YORK, JULY 11," *Aurora*, 14 July 1795.

70. *Albany Gazette*, 13 July 1795.

71. "MONMOUTH, SATURDAY, JULY 11," *Jersey Chronicle*, 11 July 1795; "QUEEN ANN'S COUNTY, MARYLAND, JULY 5, 1795," *Aurora*, 8 July 1795.

72. "WILMINGTON, JULY 8," *Aurora*, 13 July 1795; "QUEEN ANN'S COUNTY, MARYLAND. JULY 5, 1795," *Aurora*, 8 July 1795.

73. "ANNIVERSARY OF AMERICAN INDEPENDENCE" *Aurora*, 7 July 1795.

74. "BALTIMORE, JULY 7," *Aurora*, 10 July 1795.

75. "Fairhaven, July 4th, 1795," *Rutland Herald*, 13 July 1795.

76. "DOVER, JULY 4," *Aurora*, 14 July 1795; *Daily Advertiser*, 8 July 1795.

77. "GENERAL ORDERS," *Aurora*, 3 July 1795.

78. A MILITIA-MAN, "To the MILITIA of PHILADELPHIA," *Aurora*, 3 July 1795. For a full discussion of the Jay Treaty, see Jerald A. Combs, *The Jay Treaty: Political Battleground of the Founding Fathers* (Berkeley, 1970).

79. *Independent Gazetteer* (Philadelphia), 8 July 1795.

80. "PHILADELPHIA, July 9," *Gazette US*, 9 July 1795; Drinker, 4 July 1795, *Diary*, I: 700.

81. *Independent Gazetteer*, July 8, 1795.

82. OLD SOLDIER, "For the Aurora," *Aurora*, 30 June 1796.

83. "PHILADELPHIA—JULY 12," *Aurora*, 12 July 1796.

84. "FOR THE GAZETTE OF THE UNITED STATES," *Gazette US*, 14 July 1796.

85. "PHILADELPHIA, MONDAY—JULY 11. COMMUNICATION," *Aurora*, 11 July 1796.

86. TOBY SWIG, "A PROCLAMATION, FOURTH OF JULY, 1796," *Aurora*, 2 July 1796.

87. *Kentucky Gazette*, 16 July 1796; "MORRIS-TOWN, JULY 9, 1796" *New Jersey Journal*, 13 July 1796.

88. "WHIGSTOWN," *Aurora*, 18 July 1796.

89. "Celebration of the 4th of July, 1796, at Bristol, being the 21st year of the Independence of the United States of America," *Herald US*, 9 July 1796.

90. *Albany Gazette*, 8 July 1795.

91. "FOURTH OF JULY!" *Eagle*, 11 July 1796.

92. "YORK, July 5," *Lancaster Journal*, 8 July 1796.

93. Ibid.

94. Ibid.

95. James Forten, *A Series of Letters by a Man of Color* (Philadelphia, 1813), as excerpted in Herbert Aptheker, ed., *A Documentary History of the Negro People in the United States* (New York, 1951), 64. See also Jean R. Soderlund, "Black Women in Colonial Pennsylvania," *Pennsylvania Magazine of History and Biography* 107 (1983): 55–56, Gary B. Nash, *Forging Freedom: The Formation of Philadelphia's Black Community, 1720–1840* (Cambridge, 1988), 172–211, and Winthrop D. Jordan, *White over Black: American Attitudes Toward the Negro, 1550–1812* (Chapel Hill, 1968), 375–402.

96. Cited in Nash, *Forging Freedom*, 177.

97. *New-York Evening Post*, 12 July 1804.

98. Waldstreicher, *The Making of American Nationalism*, chapter six; Nash,

Forging Freedom, 172–211, Davis, *Parades and Power*, 38–48, and Jordan, *White over Black*, 403–22.

    99. Fischer, *The Revolution of American Conservatism*, 29–72

    100. *Aurora*, 13 July 1797.

    101. "JULY 4," *Aurora*, 7 July 1797.

    102. *Aurora*, 11 July 1797.

    103. "ANNIVERSARY OF AMERICAN INDEPENDENCE," *Aurora*, 14 July 1797.

    104. "COMMUNICATED FOR PUBLICATION IN THE AURORA," *Aurora*, 12 July 1797.

    105. "CARLISLE, July 5," *Carlisle Gazette*, 5 July 1797.

    106. "FOURTH OF JULY," *New-Jersey Journal*, 5 July 1797; Moffat, *Population History*, 94.

    107. *Gazette US*, 5 July 1798.

    108. *Ibid.*

    109. *Porcupine's Gazette*, 5 July 1798.

    110. *Gazette US*, 5 July 1798.

    111. Fisher Ames to Timothy Pickering, Dedham, July 1798, in *Works of Fisher Ames: With a Selection from His Speeches and Correspondence*, ed. Seth Ames (1854) (New York, 1969), I: 231; *Return of the Whole Number of Persons Within the Several Districts of the United States, According to "An act providing for the second Census or Enumeration of the Inhabitants of the UNITED STATES"* (Washington, 1801), 8.

    112. "AUGUSTA, July 7," *Augusta Chronicle*, 7 July 1798.

    113. "From Wiscasset, July 6," *Kennebeck Intelligencer*, 13 July 1798.

    114. "Funeral of Jacobinism," *Porcupine's Gazette*, 14 July 1798.

    115. "NEWPORT, July 6," *Companion*, 6 July 1798; "Schenectady, July 5, 1798," *Albany Gazette*, 9 July 1798.

    116. *Philadelphia Gazette*, 9 July 1798; "LANCASTER, July 6," *Porcupine's Gazette*, 10 July 1798.

    117. "PATRIOTIC FAIR," *Evening Courier*, 3 August 1798.

    118. "PRINCETON, July 5," *Gazette US*, 11 July 1798.

    119. "York, Pennsylvania, July 17 [sic]," *Porcupine's Gazette*, 14 July 1798.

    120. "FOURTH OF JULY," *Aurora*, 26 July 1798.

    121. "NEWBURGH, (N.Y.) AUGUST 13," *Aurora*, 3 September 1798; "Lexington, July 11," *Kentucky Gazette*, 11 July 1798.

    122. "FOURTH OF JULY," *Aurora*, 16 July 1798.

    123. "Lexington, July 11," *Kentucky Gazette*, 11 July 1798; "Celebration of the officers of 40th Regiment and other citizens at Louisa Court House Virginia," *Aurora*, 20 July 1798.

    124. Celebration at Morristown, New Jersey," *Aurora*, 12 July 1798.

    125. "Celebration in Montgomery (N.Y.)," *Aurora*, 19 July 1798; *Aurora*, 7 July 1798.

    126. "Celebration in Duchess County, State of New York," *Aurora*, 12 July 1798; "FOURTH OF JULY," *Aurora*, 16 July 1798.

    127. "EASTON, JULY 5, 1798," *Aurora*, 12 July 1798; "Celebration in Sag-

harbour (N.Y.)," *Aurora*, 21 July 1798; "Celebration at Dover," *Aurora*, 12 July 1798.

128. "NEW-HAVEN, July 4," *Connecticut Courant*, 15 July 1799.

129. "July 5," *Porcupine's Gazette*, 5 July 1799.

130. "WARREN, SATURDAY, JULY 6," *Herald US*, 6 July 1799.

131. *Vermont Gazette*, 8 August 1799.

132. *Aurora*, 18 July 1799.

133. *Aurora*, 9 July 1799; Moffat, *Population History*, 63.

134. *Kentucky Gazette*, 25 July 1799; *Return of the Whole Number of Persons*, 2P.

135. *Carlisle Gazette*, 10 July 1799.

136. "PATERSON, JULY 4, 1799," *Aurora*, 11 July 1799.

137. *Aurora*, 6 July 1799.

138. "ANNIVERSARY FESTIVAL," *Aurora*, 11 July 1799.

139. "ANNIVERSARY FESTIVAL," *Aurora*, 11 July 1799; "Jefferson's Village, July 4, 1799," *Aurora*, 11 July 1799; "NEW-LONDON, JULY 10. FROM THE BEE," *Aurora*, 16 July 1799; "CELEBRATION OF THE IVth OF JULY," *Weekly Museum*, 6 July 1799; *Aurora*, 6 July 1799.

140. *Aurora*, 10 July 1799.

141. *Aurora*, 6 July 1799.

142. "BLOOMFIELD, FOURTH OF JULY, 1799," *Aurora*, 11 July 1799.

143. *Aurora*, 30 July 1799.

144. *Aurora*, 7 July 1798.

145. *Aurora*, 7 July 1798.

146. The political allegiances of the militia companies that participated in the 1799 July Fourth parade (listed in the *Aurora*, July 8, 1799) can be deduced from William Duane's description of Philadelphia's symbolic funeral procession for George Washington. In his account of this event, Duane listed the political affiliations of all of the militia companies that took part. See *Aurora*, 27 December 1799.

Of twenty-six Independence Day feasts held in Philadelphia between 1793 and 1801, which were reported in the *Aurora*, the *Gazette US*, and *Porcupine's Gazette*, nineteen featured toasts that were clearly Republican in sentiment.

147. W. A. Newman Dorland, "The Second Troop of Philadelphia City Cavalry," *Pennsylvania Magazine of History and Biography*, 45 (1921): 364–87; 46 (1922): 57–77, 154–72, 262–71, 346–65; 47 (1923): 67–79, 147–77, 262–76, 357–75; 48 (1924): 270–84, 372–82; "Pay roll of the Detachment of the Vol: Lt: Infantry Company . . . June 1793," Records of the Comptroller General, Military Accounts, RG-4, Microfilm Reel 363, PSA; James Hardie, *The Philadelphia Directory and Register: Containing the Names, Occupations and Places of Abode of the Citizens, Arranged in Alphabetical Order . . .* (Philadelphia, 1793); Billy G. Smith, *The "Lower Sort": Philadelphia's Laboring People, 1750–1800* (Ithaca, 1990), 164. For a general history of the militia during this period, see John K. Mahon, *The American Militia: Decade of Decision, 1789–1800* (Gainesville, 1960).

148. *Aurora*, 8 July 1799. This report listed the names and the commanders of each militia company, allowing a comparison with an account of the December 26,

1799 procession commemorating the death of Washington, which listed the party affiliations of most of Philadelphia's militia companies. See *Aurora*, 27 December 1799; *Aurora*, 7 July 1800.

149. *Aurora*, 8 July 1800, 9 July 1800.

150. *Aurora*, 9 July 1800.

151. "THE CINCINNATI," *Aurora*, 7 July 1800.

152. *Aurora*, 12 November 1799.

153. "EASTON," January 24," *Aurora*, 7 February 1801; "LANCASTER RE-PUBLICAN FESTIVAL," *Aurora*, 11 March 1801. I have found the following to be particularly useful in a consideration of the ideology and role of the Declaration of Independence in American politics: Gary Wills, *Inventing America: Jefferson's Declaration of Independence* (New York, 1978), and Daniel T. Rodgers, *Contested Truths: Keywords in American Politics Since Independence* (New York, 1987).

154. Drinker, 4 July 1801, *Diary*, II: 1424.

155. *Gazette US*, 6 July 1801.

156. "TWENTY-SIXTH ANNIVERSARY OF EMANCIPATION FROM THE BRITISH YOKE," *Aurora*, 7 July 1801.

157. *Aurora*, 7 July 1800.

158. "FESTIVITIES, ON THE FOURTH OF JULY, 1801," *Aurora*, 10 July 1801.

159. "NATIONAL FESTIVAL," *Aurora*, 12 July 1800; *Return of the Whole Number of Persons*, 2A.

160. "LEWIS-TOWN, (Mifflin County)," *Aurora*, 25 July 1800; *Return of the Whole Number of Persons*, 2E.

161. "Federal Celebration," *Guardian of Liberty*, 11 July 1801; *Return of the Whole Number of Persons*, 26.

162. "AUGUSTA, July 5," *Augusta Chronicle*, 5 July 1800; "MIFFLIN-TOWN, July 9," *Carlisle Gazette*, 16 July 1800.

163. "AT BALTIMORE," *Aurora*, 11 July 1800; "FESTIVAL OF INDEPEN-DENCE," *Aurora*, 7 July 1800.

164. "NEWPORT, Saturday, July 25, 1801," *Guardian of Liberty*, 25 July 1801.

165. Cope, *Philadelphia Merchant*, 67.

166. "CHESTERTOWN, July 4, 1801," *Aurora*, 8 July 1801.

167. "New-York, July 7," *Aurora*, 23 July 1801.

168. "HOPEROOK, MASSACHUSETTS," *Aurora*, 23 July 1801.

169. "At Suffield, Connecticut," *Aurora*, 14 July 1801.

170. "At Mendham," *Aurora*, 23 July 1801.

171. "TWENTY-SIXTH ANNIVERSARY OF EMANCIPATION FROM THE BRITISH YOKE," *Aurora*, 7 July 1801.

172. "PHILADELPHIA, July 9," *Guardian of Liberty*, 18 July 1801.

173. *Aurora*, 8 July 1800.

174. The *New-York Evening Post* article was reprinted and commented on in the *Aurora*, 11 July 1804.

175. *Aurora*, 11 July 1804; "FROM THE BOSTON DEMOCRAT," *Aurora*, 18 July 1808.

176. Theodore Dwight, *An Oration, Delivered at New-Haven on the 7th of July, A.D., Before the Society of the Cincinnati, For the State of Connecticut, Assembled to Celebrate the Anniversary of American Independence* (Hartford, 1801), 15.

Chapter Four

1. Although he did not deal with popular political culture as such, it was Richard Hofstadter who pointed out that the lack of so much as a concept of a loyal opposition made oppositional politics particularly difficult for the Democratic Republicans. See Hofstadter, *The Idea of a Party System: The Rise of Legitimate Opposition in the United States, 1780–1840* (Berkeley, 1969), 1–39, 74–121.

2. See Charles Fraser, *Reminiscences of Charleston, Lately Published in the Charleston Courier, and Now Revised and Enlarged by the Author* (Charleston, 1854), 40–41; *New-York Journal*, 29 December 1792, and *Daily Advertiser*, 29 December 1792; *New-York Journal*, 6 February 1793; "RHODE-ISLAND," *Herald US*, 9 February 1793; *Gazette of Georgia*, 31 January 1793; "LEXINGTON, Feb. 16," *Kentucky Gazette*, 16 February 1793; "Celebration of the FEAST of LIBERTY and EQUALITY," *Independent Chronicle*, 31 January 1793.

For more on the festivals in France that to some degree inspired these American celebrations, see Mona Ozouf, *Festivals and the French Revolution* (1976), trans. Alan Sheridan (Cambridge, 1988); Noel Parker, *Portrayals of Revolution: Images, Debates and Patterns of Thought on the French Revolution* (Carbondale, 1990); Yves-Marie Bercé, *Fête et révolte: des mentalités populaires de XVIme au XVIIIme siècle* (Paris, 1976); Jean Ehard and Paul Villeneix, *Les fêtes de la révolution* (Paris, 1977).

3. "Celebration of the FEAST of LIBERTY and EQUALITY," *Independent Chronicle*, 31 January 1793.

4. *Life, Journals and Correspondence of Rev. Manasseh Cutler, LL.D.*, ed. William Parker Cutler and Julia Perkins Cutler (Cincinnati, 1888), I: 489.

5. "BOSTON, January 22," *New-York Journal*, 6 February 1793. This was the most complete account of the festival, combining as it did accounts from a variety of Boston newspapers, together with what may well have been letters from people who had witnessed the event.

6. "Celebration of the FEAST of LIBERTY and EQUALITY," *Independent Chronicle*, 31 January 1793.

7. "BOSTON, January 22," *New-York Journal*, 6 February 1793. See also "Celebration of the FEAST of LIBERTY and EQUALITY," *Independent Chronicle*, 31 January 1793.

For a complete discussion of the context and significance of this festival, See Simon P. Newman, "'Tis the Worlds Jubilee and Mankind Must Be Free: Boston Celebrates the Victory at Valmy," unpublished paper presented at the annual meeting of the American Historical Association, Chicago, 1991.

8. "Celebration of the FEAST of LIBERTY and EQUALITY," *Independent Chronicle*, 31 January 1793.

9. *Gazette US*, 6 February 1793.

10. *Massachusetts Mercury*, 26 January 1793.

11. "THE DAY. LIBERTY AND EQUALITY," *Independent Chronicle*, 24 January 1793.

12. Ibid.

13. "BOSTON, January 22," *New-York Journal*, 6 February 1793.

14. "CIVIC FESTIVAL!," *Columbian Centinel*, 26 January 1793.

15. "THE DAY. LIBERTY AND EQUALITY," *Independent Chronicle*, 24 January 1793.

16. "CIVIC FESTIVALS," *Columbian Centinel*, 30 January 1793.

17. "BOSTON, January 22," *New-York Journal*, 6 February 1793.

18. "CIVIC FESTIVALS," *Columbian Centinel*, 30 January 1793.

19. "Remarks," *Independent Chronicle*, 31 January 1793. For a brief discussion of American reactions to the debate between Edmund Burke and Thomas Paine in the context of party development and popular political culture, see Alfred F. Young, *The Democratic Republicans of New York: The Origins, 1763–1797* (Chapel Hill, 1967), 207–8.

20. I have surveyed well over one hundred French Revolutionary festivals and celebrations that took place all over the country, and were reported in newspapers from the *Farmer's Library* in Vermont to the Philadelphia *Aurora* to the *Gazette of Georgia*. Federalist leaders rarely attended or participated in these events, and after the early spring of 1793 only Pennsylvania Governor Thomas Mifflin (who might be described as pro-Federalist) attended and in any way sanctioned these events.

21. "THE DAY. LIBERTY AND EQUALITY," *Independent Chronicle*, 24 January 1793.

22. John Adams to Abigail Adams, 31 January 1793, *Letters of John Adams Addressed to His Wife*, ed. Charles Francis Adams (Boston: 1841), II: 124; John Quincy Adams to John Adams, 10 February 1793, *Writings of John Quincy Adams*, ed. Worthington Chauncey Ford (New York, 1913), I: 134–35.

23. William Bentley, *The Diary of William Bentley, D.D. Pastor of the East Church, Salem, Massachusetts* (1905) (Gloucester, 1962), II: 3.

24. Joseph Dennie to his parents, 25 April 1793, Joseph Dennie Papers, Houghton Library, HU.

25. "BOSTON, January 22," *New-York Journal*, 6 February 1793.

26. *Massachusetts Centinel*, 9 April 1785.

27. For more information on the economic situation, see Allan Kulikoff, "The Progress of Inequality in Revolutionary Boston," *William and Mary Quarterly* 3d. ser. 28 (1971): 375–411, and James A. Henretta, "Economic Development and Social Structure in Colonial Boston," *William and Mary Quarterly* 3d. ser. 22 (1965): 75–92.

28. *Massachusetts Centinel*, 12 May 1785.

29. *Independent Ledger*, 17 June 1784. The proposals to reform the Town Meeting are discussed in Matthew Secombe, "From Revolution to Republic: The Later Political Career of Samuel Adams, 1774–1803" (Ph.D. diss., Yale University, 1978), 31; Gary John Kornblith, "From Artisans to Businessmen: Master Mechanics in New England, 1789–1803" (Ph.D. diss., Princeton University, 1983), 105; Myron Floyd Wehtje, "A Town in the Confederation: Boston, 1783–1787" (Ph.D. diss.,

University of Virginia, 1978), 154–90. The controversy degenerated into a verbal and eventually a physical confrontation between two of the city's leading newspaper editors, the Democratic Republican Benjamin Austin, Jr. of the *Independent Chronicle*, and the Federalist Benjamin Russell of the *Columbian Centinel*. Russell's alleged assault on Austin resulted in legal action and a prolonged newspaper battle, both of which increased tension in Boston. See Kornblith, "From Artisans to Businessmen," 105–6.

Boston's population in 1790 stood at 18,038, including 4,325 "free white males" aged sixteen and over. *Return of the Whole Number of Persons Within The Several Districts of the United States, According to "An Act Providing For The Enumeration of the Inhabitants of the United States," Passed March the First, One Thousand Seven Hundred and Ninety-One* (Philadelphia, 1791), 23.

30. The "Honestus" essays appeared in the *Independent Chronicle* between March and June of 1786, and were then republished as *Observations on the Pernicious Practice of the Law, as Published Occasionally in the Independent Chronicle in the Year 1786 and Republished at the Request of a Number of Respectable Citizens* (Boston, 1814). For examples of responses to "Honestus" see *Columbian Centinel*, 8, 12, 19, 22, 26 April, 20 May 1786, and for a full discussion of the controversy see Kornblith, "From Artisans to Businessmen," 70–71.

31. "ANTI-ARISTOCRAT," *Boston Gazette*, 2 March 1789; "In Favor of Titles," *Independent Chronicle*, 18 February 1790.

32. "A MOURNER," *Boston Gazette*, 11 October 1790.

33. "A True Republican," *Massachusetts Mercury*, 4 April 1794. A detailed account of these elections can be found in Winfred E.A. Bernhard, *Fisher Ames: Federalist and Statesman, 1758–1808* (Chapel Hill, 1965), 69–73, 159–161, 204–207.

34. "BOSTON, Monday, January 14," *Boston Gazette*, 14 January 1793. One Bostonian noted that rank "is abolished by the title of Citizens," and hoped that "a numerous collection" would assemble for "this republican entertainment." See "CIVIC FEAST," *Massachusetts Mercury*, 17 January 1793.

35. "CIVIC FEAST," *Massachusetts Mercury*, 17 January 1793.

36. For discussions of women's presence, participation, and wearing of cockades see "CIVIC FESTIVALS," *Columbian Centinel*, 30 January 1793; "Celebration of the FEAST of LIBERTY and EQUALITY," *The Independent Chronicle*, 31 January 1793. In 1790 the Boston population totalled 18,038, which included a total of 7,701 males, and 9,576 females. See *Return of the Whole Number of Persons*. For more on this subject see Kulikoff, "The Progress of Inequality." Alfred F. Young has explored the role of Boston women in America's revolutionary struggle in "The Women of Boston: 'Persons of Consequence' in the Making of the American Revolution, 1765–76," in *Women and Politics in the Age of the Democratic Revolution*, ed. Harriet B. Applewhite and Darline G. Levy (Ann Arbor, 1990), 181–226.

37. "CIVIC FESTIVALS," *Columbian Centinel*, 30 January 1793.

38. *Pittsburgh Gazette*, 23 February 1793.

39. John Adams to Abigail Adams, Philadelphia, 31 January 1793, *Letters of John Adams, Addressed To His Wife*, II: 123.

40. "On the Meeting of the *Citizens of Boston* round the *Liberty-Stump* in the late Procession," *Connecticut Courant*, 11 February 1793.

41. "Extract of a latter from a gentleman in Connecticut, to his friend in this town," *Pittsburgh Gazette*, 30 March 1793.

42. Citess, *Columbian Centinel*, 16 March 1793. The practice of using "citess" was surprisingly widespread: see Susan Branson, " 'Fiery Frenchified Dames': American Women and the French Revolution," unpublished paper delivered at the annual meeting of the American Historical Association, 1991.

Men's practice of labeling women who ventured too far out into the male-dominated public sphere has a long history. See Glenna Matthews, *The Rise of Public Woman: Woman's Power and Woman's Place in the United States, 1630 –1970* (New York, 1992), 3–8. Perhaps the most famous case occurred in May of 1862, when Major General Benjamin Butler used the same tactic of branding oppositional women as prostitutes in his infamous General Order Number 28. See Mary P. Ryan, *Women in Public: Between Banners and Ballots, 1825 –1880* (Baltimore, 1990), 2–4, 130–32.

43. The official was Benjamin Nones. See Simon P. Newman, "Eagles, Hearts, and Crucifixes: The Mentalités of Philadelphia Seafarers in the New Republic," paper presented at the Philadelphia Center for Early American Studies, January 1994, 28. See also Linda K. Kerber, "The Paradox of Women's Citizenship in the Early Republic: The Case of *Martin vs. Massachusetts*, 1805," *American Historical Review* 97 (1992): 378.

44. *Gazette US*, 2 February 1793.

45. *Boston Gazette*, 1 April 1793.

46. "Tribute of Respect," *Gazette US*, 13 April 1793.

47. See J. David Harden, "Liberty Caps and Liberty Trees," *Past and Present* 146 (1995): 66–102 for a thoughtful discussion of the evolution and significance of liberty poles and trees in America, Britain and France. However, Harden restricts his discussion of American liberty poles and trees to the 1760s and 1770s, and he fails to acknowledge the large number and significance of these symbols in the 1790s.

48. Seafarers played a vital role in the transmission of revolutionary ideology and culture among the laboring poor of the Atlantic world. Although his work deals with the first half of the eighteenth century, Marcus Rediker's is the single best study of the political culture of seafarers. See Rediker, *Between the Devil and the Deep Blue Sea: Merchant Seamen, Pirates, and the Anglo-American Maritime World, 1700 –1750* (New York, 1987). See also Norman E. Saul, "Ships and Seamen as Agents of Revolution," in *The Consortium on Revolutionary Europe, 1750 –1850: Proceedings 1986*, ed. Warren Spencer (Athens, 1987), 248–58, and Peter Linebaugh and Marcus Rediker, "The Many-Headed Hydra: Sailors, Slaves and the Atlantic Working Class in the Eighteenth Century," *Journal of Historical Sociology* 3 (1990): 225–51.

49. "FOR THE EAGLE," *Eagle*, 27 October 1794.

50. "The Autobiography of Benjamin Tappan," ed. Donald J. Ratcliffe, *Ohio History* 85 (1976): 115. Tappan, the son of an artisan, spent the late 1780s and early 1790s as an apprentice in a variety of different crafts and trades.

51. The most comprehensive study of the impact of the French Revolution on the United States remains Charles Downer Hazen, *Contemporary American Opinion of the French Revolution* (Baltimore, 1897). However, James Tagg of the

University of Lethbridge in Alberta and Larry Tise of the Franklin Institute in Philadelphia are each working on new studies of the subject.

52. Elizabeth Drinker, 6 August 1799, *The Diary of Elizabeth Drinker*, ed. Elaine Forman Crane (Boston, 1991), II: 1196, and 28 January 1794, I: 542. The entry for 6 August 1799 referred to newspaper reports that the French fleet had been trapped at Toulon, while the entry for 28 January 1794 chronicled newspaper accounts of the trial and execution of Jacques-Pierre Brissot de Warville.

53. In 1775 the American colonial population of about 3 million was served by about 40 newspapers (most of them weeklies) with an average circulation of between 200 and 600. But by 1790 there were some 106 newspapers, quite a few of them dailies, for a population of about 4 million, and by 1800 that number had doubled again, giving the United States the highest number of newspapers in proportion to population of any nation on earth. See James D. Tagg, *Benjamin Franklin Bache and the Philadelphia Aurora* (Philadelphia, 1991), 90–97; Donald H. Stewart, *The Opposition Press of the Federalist Period* (Albany, 1969), 16; Arthur Schlesinger, Sr., *Prelude to Independence: The American Newspaper War on Britain, 1764–1776* (New York, 1958).

The best examinations of American newspaper coverage of the French Revolution are Beatrice F. Hyslop, "American Press Reports of the French Revolution, 1789–1794," *New York Historical Society Quarterly Bulletin* 42 (1958): 329–48, and "The American Press and the French Revolution of 1789," *Proceedings of the American Philosophical Society* 104 (1960): 54–85; Kurt Beerman, "The Reception of the French Revolution in the New York State Press: 1788–1791" (Ph.D. diss., New York University, 1960); Huntley Dupre, "The Kentucky Gazette Reports the French Revolution," *Mississippi Valley Historical Review* 26 (1939): 163–80; William F. Keller, "The French Craze of '93 and the American Press," *Americana* 35 (1941): 473–96.

54. For an example of the political divide within the merchant class, see Alfred F. Young's analysis of the situation in New York City in *The Democratic Republicans of New York: The Origins, 1763–1797* (Chapel Hill, 1967), 345–91.

55. Peter Porcupine [William Cobbett], *A Bone to Gnaw, For the Democrats . . .* (Philadelphia, 1795), 54; Porcupine, *THE BLOODY BUOY THROWN OUT AS A Warning to the Political Pilots of America . . .* (Philadelphia, 1796), 234–35.

56. "Revolution in France," *American Minerva*, 3 November 1794.

57. Cutler, *Life, Journals and Correspondence*, I: 489.

58. "Charleston, July 23," *Columbian Herald*, 23 July 1793.

59. *Gazette US*, 20 April 1797.

60. "CIVIC FETE," *Porcupine's Gazette*, 21 July 1798. A week later Cobbett gave the names of the "two DEMOCRATS" who had been hanged "on the anniversary of the triumph of their brethren in France." See *Porcupine's Gazette*, 27 July 1798.

61. *Gazette US*, 13 April 1793.

62. *Gazette US*, 31 October 1792.

63. A Farmer, "For the Gazette of the United States," *Gazette US*, 11 February 1794.

64. John Adams to Thomas Jefferson, 30 June 1813, in *The Adams-Jefferson Letters: The Complete Correspondence Between Thomas Jefferson and Abigail and John Adams*, ed. Lester J. Cappon (Chapel Hill, 1959), II: 346–47.

65. See R. R. Palmer, *The World of the French Revolution* (New York, 1971), II: 94, and Gary B. Nash, "The American Clergy and the French Revolution," *William and Mary Quarterly* 3d ser. 22 (1965): 403–5.

66. "FRENCH REVOLUTION," *Aurora*, 7 July 1792.

67. "BIRTH-DAY OF THE FRENCH REPUBLIC," *Aurora*, 1 August 1794.

68. "Glorious and Interesting Advices," *Carlisle Gazette*, 19 December 1792.

69. "Patriots!!!," *Columbian Herald*, 27 August 1793.

70. "New-London, April 27, 1795," *Gazette US*, 4 June 1795.

71. *Democrat*, 1 April 1807.

72. Peter Porcupine [William Cobbett], *A Bone to Gnaw, For the Democrats... Part II* (Philadelphia, 1795), 50–51. It is possible that Cobbett exaggerated, but my survey of early national newspapers suggests that French Revolutionary celebrations were as pervasive as Cobbett believed them to be.

73. In the course of researching this book I surveyed some 45 newspapers that were printed during some or all of the period between 1789 and 1801, from each of the original 13 states, and from Vermont, Kentucky, and the district of Maine.

74. See, for example, "PHILADELPHIA, February 12," *Virginia Gazette* (Dixon), 5 March 1779, and "FISH-KILL, February 6," *Virginia Gazette Or Advertiser*, 1 March 1783.

75. Susan Branson is currently working on the French in Philadelphia. See her unpublished paper "'Comme l'Arche de Noe': The French in Philadelphia in the 1790s," presented at the Pennsylvania Historical Association annual meeting, October 1994. See also Frances Sergeant Childs, *French Refugee Life in the United States, 1790–1800: An American Chapter of the French Revolution* (Baltimore, 1940), 103–21, 141–60; Melvin H. Jackson, *Privateers in Charleston, 1793–1796: An Account of a Palatinate in South Carolina* (Washington, D.C., 1969); Ann Catherine Hébert, "The Pennsylvania French in the 1790s: The Story of Their Survival" (Ph.D. diss., University of Texas at Austin, 1971); Thomas C. Sosnowski, "Bitter Farewells: Francophobia and the French Emigres in America," *Consortium on Revolutionary Europe 1750–1850: Proceedings* 21 (1992): 276–83.

76. On August 10, 1791 an insurrection in Paris and an attack on the Tuileries resulted in the suspension of Louis XVI by the revolutionaries; one month later, on September 22, the National Convention formally abolished the monarchy.

77. A great deal of contemporary evidence illustrates how the fall of the Bastille captured the imagination of Americans. When Michel Ange Bernard de Mangourit, the French consul in Charleston, attended or participated in festivals staged by Americans in that city, he was hailed as a veteran of the assault on the Bastille, with full attention paid to "the Mural Crown embroidered on his left breast, decreed him by the National Assembly, as conqueror of the Bastile": see "CHARLESTON, Nov. 14," *Aurora*, 22 February 1793. And if veterans of the Bastille were unavailable, Americans in larger towns and cities were able to enjoy recreations of the historic event. Moreau de St. Mery described a performance of the play "The

Bastile, or Liberty Triumphant," which he attended in New York City in the summer of 1795: see St. Mery to Albert Briois Beaumetz, New York, 26 June 1795, in *Moreau de St. Mery's American Journey: 1793–1798*, ed. Kenneth and Anna M. Roberts (Garden City, 1947), 187. Along similar lines, in Philadelphia and perhaps elsewhere citizens could pay either twenty-five or fifty cents to see "automatons" in "a representation of THE STORMING OF THE BASTILE" which used fireworks for dramatic effect: see *Aurora*, 22 August 1794.

78. See *Gazette of Georgia*, 31 January 1793; "LEXINGTON, Feb. 16," *Kentucky Gazette*, 16 February 1793; *New-Jersey Journal*, 19 March 1794; *Farmer's Library*, 13 January 1794.

79. "NEW YORK, December 29," *Weekly Museum*, 29 December 1792. The discussion about how best to celebrate Valmy can be found in the Society of Tammany or Columbia Order, Committee of Amusement Minutes, October 24, 1791–February 23, 1795, Minutes for 24 December 1792, 27 December 1792, Manuscripts Collection, NYPL. The best description of the celebration itself is "New-York, December 29," *New-York Journal*, 29 December 1792.

80. "NEW-YORK, December 29," *Weekly Museum*, 29 December 1792.

81. *New-York Journal*, 29 December 1792.

82. *New-York Journal*, 26 January 1793.

83. "Washington (on the frontiers of Pennsylvania)," *Pittsburgh Gazette*, 16 February 1793.

84. "PETERSBURGH, Jan. 24," *Aurora*, 7 February 1793.

85. "New-York, December 29," *New-York Journal*, 29 December 1792. For more on the popularity of Paine during these years see Alfred F. Young, "*Common Sense* and *The Rights of Man* in America: The Celebration and Damnation of Thomas Paine," in *Science, Mind, and Art: Essays on Science and the Humanistic Understanding in Art, Epistemology, Religion, and Ethics in Honor of Robert S. Cohen*, ed. Kostas Gavroglu et al. (Dordrecht, 1995), III: 418–28.

86. "Washington," *Pittsburgh Gazette*, 16 February 1793.

87. "PETERSBURGH, Jan. 24," *Aurora*, 7 February 1793.

88. *Aurora*, 2 January 1793.

89. "THE FRIENDS OF FRANCE," *New-York Journal*, 2 February 1793.

90. *Carlisle Gazette*, 19 December 1792.

91. "RHODE-ISLAND," *Herald US*, 9 February 1793.

92. "LEXINGTON, Feb. 16," *Kentucky Gazette*, 16 February 1793.

93. "RIGHTS OF WOMEN," *New-York Journal*, 1 May 1793.

94. "Civic Ball—AT PORTSMOUTH," *Massachusetts Mercury*, 5 February 1793.

95. See Childs, *French Refugee Life in the United States*, 62–83, and Harry Ammon, *The Genet Mission* (New York, 1973), 44–46, 51–59.

96. Thomas Jefferson to James Monroe, 5 May 1793, in *The Writings of Thomas Jefferson . . .* , ed. Albert Ellery Bergh (Washington, 1907), VI: 238.

97. "VIVE L'AMBUSCADE!!!," *Weekly Museum*, 3 August 1793.

98. "Extract of a letter from a Gentleman in *New-York* to his friend in this city, dated August 3d," *Aurora*, 4 August 1793.

99. "LA CONCORD FRIGATE," *Connecticut Courant*, 12 August 1793.

100. "PHILADELPHIA, May 17," *Aurora*, 17 May 1793. An earlier meeting was reported in *Aurora*, 14 May 1793.

101. "Minutes of the proceedings of the citizens of Philadelphia," *Aurora*, 14, 17, 20 May 1793.

102. See "BOSTON, August 15," *Aurora*, 22 August 1793; S.S. Gibson to Elizabeth Meredith, Princeton, 18 July 1793, reprinted in John M. Murrin, "Introduction," *Princetonians, 1791–1794: A Biographical Dictionary*, ed. J. Jefferson Looney and Ruth L. Woodward (Princeton, 1991), 2–3; "PHILADELPHIA, TUESDAY, AUGUST 13, 1793," *Aurora*, 13 August 1793; "RICHMOND, August 12," *Aurora*, 19 August 1793.

103. *Aurora*, 7 February 1793.

104. "PHILADELPHIA, AUGUST 14, 1793," *Aurora*, 14 August 1793.

105. "RICHMOND, August 12," *Aurora*, 19 August 1793.

106. "RICHMOND, August 14," *Aurora*, 21 August 1793.

107. Alexander Anderson, Diary entry for 15 July 1793, copy of original manuscript, NYHS; Gibson to Meredith, *Princetonians*, 2.

108. Peter Livingston to Robert Livingston, New York City, 26 January 1794, Robert Livingston Collection, NYHS.

109. "BOSTON, MARCH 24," *Aurora*, 1 April 1794.

110. See *Farmer's Library*, 13 January 1794; "RUTLAND, FEBRUARY 3," *Farmer's Library*, 3 February 1794; "VERMONT. Bennington, March 7," *Farmer's Library*, 12 March 1794.

111. *Farmer's Library*, 13 January 1794.

112. "VERMONT. Bennington, March 7," *Farmer's Library*, 12 March 1794.

113. "RUTLAND, FEBRUARY 3," *Farmer's Library*, 3 February 1794.

114. "RUTLAND, JANUARY 13," *Farmer's Library*, 13 January 1794; "To the Committee appointed to draught [sic] Toasts," *Farmer's Library*, 27 January 1794.

115. "BALTIMORE, JANUARY 23," *Aurora*, 12 February 1794.

116. "SPRINGFIELD, April 1," *Eagle*, 7 April 1794.

117. "Norfolk, Feb. 8, Civil Festival," *Independent Chronicle*, 17 March 1794.

118. "CIVIC FESTIVAL," *Gazette US*, 3 May 1794. According to the Federal census of 1790, the total population of the city of Philadelphia was 28,522, which included 7,739 "free white males" aged sixteen and over. The city and suburbs together were home to 11,360 adult white men: the 800 diners would have constituted just over 7% of this larger group. *Return of the Whole Number of Persons*, 45.

119. "CIVIC FESTIVAL," *Gazette US*, 3 May 1794.

120. *Aurora*, 13 May 1794.

121. "For the GAZETTE of the UNITED STATES," *Gazette US*, 13 May 1794.

122. *New-Jersey Journal*, 26 March 1794.

123. *Aurora*, 8 February 1794.

124. "Charleston, February 15," *Daily Advertiser*, 26 February 1794.

125. "Charleston, Feb. 17," *Columbian Herald*, 17 February 1794.

126. The names of one hundred and nine members of the Charleston Republican Society are recorded on a list dated 13 July 1793, which together with other materials relating to the Society are located in the Manuscripts Collection, BPL.

The tax records for Charleston in this period are incomplete and of relatively little value, so I have attempted to establish the occupations of as many of these members as possible by surveying Jacob Milligan, *The City Directory. By Jacob Milligan, harbour master. September, 1794* (Charleston, 1794).

127. "THE SONS OF FRANCE AND AMERICA," *Porcupine's Gazette*, 27 April 1797.

128. The Franco-American alliance was celebrated in Philadelphia and Charleston in February; the French victory at Toulon prompted celebrations in February, March, April, and May; the three constitutional anniversaries were commemorated on the appropriate days in July, August, and September.

129. "BIRTH-DAY OF THE FRENCH REPUBLIC," *Aurora*, 1 August 1794.

130. "Arrangements for the Festival of the 10th of August which is to be celebrated on Monday 11th instant," *Aurora*, 9 August 1794.

131. *Aurora*, 28 August 1794.

132. "Arrangements for the festival of the 10th of August which is to be celebrated on Monday 11th instant," *Aurora*, 9 August 1794.

133. *Aurora*, 28 August 1794.

134. Ibid.

135. Ibid.

136. See "BOSTON, Monday, July 21," *Boston Gazette*, 21 July 1794; "BOSTON, Monday August 18," *Boston Gazette*, 18 August 1794; "BALTIMORE, JULY 15," *Aurora*, 18 July 1794; "BALTIMORE, SEPT. 25," *Aurora*, 27 September 1794; "NEW-YORK, SEPT. 24," *Aurora*, 26 September 1794; "CAMDEN, July 15," *South Carolina Gazette*, 1 August 1794.

137. "PHILADELPHIA, WEDNESDAY JULY 16," *Aurora*, 16 July 1794; "BOSTON, Monday August 18," *Boston Gazette*, 18 August 1794.

138. "FROM A CORRESPONDENT," *Aurora*, 3 April 1795.

139. Marginal notation on invitation dated 11 April 1795, in George Washington, *The Writings of George Washington from the Original Manuscript Sources, 1745–1799*, ed. John C. Fitzpatrick (Washington, 1940), XXXIV: 174, fn.

140. "Fraternal Feast," *Boston Gazette*, 13 April 1795.

141. *"The Fraternal Feast,"* *Columbian Herald*, 18 May 1795.

142. "PORTSMOUTH, April 4," *Gazette US*, 17 April 1795.

143. "New-London, April 27, 1795," *Gazette US*, 4 June 1795.

144. [William Cobbett], "SACRED TO THE MEMORY OF THE Partiality, Ignorance, and baseness of the American Sans-Culottes, AS EXEMPLIFIED IN THEIR CIVIC FESTIVALS, IN HONOR OF THE BIRTH OF BATAVIA, Our Younger Sister Republic," *Porcupine's Gazette*, 22 December 1797.

145. "NEW-YORK, April 9," *Daily Advertiser*, 9 April 1795.

146. See "STATE [of] SOUTH CAROLINA. CHARLESTON, July 14," *Norwich Packet*, 7 August 1795; "BALTIMORE, JULY 15," *Aurora*, 20 July 1795; "NORFOLK, JULY 15," *Aurora*, 24 July 1795; *Aurora*, 15 July 1795; "Anniversary of the French Republic," *Mercury*, 22 September 1795.

147. "STATE [of] SOUTH CAROLINA, CHARLESTON, July 14," *Norwich Packet*, 7 August 1795.

148. "BOSTON, SEPT. 22," *Aurora*, 29 September 1795.

149. Dubois Chotard, "Notice to the friends of the republic," *Aurora*, 30 July 1795.

150. For discussion of these kinds of reactions to the American and French Revolutions, see William Appleman Williams, *America Confronts a Revolutionary World, 1776–1976* (New York, 1976), 25–43, 45–58, 60.

151. Nash, "The American Clergy and the French Revolution," 392–412.

152. "FRENCH REVOLUTION," *Aurora*, 21 July 1796.

153. "CELEBRATION OF THE VICTORIES OF THE FRENCH RE-PUBLIC IN ITALY," *Aurora*, 14 April 1797.

154. "FOR PORCUPINE'S GAZETTE," *Porcupine's Gazette*, 15 April 1797.

155. *Kentucky Gazette*, 30 January 1800.

156. "REPUBLICANISM," *Gazette US*, 3 March 1800; Drinker, 12 April 1797, *Diary*, II: 907.

157. On the impact of the Haitian Revolution on Jefferson and the Democratic Republican party, see Michael Zuckerman, "The Power of Blackness: Thomas Jefferson and the Revolution in St. Domingue," in *Almost Chosen People: Oblique Biographies in the American Grain* (Berkeley, 1993), 175–218. See also Donald R. Hickey, "America's Response to the Slave Revolt in Haiti, 1791–1806," *Journal of the Early Republic* 2 (1982): 361–80, and Alfred N. Hunt, *Haiti's Influence on Antebellum America: Slaveholding Volcano in the Caribbean* (Baton Rouge, 1988).

158. Lyman Beecher, *The Autobiography of Lyman Beecher*, ed. Barbara M. Cross (Cambridge, 1961), I: 27.

Chapter Five

1. John R. Elting, ed., *Military Uniforms in America: The Era of the American Revolution, 1755–1795* (San Rafael, 1974), 70–98; Minor Myers, Jr., *Liberty Without Anarchy: A History of the Society of the Cincinnati* (Charlottesville, 1983), 33–34.

2. "Paris, July 30," *Gazette US*, 26 September 1789.

3. See, for example, *Boston Gazette*, 19 October, 7 December 1789; *Gazette US* 12 December 1789; *Virginia Gazette or Advertiser*, 14 September 1791; *Massachusetts Mercury*, 27 July 1798. For a discussion of cockades in Revolutionary France, see Aileen Ribeiro, *Fashion in the French Revolution* (New York, 1988), 53–56.

4. Henry Wansey, *Henry Wansey and His American Journal: 1794*, ed. David John Jeremy (Philadelphia, 1970), 175.

5. Ibid., 76.

6. John F. Watson, *Annals of Philadelphia, and Pennsylvania, in the Olden Time*, ed. Willis P. Hazard (Philadelphia, 1884), I: 179–80.

7. Charles Fraser, *Reminiscences of Charleston, Lately Published in the Charleston Courier, and Now Revised and Enlarged by the Author* (Charleston, 1854), 39.

8. *Massachusetts Mercury*, 5 February 1793. See also John W. Francis, *Old New York: Or, Reminiscences of the Past Sixty Years* (New York, 1866), 115–16; Theo-

phile Cazenove, *Cazenove Journal 1794: A Record of the Journey of Theophile Cazenove Through New Jersey and Pennsylvania*, ed. Rayner Wickersham Kelsey, Haverford College Studies 13 (Haverford, 1922), 10; Watson, *Annals of Philadelphia*, I: 179.

9. Annis Boudinot Stockton to Julia Stockton Rush Morven, 22 March, Philadelphia, Rush—Williams—Biddle Family Papers, Rosenbach.

10. Elizabeth Drinker, 22 April 1796, *The Diary of Elizabeth Drinker*, ed. Elaine Forman Crane (Boston, 1991), II: 795; John Adams to Abigail Adams, 1794, as cited in Charles W. Akers, *Abigail Adams, An American Woman* (Boston, 1980), 116. See also Susan Branson, *Women and Public Space: Gender, Politics, and Society in the 1790s* (forthcoming), chapter one.

11. "Paris, July 3," *Virginia Gazette or Advertiser*, 14 September 1791.

12. C., Letter to the Editor, *Aurora*, 20 January 1791. For more on the political culture of women's literary salons and networks, see Susan Stabile, "'By a Female Hand': Letters, Belles Lettres, and the Philadelphian Culture of Performance, 1760–1820" (Ph.D. diss., University of Delaware, 1996).

13. *Massachusetts Mercury*, 5 February 1793.

14. Watson, *Annals of Philadelphia*, I: 179–80.

15. "English Flag," *Porcupine's Gazette*, 3 May 1798.

16. For further discussion of the politics of seafaring patriotism in the early republic, see Simon P. Newman, "Eagles, Hearts, and Crucifixes: The Mentalités of Philadelphia Seafarers in the New Republic," paper presented at the Philadelphia Center for Early American Studies, January 1994.

17. Samuel Coates to W. Moyer, Jr., 4 November 1796, Samuel Coates Letter Book, Coates Family Papers, HSP.

18. "Bennington, July 19," *Aurora*, 31 July 1793.

19. "COMMUNICATION," *Porcupine's Gazette*, 6 April 1797.

20. "Communication," *Vermont Gazette*, 16 November 1798.

21. Drinker, 31 December 1796, *Diary*, II: 874. For more on the fear that Haiti inspired among white Americans see Gary B. Nash, *Forging Freedom: The Formation of Philadelphia's Black Community, 1720–1840* (Cambridge, 1988), 174–76; Donald R. Hickey, "America's Response to the Slave Revolt in Haiti, 1791–1806," *Journal of the Early Republic* 2 (1982): 361–80; Michael Zuckerman, "The Power of Blackness: Thomas Jefferson and the Revolution in St. Domingue," in *Almost Chosen People: Oblique Biographies in the American Grain* (Berkeley, 1993), 175–218; Alfred N. Hunt, *Haiti's Influence on Antebellum America: Slaveholding Volcano in the Caribbean* (Baton Rouge, 1988).

22. "NEW YORK, April 22," *American Minerva*, 22 April 1795.

23. For more on Gabriel's Rebellion, see Douglas R. Egerton, *Gabriel's Rebellion: The Virginia Slave Conspiracies of 1800 and 1802* (Chapel Hill, 1993), and "Gabriel's Conspiracy and the Election of 1800," *The Journal of Southern History* 56 (1990): 191–214.

24. Egerton, *Gabriel's Rebellion*, 102–115

25. *Richmond Recorder*, 10 November 1802.

26. For references to the continued influence of revolutionary Haiti, revealed in the testimony of Denmark Vesey and his associates after their failed attempt at

conspiracy in Charleston in 1822, see *The Trial Record of Denmark Vesey* (1822) (Boston, 1970), 42, 43, 46, 89.

27. Absalom Jones, *A Thanksgiving Sermon, Preached January 1, 1808, In St. Thomas's, or the African Episcopal Church, Philadelphia: On Account of the Abolition of the African Slave Trade, On That Day, By the Congress of the United States* (Philadelphia, 1808), 15, 19. See also Nash, *Forging Freedom*, 172–211; Susan G. Davis, *Parades and Power: Street Theatre in Nineteenth-Century Philadelphia* (1986) (Berkeley, 1988); Winthrop D. Jordan, *White over Black: American Attitudes Toward the Negro, 1550–1812* (Chapel Hill, 1968), 403–22; David Waldstreicher, *The Making of American Nationalism: Celebrations and Political Culture, 1776–1820* (Chapel Hill, forthcoming), chapter six.

28. Alexander Graydon, *Memoirs of a Life, Chiefly Passed in Pennsylvania, Within the Last Sixty Years* (1811), (Edinburgh, 1822), 392; *The Two Trials of John Fries, or an Indictment for Treason; Together With a Brief report of the Trials of Several other Persons, for Treason and Insurrection, in the Counties of Bucks, Northampton and Montgomery, in the Circuit Court of the United States . . .* (Philadelphia, 1800), 46, 49.

29. Noah Webster, *The Revolution in France, Considered in Respect to its Progress and Effects* (New York, 1794), 23; *Massachusetts Mercury*, 11 September 1798.

30. "American Cockade," *Massachusetts Mercury*, 10 July 1798.

31. *Gazette US*, 22 May 1798.

32. "Death of the National Cockade," *Porcupine's Gazette*, 24 May 1798.

33. *Porcupine's Gazette*, 1 August 1798.

34. Benjamin Austin, Jr., *Constitutional Republicanism, In Opposition to Fallacious Federalism; As Published Occasionally in the Independent Chronicle, Under the Signature of Old South . . .* (Boston, 1803), 145.

35. "ANTIFEDERALISTS," *Connecticut Courant*, 20 August 1798.

36. Donald J. Ratcliffe, ed., "The Autobiography of Benjamin Tappan," *Ohio History* 85 (1976): 120, 121.

37. "PHILADELPHIA, THURSDAY EVENING, May 10," *Gazette US*, 10 May 1798.

38. *Boston Gazette*, 16 July 1798.

39. "A Hater of Traitors," *Massachusetts Mercury*, 13 July 1798. See also "American Cockade," *Massachusetts Mercury*, 10 July 1798.

40. "Extract of a Letter from Greenville, Tennessee, 26 July," *Porcupine's Gazette*, 13 August 1798.

41. Advertisement by the Philadelphia silversmiths George Armitage and James Bearley in *Porcupine's Gazette*, 6 February 1799. See also Elting, *Military Uniforms in America*, 128–29, and Myers, *Liberty Without Anarchy*, 60–63. The "Cincinnati Eagle" and popular reactions to it were recorded in the contemporary novel by Hugh Henry Brackenridge, *Modern Chivalry: Containing the Adventures of Captain John Farrago, and Teague Oregan, His Servant* (Philadelphia, 1792), I: 140.

42. *Gazette US*, 6 November 1800.

43. "Funeral Procession of the Black Cockade," in *Lewis Miller, Sketches and*

Chronicles: The Reflections of a Nineteenth Century Pennsylvania German Folk Artist (York, 1966), 76.

44. The liberty cap appears to have been known to Americans well before the revolutionary era. One of the flags carried by members of the Association in Philadelphia in the middle years of the century, for example, featured a representation of a liberty cap. See *Pennsylvania Gazette*, 12 January 1747. The most recent survey of the literature on the liberty cap in revolutionary America, France, and also Britain is J. David Harden, "Liberty Caps and Liberty Trees," *Past and Present* 146 (1995): 66–102.

45. Mona Ozouf, *Festivals of the French Revolution*, (1976), trans. Alan Sheridan (Cambridge, 1988), 205–12; Jennifer Harris, "The Red Cap of Liberty: A Study of Dress Worn by French Revolutionary Partisans, 1789–1794," *Eighteenth-Century Studies* 14 (1980–1981): 283–312; Ribeiro, *Fashion in the French Revolution*, 85–147.

46. See, for example, "Charleston, Feb. 17,' *Columbian Herald*, 17 February 1794, and "FOR THE EAGLE," *Eagle*, 27 October 1794.

47. For a discussion of conservative European opposition to both the liberty pole and the tri-colored cockade, see Ribeiro, *Fashion in the French Revolution*, 53–56, 85, 147.

48. "REAL REPUBLICAN," *American Minerva*, 8 February 1794.

49. *Museum*, 18 August 1794. For another example of a strikingly similar motif, see the new masthead adopted by the *New-Jersey Journal* in the summer of 1798, which featured a standing female liberty figure in a long flowing robe and with long, flowing hair, holding a liberty pole topped by a liberty cap.

50. *Catalogue of Coins, Tokens, and Medals in the Numismatic Collection of the Mint of the United States at Philadelphia, PA* (Washington, 1912), 11–13, plates II, V.

51. "UNION COLLEGE," *Gazette US*, 6 March 1795. A copy of the seal can be found in the Hubbell Papers, Firestone Library, Princeton University.

52. Stephen Drayton to Michel Ange Bernard de Mangourit, Charleston, 15 February 1794, Manuscripts Collection, BPL.

53. Paul Revere's engraving of *The Able Doctor, or America Swallowing the Bitter Draught*, shows America as the naked and vulnerable victim of tyrannical British males, who poured tea down her throat, fired on her native land, and leered over her helpless body. The only other female in the picture was Britannia, who stood by distressed and helpless. See Linda K. Kerber, *Women of the Republic: Intellect and Ideology in Revolutionary America* (Chapel Hill, 1980), 40, and Peter Shaw, *American Patriots and the Rituals of Revolution* (New York, 1981), 181–182.

54. "GOLD COINAGE," *Jersey Chronicle*, 7 November 1795. One of the best discussions of the French images of Liberty and Republicanism can be found in Maurice Agulhon, *Marianne into Battle: Republican Imagery and Symbolism in France, 1789–1880*, (1979), trans. Janet Lloyd (New York, 1981), 9–37. For an excellent discussion of "female civic allegories," see Mary P. Ryan, *Women in Public: Between Banners and Ballots, 1825–1880* (Baltimore, 1990), 26–29.

55. "RUTLAND, JANUARY 13," *Farmer's Library*, 13 January 1793.

56. See also Ryan, *Women in Public*, 28–29, 52.

57. "GOLD COINAGE," *Jersey Chronicle*, 7 November 1795.

58. William Cobbett, in his introduction to William Playfair, *The History of Jacobinism, Its Crimes, Cruelties and Perfidies . . . With an Appendix by Peter Porcupine, Containing a History of the American Jacobins, Commonly Denominated Democrats* (Philadelphia, 1796), 25; *American Minerva*, 24 January 1795; *Porcupine's Gazette*, 27 July 1798.

59. John Alexander, SPCA, 21 December 1804; John Peterson, Seamen's Protection Certificate Application, 2 July 1806; Abraham Carson, SPCA, 24 December 1803, Record Group 36, NA.

60. Herman Melville describes the ship the *Rights-of-Man* and the ideology shared by her crew in "Billy Budd, Sailor." See Melville, *Billy Budd, Sailor & Other Stories* (New York, 1970), 326–27. See also Newman, "Wearing Their Hearts on Their Sleeves."

61. *Aurora*, 15 June 1793.

62. Peter R. Livingston to Robert R. Livingston, 26 January 1794, cited in Alan L. Blau, "New York City and the French Revolution, 1789–1797; A Study of French Revolutionary Influence" (Ph.D. diss., City University of New York, 1973), 262. .

63. "Extract of a Letter from New-York, dated May 21," *Gazette US*, 22 May 1795. See also *Daily Advertiser*, 19 May 1795; "NEW-YORK, May 18," *Gazette US*, 20 May 1795; "NEW-YORK, May 19," *American Minerva*, 19 May 1795; *American Minerva*, 20, 22 May 1795. Two years later French attacks on American shipping gave Federalists the opportunity they wanted to attack these "offensive" emblems, which were promptly removed by the proprietors. See *Boston Gazette*, 27 March 1797.

64. "NEW-YORK, May 21," *Daily Advertiser*, 21 May 1795.

65. See, for example, Cazenove's descriptions of liberty poles in Paterson, Springfield and Morristown. Cazenove, *Cazenove Journal*, 1, 2, 10.

66. "Celebration of the FEAST of LIBERTY and EQUALITY," *Independent Chronicle*, 31 January 1793; the erection of the liberty tree in New York City is described in Blau, "New York City and the French Revolution," 437–38.

67. For a list of the liberty poles in western Pennsylvania, see the *Aurora*, 20 September 1794; Brackenridge, *Modern Chivalry*, IV, 112, 114; *Gazette US*, 3 October 1794.

68. Graydon, *Memoirs of a Life*, 392.

69. The erection of one such pole in Pennsylvania is recounted in James Craft, Daily Occurrence Book, entry for 29 January 1799, HSP; for a description of the erection of a liberty pole in New Hampshire see an article based upon a letter from Albany entitled "Liberty Poles! No Stamp Act," *Kentucky Gazette*, 4 April 1798.

70. For the Fries Rebellion see William W.H. Davis, *The Fries Rebellion, 1798–1799* (New York, 1969), and Paul Douglas Newman, "Fries Rebellion and American Political Culture, 1798–1800," *Pennsylvania Magazine of History and Biography* 119 (1995): 37–73.

71. Theodore Sedgwick, quoted in James Morton Smith, *Freedom's Fetters: The Alien and Sedition Laws and American Civil Liberties* (Ithaca, 1966), 21. See

also John C. Miller, *Crisis in Freedom: The Alien and Sedition Acts* (Boston, 1951), and Simon P. Newman, "'To Defame or Weaken the Government': The Alien and Sedition Acts and American Political Culture," paper presented at the annual meeting of the Organization of American Historians, Chicago, 1992.

72. "NEWBURGH, July 9," *Aurora*, 18 July 1798; *Bee*, 12 December 1798; "Bridgehampton, (L.I.) Dec. 22," *Bee*, 16 January 1799.

73. *Aurora*, 3 May 1798.

74. *Aurora*, 18 July 1798.

75. Ronald Hutton, *The Rise and Fall of Merry England: The Ritual Year, 1400–1700* (Oxford, 1994), 163, 30, 134, 158.

76. *Bee*, 12 December 1798.

77. *Bee*, 15 August 1798.

78. "Bridgehampton, N.Y. Dec. 22," *Independent Chronicle*, 17 January 1799.

79. "Sedition Poles," *Porcupine's Gazette*, 2 February 1799.

80. "SATURDAY, AUGUST 11," *Commercial Advertiser*, 11 August 1798.

81. Fisher Ames to Timothy Pickering, 22 November 1798, in Fisher Ames, *Works of Fisher Ames: With A Selection From His Speeches and Correspondences*, ed. Seth Ames (1854) (New York, 1969), I: 242.

82. "Firm Support of the Laws, by Energetic Measures," *Kennebeck Intelligencer*, 1 December 1798.

83. "Loyalty Triumphant Over Sedition," *Massachusetts Mercury*, 11 December 1798.

84. Witnesses suggested that Brown was a revolutionary rabble rouser, and a danger to his country and its government. Joseph Kingsbury, for example, deposed that prior to the raising of the Liberty Pole Brown had visited his house and discussed the merits of Paine's *Age of Reason*. See "CIRCUIT COURT," *Independent Chronicle*, 17 June 1799.

85. James Morton Smith, "The Federalist 'Saints' Versus 'The Devil of Sedition': The Liberty Pole Cases of Dedham, Massachusetts, 1798–1799," *New England Quarterly* 28 (1955): 202, 212.

86. The best discussion of the ways in which songs functioned in late eighteenth-century society can be found in the introduction to Laura Mason, *Singing the French Revolution: Popular Culture and Politics, 1787–1799* (Ithaca, 1996).

87. Francis, *Old New York*, 115–16; Alexander Anderson, Diary, 1793–1799, Manuscripts Copy, from Manuscript Original in Library of Columbia College, NYHS.

88. Watson, *Annals of Philadelphia*, I: 179–80.

89. "BOSTON, Monday, January 21," *Boston Gazette*, 21 January 1793.

90. Charles Biddle, *Autobiography of Charles Biddle*, 253. The "Marseillaise" appeared in print more than any other French revolutionary song. See, for example, *New York Journal*, 19 January 1793, *Daily Advertiser*, 16 July 1793, the *Massachusetts Mercury*, 2 February 1793, *Farmer's Library*, 15 July 1794, and the *Aurora*, 13 July 1793. A translation of "Ça Ira" appeared in, for example, *Boston Gazette*, 9 July 1792, while one of "La Carmagnole" was published in *Museum*, 29 December 1794 and another in the *Columbian Herald*, 22 October 1794.

This battle hymn of the French Republic retained some currency in America during the nineteenth century, and continued to appear in song books such as Timothy Swan, *The Songster's Museum; Or, A Trip to Elysium. A Selection of the Most Approved Songs, Duets, &c.* (Northampton, 1803). Firmly ensconced in the Democratic South, the "Marseillaise" became popular with Confederate armies during the Civil War. See Drew Gilpin Faust, *The Creation of Confederate Nationalism: Ideology and Identity in the Civil War South* (Baton Rouge, 1988), 11–13.

91. Laura Mason, "'Ça Ira' and the Birth of the Revolutionary Song," *History Workshop: A Journal of Socialist and Feminist Historians* 28 (1989): 22–38.

92. "RIGHTS OF WOMAN," *Weekly Museum*, 25 April 1795; see also "Rights of Woman," *Philadelphia Minerva*, 17 October 1795. The song was most recently performed by a group of early American historians in 1991, in the library of the American Philosophical Society.

93. Sarah Bache to Benjamin Franklin Bache, London, 12 September 1792, Bache Papers—Castle Collection, APS.

94. "A NEW SONG," *New-York Journal*, 11 May 1793.

95. "ODE On the Revolution of France," *Gazette US*, 1 October 1794. This article reported that Mrs. Marriot's "Ode was performed by her spouse "at the Old American Theatre" in Philadelphia.

96. "A NEW SONG, CALLED THE GUILLOTINE," *Boston Chronicle*, 9 October 1794.

97. "A NEW SONG, Called, 'THE GUILLOTINE,'" *Boston Chronicle*, 9 October 1794.

98. "NEW THEATRE," *Aurora*, 28 February 1794.

99. William Dunlap, *A History of the American Theater* (New York, 1832), 106.

100. *Boston Gazette*, 10 February 1794.

101. Dunlap, *A History of the American Theater*, 140–41.

102. William B. Wood, *Personal Recollections of the Stage, Embracing Notices of Actors, Authors, and Auditors, During a Period of Forty Years* (Philadelphia, 1855), 118–19.

103. Dunlap, *A History of the American Theatre*, 271–72.

104. Liam Riordan, "'O Dear, What Can the Matter Be?': Politics and Popular Song in the *Federal Overture* (1794)," unpublished paper, 1995.

105. "THE MANAGERS OF THE THEATRE," *Gazette US*, 17 April 1798.

106. "BALTIMORE, April 17," *Pittsburgh Gazette*, 28 April 1798.

107. "THEATRICAL INTELLIGENCE," *Gazette US*, 14 July 1798.

108. *Gazette US*, 17 April 1798. For a discussion of the origins of these Federalist songs, see Charles Warren, *Jacobin and Junto, or, Early American Politics as Viewed in the Diary of Dr. Nathaniel Ames, 1758–1822* (Cambridge, 1931), 76.

109. "National Gratitude," *Porcupine's Gazette*, 2 May 1798.

110. "BALTIMORE, April 17," *Gazette US*, 19 April 1798.

111. "THEATRICAL INTELLIGENCE," *Gazette US*, 14 July 1798.

112. *Gazette US*, 26 April 1798.

113. Ibid.

114. *Massachusetts Mercury*, 19 July 1799.

115. This particular version of 'Adams and Liberty' was published in *Connecticut Courant*, 18 June 1798.

116. *Porcupine's Gazette*, 31 July 1798.

117. *Porcupine's Gazette*, 1 August 1798. This piece was extracted from the *Commercial Advertiser*.

118. "Autobiography of Benjamin Tappan," 121.

Conclusion

1. For a brief discussion of the invention of national traditions, see Eric Hobsbawm, "Introduction: Inventing Traditions," in *The Invention of Tradition*, ed. Eric Hobsbawm and Terence Ranger (New York, 1983), 1–14.

2. Nathaniel Cutting to Harrison Gray Otis, Le Havre, 18 July 1789, Nathaniel Cutting Letter Books, Nathaniel Cutting Papers, MHS, I: 53.

3. Gino Germani, *Marginality* (New Brunswick, 1980), 22. See also Roger Chartier, "La naissance de la marginalité: entretien avec Roger Chartier," *L'Histoire* 43 (1982): 106–11; P. N. Medvedev and M. M. Bakhtin, *The Formal Method in Literary Scholarship: A Critical Introduction to Sociological Poetics*, (1928), trans. Albert J. Wehrle (Baltimore, 1977), 8–9, 118–22, and David Cannadine, "Introduction: Divine Right of Kings," in *Rituals of Royalty: Power and Ceremonial in Traditional Societies*, ed. David Cannadine and Simon Price (New York, 1987), 2.

4. David Hackett Fischer has made a somewhat similar argument, proposing that the political beliefs of elite Federalist leaders led them to reject a descent into the fray of democratic politics: only in the early nineteenth century did a young group of Federalist leaders emerge who were willing to play the modern political game. See Fischer, *The Revolution of American Conservatism: The Federalist Party in the Age of Jefferson* (New York, 1965), 182–99.

5. The ways in which popular political culture allowed for a negotiation between rulers and ruled seems to fit Gramscian hegemony theory, and I have found Gramsci useful in explicating the meaning and significance of early national popular politics. See Antonio Gramsci, *Selections from the Prison Notebooks of Antonio Gramsci*, ed. and trans. Quintin Hoare and Geoffrey Nowell Smith (New York, 1971), 57–58, 160–61, 181–82; Louis Althusser, *Lenin and Philosophy and Other Essays*, trans. Ben Brewster (New York, 1971), and *For Marx*, trans. Ben Brewster, (London, 1979); Anne Showstack Sassoon, ed., *Approaches to Gramsci* (London, 1982); Perry Anderson, "The Antinomies of Antonio Gramsci," *New Left Review* 100 (1976–1977): 5–78; Cary Nelson and Lawrence Grossberg, eds., *Marxism and the Interpretation of Culture* (Urbana, 1988).

Other historians who have found hegemony theory useful include E. J. Hobsbawm, *The Age of Capital, 1848–1875* (New York, 1975), E. P. Thompson, *Whigs and Hunters: The Origins of the Black Act* (New York, 1975), and Eugene D. Genovese, *Roll, Jordan, Roll: The World the Slaves Made* (New York, 1974).

6. An Althusserian reading of this process suggests that the continued use

of an ever more shallow rhetoric of liberty, equality, and popular rights functioned to dispel the contradictions between the values espoused in this rhetoric and the lived experiences of those Americans who articulated them. See Althusser, "Marxism and Humanism," in *For Marx*, 233–34.

7. This point has been made very forcefully by Robin D. G. Kelley in his response to Lawrence Levine's somewhat sweeping dismissal of hegemony theory. See Kelley, "Notes on Deconstructing 'The Folk,' " *American Historical Review* 97 (1992): 1404–5. Levine's essay appeared in the same issue of the *American Historical Review*: see Levine, "The Folklore of Industrial Society: Popular Culture and Its Audiences," *American Historical Review* 97 (1992): 1369–99.

8. In the wake of the Federal Constitution of 1787, eight states followed this trend with by introducing new or revised constitutions between 1790 and 1805. See Albert L. Sturm, "The Development of American State Constitutions," *Publius: The Journal of Federalism* 12 (1982): 58.

On Gabriel's Rebellion see Douglas R. Egerton, *Gabriel's Rebellion: The Virginia Slave Conspiracies of 1800 and 1802* (Chapel Hill, 1993).

For more on the disenfranchisement of propertied white women and black men in New Jersey, see Judith Apter and Lois Elkis, " 'The Petticoat Electors': Women's Suffrage in New Jersey, 1776–1807," *Journal of the Early Republic* 12 (1992): 159–93, and Irwin N. Gertzog, "Female Suffrage in New Jersey, 1790–1807," in *Women, Politics and the Constitution*, ed. Naomi Lynn (New York, 1990), 47–58.

9. For discussion of a similar process of co-option, see Robert Muchembled, *Popular Culture and Elite Culture in France, 1700–1750*, trans. Lydia Cochrane (Baton Rouge, 1985), 315–16, and Pierre Bourdieu, *Language and Symbolic Power*, ed. John B. Thompson, trans. Gino Raymond and Matthew Adamson (Cambridge, 1991).

Bibliography

Manuscripts

Anderson, Alexander. Diary. Columbia University.

Bache Papers—Castle Collection. American Philosophical Society (microfilm).

Coates, Samuel. Letterbook. Coates Family Papers. Historical Society of Pennsylvania.

Craft, James. Daily Occurrence Book. Historical Society of Pennsylvania.

Cutting, Nathaniel. Letter Books. Nathaniel Cutting Papers. Massachusetts Historical Society.

Dana Family Papers. Massachusetts Historical Society.

Dennie, Joseph. Papers. Houghton Library. Harvard University.

Ewing, Jane to James Hunter, Jr., 23 April 1789. New Jersey State Archives.

Livingston, Robert. Collection. New York Historical Society.

Mills, Robert. "Description of George Washington's Visit to Charleston, S.C. 2–9 May, 1791." South Carolina Historical Society.

Minutes and Proceedings of the Joint Committee on the Removal of the Old Post Office Building, and the Erection of a LIBERTY POLE On the Site of the First LIBERTY POLE, erected June 4, 1776, in "the Commons," the Present City Hall Park, 1919–1921. New York Historical Society.

Minutes of the Democratic Society of Pennsylvania. Historical Society of Pennsylvania.

Minutes of the Society of Tammany or Columbian Order. New York Public Library.

Records of the Comptroller General, Military Accounts. Pennsylvania State Archives. RG-4, Microfilm Reel 363.

Republican Society of Charleston, South Carolina. Papers. Boston Public Library.

Rush-Williams-Biddle Family Papers. Rosenbach Museum and Library.

Seamen's Protection Certificate Applications. Record Group 36. National Archives.

Smith, William Loughton. Papers. South Carolina Historical Society.

Yates, Peter W. "Opinion of the Justices at Schenectady—as to a number of persons erecting a liberty pole in the public highway February 7, 1774." New York Historical Society.

Published Papers

Adams, John. *Adams Family Correspondence*. Ed. L. H. Butterfield et al. 6 vols. to date. Cambridge, Mass.: Belknap Press, 1963–1993.

————. *Diary and Autobiography of John Adams.* Ed. L. H. Butterfield. 4 vols. Cambridge, Mass.: Belknap Press, 1961.

————. *Letters of John Adams Addressed to His Wife.* Ed. Charles Francis Adams. 2 vols. Boston: C. C. Little and J. Brown, 1841.

————. *The Adams-Jefferson Letters: The Complete Correspondence Between Thomas Jefferson and Abigail and John Adams.* Ed. Lester J. Cappon. 2 vols. Chapel Hill: University of North Carolina Press, 1959.

Adams, John Quincy. *Writings of John Quincy Adams.* Ed. Worthington Chauncey Ford. 6 vols. New York: Macmillan, 1913–1917.

Ames, Fisher. *Works of Fisher Ames: With a Selection From His Speeches and Correspondence.* Ed. Seth Ames. 2 vols. 1854. New York: Da Capo, 1969.

Austin, Benjamin, Jr. *Constitutional Republicanism, In Opposition to Fallacious Federalism; As Published Occasionally in the Independent Chronicle, Under the Signature of Old South . . . .* Boston: Adams and Rhoades, 1803.

————. *Observations on the Pernicious Practice of the Law, as Published Occasionally in the Independent Chronicle in the Year 1786 and Republished at the Request of a Number of Respectable Citizens.* Boston: Joshua Belcher, 1814.

Beecher, Lyman. *The Autobiography of Lyman Beecher.* Ed. Barbara M. Cross. 2 vols. Cambridge, Mass.: Belknap Press, 1961.

Bentley, William. *The Diary of William Bentley, D.D. Pastor of The East Church, Salem, Massachusetts.* 2 vols. 1905. Gloucester, Mass.: P. Smith, 1962.

Biddle, Charles. *Autobiography of Charles Biddle, Vice-President of the Supreme Executive Council of Pennsylvania, 1745–1821.* Ed. Charles Biddle. Philadelphia: E. Claxton, 1883.

Brackenridge, Hugh Henry. *Modern Chivalry: Containing the Adventures of Captain John Farrago, and Teague Oregan, His Servant.* Philadelphia: John M'Culloch, 1797.

Brooks, John M. *A Eulogy on General Washington: Delivered Before the Inhabitants of the Town of Medford, Agreeably to their Vote, and at the Request of their Committee. on the 13th of January, 1800 . . . .* Boston: Samuel Hall, 1800.

Byrd, William. *Another Secret Diary of William Byrd of Westover, 1739–1741: With Letters and Literary Exercises, 1696–1726.* Ed. Maude H. Woodfin and Marion Tinling. Richmond: Dietz Press, 1942.

————. *The Secret Diary of William Bird of Westover, 1709–1712.* Ed. Louis B. Wright and Marion Tinling. Richmond: Dietz Press, 1941.

Cazenove, Theophile. *Cazenove Journal 1794: A Record of the Journey of Theophile Cazenove Through New Jersey and Pennsylvania.* Ed. Rayner Wickersham Kelsey. Haverford College Studies 13. Haverford: Pennsylvania History Press, 1922.

Cope, Thomas. *Philadelphia Merchant: The Diary of Thomas P. Cope, 1800–1851.* Ed. Eliza Cope Harrison. South Bend, Ind.: Gateway Editions, 1978.

Coverly, Nathaniel. *The Death of General Washington, With Some Remarks on Jeffersonian Policy.* Boston: N. Coverly, n.d.

Cutler, Manasseh. *Life, Journals and Correspondence of Rev. Manasseh Cutler, LL.D..* Ed. William Parker Cutler and Julia Perkins Cutler. 2 vols. Cincinnati, Oh.: Robert Clarke, 1888.

Dana, Joseph. *A Discourse on the Character and Death of General George Washington . . . Delivered at Ipswich on the 22D. February, A.D. 1800 . . . .* Newburyport, Mass.: Edmund M. Blunt, 1800.

Drinker, Elizabeth. *The Diary of Elizabeth Drinker.* Ed. Elaine Forman Crane. 2 vols. Boston: Northeastern University Press, 1991.

Dwight, Theodore. *An Oration, Delivered at New-Haven on the 7th of July, A.D., Before the Society of the Cincinnati, For the State of Connecticut, Assembled to Celebrate the Anniversary of American Independence.* Hartford, Conn.: Hudson and Goodwin, 1801.

Ellery, Henrietta C. "Diary of the Hon. William Ellery of Rhode Island, June 28–July 23, 1778." *Pennsylvania Magazine of History and Biography* 11 (1887): 477–78.

Fithian, Philip Vickers. *Journal & Letters of Philip Vickers Fithian, 1773–1774: A Plantation Tutor of the Old Dominion.* Ed. Hunter Dickinson Farish. Williamsburg, Va.: Colonial Williamsburg, 1943.

Foster, Augustus John. *Jeffersonian America: Notes on the United States of America Collected in the Years 1805–6–7 and 11–12 by Sir Augustus John Foster, Bart.* Ed. Richard Beale Davis. San Marino, Calif.: Huntington Library, 1954.

Francis, John W. *Old New York: Or, Reminiscences of the Past Sixty Years.* New York: W. J. Widdleton, 1866.

Franklin, Benjamin. *The Autobiography.* New York: Vintage Books, 1990.

———. *The Papers of Benjamin Franklin.* Ed. Leonard W. Labaree et al. 31 vols. to date. New Haven, Conn.: Yale University Press, 1959–1995.

Fraser, Charles. *Reminiscences of Charleston, Lately Published in the Charleston Courier, and Now Revised and Enlarged by the Author.* Charleston, S.C.: John Russell, 1854.

Graydon, Alexander. *Memoirs of a Life, Chiefly Passed in Pennsylvania, Within the Last Sixty Years.* 1811. Edinburgh: George Ramsay, 1822.

Hamilton, Alexander. *The Papers of Alexander Hamilton.* Ed. Harold C. Syrett et al. 27 vols. New York: Columbia University Press, 1961–1987.

Hotchkiss, Frederick W. *An Oration Delivered at Saybrook on Saturday February 22d, 1800; the Day Set Apart by the Recommendation of Congress for the People of the United States to Testify Their Grief for the Death of General George Washington; Who Died December 14, 1799.* New London, Conn.: S. Green, 1800.

Jefferson, Thomas. *The Papers of Thomas Jefferson.* Ed. Julian P. Boyd et al. 28 vols. to date. Princeton, N.J.: Princeton University Press, 1950–1996.

———. *The Writings of Thomas Jefferson.* Ed. Albert Ellery Burgh. 20 vols. Washington, D.C.: Thomas Jefferson Memorial Association, 1903–1904.

Jones, Absalom. *A Thanksgiving Sermon, Preached January 1, 1808, In St. Thomas's, or the African Episcopal Church, Philadelphia: On Account of the Abolition of the African Slave Trade, On That Day, By the Congress of the United States.* Philadelphia: Fry and Kammerer, 1808.

Maclay, William. *The Diary of William Maclay And Other Notes On Senate Debates.* Ed. Kenneth R. Bowling and Helen E. Veit. Baltimore: Johns Hopkins University Press, 1988.

Marshall, Christopher. *Passages from the Remembrances of Christopher Marshall, Member of the Committee of Observation and Inspection, of the Provincial Conference, And of the Council of Safety*. Ed. William Duane. Philadelphia: J. Crissy, 1839.

Moreau de Saint Méry, Médéric Louis Élie. *Moreau de St. Méry's American Journey*. Ed. Kenneth Roberts and Anna B. Roberts. Garden City, N.Y.: Doubleday, 1947.

Nicholls, James C. "Lady Henrietta Liston's Journal of Washington's 'Resignation,' Retirement, and Death." *Pennsylvania Magazine of History and Biography* 95 (1971): 511–20.

Playfair, William. *The History of Jacobinism, Its Crimes, Cruelties and Perfidies . . . With an Appendix by Peter Porcupine, Containing a History of the American Jacobins, Commonly Denominated Democrats*. Philadelphia: for William Cobbett, 1796.

Porcupine, Peter [William Cobbett]. *The Bloody Buoy Thrown Out As A Warning to the Political Pilots of America . . . .* Philadelphia: Thomas Bradford, 1795.

———. *A Bone to Gnaw, For the Democrats . . . .* Philadelphia: Thomas Bradford, 1795.

———. *A Bone to Gnaw, For the Democrats . . . Part II*. Philadelphia: Thomas Bradford, 1795.

Ratcliffe, Donald J. "The Autobiography of Benjamin Tappan." *Ohio History* 85 (1976): 109–57.

Riedesel, Frederike Charlotte Luise. *Letters and Journals Relating to the War of the American Revolution, And the Capture of the German Troops at Saratoga*. Trans. William L. Stone. Albany, N.Y.: J. Munsell, 1867.

Rush, Benjamin. *The Autobiography of Benjamin Rush: His "Travels Through Life" together with his Commonplace Book for 1789–1813*. Ed. George W. Corner. Princeton, N.J.: Princeton University Press, 1948.

Smith, Paul H. et al., eds. *Letters of Delegates to Congress, 1774–1789* 23 vols. to date. Washington, D.C.: Library of Congress, 1976–1995.

Stiles, Ezra. *The Literary Diary of Ezra Stiles*. Ed. Franklin Bowditch Dexter. 3 vols. New York: Charles Scribner, 1901.

Swan, Timothy. *The Songster's Museum; Or, A Trip to Elysium. A Selection of the Most Approved Songs, Duets, &c*. Northampton, Mass.: Andrew Wright, 1803.

Wainwright, Nicholas B., ed. "'A Diary of Trifling Occurrences': Philadelphia, 1776–1778." *Pennsylvania Magazine of History and Biography* 82 (1958): 411–65.

Wansey, Henry. *Henry Wansey and His American Journal: 1794*. Ed. David John Jeremy. Philadelphia: American Philosophical Society, 1970.

Washington, George. *The Diaries of George Washington*. Ed. Donald Jackson. 5 vols. Charlottesville: University Press of Virginia, 1976–1979.

———. *The Papers of George Washington: Presidential Series*. Ed. W. W. Abbot et al. 6 vols. to date. Charlottesville: University Press of Virginia, 1987–1996.

———. *The Writings of George Washington*. Ed. John C. Fitzpatrick. 37 vols. Washington, D.C.: U.S. Government Printing Office, 1931–1944.

Watson, John F. *Annals of Philadelphia, and Pennsylvania, in the Olden Time.* 2 vols. Philadelphia: Edwin S. Stuart, 1905.

Webster, Noah. *The Revolution in France, Considered in Respect to its Progress and Effects.* New York: George Bunce, 1794.

DOCUMENTS

The Debates And Proceedings In The Congress Of The United States; With An Appendix, Containing Important State Papers And Public Documents, And All The Laws Of A Public Nature; With A Copious Index, 42 vols. Washington, D.C.: Gales and Seaton, 1834–1856.

Austin, William. *A Selection of the Patriotic Addresses, To the President of the United States. Together With The President's Answers. Presented in the Year One Thousand Seven Hundred and Ninety-Eight, and the Twenty-Second of the Independence of America.* Boston: John W. Folsom, 1798.

Farrand, Max, ed. *The Records of the Federal Convention of 1787.* New Haven, Conn.: Yale University Press, 1966.

Foner, Philip S., ed. *The Democratic Republican Societies, 1790 – 1800, a Documentary Sourcebook of Constitutions, Declarations, Addresses, Resolutions, and Toasts.* Westport, Conn.: Greenwood Press, 1976.

Hardie, James. *The Philadelphia Directory and Register: Containing the Names, Occupations and Places of Abode of the Citizens, Arranged in Alphabetical Order . . . .* Philadelphia: T. Dobson, 1793.

Maclay, William. *Sketches of Debate in the First Senate of the United States in 1789 – 90 –91.* 1880. New York: Burt Franklin, 1969.

Milligan, Jacob. *The City Directory. By Jacob Milligan, harbour master. September, 1794.* Charleston, S.C.: William P. Young, 1794.

Return of the Whole Number of Persons Within the Several Districts of the United States, According to "An act Providing for the Enumeration of the Inhabitants of the United States," Passed March the First, One Thousand Seven Hundred and Ninety-One. Philadelphia: Childs and Swaine, 1791.

Return of the Whole Number of Persons Within the Several Districts of the United States, According to "An act providing for the second Census or Enumeration of the Inhabitants of the UNITED STATES." Washington, D.C.: William Duane, 1801.

The Two Trials of John Fries, or an Indictment for Treason; Together With a Brief Report of the Trials of Several Other Persons, for Treason and Insurrection, in the Counties of Bucks, Northampton and Montgomery, in the Circuit Court of the United States . . . . Philadelphia: William H. Woodward, 1800.

The Trial Record of Denmark Vesey, 1822. Boston: Beacon Press, 1970.

NEWSPAPERS AND MAGAZINES

The Albany Gazette (Albany).

The American Minerva, Patroness of Peace, Commerce, and the Liberal Arts (New York City).

The Augusta Chronicle and Gazette of the State (Augusta, Ga).

Aurora. General Advertiser (Philadelphia).

The Bee (New London).

The Boston Chronicle (Boston).

Boston Daily Advertiser (Boston).

The Boston-Evening Post (Boston).

The Boston Gazette (Boston).

The Boston News-Letter (Boston).

The Carlisle Gazette, and the Western Repository of Knowledge (Carlisle, Penna).

Columbian Centinel (Boston).

Columbian Magazine (Philadelphia).

The Columbian Herald, or the Independent Courier of North-America (Charleston, S.C.).

The Columbian Magazine or Monthly Miscellany (Philadelphia).

Commercial Advertiser (New York).

The Companion; and Commercial Advertiser (Newport, R.I.).

The Connecticut Courant (Hartford, Conn.).

The New-York Daily Advertiser (New York).

The Delaware Gazette (Wilmington, Del.).

The Democrat (Boston).

The Eagle: or, Dartmouth Centinel (Hanover, N.H.).

Vesper; or, the Evening Courier (Charleston, S.C.).

The Farmer's Library: Or, Vermont Political & Historical Register (Rutland, Vt.).

The Gazette of the State of Georgia (Savannah, Ga.).

Gazette of Maine (Portland, Me.).

The Gazette, of the State of South-Carolina (Charleston, S.C.).

Gazette of the United States (Philadelphia).

The Guardian; or, New-Brunswick Advertiser (New Brunswick, N.J.).

The Guardian of Liberty (Newport, R.I.).

Herald of the United States (Warren, R.I.).

The Independent Chronicle (Boston).

The Independent Gazetteer; or, the Chronicle of Freedom (Philadelphia).

The Independent Ledger, and the American Advertiser (Boston).

Jersey Chronicle (Mount Pleasant, N.J.).

Kennebeck Intelligencer (Augusta, Me.).

The Kentucky Gazette (Lexington, Ky.).

The Lancaster Journal (Lancaster, Penna.).

The Massachusetts Centinel (Boston).

The Maryland Gazette, and Baltimore General Advertiser (Baltimore).

Massachusetts Mercury (Boston).

National Gazette (Philadelphia).

The New-Jersey Journal, and Political Intelligencer (Elizabethtown, N.J.).

The New-London Summary (New London, Conn.).

The Newport Mercury (Newport, R.I.).

The New-York Gazette (New York).

The New-York Journal, or General Advertiser (New York).

The New-York Mercury (New York).
The Norwich Packet (Norwich, Conn.).
The New-York Evening Post (New York).
The Pennsylvania Gazette (Philadelphia).
The Pennsylvania Packet; and the General Advertiser (Philadelphia).
The Philadelphia Minerva (Philadelphia).
The Pittsburgh Gazette (Pittsburgh).
Porcupine's Gazette and United States Daily Advertiser (Philadelphia).
The Recorder (Richmond, Va.).
The Rhode-Island Museum (Newport, R.I.).
The Rutland Herald; Or, Vermont Mercury (Rutland, Vt.).
The South-Carolina Gazette (Charleston, S.C.). .
The South-Carolina Gazetteer; and Country Journal (Charleston, S.C.).
The State Gazette of North Carolina (Edenton, N.C.).
The Vermont Gazette (Bennington, Vt.).
The Virginia Gazette (Williamsburg, Va.), pub. John Dixon and William Hunter.
The Virginia Gazette (Williamsburg, Va.), pub. William Hunter.
The Virginia Gazette (Williamsburg, Va.), pub. John Dixon and Thomas Nicholson.
The Virginia Gazette (Williamsburg, Va.), pub. William Parks.
The Virginia Gazette (Williamsburg, Va.), pub. Alexander Purdie and John Dixon.
The Virginia Gazette (Williamsburg, Va.), pub. Clementina Rind.
The Virginia Gazette (Williamsburg, Va.), pub. William Rind.
The Virginia Gazette, or, the American Advertiser (Richmond, Va.).
The New-York Weekly Museum (New York).

BOOKS AND ARTICLES

Agulhon, Maurice. *Marianne into Battle: Republican Imagery and Symbolism in France, 1789–1880* 1979. Trans. Janet Lloyd. New York: Cambridge University Press, 1981.

Albanese, Catherine L. *Sons of the Fathers: The Civil Religion of the American Revolution.* Philadelphia: Temple University Press, 1976.

Althusser, Louis. *For Marx.* Trans. Ben Brewster. London: Verso, 1979.

———. *Lenin and Philosophy and Other Essays.* Trans. Ben Brewster. New York: Monthly Review Press, 1971.

Ammon, Harry. *The Genet Mission.* New York: W. W. Norton, 1973.

Anderson, Perry. "The Antinomies of Antonio Gramsci." *New Left Review* 100 (1976–1977): 5–78.

Andrews, Charles M. "The Boston Merchants and the Non-Importation Movement." *Transactions of the Colonial Society of Massachusetts* 19 (1916–17): 159–259.

Applebaum, Diana Karter. *The Glorious Fourth: An American Holiday.* New York: Facts on File, 1989.

Appleby, Joyce. *Capitalism and a New Social Order: The Republican Vision of the 1790s*. New York: New York University Press, 1984.

Apter, Judith and Lois Elkis. "'The Petticoat Electors': Women's Suffrage in New Jersey, 1776–1807." *Journal of the Early Republic* 12 (1992): 159–93.

Aptheker, Herbert, ed. *A Documentary History of the Negro People in the United States*. New York: Citadel Press, 1951.

Bailyn, Bernard. *The Ideological Origins of the American Revolution*. Cambridge, Mass.: Belknap Press, 1967.

Baker, Paula. "The Domestication of Politics: Women and American Political Society, 1780–1920." *American Historical Review* 89 (1984): 620–47.

Bakhtin, Mikhail. *The Dialogic Imagination: Four Essays by M. M. Bakhtin*. Ed. Michael Holquist, trans. Caryl Emerson and Michael Holquist. Austin: University of Texas Press, 1981.

Banner, James M. *To the Hartford Convention: The Federalists and the Origins of Party Politics in Massachusetts, 1789–1815*. New York: Alfred A. Knopf, 1970.

Banning, Lance. *The Jeffersonian Persuasion: Evolution of a Party Ideology*. Ithaca, N.Y.: Cornell University Press, 1978.

Beard, Charles A. *An Economic Interpretation of the Constitution of the United States*. New York: Macmillan, 1913.

Becker, Carl. *The History of Political Parties in the Province of New York, 1760–1776*. Madison: University of Wisconsin Press, 1909.

Beerman, Kurt. "The Reception of the French Revolution in the New York State Press: 1788–1791." Ph.D. diss., New York University, 1960.

Bell, Whitfield J., Jr. "The Federal Processions of 1788," *The New-York Historical Society Quarterly* 46 (1962): 5–39.

Bercé, Yves-Marie. *Fête et révolte: des mentalités populaires de XVIme au XVIIIme siècle*. Paris: Hachette, 1976.

Bergeron, David M. *English Civic Pageantry, 1558–1642*. Columbia: University of South Carolina Press, 1971.

Bernhard, Winfred E.A. *Fisher Ames: Federalist and Statesman, 1758–1808*. Chapel Hill: University of North Carolina Press, 1965.

Blau, Alan L. "New York City and the French Revolution, 1789–1797." Ph.D. diss., City University of New York, 1973.

Boorstin, Daniel J. *The Americans: The National Experience*. New York: Random House, 1965.

Bourdieu, Pierre. *Language and Symbolic Power*. Ed. John B. Thompson, trans. Gino Raymond and Matthew Adamson. Cambridge, Mass.: Harvard University Press, 1991.

Branson, Susan. "'Comme l'Arche de Noe': The French in Philadelphia in the 1790s." Presented at the annual meeting of the Pennsylvania Historical Association, October 1994.

———. "'Fiery Frenchified Dames': American Women and the French Revolution." Paper presented at the annual meeting of the American Historical Association, 1991.

———. *Women and Public Space: Gender, Politics, and Society in the 1790s*. Forthcoming.

Brewer, John. *The Common People and Politics, 1750s–1790s*. Cambridge: Chadwyck-Healey, 1986.

———. "The Number 45: A Wilkite Political Symbol." In Stephen B. Baxter, ed., *England's Rise to Greatness* Berkeley: University of California Press, 1983. 349–80.

———. *Party Ideology and Popular Politics at the Accession of George III*. New York: Cambridge University Press, 1976.

Brooke, John L. "Ancient Lodges and Self-Created Societies: Voluntary Associations and the Public Sphere in the Early Republic." Paper presented at the United States Capitol Historical Society Conference, Washington, D.C., 1990.

Broussard, James H. *The Southern Federalists, 1800–1816*. Baton Rouge: Louisiana State University Press, 1978.

Brown, Richard D. *Knowledge Is Power: The Diffusion of Information in Early America, 1700–1865*. New York: Oxford University Press, 1989.

———. *Revolutionary Politics in Massachusetts: The Boston Committee of Correspondence and the Towns*. Cambridge, Mass.: Harvard University Press, 1970.

Brown, Richard M. *The South Carolina Regulators: The Story of the First American Vigilante Movement*. Cambridge, Mass.: Belknap Press, 1963.

Buel, Richard, Jr. *Securing the Revolution: Ideology in American Politics, 1789–1815*. Ithaca, N.Y.: Cornell University Press, 1972.

Burrows, Edwin G. "Military Experience and the Origins of Federalism and Anti-Federalism." In Jacob Judd and Irwin Polishook, eds., *Aspects of Early New York Society and Politics*. Tarrytown, N.Y.: Sleepy Hollow Restorations, 1974. 83–92.

Bushman, Richard L. *King and People in Provincial Massachusetts*. Chapel Hill: University of North Carolina Press, 1985.

Cannadine, David and Simon Price, eds. *Rituals of Royalty: Power and Ceremonial in Traditional Societies*. New York: Cambridge University Press, 1987.

Catalogue of Coins, Tokens, And Medals in The Numismatic Collection of the Mint of the United States at Philadelphia, PA. Washington, D.C.: U.S. Government Printing Office, 1912.

Chartier, Roger. "La naissance de la marginalité: entretien avec Roger Chartier." *L'Histoire* 43 (1982): 106–11.

Childs, Frances Sergeant. *French Refugee Life in the United States, 1790–1800: An American Chapter of the French Revolution*. Baltimore: Johns Hopkins University Press, 1940.

Clark, Charles E. *The Public Prints: The Newspaper in Anglo-American Culture, 1665–1740*. New York: Oxford University Press, 1994.

Clawson, Mary Ann. *Constructing Brotherhood: Class, Gender, and Fraternalism*. Princeton, N.J.: Princeton University Press, 1989.

Cogliano, Francis D. "No King No Popery: Anti-Popery and Revolution in New England, 1745–1791." Ph.D. diss., Boston University, 1993.

Combs, Jerald A. *The Jay Treaty: Political Battleground of the Founding Fathers*. Berkeley: University of California Press, 1970.

Conroy, David W. "Puritans in Taverns: Law and Popular Culture in Colonial Massachusetts, 1630–1720." In Susanna Barrows and Robin Room, eds., *Drink-*

ing: Behavior and Belief in Modern History. Berkeley: University of California Press, 1991. 29–60.

Cornell, Saul. "Aristocracy Assailed: The Ideology of Backcountry Anti-Federalism." *Journal of American History* 76 (1990): 1148–72.

Cunliffe, Marcus. *George Washington: Man and Monument*. Boston: Little, Brown and Company, 1958.

Cunningham, Noble, E. Jr. *The Jeffersonian Republicans: The Formation of Party Organization, 1789–1801*. Chapel Hill: University of North Carolina Press, 1957.

Davis, Natalie Zemon. "Toward Mixtures and Margins." *American Historical Review* 97 (1992): 1409–1416.

Davis, Susan G. *Parades and Power: Street Theatre in Nineteenth Century Philadelphia*. 1986. Berkeley: University of California Press, 1988.

Davis, William W.H. *The Fries Rebellion, 1798–1799*. New York: Arno Press, 1969.

Dorland, W.A. Newman. "The Second Troop of Philadelphia City Cavalry." *Pennsylvania Magazine of History and Biography* 45 (1921): 364–87; 46 (1922): 57–77, 154–72, 262–71, 346– 65; 47 (1923): 67–79, 147–77, 262–76, 357–75; 48 (1924): 270–84, 372–82.

Dunlap, William. *A History of the American Theatre*. New York: J. and J. Harper, 1832.

Dupre, Huntley. "The Kentucky Gazette Reports the French Revolution." *Mississippi Valley Historical Review* 26 (1939): 163–80.

Durey, Michael. "Thomas Paine's Apostles: Radical Emigres and the Triumph of Jeffersonian Republicanism." *William and Mary Quarterly* 3d ser. 44 (1987): 661–88.

Earle, Alice Morse. *Colonial Days in Old New York*. New York: Scribner's, 1912.

Egerton, Douglas R. "Gabriel's Conspiracy and the Election of 1800." *Journal of Southern History* 56 (1990): 191–214.

———. *Gabriel's Rebellion: The Virginia Slave Conspiracies of 1800 and 1802*. Chapel Hill: University of North Carolina Press, 1993.

Erhard, Jean and Paul Villeneix. *Les fêtes de la révolution*. Paris: Société des Etudes Robespierristes, 1977.

Elkins, Stanley M. and Eric L. McKitrick. *The Age of Federalism: The Early American Republic, 1788–1800*. New York: Oxford University Press, 1993.

Elting, John R. *Military Uniforms in America: The Era of the American Revolution, 1755–1795*. San Rafael, Calif.: Presidio Press, 1974.

Epstein, James. "Radical Dining, Toasting, and Symbolic Expression in Early Nineteenth-Century Lancashire: Rituals of Solidarity." *Albion* 20 (1988): 271–91.

———. "Understanding the Cap of Liberty: Symbolic Practice and Social Conflict in Early Nineteenth-Century England." *Past and Present* 122 (1989): 75–118.

Faust, Drew Gilpin. *The Creation of Confederate Nationalism: Ideology and Identity in the Civil War South*. Baton Rouge: Louisiana State University Press, 1988.

Fischer, David Hackett. *Albion's Seed: Four British Folkways in America*. New York: Oxford University Press, 1989.

———. *The Revolution of American Conservatism: The Federalist Party in the Age of Jefferson*. New York: Harper and Row, 1965.

Fliegelman, Jay. *Declaring Independence: Jefferson, Natural Language, and the Culture of Performance*. Stanford, Calif.: Stanford University Press, 1993.

Foucault, Michel. *Power/Knowledge: Selected Interviews and Other Writings, 1972–1977*. Ed. Colin Gordon, trans. Colin Gordon, Leo Marshall, John Mepham, Kate Soper. New York: Pantheon Books, 1980.

Frey, Sylvia R. *Water from the Rock: Black Resistance in a Revolutionary Age*. Princeton, N.J.: Princeton University Press, 1991.

Furley, O. W. "The Pope-Burning Processions of the Late- Seventeenth Century." *History* 44 (1959): 16–23.

Genovese, Eugene D. *Roll, Jordan, Roll: The World the Slaves Made*. New York: Pantheon, 1974.

Germani, Gino. *Marginality*. New Brunswick, N.J.: Transaction Books, 1980.

Gertzog, Irwin N. "Female Suffrage in New Jersey, 1790–1807." In Naomi Lynn, ed. *Women, Politics and the Constitution*, New York: Haworth Press, 1990. 47–58.

Gildrie, Richard P. "The Ceremonial Puritan: Days of Humiliation and Thanksgiving." *New England Historical and Genealogical Register* 136 (1982): 3–16.

Gilje, Paul A. "The Common People and the Constitution: Popular Culture in New York City in the Late Eighteenth Century." In Paul A. Gilje and William Pencak, eds., *New York in the Age of the Constitution, 1775–1800*. Rutherford, N.J.: Fairleigh Dickinson University Press, 1992. 48–73.

———. *The Road to Mobocracy: Popular Disorder in New York City, 1763–1834*. Chapel Hill: University of North Carolina Press, 1987.

Goodman, Paul. *The Democratic-Republicans of Massachusetts: Politics in a Young Republic*. Cambridge, Mass.: Harvard University Press, 1964.

Gramsci, Antonio. *Selections from the Prison Notebooks of Antonio Gramsci*. Ed. and trans. Quintin Hoare and Geoffrey Nowell Smith. New York: International Publishers, 1971.

Grimes, Ronald L. *Ritual Criticism: Case Studies in its Practice, Essays on Its Theory*. Columbia: University of South Carolina Press, 1990.

Griswold, Rufus Wilmot. *The Republican Court: Or, American Society in the Days of Washington*. New York: D. Appleton, 1854.

Habermas, Jürgen. "The Public Sphere: An Encyclopedia Article (1964)." *New German Critique* 5 (1974): 49–55.

Hall, David D. *Days of Wonder, Days of Judgement: Popular Religious Belief in Early New England*. New York: Alfred A. Knopf, 1989.

Harden, J. David. "Liberty Caps and Liberty Trees." *Past and Present* 146 (1995): 66–102.

Harris, Jennifer. "The Red Cap of Liberty: A Study of Dress Worn by French Revolutionary Partisans, 1789–1794." *Eighteenth-Century Studies* 14 (1980–1981): 283–312.

Harris, Tim. *London Crowds in the Reign of Charles II: Propaganda and Politics From the Restoration Until the Exclusion Crisis*. New York: Cambridge University Press, 1987.

Harrison, Mark. *Crowds and History: Mass Phenomena in English Towns, 1790–1835*. New York: Cambridge University Press, 1988.

Hay, Robert Pettus. "Freedom's Jubilee: One Hundred Years of the Fourth of July, 1776 to 1876." Ph.D. diss., University of Kentucky, 1967.

———. "George Washington: American Moses." *American Quarterly* 21 (1969): 780–91.

Hazen, Charles Downer. *Contemporary American Opinion of the French Revolution*. Baltimore: Johns Hopkins University Press, 1897.

Hébert, Ann Catherine. "The Pennsylvania French in the 1790s: The Story of Their Survival." Ph.D. diss., University of Texas at Austin, 1971.

Henderson, Archibald. *George Washington's Southern Tour, 1791*. Boston: Houghton Mifflin, 1923.

Henretta, James A. "Economic Development and Social Structure in Colonial Boston." *William and Mary Quarterly* 3d ser. 22 (1965): 75–92.

Hickey, Donald R. "America's Response to the Slave Revolt in Haiti, 1791–1806." *Journal of the Early Republic* 2 (1982): 361–80.

Hill, Christopher. *The World Turned Upside Down*. 1972. Harmondsworth: Penguin, 1975.

Hindle, Brook. "The March of the Paxton Boys." *William and Mary Quarterly* 3d ser. 3 (1946): 461–86.

———. *David Rittenhouse*. Princeton, N.J.: Princeton University Press, 1964.

Hobsbawm, E. J. *The Age of Capital, 1848–1875*. New York: Scribner's, 1975.

———. *Primitive Rebels: Studies in Archaic Forms of Social Movements in the Nineteenth and Twentieth Centuries*. Manchester: Manchester University Press, 1959.

Hobsbawm, Eric and Terence Ranger, eds. *The Invention of Tradition*. New York: Cambridge University Press, 1983.

Hodges, Graham Russell. "Black Revolt in New York City and the Neutral Zone: 1775–83." In Paul A. Gilje and William Pencak, eds., *New York in the Age of the Constitution, 1775–1800*, Rutherford, N.J.: Fairleigh Dickinson University Press, 1992. 20–47.

Hoerder, Dirk. "Boston Leaders and Boston Crowds, 1765–1776." In Alfred F. Young, ed., *The American Revolution: Explorations in the History of American Radicalism*. DeKalb: Northern Illinois University Press, 1976. 233–71.

Hofstadter, Richard. *The Idea of a Party System: The Rise of Legitimate Opposition in the United States, 1780–1840*. Berkeley: University of California Press, 1969.

Hooker, Richard J. "The American Revolution Seen Through A Wine Glass." *William and Mary Quarterly* 3d ser. 11 (1954): 52–77.

Hunt, Alfred N. *Haiti's Influence on Antebellum America: Slaveholding Volcano in the Caribbean*. Baton Rouge: Louisiana State University Press, 1988.

Hutson, James H. "John Adams' Title Campaign." *New England Quarterly* 41 (1968): 30–39.

Hutton, Ronald. *The Rise and Fall of Merry England: The Ritual Year, 1400–1700*. New York: Oxford University Press, 1994.

Hyslop, Beatrice F. "The American Press and the French Revolution of 1789." *Proceedings of the American Philosophical Society* 104 (1960): 54–85.

———. "American Press Reports of the French Revolution, 1789–1794." *New York Historical Society Quarterly Bulletin* 42 (1958): 329–48.

Isaac, Rhys. *The Transformation of Virginia, 1740 –1790*. Chapel Hill: University of North Carolina Press, 1982.

Jackson, Melvin H. *Privateers in Charleston, 1793 –1796: An Account of a Palatinate in South Carolina*. Washington, D.C.: Smithsonian Institution Press, 1969.

Jacob, Margaret C. *Living the Enlightenment: Freemasonry and Politics in Eighteenth-Century Europe*. New York: Oxford University Press, 1991.

Jacobs, Wilbur R. *The Paxton Riots and the Frontier Theory*. Chicago: Rand McNally, 1967.

Johnstone, Robert M., Jr. *Jefferson and the Presidency: Leadership in the Young Republic*. Ithaca, N.Y.: Cornell University Press, 1978.

Jordan, Gerald and Nicholas Rogers. "Admirals as Heroes: Patriotism and Liberty in Hanoverian England." *Journal of British Studies* 28 (1989): 201–24.

Jordan, Winthrop. *White over Black: American Attitudes Toward the Negro, 1550 – 1812*. Chapel Hill: University of North Carolina Press, 1968.

Kaplan, Sidney. "Veteran Officers and Politics in Massachusetts, 1783–1787." *William and Mary Quarterly* 3d ser. 9 (1952): 29–57.

Karsten, Peter. *Patriot-Heroes in England and America: Political Symbolism and Changing Values over Three Centuries*. Madison: University of Wisconsin Press, 1978.

Kay, Marvin L. Michael. "The North Carolina Regulation, 1766–1776." In Alfred F. Young, ed., *The American Revolution: Explorations in the History of American Radicalism*. DeKalb: Northern Illinois University Press, 1976.

Kaye, Harvey K. and Keith McClelland, eds. *E.P. Thompson: Critical Perspectives*. Philadelphia: Temple University Press, 1990.

Keller, William F. "The French Craze of '93 and the American Press." *Americana* 35 (1941): 473–96.

Kelley, Robin D. G. "Notes on Deconstructing 'The Folk'." *American Historical Review* 97 (1992): 1400–1408.

Kerber, Linda K. *Federalists in Dissent: Imagery and Ideology in Jeffersonian America*. Ithaca, N.Y.: Cornell University Press, 1970.

———. " 'History Can Do It No Justice': Women and the Reinterpretation of the American Revolution." In Ronald Hoffman and Peter J. Albert, eds., *Women in the Age of the American Revolution*. Charlottesville: University Press of Virginia 1989. 3–42.

———. " 'I Have Don . . . much to carrey on the Warr': Women and the Shaping of Republican Ideology after the American Revolution." In Harriet B. Applewhite and Darline G. Levy, eds., *Women and Politics in the Age of Democratic Revolution*. Ann Arbor: University of Michigan Press, 1990. 227–58.

———. "The Paradox of Women's Citizenship in the Early Republic: The Case of *Martin vs. Massachusetts*, 1805." *American Historical Review* 97 (1992): 349–78.

———. "The Republican Mother: Women and the Enlightenment—An American Perspective." *American Quarterly* 28 (1976): 187–205.

———. *Women of the Republic: Intellect and Ideology in Revolutionary America*. Chapel Hill: University of North Carolina Press, 1980.

Kornblith, Gary John. "From Artisans to Businessmen: Master Mechanics in New England, 1789–1803." Ph.D. diss., Princeton University, 1983.

Koschnik, Albrecht. "Political Conflict and Public Contest: Rituals of National Celebration in Philadelphia, 1788–1815." *Pennsylvania Magazine of History and Biography* 98 (1994): 209–48.

Krantz, Frederick, ed. *History from Below: Studies in Popular Protest and Popular Ideology in Honor of George Rudé.* Montreal: Concordia University, 1985.

Kulikoff, Allan. "The Progress of Inequality in Revolutionary Boston." *William and Mary Quarterly* 3d ser. 28 (1971): 375–411.

Lemisch, Jesse. "Jack Tar in the Streets: Merchant Seamen in the Politics of Revolutionary America." *William and Mary Quarterly* 3d ser. 25 (1968): 371–407.

———. "Listening to the 'Inarticulate': William Widger's Dream and the Loyalties of American Revolutionary Seamen in British Prisons." *Journal of Social History* 3 (1969): 1–29.

Lewis Miller, Sketches and Chronicles: The Reflections of a Nineteenth Century Pennsylvania German Folk Artist. York, Penna.: Historical Society of York County, 1966.

Levine, Lawrence. "The Folklore of Industrial Society: Popular Culture and Its Audiences." *American Historical Review* 97 (1992): 1369–99.

Linebaugh, Peter and Marcus Rediker. "The Many-Headed Hydra: Sailors, Slaves and the Atlantic Working Class in the Eighteenth Century." *Journal of Historical Sociology* 3 (1990): 225–51.

Link, Eugene Perry. *Democratic-Republican Societies, 1790–1800.* New York: Columbia University Press, 1942.

Longmore, Paul K. "The Enigma of George Washington: How Did the Man Become the Myth?" *Reviews in American History* 13 (1985): 184–90.

———. *The Invention of George Washington.* Berkeley: University of California Press, 1988.

Looney, J. Jefferson and Ruth L. Woodward, eds. *Princetonians, 1791–1794: A Biographical Dictionary.* Princeton, N.J.: Princeton University Press, 1991.

Love, William D. *The Fast and Thanksgiving Days of New England.* Boston: Houghton Mifflin, 1895.

Lynn, Naomi, ed. *Women, Politics and the Constitution.* New York: Haworth Press, 1990.

Mahon, John K. *The American Militia: Decade of Decision, 1789–1800.* Gainesville: University of Florida Press, 1960.

Maier, Pauline. *From Resistance to Revolution: Colonial Radicals and the Development of American Opposition to Britain, 1765–1776.* New York: Alfred A. Knopf, 1972.

Manning, Frank E., ed. *The Celebration of Society: Perspectives on Contemporary Cultural Performance.* Bowling Green, Oh.: Bowling Green University Press, 1983.

Marston, Jerrilyn Greene. *King and Congress: The Transfer of Political Legitimacy, 1774–1776.* Princeton, N.J.: Princeton University Press, 1987.

Mason, Laura. "*Ça Ira* and the Birth of the Revolutionary Song." *History Workshop: A Journal of Socialist and Feminist Historians* 28 (1989): 22–38.

———. *Singing the French Revolution: Popular Culture and Politics, 1787–1799*. Ithaca, N.Y.: Cornell University Press, 1996.

Matthews, Glenna. *The Rise of Public Woman: Woman's Power and Woman's Place in the United States, 1630–1970*. New York: Oxford University Press, 1992.

Mayo, Bernard. *Myths and Men: Patrick Henry, George Washington, Thomas Jefferson*. Athens: University of Georgia Press, 1959.

McGlynn, Frank and Arthur Tuden, eds. *Anthropological Approaches to Political Behavior*. Pittsburgh: University of Pittsburgh Press, 1991.

Medvedev, P. N. and M. M. Bakhtin. *The Formal Method in Literary Scholarship: A Critical Introduction to Sociological Poetics*. 1928. Trans. Albert J. Wehrle. Baltimore: Johns Hopkins University Press, 1977.

Melville, Herman. *Billy Budd, Sailor & Other Stories*. New York: Penguin, 1970.

Middlekauf, Robert. "The Ritualization of the American Revolution." In Stanley Coben and Lorman Ratner, eds., *The Development of an American Culture*. Englewood Cliffs, N.J.: Prentice Hall, 1970. 31–43.

Miller, John C. *Crisis in Freedom: The Alien and Sedition Acts*. Boston: Little, Brown, and Company, 1951.

Miller, Richard G. "The Federal City, 1783–1800." In Russell F. Weigley, ed., *Philadelphia: A 300-Year History*. New York: W. W. Norton, 1982. 155–205.

Moffat, Riley. *Population History of Eastern U.S. Cities and Towns, 1790–1870*. Metuchen, N.J.: Scarecrow Press, 1992.

Morgan, Edmund S. *American Slavery, American Freedom: The Ordeal of Colonial Virginia*. New York: W. W. Norton, 1975.

———. *Inventing the People: The Rise of Popular Sovereignty in England and America*. New York: W. W. Norton, 1988.

Morgan, Edmund S. and Helen M. Morgan. *The Stamp Act Crisis: Prologue to Revolution*. 1953. New York: W. W. Norton, 1963.

Muchembled, Robert. *Popular Culture and Elite Culture in France, 1700–1750*. Trans. Lydia Cochrane. Baton Rouge: Louisiana State University Press, 1985.

Murrin, John M. "Anglicizing an American Colony: The Transformation of Provincial Massachusetts." Ph.D. diss., Yale University, 1966.

———. "Escaping Perfidious Albion: Federalism, Fear of Aristocracy, and the Democratization of Corruption in Postrevolutionary America." In Richard K. Matthews, ed., *Virtue, Corruption, and Self-Interest: Political Values in the Eighteenth Century*. Bethlehem, Penna.: Lehigh University Press, 1994.

———. "The Great Inversion, or Court versus Country: A Comparison of the Revolution Settlements in England (1688–1721) and America (1776–1816)." In J.G.A. Pocock, ed., *Three British Revolutions: 1641, 1688, 1776*. Princeton, N.J.: Princeton University Press, 1980. 368–453.

Myers, Minor, Jr. *Liberty Without Anarchy: A History of the Society of the Cincinnati*. Charlottesville: University Press of Virginia, 1983.

Nash, Gary B. "The American Clergy and the French Revolution." *William and Mary Quarterly* 3d ser. 22 (1965): 392–412.

———. *Forging Freedom: The Formation of Philadelphia's Black Community, 1720–1840*. Cambridge, Mass.: Harvard University Press, 1988.

———. *The Urban Crucible: Social Change, Political Consciousness, and the Ori-*

gins of the American Revolution. Cambridge, Mass.: Harvard University Press, 1979.

Nelson, Cary and Lawrence Grossberg, eds. *Marxism and the Interpretation of .Culture*. Urbana: University of Illinois Press, 1988.

Nelson, Paul David. *William Tryon and the Course of Empire: A Life in British Imperial Service*. Chapel Hill: University of North Carolina Press, 1990.

Newman, Paul Douglas. "Fries Rebellion and American Political Culture, 1798–1800." *Pennsylvania Magazine of History and Biography* 119 (1995): 37–73.

Newman, Simon P. "Eagles, Hearts, and Crucifixes: The Mentalités of Philadelphia Seafarers in the New Republic." Paper presented at the Philadelphia Center for Early American Studies, 1994.

———. "'Tis the Worlds Jubilee and Mankind Must Be Free': Boston Celebrates the Victory at Valmy." Paper presented at the annual meeting of the American Historical Association, Chicago, 1991.

———. "'To Defame or Weaken the Government': The Alien and Sedition Acts and American Political Culture." Paper presented at the annual meeting of the Organization of American Historians, 1992.

Nord, David Paul. "Newspapers and American Nationhood." In John B. Hench, ed., *Three Hundred Years of the American Newspaper*. Worcester, Mass.: American Antiquarian Society, 1991. 391–405.

Norton, Mary Beth. *Liberty's Daughters: The Revolutionary Experience of American Women, 1750–1800*. Boston: Little, Brown, and Company, 1980.

Ozouf, Mona. *Festivals and the French Revolution*. 1976. Trans. Alan Sheridan. Cambridge, Mass.: Harvard University Press, 1988.

Paine, Ralph D. *The Ships and Sailors of Old Salem: The Record of a Brilliant Era of American Achievement*. New York: Outing Publishing, 1909.

Palmer, R. R. *The World of the French Revolution*. 2 vols. New York: Harper and Row, 1971.

Parker, Noel. *Portrayals of Revolution: Images, Debates and Patterns of Thought on the French Revolution*. Carbondale: Southern Illinois University Press, 1990.

Piersen, William G. *Black Yankees*. Amherst: University of Massachusetts Press, 1988.

Procter, David E. *Enacting Political Culture: Rhetorical Transformations of Liberty Weekend 1986*. New York: Praeger, 1991.

Rediker, Marcus. *Between the Devil and the Deep Blue Sea: Merchant Seamen, Pirates, and the Anglo-American Maritime World, 1700–1750*. New York: Cambridge University Press, 1987.

Reidy, Joseph P. "'Negro Election Day' & Black Community Life in New England, 1750–1860." *Marxist Perspectives* 1 (1978): 102.

Ribeiro, Aileen. *Fashion in the French Revolution*. New York: Holmes and Meier, 1988.

Riordan, Liam. "'O Dear, What Can the Matter Be': Politics and Popular Song in the *Federal Overture* (1794)." Unpublished paper, 1995.

Rodgers, Daniel T. *Contested Truths: Keywords in American Politics Since Independence*. New York: Basic Books, 1987.

Roeber, A. G. *Palatines, Liberty, and Property: German Lutherans in Colonial British America*. Baltimore: Johns Hopkins University Press, 1993.

Rogers, Nicholas. *Whigs and Cities: Popular Politics in the Age of Walpole and Pitt*. Oxford: Clarendon Press, 1989.

Rosswurm, Steven. *Arms, Country, and Class: The Philadelphia Militia and the "Lower Sort" During the American Revolution, 1775–1783*. New Brunswick, N.J.: Rutgers University Press, 1987.

Rudé, George E. *The Crowd in History: A Study of Popular Disturbances in France and England, 1730–1848*. New York: Wiley, 1964.

———. *The Face of the Crowd: Studies in Revolution, Ideology, and Popular Protest. Selected Essays of George Rudé*. Ed. Harvey J. Kaye. Atlantic Highlands, N.J.: Humanities Press International, 1988.

———. *Wilkes and Liberty: A Social Study of 1763 to 1774*. Oxford: Oxford University Press, 1962.

Ryan, Mary P. *Women in Public: Between Banners and Ballots, 1825–1880*. Baltimore: Johns Hopkins University Press, 1990.

Ryerson, Richard Alan. *The Revolution Is Now Begun: The Radical Committees of Philadelphia, 1765–1776*. Philadelphia: University of Pennsylvania Press, 1978.

Sassoon, Anne Showstack, ed. *Approaches to Gramsci*. London: Writers and Readers, 1982.

Saul, Norman E. "Ships and Seamen as Agents of Revolution." In Warren Spencer, ed. *The Consortium on Revolutionary Europe, 1750–1850: Proceedings 1986*. Athens: University of Georgia Press, 1987. 248–58.

Schama, Simon. *The Embarrassment of Riches*. Berkeley: University of California Press, 1988.

Scharf, J. Thomas and Thompson Westcott. *History of Philadelphia, 1609–1884*. 2 vols. Philadelphia: L. H. Everts, 1884.

Schlesinger, Arthur, Sr. "Liberty Tree: A Genealogy." *New England Quarterly* 25 (1952): 435–58.

———. *Prelude to Independence: The American Newspaper War on Britain, 1764–1776*. New York: Knopf, 1958.

Schwartz, Barry. *George Washington: The Making of an American Symbol*. New York: Free Press, 1987.

Secombe, Matthew. "From Revolution to Republic: The Later Political Career of Samuel Adams, 1774–1803." Ph.D. diss., Yale University, 1978.

Sharp, James Roger. *American Politics in the Early Republic: The New Nation in Crisis*. New Haven, Conn.: Yale University Press, 1993.

Shaw, Peter. *American Patriots and the Rituals of Revolution*. Cambridge, Mass.: Harvard University Press, 1981.

Smith, Barbara Clark. "Food Rioters and the American Revolution." *William and Mary Quarterly* 3d ser. 51 (1994): 3–38.

Smith, Billy G. *The "Lower Sort": Philadelphia's Laboring People, 1750–1800*. Ithaca, N.Y.: Cornell University Press, 1990.

Smith, James Morton. "The Federalist 'Saints' Versus 'The Devil of Sedition': The Liberty Pole Cases of Dedham, Massachusetts, 1798–1799." *New England Quarterly* 28 (1955): 198–215.

———. *Freedom's Fetters: The Alien and Sedition Laws and American Civil Liberties*. Ithaca, N.Y.: Cornell University Press, 1966.

Soderlund, Jean R. "Black Women in Colonial Pennsylvania." *Pennsylvania Magazine of History and Biography* 107 (1983): 49–68.

Sosnowski, Thomas C. "Bitter Farewells: Francophobia and the French Emigres in America." *Consortium on Revolutionary Europe 1750–1850: Proceedings* 21 (1992): 276–83.

Sprinkle, John Harold, Jr. "Loyalists and Baconians: The Participants in Bacon's Rebellion in Virginia, 1676–1677." Ph.D. diss., College of William and Mary, 1992.

Stabile, Susan. "'By a Female Hand': Letters, Belles Lettres, and the Philadelphia Culture of Performance, 1760–1820." Ph.D. diss., University of Delaware, 1996.

———. "'I Saw Great Fabius Come in State': Philadelphia Women's Court Poetry in the Age of Washington." Paper presented at the annual meeting of the Society of Historians of the Early American Republic, Chapel Hill, N.C., July 1994.

Stewart, Donald H. *The Opposition Press of the Federalist Period*. Albany: State University of New York Press, 1969.

Stinchcombe, William C. "Americans Celebrate the Birth of the Dauphin." In Ronald Hoffman and Peter J. Albert, eds., *Diplomacy and Revolution: The Franco-American Alliance of 1778*. Charlottesville: University Press of Virginia, 1981.

Sturm, Albert L. "The Development of American State Constitutions." *Publius: The Journal of Federalism* 12 (1982): 57–98.

Tagg, James D. *Benjamin Franklin Bache and the Philadelphia Aurora*. Philadelphia: University of Pennsylvania Press, 1991.

Tatum, Charles T. "The Beginnings of United States Coinage." *American Journal of Numismatic and Archaeological Societies* 29 (1895): 69–76.

Taxay, Don. *The U.S. Mint and Coinage: An Illustrated History from 1776 to the Present*. New York: Arno Press, 1966.

Thompson, E. P. *Customs in Common: Studies in Traditional Popular Culture*. London: Merlin Press, 1991.

———. *The Making of the English Working Class*. London: U. Gollancz, 1963.

———. *Whigs and Hunters: The Origin of the Black Act*. New York: Pantheon, 1975.

Thompson, Peter. "'The Friendly Glass': Drink and Gentility in Colonial Philadelphia." *Pennsylvania Magazine of History and Biography* 113 (1989): 549–73.

———. "A Social History of Philadelphia's Taverns, 1683–1800." Ph.D. diss., University of Pennsylvania, 1989.

Tillson, Albert H., Jr. "The Militia and Popular Political Culture in the Upper Valley of Virginia, 1740–1775." *Virginia Magazine of History and Biography* 94 (1986): 285–306.

Travers, Len. "'The Brightest Day in Our Calendar': Independence Day in Boston and Philadelphia, 1776–1826." Ph.D. diss., Boston University, 1992.

———. "'The Brightest Day in our Calendar': Patriotism, Politics, and Independence Day in Federalist Boston, 1783–1818." *Essex Institute Historical Collections* 125 (1989): 129–61.

Ulrich, Laurel Thatcher. *A Midwife's Tale: The Life of Martha Ballard, Based On Her Diary, 1785–1812*. New York: Knopf, 1991.

Vermeule, Cornelius. *Numismatic Art in America: Aesthetics of the United States Coinage*. Cambridge, Mass.: Belknap Press, 1971.

Wade, Melvin C. "'Shining in Borrowed Plumage': Affirmation of Community in Black Coronation Festivals of New England, ca. 1750–1850." In Robert Blair St. George, ed., *Material Life in America*. Boston: Northeastern University Press, 1988. 171–81.

Waldstreicher, David. *The Making of American Nationalism: Celebrations and Political Culture, 1776–1820*. Chapel Hill: University of North Carolina Press, forthcoming.

———. "Rites of Rebellion, Rites of Assent: Celebrations, Print Culture, and the Origins of American Nationalism." *Journal of American History* 82 (1995): 37–61.

Warner, Michael. *The Letters of the Republic: Publication and the Public Sphere in Eighteenth-Century America*. Cambridge, Mass.: Harvard University Press, 1990.

Warren, Charles. *Jacobin and Junto, or, Early American Politics as Viewed in the Diary of Dr. Nathaniel Ames, 1758–1822*. Cambridge, Mass.: Harvard University Press, 1931.

Washburn, Wilcomb E. *The Governor and the Rebel: A History of Bacon's Rebellion in Virginia*. Chapel Hill: University of North Carolina Press, 1957.

Webb, Stephen Saunders. *1676: The End of American Independence*. 1984. Cambridge, Mass.: Harvard University Press, 1985.

Weems, Mason L. *The Life of Washington*. 1800. Ed. Marcus Cunliffe. Cambridge, Mass.: Belknap Press, 1962.

Wehtje, Myron Floyd. "A Town in the Confederation: Boston, 1783–1787." Ph.D. diss., University of Virginia, 1978.

White, Shane. "'It Was a Proud Day': African Americans, Festivals, and Parades in the North, 1741–1834." *Journal of American History* 81 (1994): 13–50.

———. "Pinkster: Afro-Dutch Syncretization in New York City and the Hudson Valley." *Journal of American Folklore* 102 (1989): 68–75.

Wilentz, Sean. "Artisan Republican Festivals and the Rise of Class Conflict in New York City, 1788–1837." In Michael H. Frisch and Daniel J. Walkowitz, eds., *Working-Class America: Essays on Labor, Community, and American Society*. Urbana: University of Illinois Press, 1983. 37–77.

———. *Chants Democratic: New York City and the Rise of the American Working Class, 1788–1850*. New York: Oxford University Press, 1984.

Williams, Raymond. *Keywords: A Vocabulary of Culture and Society* Revised edition. New York: Oxford University Press, 1983.

Williams, William Appleman. *America Confronts a Revolutionary World, 1776–1976*. New York: Morrow, 1976.

Williams-Myers, A. J. "Pinkster Carnival: Africanisms in the Hudson River Valley." *Afro-Americanisms in New York Life and History* 9 (1985): 7–17.

Wills, Gary. *Cincinnatus: George Washington and the Enlightenment*. Garden City, N.Y.: Doubleday, 1984.

————. *Inventing America: Jefferson's Declaration of Independence*. New York: Doubleday, 1978.

Withington, Ann Fairfax. *Toward a More Perfect Union: Virtue and the Formation of American Republics*. New York: Oxford University Press, 1991.

Wood, Gordon S. *The Creation of the American Republic, 1776–1787*. Chapel Hill: University of North Carolina Press, 1969.

————. *The Radicalism of the American Revolution*. New York: Alfred A. Knopf, 1992.

Wood, Peter H. "'Liberty is Sweet': African-American Freedom Struggles in the Years Before White Independence." In Alfred F. Young, ed., *Beyond the American Revolution: Explorations in the History of American Radicalism*. DeKalb: Northern Illinois University Press, 1993. 149–84.

Wood, William B. *Personal Recollections of the Stage, Embracing Notices of Actors, Authors, and Auditors, During a Period of Forty Years*. Philadelphia: Henry Carey Baird, 1855.

Young, Alfred F. "*Common Sense* and *The Rights of Man* in America: The Celebration and Damnation of Thomas Paine." In Kostas Gavroglu, John Stachel and Max W. Wartofsky, eds., *Science, Mind, and Art: Essays on Science and the Humanistic Understanding in Art, Epistemology, Religion, and Ethics in Honor of Robert S. Cohen*. Dordrecht: Kluwer Academic Publishers, 1995. III: 411–39.

————. "The Crowd and the Coming of the American Revolution: From Ritual to Rebellion in Boston." Paper presented to the Shelby Cullom Davis Center for Historical Studies, Princeton University, 23 January 1976.

————. *The Democratic Republicans of New York: The Origins, 1763–1797*. Chapel Hill: University of North Carolina Press, 1967.

————. "George Robert Twelves Hewes (1742–1780): A Boston Shoemaker and the Memory of the American Revolution." *William and Mary Quarterly* 3d ser. 38 (1981): 561–623.

————. "The Women of Boston: 'Persons of Consequence' in the Making of the American Revolution." In Harriet B. Applewhite and Darline G. Levy, eds., *Women and Politics in the Age of Democratic Revolution*. Ann Arbor: University of Michigan Press, 1990. 181–226.

Zuckerman, Michael. *Almost Chosen People: Oblique Biographies in the American Grain*. Berkeley: University of California Press, 1993.

Index